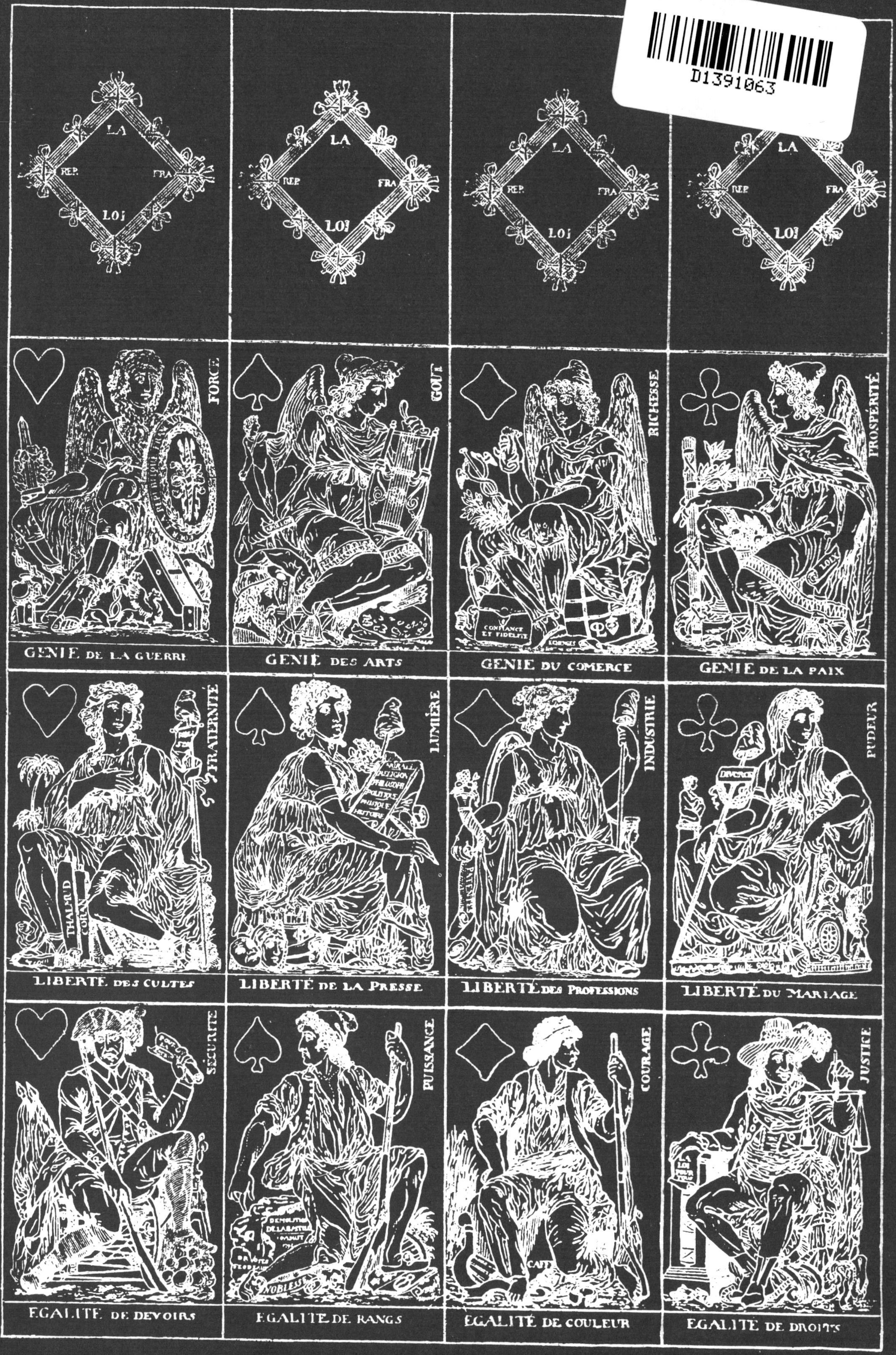
LA
REP.
FRA
LOI
FORCE
GENIE DE LA GUERRE
GOUT
GENIE DES ARTS
RICHESSE
CONFIANCE ET FIDELITÉ
GENIE DU COMERCE
PROSPÉRITÉ
GENIE DE LA PAIX
FRATERNITÉ
LIBERTÉ DES CULTES
LUMIÈRE
LIBERTÉ DE LA PRESSE
INDUSTRIE
LIBERTÉ DES PROFESSIONS
PUDEUR
LIBERTÉ DU MARIAGE
SÉCURITÉ
EGALITÉ DE DEVOIRS
PUISSANCE
EGALITÉ DE RANGS
COURAGE
EGALITÉ DE COULEUR
JUSTICE
EGALITÉ DE DROITS

THE FRENCH REVOLUTION

DÉCLARATION
DES DROITS DE L'HOMME
ET DU CITOYEN,
Décretés par l'Assemblée Nationale dans les séances des 20, 21, 23, 24 et 26 aoûst 1789, acceptés par le Roi
PRÉAMBULE
LES représantans du peuple Francois, constitués en assemblée nationale, considérant que l'ignorance, l'oubli ou le mépris des droits de l'homme sont les seules causes des malheurs publics et de la corruption des gouvernemens ont résolu d'exposer dans une déclaration solemnelle, les droits naturels, inaliénables et sacrés de l'homme: afin que cette déclaration constamment présente a tous les membres du corps social, leur rappelle sans cesse leurs droits et leurs devoirs; afin que les actes du pouvoir legislatif et ceux du pouvoir exécutif, pouvant être a chaque instant comparés avec le but de toute institution politique, en soient plus respectés; afin que les reclamations des citoyens, fondées désormais sur des principes simples et incontestables, tournent toujours au maintien de la constitution et du bonheur de tous.
EN conséquence, l'assemblée nationale reconnoit et déclare, en presence et sous les auspices de l'Etre suprême les droits suivans de l'homme et du citoyen.
ARTICLE PREMIER.
LES hommes naissent et demeurent libres et égaux en droits; les distinctions sociales ne peuvent être fondées que sur l'utilité commune.
II.
LE but de toute association politique est la conservation des droits naturels et inprescriptibles de l'homme; ces droits sont la liberté, la proprieté, la sureté, et la résistance à l'oppression.
III.
LE principe de toute souveraineté réside essentiellement dans la nation, nul corps, nul individu ne peut exercer d'autorite qui n'en émane expressement.
IV.
LA liberté consiste a pouvoir faire tout ce qui ne nuit pas à autrui Ainsi, l'exercice des droits naturels de chaque homme, n'a de bornes que celles qui assurent aux autres membres de la société la jouissance de ces mêmes droits; ces bornes ne peuvent être déterminées que par la loi
V.
LA loi n'a le droit de défendre que les actions nuisibles a la société. Tout ce qui n'est pas défendu par la loi ne peut être empêché, et nul ne peut être contraint à faire ce qu'elle n'ordonne pas.
VI.
LA loi est l'expression de la volonté générale; tous les citoyens ont droit de concourir personnellement, ou par leurs représentans, a sa formation; elle doit être la même pour tous, soit qu'elle protege, soit qu'elle punisse. Tous les citoyens étant égaux a ses yeux, sont également admissibles a toutes dignités, places et emplois publics, selon leur capacité, et sans autres distinction que celles de leurs vertus et de leurs talens
VII.
NUL homme ne peut être accusé, arreté, ni détenu que dans les cas déterminés par la loi, et selon les formes qu'elle a prescrites, ceux qui sollicitent, expédient, exécutent ou font exécuter des ordres arbitraires, doivent être punis; mais tout citoyen appelé ou saisi en vertu de la loi, doit obéir a l'instant, il se rend coupable par la résistance.
VIII.
LA loi ne doit établir que des peines strictement et évidemment nécessaire, et nul ne peut être puni qu'en vertu d'une loi établie et promulguée antérierement au délit, et légalement appliquée.
IX.
TOUT homme étant présumé innocent jusqu'à ce qu'il ait été déclaré coupable, s'il est jugé indispensable de l'arrêter, toute rigueur qui ne serait pas nécessaire pour s'assurer de sa personne doit être sévérement réprimée par la loi.
X.
NUL ne doit être inquiété pour ses opinions, mêmes religieuses pourvu que leur manifestation ne trouble pas l'ordre public établi par la loi.
XI.
LA libre communication des pensées et des opinions est un des droits les plus precieux de l'homme; tout citoyen peut dont parler écrire, imprimer librement: sauf à répondre de l'abus de cette liberté dans les cas déterminés par la loi.
XII.
LA garantie des droits de l'homme et du citoyen nécessite une force publique; cette force est donc instituée pour l'avantage de tous, et non pour l'utilité particuliere de ceux a qui elle est confiée.
XIII.
POUR l'entretien de la force publique, et pour les dépenses d'administration, une contribution commune est indispensable; elle doit être également répartie entre les citoyens en raison de leurs facultées
XIV.
LES citoyens ont le droit de constater par eux même ou par leurs représentans, la nécessité de la contribution publique, de la consentir librement, d'en suivre l'emploi, et d'en déterminer la quotité, l'assiette, le recouvrement et la durée.
XV.
LA société a le droit de demander compte a tout agent public de son administration.
XVI.
TOUTE société, dans laquelle la garantie des droits n'est pas assurée, ni les séparation des pouvoirs déterminée, n'a point de constitution
XVII.
LES propriétés étant un droit inviolable et sacré, nul ne peut en être privé, si ce n'est lorsque la nécessité publique, légalement constatée, l'exige evidemment, et sous la condition d'une juste et préalable indemnité.
AUX REPRESENTANS DU PEUPLE FRANCOIS

THE FRENCH REVOLUTION

Voices from a momentous epoch

1789–1795

Richard Cobb

General Editor

Colin Jones

Editor

Guild Publishing London

This edition published 1988 by
GUILD PUBLISHING

by arrangement with
Phoebe Phillips Editions and
Simon & Schuster Ltd

First published 1988

CN 8039

Phototypesetting:
Tradespools Ltd, Frome, Somerset
Origination:
Columbia Offset Limited, Singapore
Printed and bound in Great Britain by:
Purnell Book Production Limited

FRONTISPIECE The Declaration of the Rights of Man and the Citizen, composed by the National Assembly and decreed by them in August 1789. It prefaced the 1791 Constitution and remains of great historical importance.

Created and produced by PHOEBE PHILLIPS EDITIONS

Editorial Director: Tessa Clark

Editorial

Editor: Cecilia Walters
Sheila Mortimer
Timothy Probart
Paul Mackintosh
Richard & Hilary Bird
Yvonne Ibazebo
Liliane Reichenbach
Picture Research:
Agnès Viterbi

Design and Production

Harry Green
Rachael Foster
Rebecca Bone

Specially commissioned photographs
Marianne Majerus

Maps
Jeff Edwards

General Editor

Professor Richard Cobb, *former Professor of Modern History, Oxford University*

Editor

Colin Jones, *Senior Lecturer in History, University of Exeter*

Translators

Helen McPhail
Janet Shirley
Kate Westoby

Contributors to illustrated spreads

DR. NIGEL ASTON, Department of History, Open University, United Kingdom

DR. JEREMY BLACK, Department of History, University of Durham, United Kingdom

DR. MICHAEL BROERS, School of History, University of Leeds, United Kingdom

DR. PETER CAMPBELL, School of European Studies, University of Sussex, United Kingdom

DR. MALCOLM CROOK, Department of History, University of Keele, United Kingdom

DR. GEOFFREY CUBITT, Jesus College, Oxford University, United Kingdom

DR. MICHAEL DUFFY, Department of History and Archaeology, University of Exeter, United Kingdom

ANDREW FREEMAN, writer and journalist

PROFESSOR DAVID GARRIOCH, Department of History, Monash University, Victoria, Australia.

DR. HUGH GOUGH, Department of Modern History, University College, Dublin, Republic of Ireland

DR. JENNIFER HARRIS, The Whitworth Art Gallery, University of Manchester, United Kingdom

PROFESSOR ROBERT D. HARRIS, College of Letters and Science, Department of History, University of Idaho, United States of America

MAURICE HUTT, School of European Studies, University of Sussex, United Kingdom

PROFESSOR GARY KATES, Department of History, Trinity University, Texas, United States of America

PROFESSOR MARTYN LYONS, School of History, University of New South Wales, Australia

DR. STEPHEN MENNELL, Department of Sociology, University of Exeter, United Kingdom.

DR. DORINDA OUTRAM, Department of Modern History, University College, Cork, Republic of Ireland

PROFESSOR ALISON PATRICK, Department of History, University of Melbourne, Victoria, Australia

PROFESSOR SAMUEL F. SCOTT, College of Liberal Arts, Wayne State University, Michigan, United States of America

DR. WILLIAM SCOTT, Department of History, University of Aberdeen, United Kingdom

DR. MICHAEL SONENSCHER, King's College, Cambridge University, United Kingdom

PROFESSOR DONALD SUTHERLAND, Department of History, University of Maryland, United States of America

DR. FRANK TALLET, Faculty of Letters and Social Sciences, Department of History, University of Reading, United Kingdom

RICHARD WRIGLEY, writer and journalist

Contents

Editor's Note

One of the most significant and influential events in world history, the French Revolution continues to fascinate 200 years after the people of France rebelled against their rulers. Many key episodes still exert a strong appeal: the storming of the Bastille is a potent symbol of resistance to oppression and the decapitation of the Bourbon Louis XVI – 'Louis Capet', as the revolutionaries derisively called him, evoking the 'first race' of French kings, the Capetian monarchs – retains its chillingly levelling edge. Generations of revolutionaries from Marx and Engels through to Lenin, Trotsky and their 20th-century heirs claimed inspiration from the radicals and *sans-culottes* of the 1790s, and saw the French example as the prototype of all modern revolutions.

Much of the common currency of our political vocabulary was coined, or acquired its contemporary connotations, in the Revolution. 'Left' and 'right' were first used to describe radicals and reactionaries seated on either side of the President of the National Assembly in 1790. 'Terror' and 'terrorist' are two other heavily charged terms that date from the 1790s. So too are 'aristocrat', 'anarchist', 'bureaucrat', '*ancien régime*', 'reaction' . . .

The French Revolution is one of the foundation stones of contemporary political culture and the modern state. Yet its archetypal status can be a drawback. It encourages us to think in generalities which contemporary historical research would not support. France was far from being the most oppressive society in 18th-century Europe. By 1789, the infamous *lettres de cachet* were used less against the crown's political opponents than against sexual deviants and family miscreants. The press was not entirely free; but it was free enough to have produced the Enlightenment, and skirted around royal censorship with some agility. French peasants endured the vexations of the seigneurial regime, but not the onerous personal servitude imposed on the serfs of eastern Europe. French townsmen did not enjoy the status of their prosperous English counterparts, but, in spite of its continuing inability to guarantee that the poor were properly fed, the French economy had boomed in the 18th century. Louis XVI was no ogre, but a sensitive and kindly (if rather dim) family man.

When the Bastille was stormed on 14 July 1789, this towering symbol of political tyranny and oppression yielded seven prisoners, of whom two were irrefutably and classifiably insane – an example of how, behind the images and myths of the Revolution, there are less heroic, but no less engaging social realities.

The aim of this book is to convey the importance of the French Revolution in world history; and to show how the human and the humdrum persisted in the welter of events. The Revolution was made, lived, celebrated, condemned, resisted and suffered by men and women whose hopes and aspirations were hardly different from their 20th-century counterparts. And we have used their voices – in letters, diaries, newspaper articles, speeches, memoirs, poems – to compile our narrative.

International statesmen and politicians, monarchs, diplomats and men of letters from France and from the world outside (Britain, the United States of America, Germany) are here; but so are paupers and peasants, merchants and lawyers, priests and booksellers, journalists and

LEFT Only seven prisoners were found inside the Bastille on 14 July. Rumours – and pictures like this – invented many more.

writers of every political hue, émigré noblemen and women, Parisian *sans-culottes* and militant feminists, housewives and princesses. The anonymous and the little-known rub shoulders in these pages with more familiar figures like Mirabeau, Marie-Antoinette, Danton, Robespierre, Goethe and George Washington. Through the chorus of their often wildly differing voices, we have tried to penetrate beneath the surface glamour of events into the mundane hopes and fears, the reactions and aspirations of ordinary people. The Revolution is seen not simply as a clash of myths, concepts, abstractions and principles; but also as the product of human dealings and emotions.

Most of the documents are translated into English for the first time and are linked with explanatory texts which have, however, been kept as concise as clarity would allow, so that the documents themselves do most of the talking. Editorial trimming of the texts has sometimes been necessary, but this has been kept to a minimum. Full details of the extracts that have been used are given at the back of the book, together with a glossary of Revolutionary terms, and brief biographical details on many of the people whose voices are recorded in the text. There is also a guide to further reading.

The documentary narrative is complemented throughout by short notes and essays on key topics and invididuals, written by a team of experts drawn from three continents. And, to reflect the interest the Revolution engendered – as far afield as America – who had been helped by the French in its own revolution – we have included comments from contemporary British and American magazines and newspapers. Illustrations of the images – and some of the artefacts – of the period highlight the human realities behind one of the most resonant and inspiring events of modern times.

LEFT The fall of the Bastille on 14 July 1789; stormed by soldiers and civilians with the aid of cannon from the Invalides.

THE REVOLUTIONARY CALENDAR

Introduced by decree of the Convention, October 1793. The following names of months were decreed:

Vendémiaire	= 22 September – 21 October
Brumaire	= 22 October – 20 November
Frimaire	= 21 November – 20 December
Nivôse	= 21 December – 19 January
Pluviôse	= 20 January – 18 February
Ventôse	= 19 February – 20 March
Germinal	= 21 March – 19 April
Floréal	= 20 April – 19 May
Prairial	= 20 May – 18 June
Messidor	= 19 June – 18 July
Thermidor	= 19 July – 17 August
Fructidor	= 18 August – 16 September

YEAR I
(21 September 1792 – 21 September 1793)
In retrospect only: dated from the declaration of the Republic, 21 September 1792.

YEAR II
(22 September 1793 – 21 September 1794)
Followed from the introduction of the Revolutionary Calendar, October 1793.

YEAR III
(22 September 1794 – 21 September 1795)

YEAR IV
(22 September 1795 – 21 September 1796)

GREGORIAN CALENDAR

1789
5 May: Opening of the Estates General
14 July: Fall of the Bastille
4 August: Abolition of feudalism
26 August: Declaration of the Rights of Man
5-6 October: March on Versailles

1790
14 July: Fête de la Fédération

1791
20 June: Flight to Varennes
17 July: Champ-de-Mars massacre

1792
20 April: War on Austria
20 June: Invasion of the Tuileries
10 August: Overthrow of the king
2-6 September: September massacres
20 September: Battle of Valmy
6 November: Battle of Jemappes; French conquer Belgium

1793
21 January: Execution of Louis XVI
1 February: War on Britain and the United Provinces (soon on most European states)
10 March: Vendée rising
18 March: Battle of Neerwinden; loss of Belgium
6 April: Committee of Public Safety established
Summer: sans-culotte pressure
2 June: Expulsion of Girondin deputies from the Convention
June: Federalist revolt
27 August: Toulon surrenders to the British
Autumn: Robespierre in control of Committee of Public Safety
16 October: Battle of Wattignies
19 December: British evacuate Toulon

1794
24 March: Hébertists executed
6 April: Dantonists executed
18 May: Battle of Tourcoing; Belgium reoccupied
8 June: Festival of the Supreme Being
26 June: Battle of Fleurus
27 July: Coup of 9 Thermidor

1795
April-July: Peace with Prussia, United Provinces, Spain
8 June: Death of Louis XVII
22 August: "Law of the Two-Thirds" passed
4 October: Vendémiaire rising

PRESSURE GROUPS

OTHER

PARIS SECTIONS
(1790 – 5)
Especially powerful between the overthrow of the king, 1792, and early 1794.

PROVINCIAL JACOBIN CLUBS
(c.*5500 in all*)

CORDELIERS CLUB
More extreme than Jacobins.
Leading members include Danton, Desmoulins, Hébert, etc.

DIRECTORS
Committee of five elected by the Councils.
Replaceable one per annum. Most important figures: Barras (1795 – 9), Carnot (1795 – 7), La Révellière-Lépeaux (1795 – 9), Sieyès (1799).

PRESS
Royalist newspapers (*L'Ami du Roi*, *Actes des Apôtres*, etc.) influential 1789 – 92.

Left-wing press: notably Marat's *L'Ami du peuple* (1789 – 94), Fréron's *L'Orateur du peuple* (1790 – 95), Brissot's *Le Patriote français* (1789 – 93), Hébert's *Le Père Duchesne* (1790 – 94), Prudhomme's *Les Révolutions de Paris* (1789 – 94).

JACOBINS

At first liberal; then increasingly radical.

BRETON CLUB
(April – November 1789)

JACOBIN CLUB
Dominated by Lameth, Dupont, Barnave until July 1791.

Girondin deputies dominate, but are expelled for criticising the Paris Commune, late 1793.

Robespierre faction increasingly powerful until July 1794.

Club closed 12 November 1794.

The French political structure 1789 – 1795

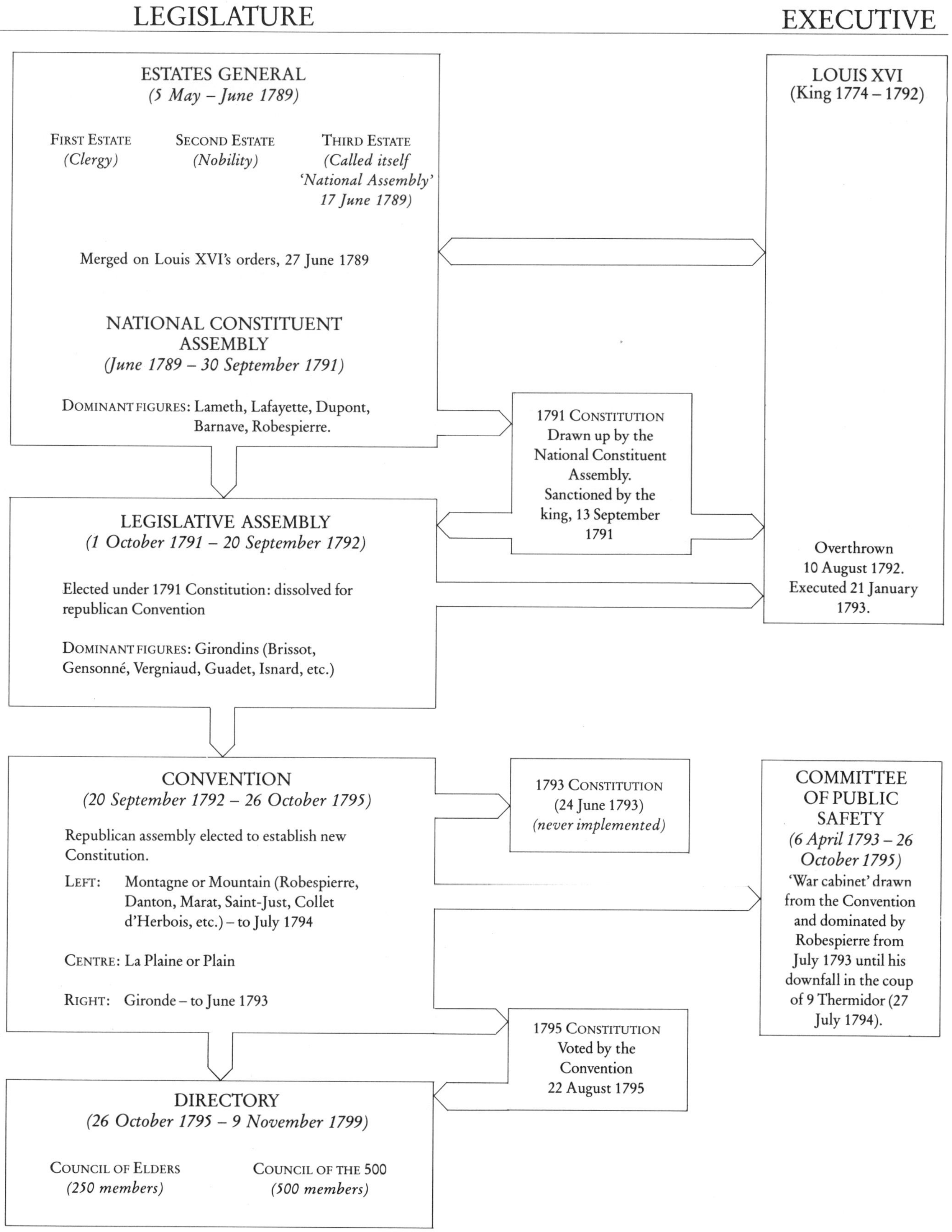
LEGISLATURE
EXECUTIVE
ESTATES GENERAL
(5 May – June 1789)
First Estate
(Clergy)
Second Estate
(Nobility)
Third Estate
(Called itself 'National Assembly' 17 June 1789)
Merged on Louis XVI's orders, 27 June 1789
NATIONAL CONSTITUENT ASSEMBLY
(June 1789 – 30 September 1791)
Dominant figures: Lameth, Lafayette, Dupont, Barnave, Robespierre.
LOUIS XVI
(King 1774 – 1792)
Overthrown 10 August 1792. Executed 21 January 1793.
1791 Constitution
Drawn up by the National Constituent Assembly. Sanctioned by the king, 13 September 1791
LEGISLATIVE ASSEMBLY
(1 October 1791 – 20 September 1792)
Elected under 1791 Constitution: dissolved for republican Convention
Dominant figures: Girondins (Brissot, Gensonné, Vergniaud, Guadet, Isnard, etc.)
CONVENTION
(20 September 1792 – 26 October 1795)
Republican assembly elected to establish new Constitution.
Left: Montagne or Mountain (Robespierre, Danton, Marat, Saint-Just, Collet d'Herbois, etc.) – to July 1794
Centre: La Plaine or Plain
Right: Gironde – to June 1793
1793 Constitution
(24 June 1793)
(never implemented)
COMMITTEE OF PUBLIC SAFETY
(6 April 1793 – 26 October 1795)
'War cabinet' drawn from the Convention and dominated by Robespierre from July 1793 until his downfall in the coup of 9 Thermidor (27 July 1794).
1795 Constitution
Voted by the Convention 22 August 1795
DIRECTORY
(26 October 1795 – 9 November 1799)
Council of Elders
(250 members)
Council of the 500
(500 members)

ABOVE In the heady days of revolutionary fervour following the fall of the Bastille, each section of Paris planted a Liberty tree to commemorate the winning of liberty. Here, the mayor, flanked by National Guards, oversees the planting to the accompaniment of music and appropriate ditties.

TOP RIGHT The Revolution set the pattern for similar future regimes not only in political terms, but also in the variety and pervasiveness of its propaganda. The fasces on this pot were adapted under the Revolution from the ancient Roman axes that signified law and order, and used to show the new Republic's virtues.

ans l'enthousiasme de cette Liberté que l'on croyoit
être donné, on imagina de planter des arbres pour
perpetuer la mémoire, ce qui ce fit dans chaque
tion avec grand appareil, les Gardes nationaux
compagnoient le Maire, et une Musique brillante
doit cette fête interessante.

RIGHT Another everyday item made to serve the Revolution: a clock face with figures of Union and Peace supporting the dial. Furniture, ornaments, clothes and items of all kinds were embellished with such emblems; designed to spread the new regime's ideology and inculcate civic virtue in all French citizens. However, as the Federalist and Vendean revolts spread, sentiments of peace and union began to ring ever more hollow.

Ancien régime Europe, 1789

ANGLO-FRENCH rivalry dominated international relations in the 18th century. Britain, however – Europe's leading colonial and commercial power – was defeated by its own colonists (with French aid) in the American War of Independence (1776–83). France remained the major land power of western and southern Europe: Spain, ruled by a cadet branch of the French Bourbon dynasty, was in eclipse, while divided Italy posed no great threat.

In the east, the Austrian Habsburg dynasty was challenged by two new major powers: Prussia, under the Hohenzollern ruler, Frederick the Great (1740–86), the most militaristic state in Europe; and Catherine the Great's Russia.

The political geography of *ancien régime* Europe was complex and overlapping. Austrian and Prussian territory, for example, straddled the boundaries of the ramshackle Holy Roman Empire, which comprised hundreds of German mini-states. France too had several foreign enclaves within its territory, most notably Avignon, a papal possession.

The Revolution allowed a greater consolidation of French territory, a process helped by the introduction of the departmental system. It also saw France expand its boundaries. That expansion was achieved only by force of arms, and indeed in 1793 had looked unlikely as the allied armies of the First Coalition penetrated French territory on all fronts. By 1794–5, however, France had rolled her enemies back and was beginning an era of unparalled expansion.

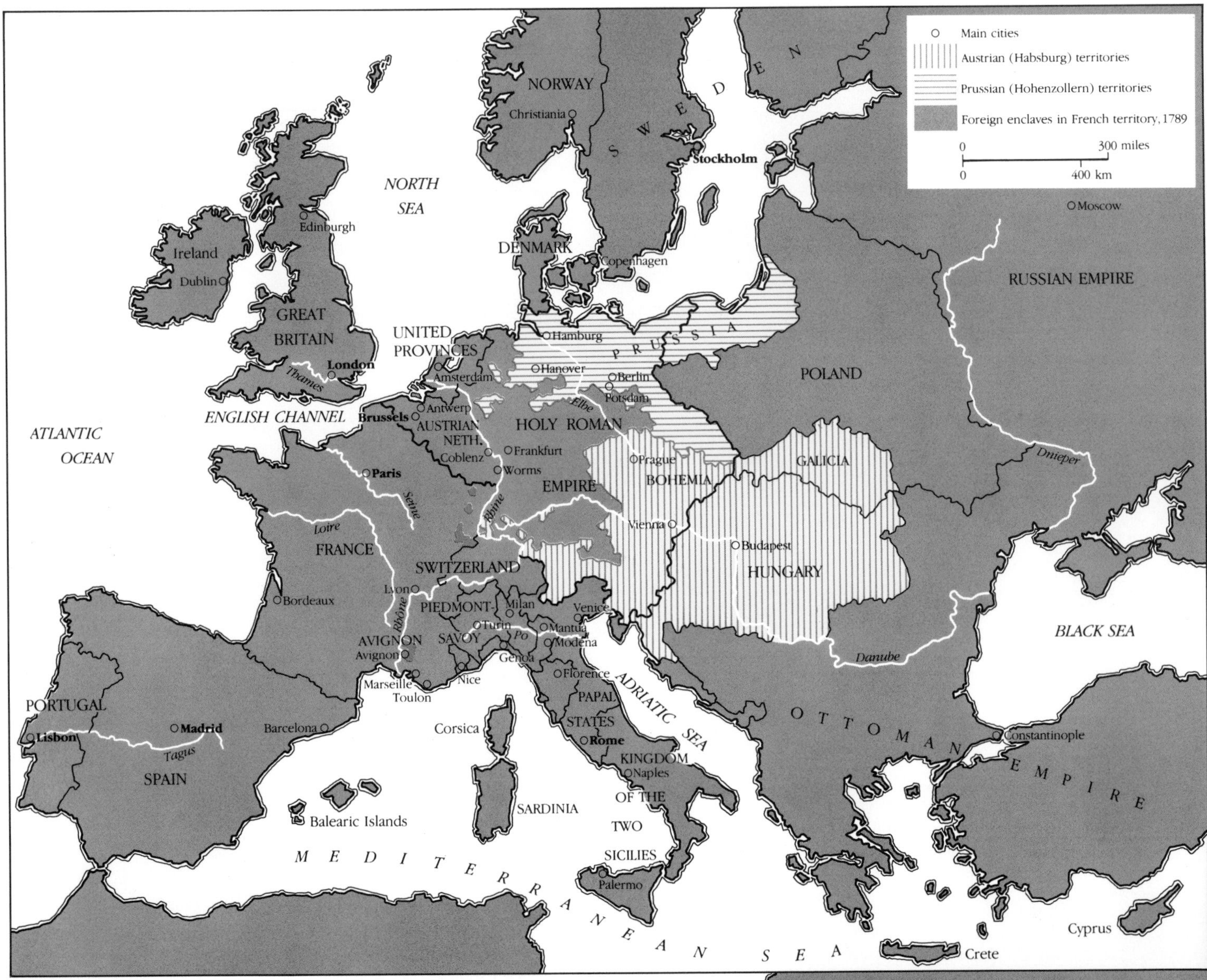

France, 1789–1795

CHAPTER ONE: 1788–1789

The Great Hope

France was close to bankruptcy when Louis XVI, prompted by the need to raise money, decided to convoke the Estates General – an archaic representative body which had not met since 1614 – hoping that it would agree to an increase in taxation in return for limited royal reforms. His gamble failed. Elections to the assembly, accompanied by the drawing up of lists of grievances (*cahiers de doléances*), raised expectations for radical change at every level of French society. When the Estates General met at Versailles in early May 1789, they embodied a new form of political awareness, which the king would be unable to keep in check.
(*18th-century Versailles*)

THE turning point was 1789. It was in that year that the Revolution, already apparent in the minds, customs and way of life of the French nation, began to take effect in government. I will describe the principal reasons for this and some of the events to which it led.

The king had placed his confidence in M. de Vergennes, an anxious minister, frightened of the court and of the great men, lacking character or talent, and yet wise and enlightened; he influenced rather than directed the king's conduct. Alarmed by the dangerous situation of the kingdom, he made it clear to the king and convinced him of the need for extraordinary measures and a new system of administration if disaster was to be avoided.

The most striking of the country's troubles was the chaos in its finances, the result of years of extravagance intensified by the expense of the American War of Independence, which had cost the state over twelve hundred million livres.

No one could think of any remedy but a search for fresh funds, as the old ones were exhausted. M. de Calonne, Minister of Finance, had conceived a bold and wide-ranging plan. This was put to the king, who gave it his approval and promised to support its implementation with the full weight of his authority.

Without either threatening the basis of the French monarchy or damaging the sovereign's authority, this plan changed the whole previous system of financial administration and attacked all its vices at their root. The worst of these were: the arbitrary system of allocation, the oppressive cost of collection, and the abuse of privilege by the richest section of taxpayers. This abuse extended not merely to the great and influential of the realm, but to the first orders of the state, that is, the clergy and the nobility, to the provinces, and to the towns, so that the whole weight of public expenditure was borne by the most numerous but least wealthy part of the nation, which was crushed by the burden.

The plan was to be endorsed by an Assembly of Notables of the kingdom which was to circumvent the need to consult the parlements. It was the more welcome to the king in that it fulfilled his dearest wish: the relief of the most numerous class of his subjects. The Notables were thus summoned for 29 January 1787; I was appointed to this Assembly; it had not met since 1626, in the reign of Louis XIII.

The Notables, who comprised the leading figures among the clergy, nobility, magistracy and the principal towns, were naturally bound to oppose the ending of abuses from which they profited. Nevertheless,

The American War of Independence

IN January 1775, Britain's thirteen American colonies rose in revolt against the mother country. Hostilities lasted until 1782, and American independence was formally recognized in 1783. In their struggle against Britain, the American colonists found crucial support from an alliance with the European powers, most notably the French.

Some of the themes later to resonate in the French Revolution – such as the need for representative assemblies to consent to taxation – were in this earlier one. But France's involvement owed less to such principles than to a desire to see Britain defeated.

Britain and France were serious rivals for most of the period 1689-1815. The crushing French defeat in the Seven Years War (1756-63) inspired a desire both for revenge and for the recovery of France's maritime and colonial position. However, when Choiseul led her to the brink of war in 1770, in support of her ally Spain in her clash with Britain over claims to the Falkland Islands, he was dismissed. His replacement, d'Aiguillon, sought agreement with Britain, especially as he was concerned to counter the Russian threat to the European balance of power. He failed, and the accession of Louis XVI in 1774 was followed by the creation of a new ministry, in which Vergennes was Foreign Minister, less inclined to heed British wishes. He and his colleagues, however, would no more have wanted war with Britain than had their predecessors over the Falklands in 1770, but for American developments.

LEFT A French china cup of the 1770s celebrating Benjamin Franklin, friend of the *philosophes*.

France secretly welcomed the open resistance put up by the American colonies against their English overlords. But this did not necessarily mean that she would go to war. Her recent experience of North American conflict was not favourable: she had lost

Canada during the Seven Years War. French policy hardened after the news of the British defeat by the American colonists, at Saratoga in October 1777, reached Europe. By February 1778, France and the American rebels had signed a treaty of alliance. British and French envoys were called back the following month and fighting began that summer.

French intervention was to tilt the military balance in the New World. Although French troops were sent, it was naval assistance that was particularly valuable. An attempt by France and her ally Spain to invade Britain in 1779 failed, but in 1781 the French fleet helped to force the surrender of the army commanded by General Cornwallis, blockaded at Yorktown. This led to a crisis of confidence in Britain, the fall of Lord North's ministry in early 1782, and the decision to negotiate peace on the basis of American independence.

Britain's defeat in the war was not as serious as it could have been. But the loss of America was a serious blow and this was reflected in the Anglo-French peace treaty signed at Versailles in September 1783: George III ceded to Louis XVI a number of colonial possessions. The war represented a military triumph for France and also a diplomatic one – Britain had been isolated in the conflict, France supported by Spain and the United Provinces. There had also been domestic turmoil in Britain; a perceptive commentator, asked in 1780 to state which European country would probably experience revolution before the end of the decade, would probably have replied Britain.

The American war helped to undermine France. Though some taxes were increased, Jacques Necker, the Minister of Finance, funded the war mainly through borrowing and the increasing cost of servicing that debt placed a major strain on the nation's economy. By the autumn of 1780 the situation had become so serious that the Council of State was forced to consider the possibility of a truce which would leave the British in occupation of part of the American colonies.

If the financial burden of the war led to the summoning of the Assembly of Notables in 1787, the response to ministerial demands was influenced by the success of the American Revolution, which showed that it was possible to create a new political order and, by applying the laws of reason, to formulate a new constitution.

ABOVE The victorious George Washington; from a portrait in a French collection.

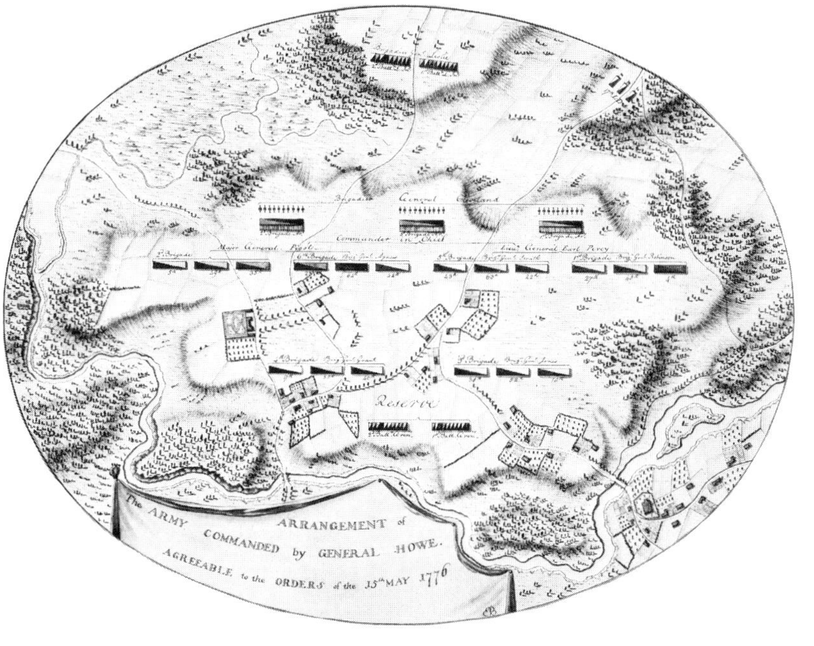

RIGHT The English forces in America commanded by General Howe, who won many battles, but lost the war.

most of the nobles, and others under direct government influence, were well intentioned.

They would have carried the rest with them but for the intrigues of the archbishop of Toulouse, Loménie de Brienne, one of the Notables. All the assembly did was to destroy the minister who had set up the plan, M. de Calonne; he, abandoned by the king, was disgraced and forced to go into exile for fear of being given up to the fury of the people.

Loménie de Brienne was put in charge of the administration of finance. Shortly afterwards the king was imprudent enough to make him principal minister. Brienne dismissed the Notables and was soon at the mercy of the parlements. He gathered a few remnants of M. de Calonne's plans, containing some useful insights and suggestions for solving the immediate problems; but the magistracy opposed a stubborn resistance to their execution.

Then the troubles began. They broke out first in Brittany, where the government was compelled to bring in armed forces, but did not dare use them owing to the reluctance shown by the troops, especially the officers.

In Paris the people's discontent, already raised to the point of rebellion by factious members of the parlement, gave rise to riots which had to be put down by military force.

The upheavals were even more violent in 1788. Tired of opposition from the parlements, Brienne persuaded the king to adopt the fanciful idea of setting up a plenary court intended to prevent them from achieving that share in the legislature they were trying to grasp.

Then the parlements, inspired by the idea of the Assembly of Notables, demanded the convocation of the Estates General. They were quite sure the court would refuse it. The clergy made the same request – and the same mistake.

The government made a still greater one: it promised to call the Estates General. They had not met for almost two hundred years, and in this long period of time there had been such great changes in the minds, the way of life, in the character, customs and government of the French nation that their meeting now could only produce upheaval.

The above description of the origins of the Revolution was recorded by the marquis de Bouillé, military commander in 1789 who later emigrated.

The pre-Revolution

A FINANCIAL crisis started the chain of events that led to the upheaval of 1789. For several years the royal government had covered its deficits with loans. In 1783 the parlement of Paris – the most prestigious of France's 13 high courts of appeal, whose decisions gave royal decrees the force of law – began to remonstrate against such loans, stating that the deficit could be eliminated by curtailing expenditure. Public opinion, fuelled by publicity given to lavish court spending, seemed to share this view.

The Controller-General, Charles-Alexandre de Calonne, denied that extravagance was the problem. He argued that more money could be raised through

ABOVE Calonne. Dismissed, he fled to England in 1787, where he wrote several works on the state of France and Europe.

taxation if the privileged classes would only give up their exemptions and pay their fair share. He maintained that the country's financial difficulties stemmed from the heavy costs incurred by France during the American War of Independence.

Whatever the cause of the deficit, Calonne realized during 1786 that the country must find new sources of revenue or face bankruptcy the following year. He persuaded Louis XVI to convene an Assembly of Notables before whom he would explain the government's predicament, and propose a series of reforms to increase income by levying more taxes on the wealthy. He assured the king that no additional burden would be laid on the poorer classes.

The Assembly of Notables consisted of 144 delegates drawn from the most distinguished members of the aristocracy, the prelates of the French Catholic church and government officials; all were appointed by the king. Calonne assumed that as soon as he had explained the financial situation to them, their patriotism and sense of responsibility would lead them to approve his reforms. With their moral support he could ignore any objections – or any remonstrances the parlement of Paris might make.

The Assembly sat from 22 February to 25 May 1787. It agreed to most of Calonne's reforms, subject to important revisions, and, in addition, that taxes should be levied more equitably, based upon ability to pay. But the Notables distrusted Calonne's explanation for the origins of the deficit, and demanded that they be allowed to inspect the relevant financial records. This behaviour, more like that of an English parliament than of a consultative assembly, took Calonne by surprise. He tried to appeal to public opinion, claiming that the Notables' motives were dictated by an unwillingness to pay their fair share of taxes. But the tactic failed: public opinion was overwhelmingly on the side of the Assembly. The impasse was broken only by Louis XVI's dismissal of Calonne on 8 April 1787.

Calonne's successor was the archbishop of Toulouse, Loménie de Brienne. An enlightened prelate, he sincerely desired to carry out the reforms stipulated by the Assembly. He persuaded the king to make many concessions, including turning over the financial accounts to the Notables' scrutiny. However, the Assembly demanded that a permanent commission, independent of the royal government, be established to supervise the administration of finances. The king could not consent to such a restriction on his power; the Assembly was dismissed on 26 May.

Brienne went ahead with his reforms, which now had to be passed by the parlement of Paris. In July it refused to register his tax edicts, declaring that only the Estates General – France's national parliament, which had not even met since 1614 – had the authority to approve such measures.

The cry for the Estates General swept across the kingdom. After trying to reach a compromise with the parlement, Brienne resorted to force. By the edicts of May 1788, the parlement of Paris was shorn of its right to register edicts and present remonstrances; these were transferred to a new plenary court, whose members were appointed by the king.

The May edicts aroused opposition throughout the kingdom. Violence flared in some provinces and threatened to spread to others. Brienne realized it was impossible to resist the public demand for the Estates General and on 5 July 1788, Louis XVI promised to summon them. Although Brienne still hoped for a delay, the threat of bankruptcy forced his hand and on 8 August the king promised to convoke the Estates General no later than 1 May 1789.

A week later the government was compelled to renege on the interest payments on some of its loans and resort to paper money. Now the king's closest advisers persuaded him to accept Brienne's resignation and to call upon the Swiss banker Jacques Necker, who had been finance minister from 1777 to 1781, to lead the country out of the crisis.

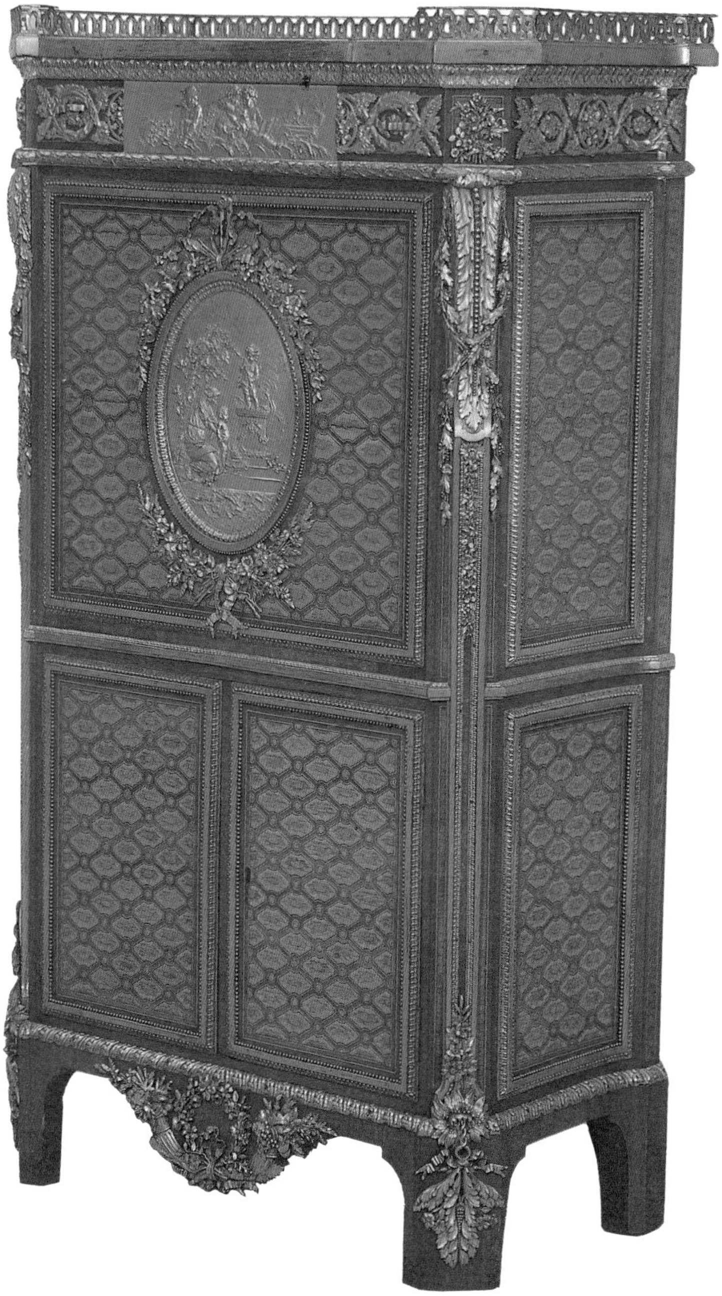

RIGHT Marie-Antoinette's secretaire from Versailles; an example of the royal extravagance opposed by the Notables.

Whilst awaiting execution under the Terror in 1793, the Grenoblois lawyer Barnave, a dominant figure in national politics, put down his thoughts on the government crisis of 1789.

THE democratic ideal, virtually stifled under all European governments while the feudal system remained powerful, has gathered strength and continues to grow. As the arts, trade and the pursuit of luxury enrich the industrious section of the people, impoverish the big land-owners and bring the different classes closer together through money, so science and education bring them closer in their daily lives, and recall men to the basic idea of equality.

To these natural causes can be added the influence of royal power: long undermined by the aristocracy, it has called the people to its aid.

Conditions in France were ripe for a democratic revolution when the unfortunate Louis XVI ascended the throne; the government's actions favoured its explosion.

The two privileged orders who still retained control of the government were ruined through their taste for luxury and had degraded themselves by their way of life. The Third Estate, in contrast, had produced enlightened thinkers and acquired enormous wealth. The people were restrained only by their habit of servitude and the limited hope they had of breaking their chains. The government had succeeded in containing this hope; but it had nevertheless flourished in the heart of the nation.

It was already apparent that, among the growing generation, the principles of Voltaire were beginning to give way, in favour of those of Helvetius and Rousseau. For royal power to remain intact in such circumstances would have required a tyrant or a great statesman on the throne.

Louis XVI was neither; he was too well intentioned not to try to remedy abuses which had shocked him, but he possessed neither the character nor the talents to control an impetuous nation in a situation which cried out for reform. His reign was a succession of feeble attempts at doing good, shows of weakness, and clear evidence of his inadequacy as a ruler.

LEEDS INTELLIGENCER (Leeds), *July 1789*

. . . we are reproached with falling short of the liberality of sentiment displayed in the kingdom of France, but I hope never to see the British National Assembly possessed by the spirit of Voltaire.

The Enlightenment

THE 18th-century Enlightenment may be represented as a new way of thinking about mankind and the environment. The main proponents of this intellectual movement, the *philosophes*, were primarily men of letters – men like Voltaire, Diderot, Montesquieu and Rousseau – but their views stemmed from the scientific revolution of the previous century. The discoveries of Galileo, Kepler and Newton in physics and cosmology revealed a universe that was infinite, yet governed by universal laws that could be discovered by the human intelligence. The *philosophes* were convinced that all creation was similarly rational, so that it was possible for man to uncover laws which regulated society, politics, the economy, even morality. Once understood, these laws would teach mankind not only what we are, but what we ought to be and to do.

For the *philosophes*, much of Western Christian civilization was incompatible with such a rational order. The absolute monarchy, the aristocratic society which dated from the Middle Ages, the established church, all came under their scrutiny. 'Despotism, feudalism, clericalism' became the objects of their criticism and satire.

Though some of their more daring ideas never passed

the censor, the *philosophes* conveyed their message to the public through the printed word. Their greatest monument was the *Encyclopédie* – entitled 'A Rational Dictionary of the Arts and the Sciences' and edited by Denis Diderot. The first volume appeared in 1752, the last of 35 in 1780, and it expressed the authors' pride in the European achievement since the Renaissance.

English civilization was particularly admired by the *philosophes*. In Voltaire's first important work, *Philosophical Letters* published in 1734, he extolled the freedoms enjoyed by all Englishmen: freedom from arbitrary arrest, freedom of speech and of the press, and religious toleration. Injustice, the abuse of power,

ABOVE The *philosophes* dining, with Voltaire in the centre with his arm raised. They frequented Paris cafés, such as the famous Café Procope.

above all the intolerance and bigotry of the Catholic church, drew Voltaire's sharpest barbs.

The *philosophes* approached religion with the same reasonableness that they brought to politics. Most believed in some form of Deism, which saw the universe and the world as deliberately created – and held that the existence of such a rational creation must imply an intelligent Creator. What they could not accept was the literal interpretation of the Bible. In their view miracles and other phenomena not explained by natural laws and reason were mere superstitions.

The most influential apostle of liberty and opponent of despotism was Charles de Secondat, baron de Montesquieu, another admirer of the English political system. In his most famous work, *The Spirit of the Laws*, published in 1748, he made a comparative study of law and forms of government since antiquity in which he expressed great admiration for the limited monarchy of the English. He recognized how such a government, by fostering patriotism among the people, was far stronger than absolute monarchy.

It is difficult to say how the *philosophes*, men of theory rather than of practical experience in politics, would have reacted to the concrete issues of the Revolution: certainly, they did not call for a violent revolution that would overthrow the monarchy and establish a republic. Most looked towards a constitutional monarchy coupled with representative institutions.

Jean-Jacques Rousseau shared Montesquieu's and Voltaire's passion for liberty and their hatred of despotism. Unlike them he believed that an individual could be free only if all men were free. In *The Social Contract*, published in 1762, he sought to show how a democratic society could function, arguing that supreme sovereignty rested with the general will, which expressed the aspirations of all citizens. He did not share the pride of the other major *philosophes* in the achievements in the arts and the sciences. He believed instead that sophisticated civilization had corrupted mankind rather than improved it. In *Emile*, also published in 1762, he claimed that humanity could be restored to its true nature only by proper education.

From the evils of 'despotism, feudalism, clericalism' the revolutionaries adapted the watchword of 'Liberty, Equality, Fraternity', drawing on notions from the Enlightenment. But because the *philosophes* lived and wrote some years before the coming of the Revolution, it is difficult directly to assess their influence on the events of 1789 and after. Yet the foundation documents of the Revolution – the Declaration of the Rights of Man, the August decrees and the Constitution of 1791 – clearly reveal the debt owed to Montesquieu, Voltaire and Rousseau.

LEFT A contemporary bust of Jean-Jacques Rousseau: already popular under the *ancien régime*, he became one of the chief idols of revolutionary ideology.

RIGHT A box with a secret miniature of Voltaire. Secrecy was sometimes necessary when the Enlightenment encountered *ancien régime* censorship and disapproval.

The royal decree of 8 August 1788, convoking the Estates General for 1 May 1789, makes only a coy allusion to the financial problems which provoked the king to take such a drastic step.

HIS Majesty has decided to provide for an immediate convocation of the Estates General of his kingdom.

His Majesty has not yet decided where the Estates General are to meet, but is able to announce to his subjects that their assembly is fixed for 1 May 1789. Certain of reaping the fruit of the representatives' enthusiasm and love, His Majesty is already looking forward to calm and peaceful days after the storm, to seeing order restored in all the provinces, to the national debt being consolidated and to France enjoying, without disturbance, the power and respect due to its size, population, wealth and the character of its people.

His Majesty commands that this present decree shall be printed, published and displayed throughout the kingdom. The lieutenant general of police of the city of Paris and the Intendants throughout the provinces are instructed to put this in hand.

Given in the king's Council of State in the presence of His Majesty at Versailles, 8 August 1788.

A radical clergyman, the abbé Sieyès, published his famous and widely circulated pamphlet 'What is the Third Estate?' in January 1789, during the run-up to the elections to the Estates General.

WE have three questions to ask ourselves:

What is the Third Estate? EVERYTHING.

What has it been in the political order until now? NOTHING.

What is it asking for? To become SOMETHING.

Who would dare to say that the Third Estate does not have in itself all that is needed to form a complete nation? It is a man who is strong and robust but still has one arm in chains. Take away the privileged order, and the nation would not be less, but more.

And so what is the Third Estate? It is EVERYTHING but an EVERYTHING shackled and oppressed. Without the privileged order, what would it be? EVERYTHING, an EVERYTHING flourishing and free. Nothing can go well without it; everything would go infinitely better without the others.

It is not enough to prove that the privileged orders are not merely useless to the nation but harmful and damaging; it must also be shown that the order of nobility has no place in the organization of society, that it can certainly be a burden to a nation but can never form part of it.

What is a nation? A body of associates living under a common law and represented by the same legislature.

As for its political rights, these too it exercises separately from the nation. The nobility has its own representatives who are in no way empowered to speak for the people. Its body of deputies sit apart; and even if they gathered in one hall with the deputies of the ordinary citizens, it is none the less true that their representation is essentially separate and distinct. It is alien to the nation by its origin, since its mission is not from the people, and by its objective, since its purpose is not the defence of the general interest but of its own.

The Third Estate, then, contains everything that makes up the nation; everything that is not part of the Third Estate cannot consider itself as belonging to the nation. What is the Third Estate? EVERYTHING.

What can the Third Estate do if it wants to gain its political rights in a way that will be beneficial to the nation?

The Third Estate must meet separately; it will not associate in any way with the clergy or nobility and will not vote with them either by order or by head.

But the Third Estate, it will be said, cannot form the Estates General. All the better! It shall compose a National Assembly.

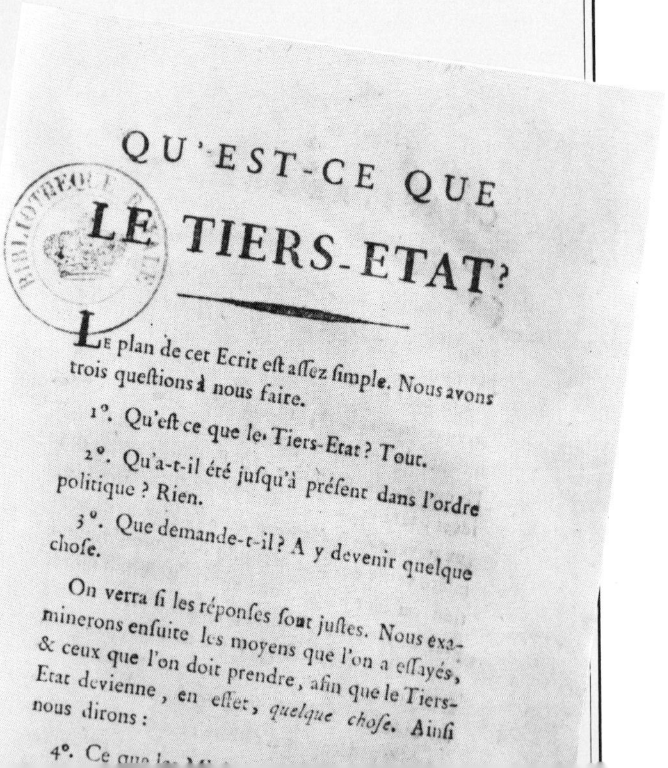

QU'EST-CE QUE LE TIERS-ETAT?

Le plan de cet Ecrit eſt aſſez ſimple. Nous avons trois queſtions à nous faire.

1°. Qu'eſt ce que le Tiers-Etat? Tout.

2°. Qu'a-t-il été juſqu'à préſent dans l'ordre politique? Rien.

3°. Que demande-t-il? A y devenir quelque choſe.

On verra ſi les réponſes ſont juſtes. Nous examinerons enſuite les moyens que l'on a eſſayés, & ceux que l'on doit prendre, afin que le Tiers-Etat devienne, en effet, *quelque choſe*. Ainſi nous dirons:

4°. Ce que

The Third Estate

In January 1789 the abbé Sieyès published his pamphlet *What is the Third Estate?* It was an inspiration to, and ammunition for, those who challenged the nobility's dominance in French society. Whereas the first two estates of the realm, the clergy and the nobility, made up less than half a million men between them, the Third Estate – the common people – represented the other 25 or so million in France. Sieyès argued that, from being of no importance politically, it should become all-important and oust the aristocracy from the running of the nation.

Sieyès was essentially concerned with the bourgeoisie – the merchants, lawyers and doctors of the towns, and the property-owners in the countryside – men of wealth and education who could provide leadership for the mass of people.

The abbé's exercise in commoner consciousness-raising – asking, 'Is it proper for the Third Estate, at the end of the 18th century, to languish in the sad and cowardly customs of ancient servitude?' – coincided with a flood of pamphlets and petitions on the same theme from the towns and cities of provincial France.

Relations between nobles and bourgeois varied from town to town. At Rouen, for instance, the nobility refused to surrender any of their privileges – and demanded more – whereas at Marseille the merchants and the nobles put forward similar demands, which reflected a common life-style and shared culture based on commercial and enlightened values. Even here, however, a rich merchant such as Dominique Audibert, academician and correspondent of Voltaire, wrote of how his 'blood boiled' to see with what contempt the nobility viewed the rest of society. In pamphlets inspired by Sieyès, his colleague Jacques Seimandy forcefully expressed the Third Estate's claim to political power, based on its wider knowledge, its greater practical experience and its more substantial contribution to the well-being of the country. He and his fellow-Marseillais totally condemned a system of government which squandered national resources on an extravagant minority.

The leading commoners paid tribute to the talents of nobles who improved their estates and aided their peasants, who served bravely in the army or who shone intellectually. But they scorned both the corrupt courtiers and the general run of impoverished and uncultivated provincial nobles.

In the electoral period prior to the meeting of the Estates General, they increasingly stressed that nobility should be accorded, as a reward for virtuous and patriotic conduct, to men who had served the nation. Anyone who bought titles, or had insinuated themselves into the aristocracy by murky financial dealings or by rashly but profitably lending money to the government, was deemed unworthy.

In the eyes of the solid bourgeoisie, only men from the Third Estate who had demonstrated competence in their own affairs could bring order to those of France. To do so, they would be prepared to co-operate with nobles who, like Mirabeau and La Fayette, had shed the prejudices and privileges of their class and were prepared to help rebuild the nation. But they would have to accept bourgeois terms, and profess allegiance to the values of equality, justice, liberty and hard work.

The Third Estate represented the national interest and rallied the labouring, productive classes under their banner. The slogan 'Long live the Third Estate!' was a genuinely popular cry during the spring and summer months of 1789.

BELOW The abbé Sieyès, who survived to hold office in the Directory.

The decree of 24 January 1789 which follows was based on the royal decree of 27 December 1788, in which the king and his principal minister, Necker, had outlined how elections to the Estates General were to be held.

THE king, in sending letters of convocation to the Estates General to the different provinces within his obedience, desires that his subjects should all be called to take part in the election of the deputies who are to form this great and solemn assembly.

His Majesty wishes that everyone, from the extremities of his realm and from the most remote dwelling places, may be assured that his desires and claims will reach His Majesty.

His Majesty has further endeavoured to achieve this especial object of his care by summoning to the assemblies of the clergy all the good and useful pastors who are in close and daily contact with the poverty and relief of the people and are most intimately acquainted with their fears and their anxieties.

The king, in arranging the order of the convocations and the structure of the assemblies, wished as far as possible to follow the old traditions. Guided by this principle, His Majesty has preserved the time-honoured privilege for all *bailliages* who had sent a representative to the 1614 Estates General to do so again.

His Majesty expects above all that only the voice of conscience will be heard in the choice of deputies to the Estates General.

Therefore His Majesty has commanded and commands the following:

Each order shall draw up a list of grievances (*cahier de doléances*) and choose its deputies separately, unless they prefer to do so jointly, in which case the consent of the three orders, obtained separately, will be needed.

Given and decreed by the king in his council at Versailles, 24 January 1789.

Signed: LOUIS.

THE CHRISTIAN'S, SCHOLAR'S, AND FARMER'S MAGAZINE (Elizabethtown, N.J.), *April and May 1789*

Feb. 16 1789. The noblemen of Roussillon, in Perpignan, came to a resolution on January 21 not to claim any more privileges in the meeting of the states General than the citizens; which resolution they recommended to be followed by the Noblesse and Clergy throughout the kingdom, on this principle, – 'That they were men and citizens, before they were raised to their present situations'.

The memoirs of Jean-Sylvain Bailly, the celebrated scientist who was to become the first president of the National Assembly and the first Revolutionary mayor of Paris, capture something of the intoxication which many felt in the elections to the Estates General. Bailly is here participating in the district elections in which Paris chose its deputies for the Estates General.

WHEN I found myself in the middle of the district assembly, I felt that I breathed a new air: it was a marvel to be something in the political system, and that merely by virtue of being a citizen, or rather a burgess of Paris, for at that time we were still burgesses, not citizens. The men who for years had been meeting in the clubs used to discuss public affairs in them, but only as topics of conversation; they had no rights, no influence whatever.

Here, we had the right to elect, we had at least, as in Estates General of former times, the right to make requests and to draw up lists of grievances (*cahiers*). Here, we had an influence – distant, certainly, but obtained for the first time in more than a century and a half; and this privilege had been won by an enlightened generation who understood its value and would be able to extend its advantages.

This assembly, such a tiny part of the nation, was nevertheless conscious of the rights and the strength of the whole; it realized that these rights and this strength lent it a kind of authority, one that may reside in the wills of individuals who are destined to form the general will.

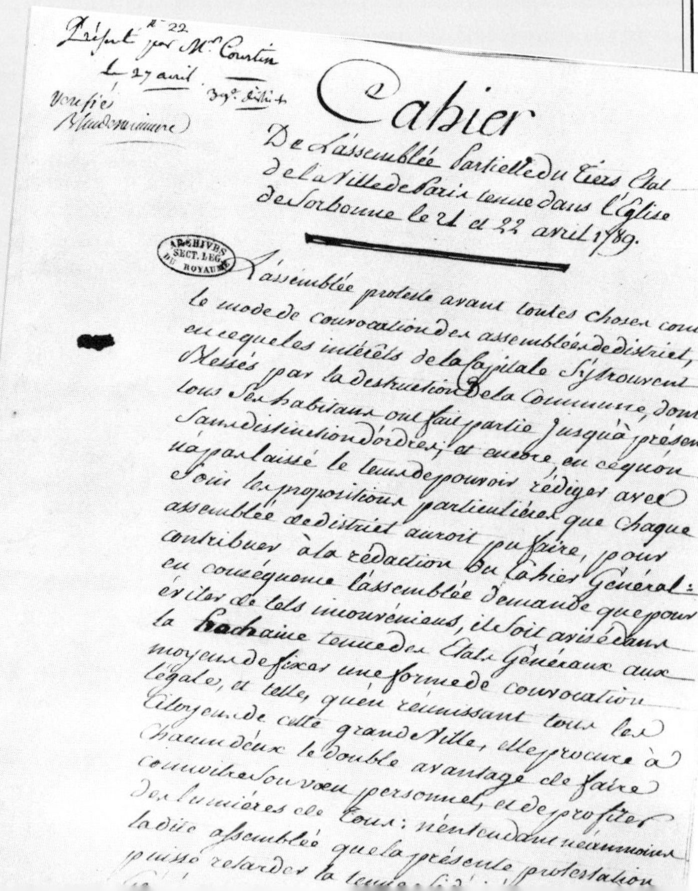

Cahier

De l'assemblée partielle du Tiers État de la Ville de Paris tenue dans l'Église de Sorbonne le 21 et 22 avril 1789.

L'assemblée proteste avant toutes choses contre le mode de convocation des assemblées de district, en ce que les intérêts de la Capitale s'y trouvent blessés par la destruction de la Commune, dont tous ses habitans ont fait partie jusqu'à présent sans distinction d'ordres; et encore en ce qu'on n'a pas laissé le temps de pouvoir rédiger avec soin les propositions particulières que chaque assemblée de district auroit pu faire, pour contribuer à la rédaction du Cahier Général: en conséquence l'assemblée demande que pour éviter de tels inconvéniens, il soit avisé dans la prochaine tenue des États Généraux aux moyens de fixer une forme de convocation légale, et telle, qu'en réunissant tous les Citoyens de cette grande Ville, elle procure à chacun d'eux le double avantage de faire connoître son vœu personnel, et de profiter des lumières de tous: n'entendant néanmoins ladite assemblée que la présente protestation puisse retarder la tenue …

The cahiers de doléances

At every stage of the multi-tiered election for the Estates General in March and April 1789, men were invited to list their grievances in collective statements, digests of which were to be taken by delegates to the Estates General when it met at Versailles. These books of grievances – *cahiers de doléances* – are a matchless social and economic record, and provide a revealing 'snapshot' of public opinion on the eve of the Revolution.

Cahiers de doléances had been an integral part of every meeting of the Estates General since the 15th century. But in 1789 they were given extra poignancy and edge: there had been no meeting since 1614; and elections were conducted in the midst of a worsening social and economic crisis.

In spite of the stark conditions which prevailed while they were being drawn up, they cannot be regarded as overtly subversive documents. Although the basic ingredients for the complete overthrow of *ancien régime* society and government were embedded within them, they were imbued with royalist sentiment. From the humblest levels of parish and guild to the final *bailliage* stage, when deputies to Versailles were elected for all three estates, *cahiers* unceasingly, and often sycophantically, protested their gratitude and fidelity to the benevolent ruler who had given them this opportunity of voicing their complaints. On the face of it, the revolutionaries of 1789 were avowed royalists.

There was a surprising degree of unanimity in the demands of the three orders listed in the general *cahiers* drawn up at *bailliage* level. Clergy, nobility and Third Estate tended overwhelmingly to accept and welcome representative assemblies and constitutional rule, and agreed about many social and economic reforms. The divisions which arose from the summer of 1789 onwards were detectable in only a small number of sensitive issues listed in the general *cahiers*. For example, the clergy and nobility often mandated their deputies to insist on voting by order rather than by head in the Estates General, so as to block radical reform initiatives by the Third Estate.

Liberal *cahiers* like those composed by the noblemen of Paris and other urban centres contrasted strikingly with the attitudes struck by the country gentry in economically backward regions. And the progressive views of many parish priests contrasted with those of the reactionary, aristocratic upper clergy. The Third Estate was even more divided. The well-fed, well-off men who dominated in the *bailliage* assemblies saw the world differently from the peasants and artisans who had contributed to the preliminary *cahiers*. Hunger, for example, was the key issue of 1789 only for the poorest groups. There were attempts to co-ordinate the Third Estate's demands: model *cahiers* were drawn up and circulated in rural areas by the duc d'Orléans and by other members of the radical caucus, the Society of Thirty. However, real conflicts of interest were involved, and many of the more radical demands of the lower classes were edited out from the general *cahiers* by the men of substance who wielded power in the *bailliage* assemblies; the list of grievances this produced was as socially slanted as the 600-odd deputies of the Third Estate, who mustered no tradesmen and one peasant.

ABOVE A contemporary satire: the commoner's prayer, to be delivered from tariffs, gamekeepers, military service, *et al.*

Peasant *cahiers* reveal the critical importance of electoral consultation in the crisis of 1789. Often composed outside the church door after a Sunday Mass, and written out in a clumsy and phonetic hand – only two males out of three could even sign their names in 1789 – the documents frequently combine specific complaints with long descriptions of the misery of their lives and mix concrete demands with vague political aspirations, attacking seigneurs, tithe-owners, excise-men, tax-farmers and much else.

The *cahier* – or list of grievances – of the nobility of the province of Roussillon, on the frontier with Spain, contains a mixture of noble intransigence (voting by order), provincial particularism (the call to reactivate local assemblies) and mild liberalism (tax reform, press freedom, regular meetings of the Estates General).

DEPUTIES to the Estates General are only delegates, agents of power, instruments of the public will. Members of the nobility of Roussillon, while working together for the general welfare of the kingdom and of all the orders, will always bear in mind what they owe to the province and to their own order in particular.

Votes shall be cast in the Estates General by order and not by head.

Deputies shall call for the Estates General to be regularly reconvened every five years at the latest.

The deputies shall deal with the general constitution of the kingdom. The main object of their discussions must be to define and regulate this in an exact and invariable way. Therefore the deputies shall ask that it be declared:

That France is a monarchy, heritable from male to male, in order of primogeniture, daughters being excluded, ruled by the king according to the laws.

That to the prince alone belongs, unshared, all executive power for the maintenance of public order and the defence of the state.

That no decree is considered law unless it has been proposed or permitted by the king, agreed or requested by the nation assembled in the Estates General.

That all new laws regarding the general constitution of the state must be sent to the parlements.

That to the nation legally assembled in the Estates General belongs exclusively the right to grant subsidies, to regulate the use made of them, to assign to each department the agreed necessary funds, and to demand an account of them.

The liberty of the citizen being the most precious of all possessions and most sacred of all rights, all arbitrary commands and all *lettres de cachet* issued by the sovereign or his ministers shall be declared illegal and their use forbidden for ever.

As an integral part of civil liberty, every kind of writing may be printed and published, on condition that the author, publisher or printer puts his name to it and answers personally for anything that may be said in them contrary to religion, morality and the honour of the citizens.

The order of nobility, faithful to the desire it has expressed to bear jointly with the other orders, in exact proportion, the burden of taxation and general contributions of the province, especially authorizes its deputies to agree to equality of assessment without any pecuniary exemptions, enjoining them none the less to take care that no attack be made upon property or upon the honorific distinctions and rights inherent in the order of nobility, which are of the essence of monarchic government.

While waiting for better times which may permit the abolition of the salt tax, or *gabelle*, the deputies shall ask for a reduction in the price of salt.

Deputies of the order shall work together to their utmost to promote the support of religion, the respect due to divine worship, the very needful restoration of morality and of national education.

Given and decreed in the general assembly of the order and signed by the commissioners and all the members present.

At Perpignan, 28 April 1789. Signed: DE LLUCIA
Secretary of the Order of Nobility.

The *cahier* of the diocesan clergy of St-Malo, in Brittany, combines liberalism in state and church matters with an archaic outlook on public morals and Breton independence.

THE clergy of the diocese of St-Malo, summoned by the king's command to consider means of promoting the prosperity of the kingdom, being anxious to respond to the benevolent intentions of the monarch and to prove to the whole nation its zeal in all that concerns public well-being, has in its various assemblies drawn up the following *cahier*.

That in the national assembly, and in all political assemblies in the provinces, votes shall be counted by head and not by order.

That it shall be laid down in the same assembly as a fundamental law of the kingdom that no tax will be imposed except by the agreement of the assembled nation.

That in future the Estates General shall meet at fixed periods.

That at each meeting of the Estates General an account shall be given to the nation of the use made of public money since the previous meeting.

That request be made for the safeguarding of all the rights, franchises and immunities of our province of Brittany.

The nobility

As the second of the three orders, or estates, of society, the nobility enjoyed extensive rights and privileges. The most significant was exemption from personal taxation, on the grounds that as members of a military caste they paid their taxes in blood. However, nobility was no longer associated only with the profession of arms. Some financial and judicial offices ennobled their owners, which added a nobility of the robe – named after the black robe worn by court officials – to that of the sword. Given the natural tendency of any family to die out in the male line after half a dozen generations, this influx of office-holders and rich bourgeoisie, who could literally buy their way into the nobility through the system of 'venality', or purchase of office, and go on to adopt the aristocratic life-style, was probably essential to the survival of the order as a

ABOVE A Sèvres porcelain panel showing the king and members of the high nobility watching a stag hunt, complete with liveried huntsmen.

powerful group. On the eve of the Revolution, nobility was therefore a question of life-style, honour, title, privilege, lineage and morality, rather than membership of a military group. The old ethic survived, but in 1789 about half the 30,000 or so privileged families could trace their noble ancestry back no further than the mid-17th century.

Economically, the nobility was characterized by great landed wealth. Their approach to estate management was often businesslike, almost 'bourgeois' in its concern for profit. Nobles were generally the richest members of society in any region, partly because the age was favourable to the accumulation of property by the moneyed, and also because the wealthiest bourgeois almost always became noble. Typical sources of income were rents, seigneurial dues and exploiting forestry and directly farmed land on estates. Even so, there were great variations within the order: Brittany, for example, was noted for its large number of poor nobles (*hobereaux*).

Differences of wealth produced a cultural split. The richest nobles acquired an expensive, enlightened education. They belonged to academies, read the *Encyclopédie* and the works of the *philosophes*, and adopted modish ideas of equality and liberty. The poorer ones were less well educated, more steeped in provincialism and more devoted to the older ethic. Similarly, there was a wide gap between the extravagant courtier and the provincial noble. Another important division was reflected in the Ségur ordinance of 1781, which restricted access to the highest ranks in the army to men able to prove four generations of nobility. The intention was to protect established nobles against losing their army posts to newcomers.

In 1789 most members of the nobility attended electoral assemblies, where they elected the 282 noble deputies to the Estates General and drew up lists of grievances (*cahiers*). Many of these *cahiers* reveal surprisingly liberal views, including demands for a constitution, individual liberty and the abolition of all fiscal privileges including their own. The parlements had been in the vanguard of the Pre-Revolution in 1787–8. Yet although, in the summer crisis of 1789, some liberal nobles like Lafayette and Noailles made common cause with the radical demands of the Third Estate, most probably never dreamed that subsequent events would end their dominance within society. The Revolution was a rude shock.

RIGHT The marquise de Gestas; a typical member of the provincial Gascon nobility of Louis XVI's reign.

REQUESTS CONCERNING THE GOOD OF THE PEOPLE.

That no attempt shall be made upon the liberty of any citizen without giving him means of defence at the very moment of his detention.

To ask for the abolition of the *corvée* (forced labour service).

To seek for means of protecting the people from the distress caused by seigneurial rights pertaining to pigeon-houses, dovecotes, warrens, hunting, mills, presses, seigneurial ovens and other feudal rights.

REQUESTS CONCERNING THE NEEDS OF THE FIRST ORDER.

That only the Catholic religion be publicly exercised in France.

To request proper and effective means of giving young people in town and country an education that will be solid and useful to religion and to the state.

Admission of the deputies of all classes of clergy to all ecclesiastical assemblies, national and provincial, as well as to the political assemblies of this province; and, in these, a proportional and adequate representation of the Third Estate.

To ask for implementation of the canons against holding benefices in plurality.

And the clergy conclude by exhorting their representatives in the Estates General to support with all the zeal in their power any other useful suggestions which may be made and which may have escaped their consideration.

The *cahier* of the little Norman town of Gisors represents the wishes of the wealthier commoners, who were liberal in economics as well as in politics.

THE Third Estate of this town invites the deputies to the Estates General to do all they can to encourage the Assembly to adopt the following resolutions, but not until they have first of all joined with all the deputies of the kingdom in demonstrating to the best of kings the gratitude, respect, love and submission of his subjects of the town of Gisors.

Resolutions shall be taken and decreed in the Estates General by the three orders jointly and votes shall be counted by head and not by order.

That in the matter of taxes and loans the sovereign's authority cannot be exercised except by the general agreement of the assembled nation, and with the assistance of its deliberations and its advice in matters of legislation.

Before giving recognition to the national debt or imposing any taxation, the deputies shall cause to be decreed, as the kingdom's permanent system of government, the regular recall of the Estates General at fixed periods.

They shall ask for the abolition of every kind of indirect tax, under whatever description it was set up, and that none be created within the interior of the kingdom.

No citizen may be made prisoner nor deprived of his liberty for any reason whatever without having been first taken before his natural judge, or before the judge of the offence of which he is accused, and without having been sentenced to that imprisonment, for which purpose all arbitrary imprisonment and especially *lettres de cachet* shall be forbidden.

Deputies will ask for:

Abolition of all forms of seigneurial justice.

Abolition of the venality of office.

The nation's right to choose its judges in all future tribunals.

Reform of the civil and criminal codes.

Game should be destroyed, or nobles who wish to preserve it should be compelled to enclose it within their parks; and the destruction of harmful animals should be encouraged.

Deputies shall ask for the abolition of immunities damaging to the Third Estate, such as exemption from troop billeting, from militia duty, coastguard duty and others of that kind.

That free schools be set up in every parish in the kingdom for the instruction of young people.

That begging be entirely prohibited, and that means be found to subsidize the feeding, maintenance and housing of the infirm poor by the establishment of charity boards in all towns, boroughs and villages.

That the *champart* (seigneurial tithe) and dues payable in kind or in labour, and other such rights which produce little for the landlord and are a grievous enslavement to the tenants, be changed to a payment in grain and straw or to money payments.

That tolls payable on goods crossing land, bridges, and on roads and others of that kind be abolished as harmful.

That dues on markets and on corn measurement be reduced to two *sous* per sack uniformly throughout the kingdom, and that steps be taken to avoid the excessive costliness of cereals.

That pigeons be kept shut up in pigeon-houses from 24 June to 1 September and from 29 September to 11 November.

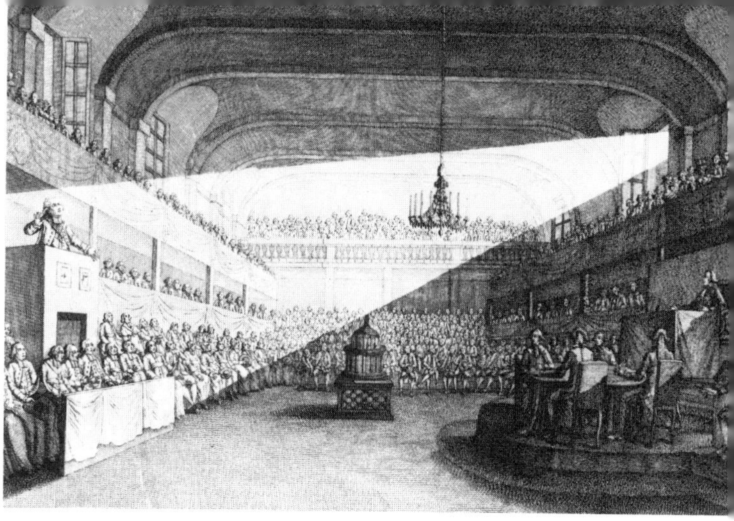

ABOVE A clerical deputy holding forth in the Assembly in 1789. Opposite him is the President of the Assembly.

The first estate

DURING the *ancien régime* the church was unrivalled in terms of its social, economic and spiritual power. The first order, or estate, of the realm owned nearly 10 per cent of all land in France, and income from land, property and tithes totalled over 150,000,000 livres a year. As the most privileged corporation in the state, it paid no direct taxes, negotiating instead a 'free gift' to the crown every five years, raised by an internally levied clerical tax; in return it held a monopoly of public worship, education and public charity.

Approximately a third of the 170,000 clergy in France served as parish priests. Better trained and more highly educated than in any previous times, the curé was generally well respected by his parishioners, and valued not merely for the religious services he provided but for his social functions too: as a dispenser of charity, expert in arbitration, arranger of marriages and link with the outside world. But there were signs of a widening gulf between the parish clergy and their superiors.

The former resented the disproportionate share of church wealth creamed off by the bishops, canons and regular orders, all of whom contributed little in clerical taxes. The curés' demands for economic justice were coupled with calls for a greater share in church government, an end to the aloofness and arbitrary power of the bishops, and to the precedence of monks and canons in the ecclesiastical hierarchy.

The church's severest lay critics were the writers of the Enlightenment – the *philosophes*. Although they offered a grudging recognition of the charitable work of women's orders, and of the curé who looked after his parishioners' welfare, they exploited the opportunities presented by other targets: idle monks, gluttonous canons and bishops involved in political intrigue.

Churchmen, in turn, blamed the *philosophes* for the growing religious indifference they claimed to detect in society. But although the writers gave expression to anti-clericalism, they did not bring it about. And if their attack on the value of the contemplative life met with general approval, their Deism – and in some cases atheism – did not. Churchmen probably exaggerated the decline in religious fervour – though decline there certainly was in clerical recruitment from the 1740s – the decrease in production of books on religious subjects, and the drop in the number of requests for requiem masses. Loss of fervour was, however, largely confined to the upper classes and the towns; overall, France was a conformist Catholic country in 1789.

The summoning of the Estates General was welcomed by the parish clergy, the group with the greatest influence in choosing the clerical deputies. All curés were allowed to attend the clerical assemblies and to vote individually, whereas chapters sent only one delegate for every ten canons, and monks one delegate for each community. Of 296 delegates elected, only 46 were bishops and 208 were parish priests.

The ecclesiastical *cahiers* reflected curés' particular concerns: reform of the church to give greater control from below, and an end to the secularization of society. But on a wider scale they saw the abolition of fiscal privilege, including the church's right to tax exemption, and greater constitutional control of government as the best means of achieving national regeneration. As a result there was a broad consensus between the parish clergy, the liberal faction of the nobility and the Third Estate. This alliance, coupled with a dislike of the aristocratic bishops, led 149 of the clerical deputies at the Estates General to vote, on 19 June, to join the Third Estate for the verification of election credentials. Four days later a majority of them again defied the king and joined the Third Estate in the National Assembly.

Though the curés did not know it, they had set in motion a Revolution which would end the existence of the clergy as the first estate in the realm.

LEFT The royal monastery of the Val-de-Grace, typical of the much envied splendour of great *ancien régime* religious institutions.

The *cahier* of the semi-literate master cobblers of the town of Pontoise in the Paris basin is more concerned with matters of livelihood than with broad principles.

ONLY one single tax, whatever name it is given.

Abolition of indirect taxes, of *gabelle*, of the mark on hides which makes it impossible for shoemakers to use the goods that they need, for the agents compel them to keep the mark and so they are not free to use their hides; if anyone is found to have a hide without the mark, because he needed to use that section of the skin, he has to undergo the most oppressive proceedings, without any counsel available, and the agents instantly demand whatever sum they feel like, you have to pay for wanting to work; and then there is a huge increase because the butchers, the tanners and the leatherworkers are out of their minds, they have forced the price of shoes up to an exorbitant height and reduced the shoemakers' trade till the masters only have half the number of workmen, just at a time when there are so many available skilled workmen. This greatly distresses all shoemakers.

The mark on a hide used to be at six deniers per pound, now it is six times that; it has become so serious that a third of leather manufacturers are perishing in prison, others have their work banned, others' whole fortunes have vanished, and in the towns, in the provinces, shoemakers now are nothing but retailers for the leatherworkers, for shoes have risen to such a price that many have to go without.

Stockpiling of grain and flour to be forbidden and import from one province to another.

Militia to be abolished.

Reform of the administration of justice and to keep it short.

Troop billeting, only municipal officials to be exempt.

Abolition of pigeon-houses, because the birds cause such waste.

Destruction of all kinds of game, and all farmers to be allowed to destroy it by any means except firearms.

A single administration for forced labour service on the roads throughout the province.

Poorhouses to be abolished, and a charity board established.

Unsigned.

Town and country

ON the eve of the Revolution only one in seven (some 15 per cent) of France's 27.9 million population lived in localities containing more than 2000 inhabitants. Yet although the proportion of the population living in urban areas was low (lower than in England, the Low Countries or the Italian states), the number of towns was itself remarkably high. There were more medium-sized towns in France than in any other territorial state in Europe. In 1700 about 55 urban districts had at least 10,000 inhabitants; by 1800 there were 78. The comparable figures were 11 and 44 for England and 30 and 53 for the German states.

The distribution of the urban population changed substantially over the 18th century. Some cities, like Bordeaux and Nîmes, almost doubled in size, while others – like Dijon or Troyes, for example – barely grew at all. Much depended on what could be drawn from the prosperity of the colonial and manufacturing sectors of the French economy.

Most manufactured goods were made or finished in towns. Trades consisted of a small number of large enterprises that could produce a relatively wide range of products throughout the year, a larger number of tiny establishments which did subcontracted work or specialized processes, and marginal firms which eked out a subsistence living from second-hand or stolen materials.

The majority of male wage-earners were single, aged between 15 and 30, and could expect to become

ABOVE A clockmaker's workshop: the type of small business that employed most of the artisan class in Paris and elsewhere.

members of a guild or establish themselves on their own account, possibly in a small town where corporate regulation did not exist. Many young men who learned a trade in the provinces left home to work in Paris or other large centres. The associations, or *compagnonnages*, that they formed in the course of their *tour de France* played an important role in the trading life of the great cities.

The rate of migration from rural to urban areas was the outcome of a complex relationship in which small and medium-sized towns acted as funnels which drew in people from nearby villages and redistributed them, or their children, to the great cities of Paris, Lyon, Rouen, Marseille and Bordeaux. Every large city was, therefore, part of a wider network which reached deep into the countryside.

The interdependence of urban and rural society and between large and small towns meant that the majority of urban dwellers were migrants. Although most people did not move very far, different members of households moved frequently.

These family networks formed by migrants from the same region were often the basis on which commercial and cultural life was conducted.

ABOVE An example of pre-revolutionary artisan's work: a porcelain figure of a Parisian *sans-culotte*, the peep-show man.

The patterns they formed owed much to the character of each town. Toulouse or Dijon, for example, with their legal, administrative and clerical institutions, housed very different networks from those that were established in commercial and manufacturing centres like Lyon and Marseille.

The importance of urban networks in the cultural life of the nation is reflected in the large number of subscribers to Diderot's *Encyclopédie*, the many members of masonic lodges, the enthusiastic readers of Rousseau's fashionable novel *La Nouvelle Héloïse*, the variegated markets for prints and engravings and the speed with which Parisian debates over Jansenism, the Jesuits, the cures by 'animal magnetism' claimed by the Austrian charlatan Mesmer, were echoed in scores of smaller towns.

The networks also played a significant part in the assemblies held to draft *cahiers de doléances* and elect deputies to the Estates General in the spring of 1789, and in transmitting Parisian divisions and conflicts to hundreds of smaller towns in subsequent years.

Here the politically ambitious duc d'Orléans, who was allied with the more radical members of the Third Estate, tries to pressurize the parish priests within his extensive domains into accepting a number of liberal principles.

CIRCULAR addressed to the parish priests in the name of the duc d'Orléans by M. de Limon, controller of the prince's finances.

7 March 1789

You will perhaps be very glad to inform your parishioners that my lord the duc d'Orléans, who prides himself in being just and generous and will always sincerely prefer the public's well-being to his own, has expressly and in writing commanded me, as having the honour to be his representative in one part of his dukedom, to do all in my power to cause the following requests to be made in the *cahiers* of the assemblies at which I may be present:

First, that the rights of property be inviolable and that no one may be deprived of his property, even for reasons of public interest, without receiving full and immediate compensation;

Second, that all taxation shall be borne equally by princes as by ploughmen, by poor as by rich;

Third, that all hunting rights and regulations be abolished;

Fourth, that the prince orders me to place no obstacle connected with his rights in the way of any just and reasonable requests which may be made by the Third Estate;

Fifth and last: that I am ready to collect all the grievances of peasants, of villagers, to listen to everything that any of them may wish to tell me, so that I shall be able to uphold their rights in the *bailliage* assembly, to support them with all my might, and, upon my return to Paris, to enable the duc d'Orléans himself to support with all his authority the well-founded grievances of his good vassals.

His Highness desires above all that the parish priests, whose task it is to procure the comfort and happiness of country districts, may obtain from the Estates General a thoroughly sufficient and decent endowment which will enable them to give their parishioners the relief they need.

I shall therefore, Sir, be deeply obliged if you would kindly provide me, from yourself and your colleagues, with all the available information on this subject.

I have, Sir, the honour to be your most humble and most obedient servant.

Philippe Egalité

THE career of Philippe, duc d'Orléans, was dictated as much by the position of his family in France as by his liberal inclinations.

Orléans, as a member of the younger branch of the Bourbon dynasty, was the king's cousin and a successor to the throne after Louis' direct male descendants and brothers. His family was prodigiously wealthy, with an annual revenue in 1787 of seven and a half million livres. It was understandable that they should harbour ambitions to rule France.

As a result, the Orléans family always differed from the king politically. In opposition at court, they attracted discontented elements.

Philippe, who became duke in 1785, was a libertine, an Anglomaniac, not very well educated and a sworn enemy of Marie-Antoinette.

Orléans' weak character, his dissolute ways, intellectual mediocrity and lack of determination made him ill-suited to the role of opposition leader and scheming pretender. But this did not prevent him from

playing an important political role, and he was often accused of attempting to bring down Louis XVI in order to succeed him or acquire a regency.

Philippe supported the Paris parlement in its opposition to royal financial reforms in 1787–8. At a *séance royale* in November 1787, at which government loans were to be approved by the parlement, the duke shocked the court by saying that the session was illegal. He was exiled, but soon returned and participated in the second Assembly of Notables in late 1788, at which he spoke in favour of increasing representation of the Third Estate. His position was liberal. He welcomed the forthcoming Estates General and threw himself into the electoral campaign with enthusiasm. His agents did the work for him: in the 1780s he had employed the future Girondin deputy Brissot; in October 1788, Choderlos de Laclos, the cynical author of *Les Liaisons dangereuses*, took over and restyled his political machine. Laclos and Sieyès drew up an electoral 'instruction', a kind of model *cahier*, readership of which reached 100,000.

The Orléanist 'machine' excelled in extra-parliamentary activity. In 1784 the Palais-Royal, the family's Parisian residence, had been remodelled and it became a centre for vice, gambling, the purchase of political pamphlets and speechmaking by fiery orators such as Camille Desmoulins. The duke belonged to the Society of Thirty, composed mainly of aristocrats and liberals who met at the house of the patriot Adrien Duport to organize propaganda for the Third Estate in the elections to the Estates General.

From 1789 onwards, Philippe was a member of the Jacobin Club. Elected to the National Convention that met to draw up a new constitution in 1792, he took the name Egalité: Orléans, a feudal name, was declared unacceptable by the revolutionaries. At Louis XVI's trial for treason he voted for the death of the king.

From this time on, Orléans was at the mercy of forces beyond his control. When General Dumouriez, his erstwhile supporter, fled to the Allies in the spring of 1793, taking with him Orléans' son the duc de Chartres (the future King Louis-Philippe), Orléans was accused by his former Jacobin friends of royalism. He was arrested on 6 April and, exactly six months later, after no serious attempt at a trial, Philippe Egalité was executed.

ABOVE Philippe Egalité as he appeared before the Revolution, in all the panoply of Bourbon magnificence, part of an order he later betrayed.

LEFT The Palais-Royal. Orléans lined its gardens with shops to recoup his squandered fortune: many sold radical political pamphlets.

Peasants' *cahiers* tended to express, in simple and concrete language, their hopes for change and their gratitude to Louis XVI; and also to chronicle their distress. The village *cahier* of Ménouville, in the Paris basin, is typical of many rural grievance lists.

IN the year 1789 on 25 February, the assembly of the inhabitants of the parish of Ménouville was called together by the sound of the bell in the usual way, and M. le Curé read out the king's letter summoning the Estates General.

We beg His Majesty to have pity on our farmland because of the hail we have had.

Also we have a great deal of waste land which is covered with juniper, and this causes much trouble on account of the rabbits which are very numerous; it is this that makes us unable to pay the dues we owe to His Majesty.

We have no help from anyone to bring us relief. Our neighbouring parishes are better off than we are, their lords have given great alms in their parishes, but we can expect help from no one but His Majesty.

We have only a few good fields very remote from the village, the rest is wretched land very full of game and this causes very small harvests.

We have one small meadow which only produces sour hay, the animals refuse to eat it, this is why we cannot raise stock.

The soil is so bad that you cannot plant fruit trees, several inhabitants have planted a few but they don't grow.

We state that salt is too dear for poor people.

We state that there should not be any tax men, there could be a levy put on drinks so that everyone would be free.

We state that there should be no militia duty, because this ruins many families; it would be better if His Majesty laid a small tax on each young man.

We inform His Majesty that our goods are too heavily burdened with seigneurial and other charges.

We inform His Majesty that there is a main road from Pontoise to Méru begun eight years ago, we did the *corvée* as we were compelled to, we have been paying out money for three years; there are stones in the said road brought by wagon eighteen months ago and no labourers to do any work there, which means that everyone has to go through the corn and grain at the side of the road, which does a lot of harm and brings complaints from the farmers who own the fields.

Given and decreed today 25 February in the presence of us, undersigned inhabitants of this parish.

The peasantry

TWENTY million peasants – about three-quarters of the population – owned only about a third of the land; the rest belonged to the church, bourgeoisie and nobility. However, the peasants cultivated almost all of it, and numerous cartoons from 1789 show a peasant carrying a noble and a priest on his back. Even when they did hold the land, it was often subject to a whole range of feudal dues: there was no outright ownership of land in the modern sense. There were various forms of tenure: principally long- or short-term leases, or the very widespread sharecropping system (*métayage*), in which half the produce went to the owner in return for use of the land and farming equipment.

Almost all peasants were free; very few bound serfs still existed, although there were nearly a million of them in the east of France, living under a regime where land without direct heirs reverted to the lord. The vast majority of peasants owned plots which were too small to support a family, and rented additional land or plied some other rural trade like ditcher or labourer. As a result, most of them were poor and only a few in each community could afford to own a plough team or take over larger rented farms. About 40 per cent were day labourers and owned no more than a tiny plot or cottage. To make a living in good years, it was necessary to use the resources of the common land (for firewood, grazing and so on), cultivate the cottage garden for fruit and vegetables, and keep a few chickens in addition to tilling the soil.

Peasants were probably better off in the south, where diversification was the rule, than in the north-east, where the land was given over to large open fields of grain. This subsistence economy was also a household economy in which women and children had to play a role in feeding the family; widows and single people found it hard to survive. In any case, life was precarious, and when the harvest was bad, vast numbers of peasants, as well as the poorer townspeople, became virtually destitute as food prices rose.

From the 1730s on there had been some improvement in farming techniques and yields, but nothing that could be described as a real agricultural revolution. The peasants had too little capital and security to take risks on innovations, while the landlords, noble or bourgeois, had little interest in improving output. The agriculturalist Arthur Young was a keen exponent of the new methods and his *Travels in France in 1787, 1788 and 1789* abounds with references to poor techniques and lack of interest: low investment, absentee landlords, sharecropping all militated against rapid development. The population increase during the 18th century added further problems. On the eve of the Revolution the population stood at 28 million; in 1700 it had been 21.5 million. Although some of this increase was absorbed by the towns, it mostly affected rural areas, leading in many districts to the subdivision of existing holdings well below the level of self-sufficiency.

The problem of rural overpopulation was compounded by the rise in prices and rents. In the half-century before 1789 rents and prices rose about 50 per cent, while wages went up by only 25 per cent, and the peasants were increasingly badly off. The state claimed an ever greater proportion of their crop in taxes, and the church tithe and seigneurial dues appeared increasingly burdensome. The peasantry of 1789 was in debt, increasingly resentful – and suffering from the catastrophic effects of the previous year's bad harvest.

RIGHT A typical old peasant woman, with her modest furniture, cat, and the revolutionary red cap (*bonnet rouge*).

BELOW A contemporary cartoon showing a peasant crushed by the levies which the monarchy and the privileged orders imposed.

The *cahier* of St-Hilaire-de-Ligné in the Poitou area.

IN consequence of the king's commands and of the order issued by the seneschal of Civray, we have proceeded to the drawing up of the *cahier* of grievances, complaints and remonstrances which our parish is entitled to make, and after due consideration we have decided only to mention the following:

We would like the roads, which are extremely bad, to be repaired, so as to facilitate communication between one parish and another and also for sending goods to market.

We hope that if in future anything is done to remedy the evils we have mentioned, it will not be at the expense of the inhabitants, most of whom are poor, and the others possess only very limited means.

As for the means of contributing to the needs of the state, as well as all that relates to the prosperity of the nation, we refer this to the understanding of those who are to form the assembly of the Estates General.

Given at St-Hilaire-de-Ligné by the undersigned inhabitants, the syndic presiding over the assembly, 4 March 1789.

The *cahier* of the village of Collan in Champagne.

THE said inhabitants affirm and declare:

That they do not possess any common land;

That they have no grazing for livestock;

That their land is dry, stony and unfertile;

That most of the land is owned by outsiders from neighbouring areas and by bourgeois of Tonnerre and Chablis;

That they are nothing but farm labourers on other people's land;

That they pay a general tithe of one in twenty-one on their crops to the seigneur of Collan;

That they also pay the same lord a quitrent by property owned and by household, as well as one hen or ten *sous*;

That this seigneur never resides in the district;

That their district is poor and wretched, and they have no one, noble or bourgeois, able to help the poor;

That their parish priest has only the basic stipend and is therefore in much distress that he cannot relieve their poverty as he would wish;

That part of their produce consists of white wine, but it sells cheaply;

That they pay heavy indirect taxes on the sale of their wine;

That after payment of these taxes, of the cost of harvesting, stakes and casks, they have very little left to repay their trouble, toil and sweat;

That all goods needed to support life are very dear, and especially salt which sells at 14 *sous* the pound;

That poor people are forced to do without soup for days at a time, not being able to buy it;

That these are all the remonstrances they have to make;

That they desire nothing but the peace and tranquillity of France, the kingdom's prosperity, the welfare of the state and of each of its members and that they will never cease to pray for the preservation of His Majesty's life.

The semi-literate *cahier* of the village of Périllos on the Spanish frontier.

THIS community complains that the seigneur does not allow the removal of vine-stakes if it does not suit him and charges for the staking that he does want. He does not let us raise wool-bearing animals or build sheep-pens in the country.

He makes us pay him the same as the tithe on all grain, so that out of six sheaves, we pay one, tithe included.

He lays claim to, he even forbids us to sell produce from the cultivated land to outsiders; in this way he gets it for almost nothing.

This community is very poor because it does not have the same rights and privileges as others, so that the lord holds us as slaves.

We ask that the tribute-moneys levied by M. de la Houlière, lieutenant and commandant at Salces, should be abolished.

Bourscheid, in eastern France on the German frontier, was a village in which the seigneurial regime was particularly harsh.

THE undersigned inhabitants believe they should begin their *cahier* by giving an idea of the different dues they pay to their seigneurs, and these are as follows:

The seigneurial system

EIGHTEENTH-century feudalism was quite different from that of the Middle Ages. It had no practical role in the political system, and no longer determined relations between nobles and king. The medieval manorial economy had gradually disappeared by the 16th century, leaving free peasants in a limited market economy. By the 1700s, although the word 'feudal' was still used very loosely, it was much more a seigneurial than a feudal system.

RIGHT A box lid illustrating a seigneur's visit to a poor family's house; true to the tradition of *noblesse oblige*.

The seigneurial network extended to virtually all land. The seigneur's personal property, called 'domain land', might be farmed directly, although it was usually rented out under various forms of tenure including sharecropping, or *métayage*. Other land was normally within the 'direct' or 'eminent' property of the seigneur; this meant that the latter was permitted a wide range of 'seigneurial rights' over other landowners. He could exact certain seigneurial dues, like the *cens* or quitrent, an annual money payment, or the (usually far more valuable) *champart*, a kind of seigneurial tithe on peasant produce. The seigneur also had the right to hold a court within the seigneurie, and enjoyed the so-called *banalités*, the right to control by monopoly the flour mill, bread oven and grape press.

These dues varied enormously according to region, and were harsher in the north than in the south; even so, the burden has been exaggerated, for they rarely amounted to as much as a twelfth of the seigneur's income. Nevertheless, in areas like Brittany and Burgundy heavy payments were exacted. The fact that justice was also in the hands of the seigneur – there were over 70,000 seigneurial courts – made protest more difficult and enabled him to protect his own interests.

Seigneuries (lordships) were no longer the preserve of the nobility, but could be bought by the clergy and bourgeoisie. The price rose fast in the 18th century, probably due as much to honorific rights as to more practical ones. The privileges of keeping pigeons, hunting, fishing and having a special pew in church were much sought after as external symbols of status and nobility.

The seigneurial system was severely criticized in the last decades of the *ancien régime*. Some *philosophes* condemned residual elements of personal servitude as contrary to human dignity. Economic thinkers attacked 'feudalism' on the grounds that it stifled economic individualism and hindered progress. Although the litigation it entailed was very profitable, some lawyers and judges argued against such a complex system. However, all educated criticism was muted, because seigneuries were a form of property, and therefore almost sacred. It would need a peasant revolution to overturn such a system.

ABOVE A gold clock presented to the marquis de Rochechouart by the city of Avignon; exemplifying reciprocal feudal ties.

They pay one hen per year per household.

Each household must spin annually two pounds of flax or three of hemp.

To pay the head-of-household tax after the death of the head of the community; this means that the lord takes the second-best beast from the dead man's stable, or, if he had no livestock, he takes from the inheritance a piece of land ploughable in one day, but not until the heir has chosen the first piece himself; and if there is no land or cattle the lord exacts payment of ten *écus*, French money.

The right to tax innkeepers four *pots* per measure of the liquor they sell, be it wine, cider or beer.

Each farmer pays annually dues in cash and in kind on ploughland, whether the land is sown or not; and six *sous* annually for each plot of meadowland.

When the subject of a seigneurie sells his property to another subject of the same lord, the seigneur is entitled to receive a tenth of the price of the goods, even if the sale is between father and son, son and father, brother and brother, etc.

The lord is also entitled to a personal due, called *Leibschafft*, or 'body labour', from his subjects, viz. 32 sols from a farmer and 16 sols from a farm worker.

Each farmer pays annually for each work-horse the sum of 40 *sous* and for each ox 30.

And each peasant also pays the seigneurs annually, in lieu of labour service, five French *livres*.

As for the other matters concerning the improvement of the finances and general welfare of the state, the community refers itself to the wisdom and goodness of His Majesty and of the Estates General.

Given and decreed in the assembled community summoned for that purpose by ourself, the appointed commissioner, and we have signed with the officers of justice and other inhabitants able to sign at Bourscheid 5 April 1789, the *cahier* having been read out and interpreted.

The *cahier* of the Norman village of Vatimesnil contains an attack on the spinning jennies, which were threatening the domestic manufacturing of many peasant households in this textile-producing area.

WE represent to His Majesty that food is too dear and that trade is not moving and that taxation is too heavy and that we can give no help to the State.

And we would like to ask His Majesty for the good of the public to abolish spinning machines because they do great wrong to all poor people.

And we represent to His Majesty some ways which could restore the state to health: such as the clergy, because we have seen communities of four or five religious enjoying thirty or forty thousand livres; above all the benefices, such as those where the clergy get between twelve hundred and twelve thousand livres without usually giving any of it away in charity; and fix a decent income for them and let His Majesty take the surplus.

And we do not know of any other ways in which His Majesty could do good to all his people.

This anonymous pamphlet was produced in Versailles just as the Estates General were gathering.

COMPLAINTS OF THE POOR PEOPLE ADDRESSED TO THE ESTATES GENERAL

The workmen, labourers, craftsmen and others who own no property, or at least none but what nature gave them, who particularly make up the class of poor people and unfortunately one-half of the French nation, find themselves compelled to address those who have been appointed their representatives in order to express their grievances and request means of bringing them relief in their precarious condition, so uncertain and often pitiable.

We have observed that the choice of deputies who are to compose the Assembly of the Estates General has been restricted to that class of persons who possess property. We do in truth belong to the order of the Third Estate which has justly won the right to appear there in numbers equal to that of the representatives of the clergy and the nobility, but among the representatives chosen from the order of the Third Estate there is not one from our class; and it seems as if everything has been done for the sake of rich men and property owners.

THE MASSACHUSETTS MAGAZINE (Boston), *April 1789*

In this kingdom the attention of all orders, ranks and descriptions of subjects, is fixed on the meeting of the Assembly of the Estates General. What advantages will result to the kingdom from this meeting, time only will determine. We may venture, however, as republicans, to predict that they will be salutary . . .

Elections to the Estates General

WHEN Louis XVI's ministers accepted the idea of representative assemblies, it was a measure of how serious the political situation had become. In 1787 the Assembly of Notables – which had not met since 1626 – was revived to curry nation-wide support for new tax reforms which threatened the financial privileges of the nobility and clergy. These stratagems did not succeed in checking the opposition to measures which, they claimed, required the sanction of the nation, embodied in the Estates General.

As the Estates General had last met in 1614, the manner in which this antiquated body was to function caused much debate. The clergy and nobility wanted voting in the assembly to follow the precedent of 1614 and to be by order – which would enable the nobility and clergy in tandem to block reform initiatives from the Third Estate. The latter, in contrast, called for the 'doubling of the Third', that is, making the representation of the Third Estate numerically equivalent to that of the other two orders combined and also for voting by head rather than by order. The Crown gave way on the former point on 27 December 1788: the Third Estate was permitted to elect about 600 deputies against the 300 each allowed the other two orders. However, no decision was made as to whether voting in the assembly would be by head or by order.

Procedures for the elections in March and April were fixed by a regulation issued on 24 January 1789. The old judicial constituency, the *bailliage*, was the framework in which all three orders held separate elections and drew up the lists of grievances – *cahiers de doléances* – which were to accompany every stage of the electoral process. All nobles could attend and vote in their native *bailliage* and all country priests were allowed to attend the ecclesiastical assemblies. As a result, two-thirds of the ecclesiastical chamber for the Estates General were from the lower clergy.

Third Estate electoral procedures were more complex. In the countryside all parishes met to elect delegates to the *bailliage* assemblies which elected deputies. In the towns there were preliminary assemblies of guilds and corporations before the town assembly met to elect delegates to the *bailliage* assembly. Despite the wide franchise, only one peasant went to Versailles as a deputy of the Third Estate and two-thirds of the deputies were lawyers.

BELOW The three Estates on their way to Versailles.

THE CHRISTIAN'S, SCHOLAR'S, AND FARMER'S MAGAZINE (Elizabethtown, N.J.), *June and July 1789*

Elizabethtown, July 31
In France – all eyes are directed to the Estates General, which assembled on 27 April at Versailles – where every accommodation is provided for them, and where galleries are erected to accommodate 3000 persons who are admitted by tickets; there are other galleries to accommodate the people.

In the following letter to his wife written in late April 1789, the noble deputy from the Poitiers region, the marquis de Ferrières, reports on the Réveillon riots in Paris of 27–8 April, occasioned by the rumour that the wealthy wallpaper manufacturer Réveillon had urged wage cuts.

They were doing Iphigenia in Aulis at the Opera; I could not miss such a delightful occasion. Oh my dearest, what exquisite feelings it aroused, what striking music!

While I gave myself up to the sweet sensations that moved my soul, blood was flowing in the Faubourg St-Antoine in Paris. Five or six thousand working men, stirred up by a hellish cabal which aims to destroy the ministry and prevent the Estates from meeting, gathered at ten o'clock in the morning armed with cudgels and launched themselves like furies on the house of a man called Réveillon, manager of the royal factory of that fine wallpaper at the Porte St-Antoine.

They scaled the walls, broke open the doors, howling, yelling, saying that they wanted to murder Réveillon, his wife and his children. They looted everything they could find, burned the papers, the designs, even bonds, laid waste the gardens, cut down the trees. The house was splendidly furnished – mirrors, books, chests, tables, everything was smashed and flung through the windows. Réveillon and his wife and children escaped over the garden walls.

This frenzied mob then attacked another house, one which belonged to Henriot, a rich manufacturer of saltpetre. This was burned and looted like the other.

The Garde Française fired several rounds but this only excited the mob still further. They climbed up on to the houses and threw stones at the troops. The Garde Française charged, firing, and many were killed. The rioting lasted until four in the morning and there were as many as seven or eight hundred dead. The Garde Française lost some of their men.

Another body of five or six hundred working men dispersed about the neighbouring streets and stopped carriages and asked everyone they encountered if they belonged to the Third Estate, heaping them with coarse insults and taking their money and their watches.

There was a meeting of three hundred and fifty nobles at the archbishop's palace in order to choose deputies for the nobility. The rabble set off in that direction; luckily most of them were drunk and they soon changed their minds and continued to infest the streets. The duc de Luynes was stopped, coming back from the racing, and compelled to shout, 'Long live the king and the Third Estate!' Gentlefolk and even the bourgeois are appalled.

There was a similar uprising at Orléans. A gang of boatmen armed with axes and long cudgels went pillaging the houses; as there is no regiment there, there was serious disorder. The young men and the bourgeois of the town had to take up arms and march against the mob. Many are reported killed on both sides; a detachment of the regiment at Blois is being brought up. Two hundred young men and the same number of bourgeois are mounting a regular guard.

All this makes one tremble for the unhappy kingdom. It is a tissue of horrors, of abominations. Everyone can guess who launched this blow. May Providence protect the king.

The pretext is the high price of bread, but this is less dear in Paris than in the provinces.

The Estates General will be stormy. There is great ill feeling between the orders. A great many people have been arrested. Yesterday the king issued an edict bringing guilty persons within the jurisdiction of police courts. The parlement has behaved as it always does, slackly. A few of these unfortunates were found dead in Réveillon's cellars; they had drunk varnish and raw alcohol, thinking it was eau-de-vie. Two of them have been hanged.

The regulations which the marquis de Brézé, the royal Master of Ceremonial, laid down as the prescribed costume of deputies to the Estates General accentuated divisions within the three orders.

CLERGY

Cardinals in red copes.
Archbishops and bishops in rochets, capes, purple cassocks and square caps.
Abbots, deans, canons, parish priests and other deputies of the second rank of clergy in cassocks, long cloaks and square caps.

The luxury trades

THE court at Versailles and the great households of the nobility were not the only markets for ornate objects. The amount of property owned by large landowners, or the administrative élites of Paris and the great cities of provincial France, was often worth twenty or thirty times as much as that owned by prosperous master artisans, but disposable wealth was far more widely distributed than this would suggest. In most cities there were several thousand households whose expenditure went well beyond ordinary necessities. Inventories reveal that many decorative objects, ornate fabrics and gilded furniture could easily be afforded by only relatively prosperous master artisans.

In Paris – by far the largest centre producing luxury goods – the number and size of the guilds associated with furnishing and decoration far outstripped those involved in textile production or the building trades. The corporation of painters and sculptors, known until 1776 as the Académie de Saint-Luc, had well over a thousand members. The joiners and cabinet-makers' corporation was of comparable size, although it did not include the many furniture producers in the Faubourg St-Antoine. The disproportionately large number of cabinet-makers, ornamental painters, fanmakers, bronze-founders, gilders, wood-carvers, gold- and silver-smiths, toymakers, jewellers, japanners and coach-makers in Paris was not just a measure of the size of the city and the wealth of some of its inhabitants; it also showed how technical expertise and commercial information were concentrated in the capital.

Many Parisian products were distributed nationally and internationally through commercial networks in which the capital's mercers – there were more than 200 of them – played a key part. The best known supplied the court at Versailles, foreign embassies in Paris and scores of tiny courts throughout Italy and the Holy Roman Empire. Others exported Parisian goods to wholesalers and retailers all over France and in most large European cities. The technical expertise and designing skills available in Paris enabled the mercers to introduce new types of ornamental objects to a variety of markets and modify many established products.

Adapting techniques and substituting cheaper materials were features of the Parisian luxury trades, and made it possible to increase the range of products and the size and type of market. Papier-mâché instead of wood; porcelain instead of gold or silver; printed textiles instead of woven silk; wallpaper instead of tapestry: all ensured that the line separating luxury from 'bourgeois' goods was always imprecise. The top end of the luxury market was supplied by manufacturers such as the Gobelins (tapestry), Sèvres (porcelain), or the relatively small number of court artisans, but many of their designs were adapted to other materials and objects by their competitors.

This variety and rapid change explains the importance to producers of luxury goods of exclusive privileges to manufacture specific products. These also allowed manufacturers to bypass the guilds' regulations and bring the different occupations associated with, for example, making coaches or wallpaper under the formal control of a single individual. Privileges were often hotly contested by competitors and by the guilds. The celebrated wallpaper manufacturer Jean-Baptiste Réveillon, whose factory was gutted in April 1789, was, at least partly, a victim of the tensions to which his privilege had given rise.

BELOW A typical piece of 18th-century furniture; a secretaire made in the 1780s when mounted Sèvres and Wedgwood plaques were popular.

NOBILITY

All the deputies of the order of nobility will wear coat and cloak of black material of the season, with gold decoration on the cloak, waistcoat to match the decoration, black breeches, white stockings, lace cravat and hat with white plumes turned up in the style of Henri IV. There is no need for the coat buttons to be gold.

THIRD ESTATE

The Deputies of the Third Estate will wear coat, waistcoat and breeches of black cloth, black stockings, with a short silk or fabric cloak such as lawyers and administrators normally wear at court, muslin cravat, and hat turned back on three sides without cords or buttons, such as churchmen wear in lay costume.

In his journal, the court aristocrat the marquis de Bombelles was impressed with the majesty of the procession and religious service which inaugurated the opening of the Estates General on 4 May 1789.

A brilliant day having succeeded the heavy rain that had fallen all night, King Louis XVI, accompanied by a splendid retinue, made his way to the parish church of Notre-Dame, in Versailles.

Two rich banners went ahead of the Recollects, who were followed by the clergy of one of the two parishes of Versailles. Next came the three orders of deputies. The archbishop of Paris carried the Holy Sacrament, and then came the king.

The bodyguards and the Cent-Suisses regiment were on duty at this church. The prayer stool for the king and queen, the chairs, all the seats for the royal family and their retinue, as well as the vast canopy suspended from the vault, were of purple velvet or satin strewn with gold-embroidered fleurs de lis.

The benches on the right were for the clergy, those on the left for the nobility, and places were reserved for the Third Estate near the choir. All these benches were taken indiscriminately, just as the Third Estate felt inclined; they then refused point blank to give them up to the nobility.

Once the king had arrived, mass began. The bishop of Nancy, deputy of the clergy, preached.

Sermon and mass done, the king went back to the palace of Versailles by carriage, as did the queen. There were frequent shouts of 'Long live the king!'; those of 'Long live the queen!' were half-hearted.

No queen of France has been less liked.

Fads and fashions

SINCE the days of Louis XIV, who had built the palace at Versailles, the French court had been a centre of conspicuous consumption and display, famous throughout Europe for its glamour and gratuitous excess. The king's ceremonial of getting up each morning – the so-called *lever* – is a perfect example: a ritual in which he was accompanied by dozens of courtiers from the highest ministers to the humblest shirt-holder.

This, like other ceremonies, was taken desperately seriously by the courtiers, who jostled for status and precedence within this sycophantic world, and who imitated their monarch. Every court figure had his mini-household, modelled on the king's; so that the number of liveried servants and the splendour of their attire was a fair gauge of status. The influence of such customs extended beyond Versailles to wealthy society in general. Solid bourgeois as well as courtiers built up their domestic households, while cooking manuals for the middle classes drew their inspiration from the court.

Court culture evolved over the century, constantly setting fresh norms and aspirations. The arrival of a young new queen in 1774 inspired bewildering changes in women's fashions. Marie-Antoinette was particularly associated with elaborately plumed headgear 'in the fashion of Henri IV', and with hair worn piled up so high that many fashionable ladies had to ride in their carriages with their heads sticking out of the window.

The court's influence on style extended to certain ways of life and leisure activities. Gambling was always a modish vice much practised at court: the queen ran up gambling debts of half a million livres in a single year. (The annual earnings of a small peasant or building worker were between 500 and 700 livres.) Other popular crazes patronized by Marie-Antoinette and her circle were billiards and horse-racing. The latter owed something to English influence – jockeys from Newmarket raced at the course in the Bois de Boulogne. Landscaped English gardens were another of the queen's fads, which also reflected a modishly Rousseau-esque desire to 'get back to nature'. She developed part of her Petit Trianon dwelling at Versailles in the English manner and created the 'Hamlet', a 'Disneyland' rural arcadia in which she dressed as a milkmaid.

Inoculation against smallpox was popularized when Louis XVI and his children underwent the treatment, and the cult of mesmerism was widely supported at court: Marie-Antoinette offered the Austrian quack Mesmer a substantial pension to establish an Institute of

Animal Magnetism in France, where his outlandish pseudo-scientific cures (condemned by a royal commission for inducing orgasm in female patients) could be developed. Ballooning also won royal approval: the brothers Montgolfier, world famed after their first successful aerial ascent in 1783, made a trial ascent at Versailles in 1784, when a sheep, a cockerel and a duck had the pleasure of a ten-minute flight.

By the late 18th century, the less stuffy, more worldly urban culture of Paris was increasingly influential. But Versailles remained an important cultural model until the end of the *ancien régime*.

RIGHT A Louis XVI tabletop with marquetry illustrating an early balloon ascent.

BELOW The mill at Le Hameau, Marie-Antoinette's arcadian playground at the Petit Trianon.

In his account of the opening session of the Estates General, at Versailles, on 5 May 1789, Bombelles is mainly concerned with questions of precedence and etiquette.

5 May. The duchesse de Polignac gave me a place in the gallery reserved for the duc de Normandie; I could only reach the hall of the Estates General at nine o'clock, and there we waited until midday before the king arrived.

The gifted architect Paris was the builder of this superb hall. On either side, nine Doric columns left spaces which were filled by tiers reaching back to the surrounding wall.

Here in this vast setting rose the king's throne, and over it a canopy as magnificent as it was elegant in its sculptures and gilding. From the canopy hung purple draperies strewn with golden fleur-de-lis and caught up to left and right by garlands attached to the columns.

The architect allowed no other colour than white and grey to intrude brightness in a building whose style should be as solemn as its purpose.

The roll-call of the deputies of the three orders took a long time. The clergy sat on the right; the nobility were here placed on the left and the Third Estate opposite the throne.

Once the king had arrived and sat down, the queen took her place on a chair under the canopy but below the throne; her aunts and sisters-in-law sat on her left at a lower level; the king's brothers and the princes of the blood were seated on the right of the throne.

The king delivered nobly and very clearly as wise and suitable a speech as could be wished. He was listened to with attention and with feeling. Only this latter emotion can excuse the fact that he was interrupted by clapping. The end of the speech, which His Majesty took up again very well, was just as strongly applauded, together with shouts of 'Long live the king!'

The Third Estate deputy, Adrien Duquesnoy, gives a commonsensical, rather sceptical, description in his journal of the first session of the Estates General.

THE opening of the Estates took place this morning. Once the deputies were listed and placed, the king arrived. At the opening he made a very concise speech in which he declared that he was summoning the Estates for the purpose of re-establishing order in the finances; he added that he was aware of and would honour his responsibility and would shun dogmatism and innovation, but spoke not a word on the constitution, etc.

The king gave his speech in a voice that was strong but had no grace or harmony; it is harsh and brusque. He was applauded several times. I tried to see why, for certainly there were no grounds for it. I was told that the first time the clapping interrupted him, he seemed upset when he began to speak again; I saw nothing of this and do not believe it.

Next came M. Necker; he was clapped the moment he rose, and spoke for at least three hours. By no means everyone can have been pleased with his speech: he praised the king at every line; no new ideas in administration or finance, but the worst was this: a clear statement that the Estates have only been convoked to re-establish the finances, to make good the deficit, which he puts as high as fifty-six million.

He was taking it for granted that the Estates are only a consultative assembly, arguing that taxes must be left as they are at present.

He took over three-quarters of an hour to prove that the French nation must avoid bankruptcy.

Necker also explained himself loftily on the question of voting by head or by order and demonstrated with determination that the court intends voting to be by order; everlastingly repeating that the king did not summon the Estates because he needed them, but out of his own good pleasure.

In a word, it all seemed prejudiced in favour of the king and the two first orders. Necker now seems to be going back on his word. His speech is being printed; it will appear on Monday, I will send it.

The galleries round the hall were full of people from Paris and from the offices at Versailles who broke into storms of applause when M. Necker talked about avoiding bankruptcy, but I thought that a third of the assembly was very displeased: no applause, often a chilly silence.

And so the battle is engaged!

The GENTLEMAN'S MAGAZINE (London), *July 1789*

Mr NECKER'S memorial on the Scarcity in France, presented to the National Assembly, and referred to the Committee for Subsistence on the present Scarcity, concludes with a high eulogium on the liberality of the sovereign, who had sold grain purchased at a great loss, that the markets might be kept down, and had also given bounties to the bakers, to indemnify them; had, in short, done all that a king and a father could do to alleviate the distress of his people.

The court and politics

THE belief that power was derived from God and held by the king, an absolute monarch, was central to the *ancien régime*. Although the ruler could impose his will summarily, for example, through *lettres de cachet* – arbitrary royal detention orders – there was a clear theoretical distinction between authority exercised legitimately according to French law and despotism, which was the abuse of power. The king was bound to exercise his authority legally and in a Christian fashion, and to respect the rights, privileges and customs of the various corporations, estates and regions.

The court was centred upon the king's household, and a courtier was a noble honoured with some task in the royal domestic service: gentleman of the bedchamber, master of the hunt, lady-in-waiting or page. Expansion under Louis XIV had fixed the court permanently at Versailles and refined it as a political instrument. There were soon thousands of court officers and Versailles became the model for all European states. Like a magnet, it drew nobles from the provinces to shine in the reflected glory of the king. It existed to exalt the monarch and concentrate the gaze of observers on itself.

The elaborate system of etiquette and hierarchy that enmeshed these aristocratic 'servants' encouraged quarrels among the courtiers, and court life became a byword for deceit, intrigue and manners honed to the point of absurdity.

This world was, nevertheless, of prime political importance: the court was the only central institution for the whole state. Patrons and clients were essential elements in society and their interests merged at court, where the king was the ultimate provider of favours. Every local élite had connections with great landowners, magistrates or governors, all of whom had places at court. Grand aristocrats, with easy access to the throne and to government ministers, intervened to secure favours for their clients or acted as go-betweens to reduce all opposition and promote compromises.

Faction was the inevitable by-product of such a system. Life was expensive at Versailles, and the great families needed royal largesse and profitable financial investments to maintain their life-style. The famous *Livre rouge*, the register of royal pensions and gratuities published in 1790, mentioned only two million livres in pensions, but in the 1780s the true figure was nearer thirty million.

Pensions, lucrative sinecures and contracts were hotly competed for by cabals of important families. This competition also extended to policy, with serious consequences for the monarchy: courtiers were more concerned to advance their families than to encourage sound government.

ABOVE The epitome of courtly magnificence: a Chevalier of the Order of the Saint Esprit, part of the machinery of Versailles.

Reforming ministers inevitably came up against powerful vested interests, especially if, like Loménie de Brienne in 1787 and 1788, they reduced the royal household allowances. The great reformer Turgot fell foul of this mentality in 1776, as did Necker in 1781. All the king could hope to do was balance the factions in order to divide and rule.

Ministers could not be above faction; as courtiers, they too needed to compete for favour and rewards and had to reckon with the long-established influence of members of the royal family as well as short-term intrigue. The houses of Orléans, Condé and the Rohan-Guémenée were powerful, and the king's extravagant brothers, the comtes de Provence and d'Artois, could not be ignored.

In the late 1780s even the queen, Marie-Antoinette, and her circle – more particularly the Polignac clan, played a decisive political role.

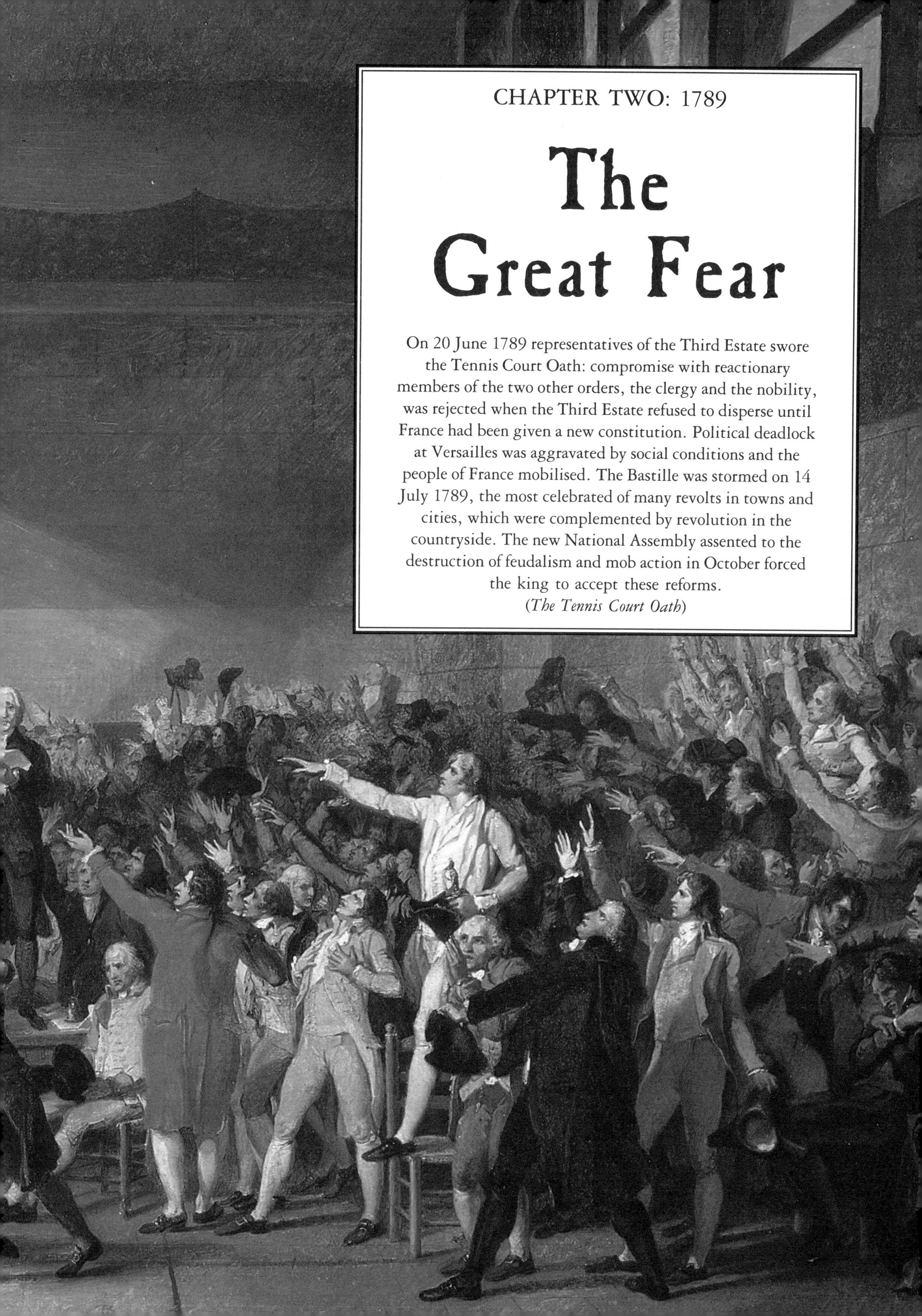

CHAPTER TWO: 1789

The Great Fear

On 20 June 1789 representatives of the Third Estate swore the Tennis Court Oath: compromise with reactionary members of the two other orders, the clergy and the nobility, was rejected when the Third Estate refused to disperse until France had been given a new constitution. Political deadlock at Versailles was aggravated by social conditions and the people of France mobilised. The Bastille was stormed on 14 July 1789, the most celebrated of many revolts in towns and cities, which were complemented by revolution in the countryside. The new National Assembly assented to the destruction of feudalism and mob action in October forced the king to accept these reforms.

(*The Tennis Court Oath*)

WALKING up a long hill to ease my mare, I was joined by a poor woman who complained of the times and that France was a sad country; demanding her reasons, she said her husband had but a morsel of land, one cow, and a poor little horse, yet they had a *franchar* (42 lbs) of wheat and three chickens to pay as a quitrent to one seigneur and four *franchar* of oats, one chicken and one sou to pay to another, besides very heavy tailles and other taxes.

She had seven children, and the cow's milk helped to make the soup. But why, instead of a horse, do not you keep another cow? Oh, her husband could not carry his produce so well without a horse; and asses are little used in the country. It was said, at present, that something was to be done by some great folks for such poor ones; she did not know who nor how, but 'God send us better, *car les tailles et les droits nous écrasent*.'

This woman, at no great distance, might have been taken for sixty or seventy; her figure was so bent, and her face so furrowed and hardened by labour – but she said she was only twenty-eight. An Englishman who has not travelled cannot imagine the figure made by infinitely the greater part of the countrywomen in France; it speaks at the first sight hard and severe labour.

That encounter between a peasant woman and the English agronomist Arthur Young, who was touring France in 1789, captures something of the people's desperate hopes for reform pinned on the Estates General.

The day after the first meeting of the Estates General, however, the court aristocrat the marquis de Bombelles noted in his diary that proceedings were instantly blocked by a dispute over the 'verification of powers' (the formal checking of deputies' credentials).

6 May 1789. The orders met today, each in their own assembly rooms. The Third Estate did nothing, because its instigators wished for the three estates to confirm their powers in common, while the clergy and the nobility apparently wish to verify their powers in their separate chambers, as in previous sessions of the Estates General such as in 1614.

The nobility voted, by 188 to 46, to continue in separate assembly on this matter.

The clergy were of the same opinion, though with a smaller majority.

The noble deputy the marquis de Ferrières, writing to his wife on 15 May, was even more scathing about the chances of anything effective emerging from the political deadlock.

Our Estates General are doing nothing. We meet together every day at nine o'clock: by the time we leave it is half-past four; we spend the whole day in useless chatter and shouting, with no one listening to anyone else. The truth is, my dear, that the Estates General is a poor sort of institution: the French have no talent for self-governance.

On 4 June 1789, the Austrian ambassador in Paris, Count Mercy, reported to Joseph II, Holy Roman Emperor, the ruler of Austria and the brother of Marie-Antoinette, that the situation seemed to call for a royal *coup de force* to get rid of the Estates General.

Since the Estates General's first meeting, there has been nothing but useless argument as to whether matters should be decided by order or by head.

The three estates differ on every point. The king tends to favour the clergy and the nobility; M. Necker has a greater inclination towards the Third Estate. Violence may be the only possible way to save the monarchy.

The secret correspondence from an undercover agent in Paris to Empress Catherine II of Russia reports the death, on 4 June, of the eldest son of Louis XVI. This loss may well have had an impact on the mental state of the king and queen over the summer.

The dauphin died yesterday at Meudon, at one o'clock in the morning.

The sad news was announced immediately, but as no instructions were given to priests or actors, the theatres remained open in Paris and churches continued to offer prayers for the prince's recovery. It was not until six o'clock in the evening that orders were received: the prayers ceased immediately, and theatre curtains came down. Official mourning will last for two months.

The duc de Normandie, aged seven, who is now dauphin, appears to enjoy a stronger constitution; but since he was inoculated he has been subject to nervous attacks which resemble epilepsy.

The royal family

In May 1770, in great splendour, Louis-Auguste, dauphin of France, not yet sixteen years old, was married to the marginally younger Habsburg archduchess, Marie-Antoinette. Their courtship was devoid of romance: the marriage was arranged by diplomats to consolidate the alliance between the royal families of France and Austria.

The two were singularly ill-matched: the dauphin was shy, awkward, and rather a misfit at the formal French court of his grandfather; the archduchess, educated in the far freer court of Vienna, was lively, attractive and uninhibited.

The marriage was not consummated for several years, and the unhappy fumblings of the royal couple as they attempted to perform their dynastic duty and conceive an heir to the throne (to which Louis had succeeded in 1774) was very much a public affair. Spies checked the royal bedlinen, the empress Maria Theresa offered detailed marital advice to her daughter, and it was soon suspected that Louis was impotent.

On one level, the king's impotence was easily explained. He had phimosis, a painful complaint involving a slightly deformed foreskin which inhibited penile erection. Physical distress and psychological pressures combined to make it impossible for him to make love to the queen. For many years he was unwilling to submit to medical examination. Eventually the Habsburg family decided to intervene and Joseph II of Austria, Marie-Antoinette's brother, visited France in 1777 to talk to the couple. Soon after, the king agreed to a minor corrective operation.

The long period of uncertainty had permanently conditioned the atmosphere at court. Because the monarchs were so young, and Louis' impotence so prolonged, factions inevitably tried to take advantage of the situation. The *arriviste* Polignac family became powerful in the queen's household, to the exclusion of other groups. As there was clearly no chance of establishing a royal mistress, each faction hoped to gain favour and influence by providing Marie-Antoinette with a lover. The Noailles put forward the vicomte de Noailles, who was rejected, and the Choiseul family proposed the duc de Lauzun. In the event, the queen took a liking to the forty-year-old duc de Coigny and to the young and handsome Swedish count Fersen. It may be that neither relationship led to infidelity, but gossip, speculation and innuendo were rife.

Marie Antoinette's first child – a little girl known later as Mme Royale – was born in 1778, to be followed by an heir in 1781 and a second son in 1785. The births were greeted by scandalous libels. Louis was a proud and devoted father and a close family life developed. The royal couple was therefore devastatd by the death of the dauphin, from tuberculosis, at the age of eight in June 1789. The king and queen withdrew to their apartments and then retired to the relative seclusion of Marly. Access to the emotionally vulnerable king was easy for the few courtiers present, and the extreme aristocratic faction took the opportunity to turn the tables on Necker at a crucial stage of the Estates General.

ABOVE Louis XVI (left) and Marie-Antoinette, who holds the future Louis XVII, with Mme Royale to her right.

Arthur Young was in Paris on 9 June and observed at first hand both the political and economic aspects of the impending crisis.

THE business going forward at present in the pamphlet shops of Paris is incredible. I went to the Palais-Royal to see what new things were published, and to procure a catalogue of all. Every hour produces something new. Thirteen came out today, sixteen yesterday, and ninety-two last week.

Nineteen-twentieths of these productions are in favour of liberty, and commonly violent against the clergy and nobility. Inquiring for whatever had appeared on the other side of the question, to my astonishment I find there are but two or three that have merit enough to be known.

Is it not wonderful, that while the press teems with the most levelling and even seditious principles that, if put in execution, would overturn the monarchy, nothing in reply appears and not the least step is taken by the court to restrain this extreme licentiousness of publication? It is easy to conceive the spirit that must thus be raised among the people.

But the coffee-houses in the Palais-Royal present yet more singular and astonishing spectacles; they are not only crowded within, but other expectant crowds are at the doors and windows, listening open-mouthed to certain orators, who from chairs or tables harangue each his little audience: the eagerness with which they are heard, and the thunder of applause they receive for every sentiment of more than common hardiness or violence against the present government, cannot easily be imagined.

I am all amazement at the ministry permitting such nests and hot-beds of sedition and revolt which disseminate amongst the people every hour principles that by and by must be opposed with vigour, and therefore it seems little short of madness to allow the propagation at present.

The Third Estate, or 'commons', took the initiative on 17 June by restyling themselves 'National Assembly' and calling on members of the other orders to join with them in proceeding to reform France. This account comes from the French equivalent of *Hansard*, the *Moniteur*.

PRESIDENT of the Assembly: I am going to put to the vote various motions relating to the way in which the assembly should be constituted.

Five motions were read out and discussed. The first to be put to the vote was that of abbé Siéyès: the others will be put to the vote in succession if the first does not receive a unanimous majority.

Abbé Sieyès' motion was passed by a majority of 491 votes to 90. The assembly therefore decreed as follows:

'Subsequent to the verification of the powers of its members, the assembly recognizes that this assembly is already made up of representatives chosen directly by at least 96 per cent of the nation.

'Further, since it is only representatives who have verified their powers who are empowered to express the wishes of the nation, and since all such representatives are present within this assembly, it is clearly evident that it is the duty of this assembly, and of this assembly alone, to interpret and present the general will of the nation: between the throne and this assembly there can be no veto, no power of prohibition.

'The assembly therefore declares that the common task of national reconstruction can and must be commenced without delay by the deputies here present, and that they must persist in this task without interruption or hindrance.

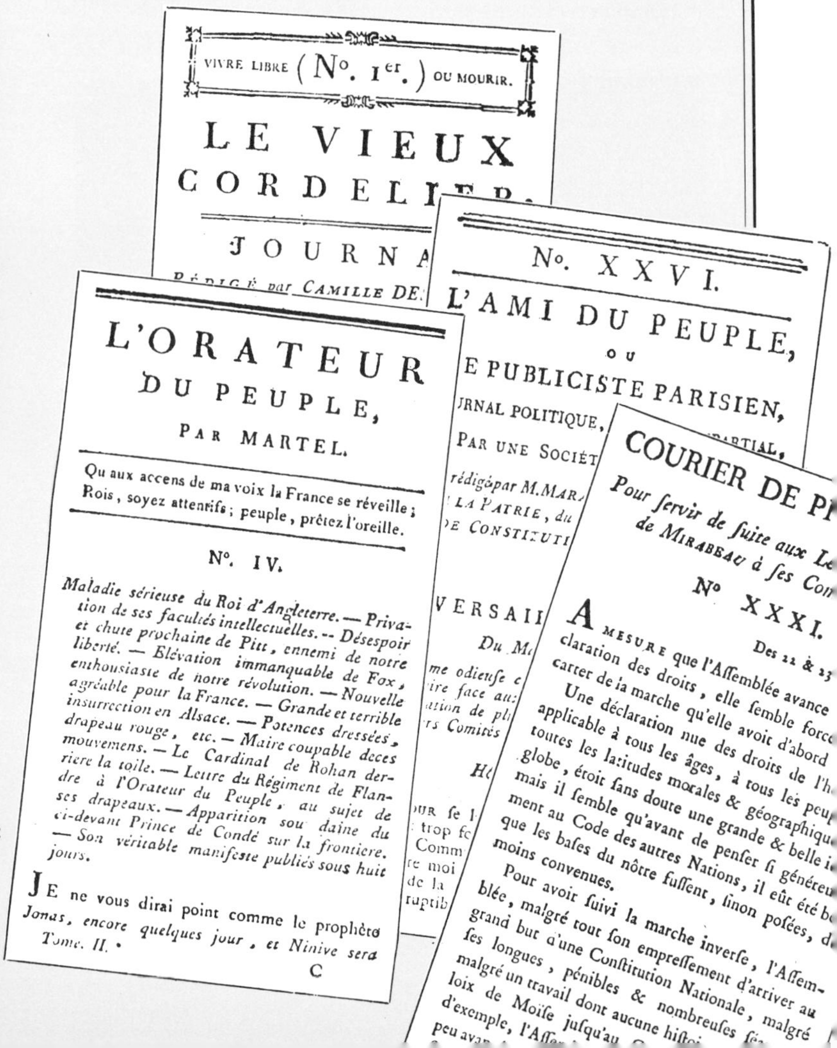

Censorship

For more than two hundred years from the 16th century it was illegal to publish a printed work – book, pamphlet or newspaper – without specific government permission, or without its content first being examined by an official censor. Writers who ignored the law ran the risk of arrest and imprisonment; in 1757 a royal decree ordered the death penalty for anyone convicted of writing or publishing anything critical of religion or government. Executions were in fact rare, but authors were often arrested.

Many works were published abroad and smuggled into France. The contraband included respectable books, banned in France because of their religious or political views. But in the years before the Revolution, there was an increasing traffic in political pamphlets which attacked social privilege and the corruption of the French political system. They were written by a 'Grub Street' of Parisian pamphleteers, embittered by their failure to build respectable literary careers for themselves and angry at the country's failure to reform. Many of their most influential works specialized in personal attacks on the royal family or on court life at Versailles, and some were openly pornographic: they ridiculed the king for his marital problems and Marie-Antoinette for her alleged sexual voracity.

Press restrictions were eased when the king was forced to call the Estates General. On 5 July 1788 a royal edict suspended censorship on pamphlets and books so that electoral procedures for the Estates General could be discussed freely, and writings on taxation, political representation and social reforms soon poured off the presses. Ministers refused to extend the same freedom to newspapers.

Insistent demands were made for journalism to be freed from intervention, and politicians like Mirabeau pointed to England and America, arguing that political reform was impossible without a free press.

Mirabeau was elected as deputy for the Third Estate of Provence and, after the opening of the Estates General on 5 May 1789, he promptly published his own newspaper, the *Etats Généraux*, giving details of the opening ceremony. The paper was banned, but Mirabeau renamed it *Lettres à ses commettants* and claimed he was exercising his right to communicate with his constituents. The government was forced to back down, and newspaper censorship soon collapsed. By the end of 1789 well over a hundred political newspapers had appeared in Paris, including Marat's *L'Ami du Peuple*, *Les Révolutions de France et de Brabant*, to which Camille Desmoulins was a major contributor, and the *Moniteur*, France's *Hansard*. They also sprang up in many provincial cities.

ABOVE The arcades of the Palais-Royal, where pamphlets were sold.

Although circulation figures were low by modern standards – the larger Parisian newspapers could count on between 5000 and 20,000 copies being sold, while provincial titles did well with sales of a few hundred – they were impressive by the standards of the 18th century, when over half the population was unable to read or write. Moreover, newspapers were shared in cafés and reading clubs, or read out aloud on street corners, so their real influence was far wider than sales figures would suggest. Leading Parisian journalists – Mirabeau, Brissot, Desmoulins and Marat – became national celebrities overnight, with great political influence.

On 20 June the king decided to suspend the meeting of all three orders until 22 June, when he would hold a 'royal session', or *séance royale*, to resolve the deadlock. The consequences led to deputies swearing the famous Tennis Court Oath, and are recounted in the journal of Creuzé-Latouche, a deputy for the Third Estate in Poitou.

It is said that the king has today ordered the official closure of the chamber, and has had a notice posted announcing a séance royale *[royal session] on Monday 22 June. This act of tyranny has caused much outcry here, although the cause is not known; it is claimed that it is intended to protect part of the clergy and the whole of the nobility from the shame of being forced to give in to the commons, apparently under pressure from the king.*

The deputies found all the doors of their chamber guarded by soldiers from the Garde Française, who prevented entry. At the same time the heralds at arms in the city proclaimed a séance royale *on Monday and the suspension of the assemblies until that day.*

This announcement created a tremendous public reaction, particularly among the common people: the news spread quickly to Paris, and caused great turmoil.

The deputies and the president of the National Assembly, however, considered that their important work should not be interrupted and moved to an empty tennis court nearby.

They all gathered there together, keenly aware both of the importance of their mission and of the unseemly manner in which a government accustomed to duping a great nation had now acted towards its representatives.

M. Mounier suggested, in moving tones, that no doubt the king had been motivated only by good intentions in his desire to hold a séance royale, *but that the way in which the session had been announced was entirely unacceptable.*

'Let us all swear,' he said, 'let us swear to God and our country that we will not disperse until we have established a sound and just constitution, as instructed by those who nominated us.'

This proposition was greeted with loud acclaim, and several members of the assembly were moved to tears. I saw several who joyfully took the heroic vow not to return home to wife and children until they had proved themselves more worthy of their loved ones by fulfilling their patriotic duty.

An official statement was suggested and the decree was drawn up, setting out the oath. The president was the first to swear; every member of the assembly took the oath after him, and all signed the decree and the statement.

A crowd of the common people had gathered outside the Tennis court where this assembly was being held, while several citizens were sitting inside, some in our midst and others in the galleries. I must also mention that there were women among the spectators.

The statement of the day's proceedings is to be printed immediately for all in the nation to see.

The session closed at seven o'clock in the evening, and the next National Assembly was set for Monday 22 June in the usual chamber.

Deputies from Brittany influenced events at the *séance royale* in ways evoked here by the abbé Grégoire, one of the most outstanding radicals in the clerical deputation. The 'Breton Club' expanded in late 1789 to become the famous Jacobin Club.

THE *séance royale* took place three days after the Tennis Court Oath on Tuesday 23 June. The previous evening we gathered together, about a dozen or fifteen deputies, at the Breton Club, so named after the Bretons who founded it. Knowing what reform measures the court was planning for the next day, we all discussed every item.

The first resolution was to remain in the usual chamber, even if the king forbade it. It was agreed that before the session opened we would go around amongst our friends to let them know what was about to happen, and what plans must be prepared in opposition. But, said one of our number, how can the wishes of twelve or fifteen people determine the actions of twelve hundred deputies? The answer was, that we use the magic word '*they*'. We will say, 'This is what the court is about to do, and as for the patriots, "*they*" have agreed on such and such measures.' '*They*' can mean 400 people just as easily as it can mean ten. Our plan worked.

THE CHRISTIAN'S, SCHOLAR'S, AND FARMER'S MAGAZINE (Elizabethtown, N.J.), *April and May 1789*

Paris February 19, 1789.
Pamphlets and handbills without number circulate as they did in America; and breathe the same spirit. The assembly of the Estates General, will be the epoch of the glory of this country, by uniting the majesty of the king with the greater majesty of the people, that union will be produced which will render this the most powerful nation in Europe.

Paris in the 18th century

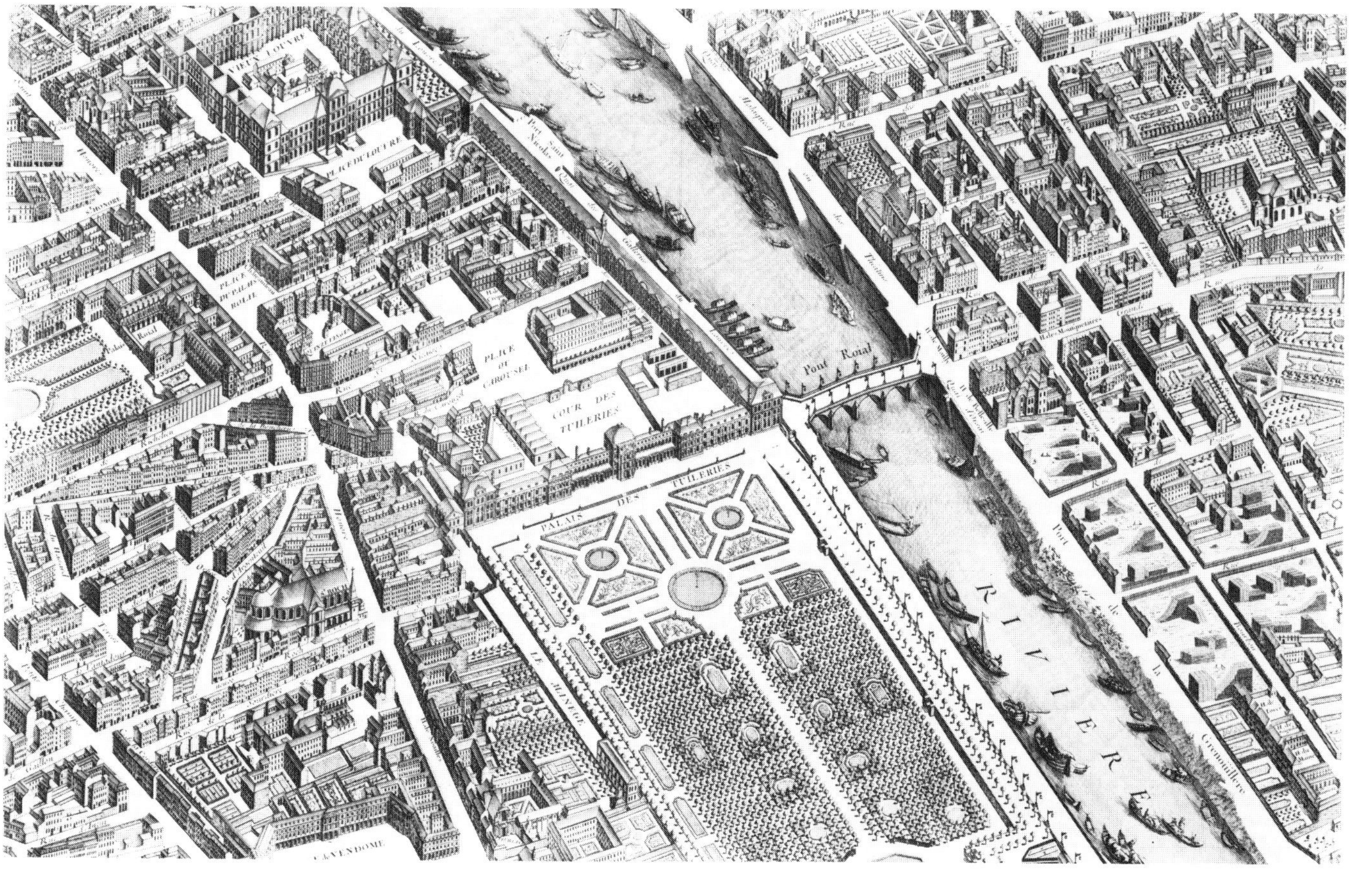

ABOVE The area of the Tuileries, from a map of Paris produced in the mid-18th century by the Provost of Merchants' office.

THE second-largest city in Europe, exceeded only by London, Paris had a population in 1789 of about 650,000. Two-thirds of Parisians were born in the provinces – the rate of immigration was so high during the 18th century that when a new wall was built in 1785, to control the entry of goods on which duty was payable, it enclosed some 3000 hectares, three times the area of the city in 1700. There were many open spaces, private gardens and numerous small farms inside the walls; market gardening was one of the main occupations in the suburbs.

Beggars were part of city life, and at times of crisis, like the hungry winter of 1788–9, the unemployed flocked into the capital in search of work. Even in good years many people were on the bread-line, and even a small increase in the price of food could be disastrous. Meanwhile, the rich led lives of conspicuous consumption. Bankers and businessmen lived in the Faubourg St-Honoré close to the stock exchange (established in 1724 on the site of the present Bibliothèque Nationale), and the great noble families congregated in the Faubourg St-Germain. In both these areas the streets were wide, flanked by graceful, spacious houses. In sharp contrast, in the city's ancient centre, six- and seven-storey tenements darkened narrow, crowded streets, and obscure passageways gave access to secondary buildings and a maze of courtyards within each block.

Luxury goods made in Paris were exported all over Europe. Furniture was produced largely in the renowned Faubourg St-Antoine, while the other major working-class area, the Faubourg St-Marcel, specialized in tanning, dyeing and brewing the internationally renowned Paris beer. Printers and booksellers were concentrated around the University on the Left Bank, textile manufacturing and dressmaking in the north-central district.

For most people life revolved around the neighbourhood. They generally found work through local networks, and were helped by neighbours when they were ill, injured or had fallen on hard times. Wells and shops were meeting-places where local gossip was exchanged, and where national events and rumours ▸

TOP The Pont-Neuf, little changed from the days of the Revolution.

ABOVE The Café Procope, believed to be the oldest in Europe, which hosted Voltaire, Benjamin Franklin, Robespierre and others.

ABOVE A narrow Parisian street, looking towards St-Gervais church. Poor areas such as this, or the Faubourg St-Antoine, were centres of disease and simmering discontent.

RIGHT Parisians on the Pont-au-Change enjoying a pattern of lower class urban life still essentially the same as that which the 15th-century poet François Villon described.

about price rises and the state of the harvest, about spectacular robberies and ministerial re-shuffles, were discussed. The police kept a close watch on cafés and wineshops and their predominantly male customers, and on the bakers' shops and markets, where crowds of women gathered and where there was a permanent danger of riot when the prices of basic necessities rose sharply.

In the prosperous Faubourg St-Honoré, life revolved around the Palais-Royal, Paris residence of the king's cousin, the duc d'Orléans. Originally it had been an extensive garden, closed to vehicles but open to strollers, a favourite promenade for respectable people. In the 1780s, when the duke enclosed the garden with a rectangle of shops and galleries, the Palais-Royal became one of the city's leisure centres, with puppets and side-shows, jewellers and watchmakers, and luxury items that attracted foreign tourists as well as local buyers. It also became a haven for prostitutes. Above all, however, the Palais was renowned for its cafés, which were to become the principal centre of agitation in late 1788 and early 1789, when the convocation of the Estates General unleashed a flood of pamphlets and press censorship virtually ceased. The palace was private property and the police could not enter without permission, so pamphlets were read aloud and orators openly expressed their views. Orléans did nothing to suppress this activity, and on 13 July 1789, the call to arms that inaugurated the insurrection in Paris was given from the Palais-Royal.

Creuzé-Latouche's account of the *séance royale*, finally held on Tuesday 23 June, highlights the sullen resentment of deputies of the National Assembly at this attempt to circumvent constitutional rule.

First of all the king read an address which was followed only by the same dismal silence in which it had been heard. People noticed that his voice trembled. During the king's speech all present remained standing; when it was finished, the king gave permission to be seated and replace hats.

A declaration of the king was read out, of several articles, without any introduction. One of the principal statements of this declaration is that the king annuls all previous decrees of the National Assembly up to this day, that he confirms that the orders are to meet separately and not in a single assembly.

The king made another speech, which included various features favourable to the privileged orders; they were acclaimed by the deputies of those orders, who immediately cried out 'Vive le roi!' But the deputies of the Third Estate remained motionless and totally silent.

After the king's second speech, the Keeper of the Seals announced the 'Declaration of the King's Intentions'. They made up the most bizarre, the most despotic, the most contradictory set of instructions ever to be found in history: the king thereby annulled all limited powers, prohibited the establishment of any future limited powers, desired that deliberation should take place by orders, etc., etc., desired that all property rights should be observed, such as tithes, seigneurial dues, feudal rights, etc., etc., and abolished mortmain (which is also a form of property), abolished lettres de cachet, *with modifications which allow the continuance of their use in the most general way – in fact, drew up the constitution by himself.*

Some features of these arrangements which favoured the privileged orders were greeted by them with cries of 'Vive le roi!' while there was unbroken silence and no response from the deputies of the Third Estate.

The king made a third speech, saying that he was familiar with all the cahiers, *that he was going to declare himself the representative of the Nation. The three orders were forbidden by the king to hold any assembly before the next day, when he wished them to assemble separately.*

During this third address the king's voice was noticeably altered, and it was generally perceived that he spoke with less assurance. He stood up, looked briefly at the silent and unmoving assembly, and departed.

The Tennis Court Oath and the séance royale

THE political deadlock which had gripped the Estates General since its opening session on 5 May, over whether deputies should meet and vote by order or in joint session (ensuring a majority for the Third Estate) was shattered by three developments: the Third Estate's decision to call itself the National Assembly on 17 June, the Tennis Court Oath of 20 June and the *séance royale*, or royal session, of 23 June.

On 10 June the Third Estate sent the nobility and clergy a final invitation to meet in joint session and turn 'from sectional interests to attend to those of the nation'. This was refused and on 17 June the Third Estate formally declared itself to constitute the National Assembly. The defection of a sprinkling of clerical deputies to the new body added credibility to its claims.

The declaration threw the court into a quandary. Necker advised Louis XVI to call a plenary session and

propose a balanced range of reforms which would isolate extremists to left and right, and rally men of good will around the throne. However, arrangements for the *séance royale* were mishandled. Deputies of the National Assembly, barred from their normal meeting-place by troops acting on royal orders to suspend all sessions until the *séance royale* convened, feared an imminent monarchical coup – and met instead at a nearby covered tennis court. Here, with a single exception – the stubborn royalist Martin d'Auch – they swore that they would not disperse until a new constitution had been established.

The Tennis Court Oath cut the ground from under the king's feet, and when the *séance royale* was eventually held, on 23 June, Louis was forced to make concessions in an attempt to defuse the situation: there was to be a new legal system; serfdom was to be abolished; *lettres de cachet* were to be ended. It was also announced that the crown would in future govern alongside an elected assembly, the Estates General, and that both would control taxation. However, his statement that 'the ancient distinction of orders is an integral part of the constitution' meant that division into orders was sacrosanct, that the vote of 17 June establishing a National Assembly was illegal, and that the two privileged orders would be able to block the Third Estate's reform initiatives in the Estates General. Moreover, Louis made matters worse by deliberately excluding from discussion everything related to 'feudal or seigneurial property and the constitutional rights of the three orders'.

When the king left the assembly hall, the deputies of the National Assembly remained and, galvanised by Mirabeau, reaffirmed their statement of 20 June. 'D— it, let them stay!' was Louis XVI's comment when told of this gesture. Over the next few days, members of the National Assembly were joined by growing numbers of deputies from the other two orders. Finally, Louis instructed the rumps of the clerical and noble orders to join together with the new body.

At the same time, he began to draw up troops around Paris and Versailles for what seemed like a final royalist *coup de force* against the Assembly. Confrontation was on the cards. The road to the Bastille lay open.

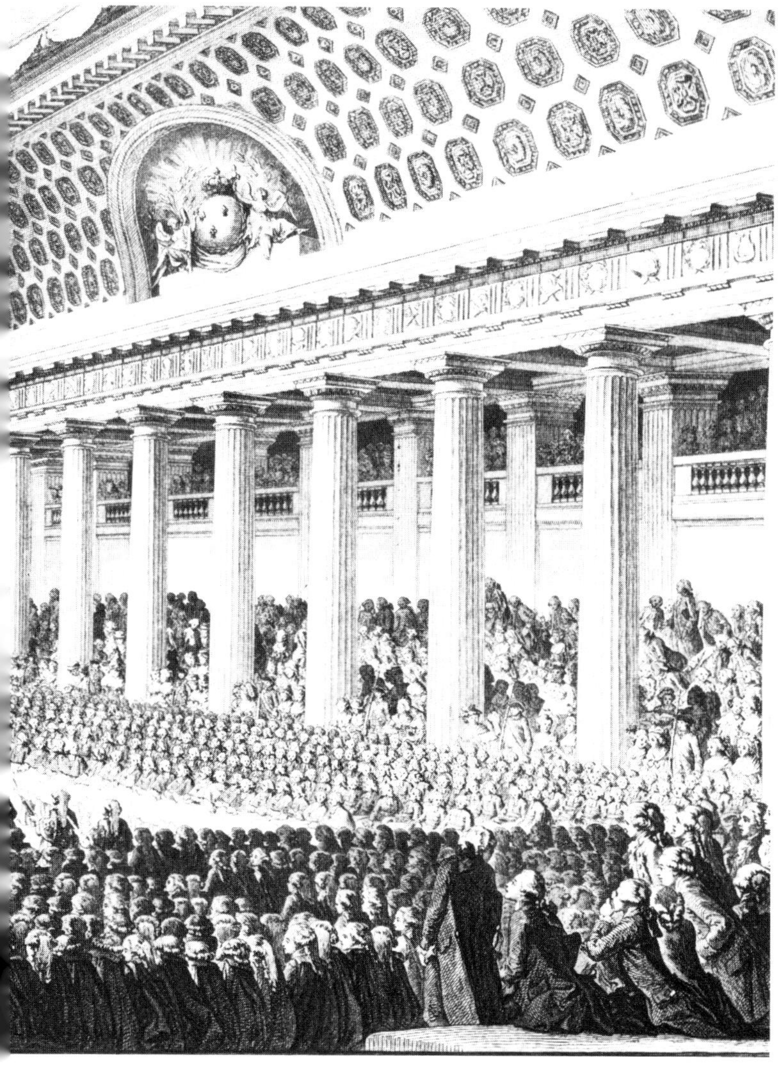

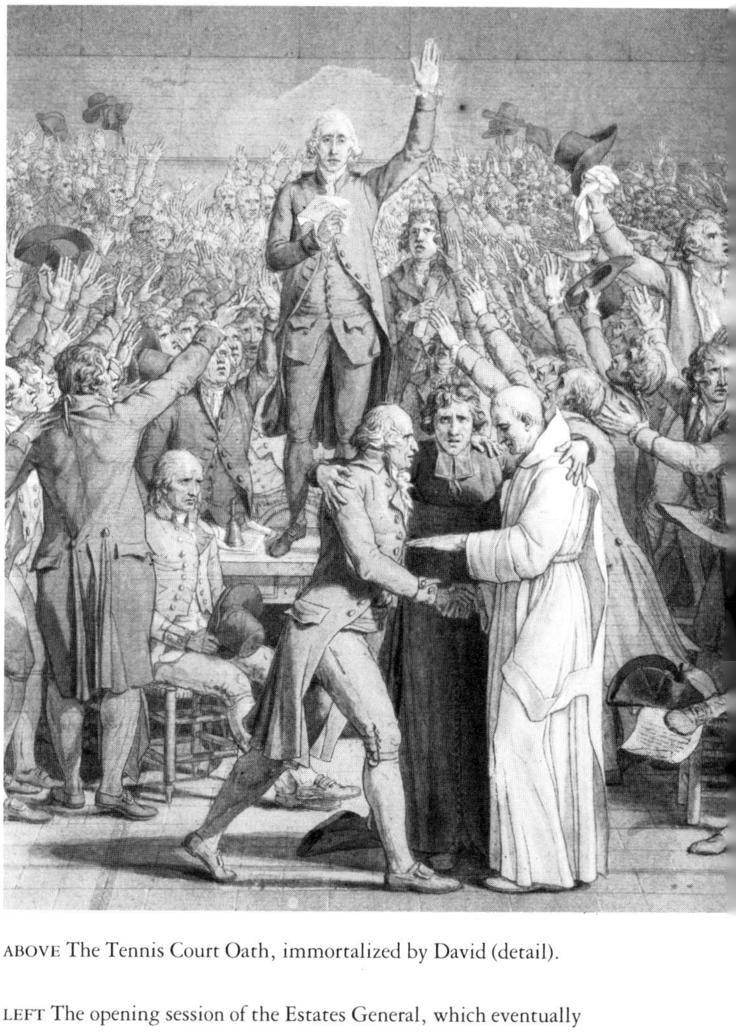

ABOVE The Tennis Court Oath, immortalized by David (detail).

LEFT The opening session of the Estates General, which eventually toppled the regime that had convened it.

The *Moniteur*'s account of events at the end of the *séance royale* shows the assembly refusing to bow to the king's will.

WHEN King Louis XVI had gone, nearly all the bishops, some of the curés and a large party of the nobility withdrew by the same door which had been opened for the court. The other deputies remained in their places: they looked at each other in astonishment, unsure as to what they should do and waiting for advice which would end their uncertainty.

Mirabeau rose. Then M. de Bréźé, the king's Master of Ceremonial, approached the assembly, and spoke a few words in a slow and hesitant voice. 'Louder!' came the cry. 'Gentlemen,' he continued, 'you have heard the king's instructions.' *M. de Mirabeau*: 'Indeed, sir, we have heard the views which have been put to the king; and you, who should not attempt to address the Estates General on his behalf, you who have no seat here, no right of speech, it is not for you to remind us of his words. However, to avoid any misunderstanding or delay, I declare that if you have been instructed to make us leave this place, you should seek permission to use force; for only the power of bayonets will dislodge us.'

'Hear hear!' shouted the deputies with one voice.

In the days following 23 June, Louis XVI appeared to give way to the Third Estate, and the National Assembly now began the work of drafting a new constitution. Arthur Young concluded that the revolution was now 'complete'.

THE whole business now seems over, and the revolution complete. The king has been frightened by the mobs into overturning his own act of the *séance royale*, by writing to the presidents of the orders of the nobility and clergy, requiring them to join the Third Estate – full in the teeth of what he had ordained before.

It was represented to him, that the want of bread was so great in every part of the kingdom that there was no extremity to which the people might not be driven; that they were nearly starving, and consequently ready to listen to any suggestions, and on the *qui vive* for all sorts of mischief: that Paris and Versailles would inevitably be burnt; and, in a word, that all sorts of misery and confusion would follow the system announced in the *séance royale*.

Mirabeau

GABRIEL-HONORÉ DE RIQUETI, comte de Mirabeau, the most controversial early leader of the Revolution, died from excess and exhaustion on 2 April 1791 at the age of 42. Rarely had so short a life been so tempestuous. His father, the marquis de Mirabeau, self-styled 'Friend of Mankind', treated him shamefully, even sadistically; he was disgusted that his eldest son, disfigured by smallpox, malformed in body and entirely lacking in elegance, should so betray his notions of a worthy nobleman.

Driven by enormous energy, the young Mirabeau acquired a wide and enlightened education. Despite this, he made himself obnoxious to the local peasantry at his family château in Provence by defending the privileges of a reactionary nobility. His turbulent love-life, extravagance and contempt for social decencies also alienated him from his own class and led to a life marked by successive spells in prison and exile. Ever resourceful, he used this time to expand his education and eventually to embrace the cause of liberty and write passionately against despotism. A visit to England in 1784 confirmed his beliefs. He admired the way in which talent flourished through a free press and in parliamentary debate. Increasingly he came to hate the French nobility as a prop of absolutism, and saw an alliance between king and people as the only hope.

A brilliant writer, able to make almost any subject fascinating, Mirabeau carved out a career in the shady world linking politics, finance – and sex – in the declining years of the *ancien régime*. But as last-ditch plans for reforming France took shape in 1787, he ruined his chances of a respectable political career by scurrilous pamphleteering against the powerful reforming minister Jacques Necker.

He looked hopefully towards the forthcoming Estates General. Like all the 'patriots of '89' he had a vision of a patriotic monarch ruling by popular consent, according to a constitution which guaranteed essential freedoms, and pledged himself to defend the monarchy if he was elected.

Confident that his day had indeed dawned, always sure that he could instantly weigh up a political situation, Mirabeau offered advice to the government – but to no avail. He saw himself as saviour of both king and country, but his past had sown seeds of deep distrust.

In Provence he confronted the nobility, who virtually expelled him from their ranks, driving him towards the Third Estate. He became enormously popular in the great port-city of Marseille where, in March 1789, his

ABOVE Mirabeau's warning to the marquis de Brézé of 23 June 1789, that the assembly would be dispersed only by bayonets.

fiery oratory, imposing manner and reputation as scourge of the aristocracy made him a hero. Although he was elected deputy in Aix, Mirabeau always defended the interests of Marseille – and that city, bastion of the Revolution in the Midi, always looked to Mirabeau.

He was much distrusted in the National Assembly, however. The English observer Arthur Young noted that Mirabeau 'is one of the first pens of France, and certainly the first orator; and yet his reputation is such that he could not carry from confidence six votes on any question in the Estates'. Nevertheless, he soon built up formidable acclaim as a campaigning journalist and powerful speaker. His superb tactical sense won over many doubters, at least temporarily. When the king tried to rescue what he could for the aristocracy, at the *séance royale* on 23 June 1789, Mirabeau rallied the Third Estate and defied an attempt to disperse them, declaring that they could be moved only by bayonets. On 8 July, he urged Louix XVI to dismiss the troops which threatened the Assembly; if heeded, his warning might have forestalled the taking of the Bastille.

He was suspected of helping to organize the *journée* of 6 October, when the common women of Paris marched to Versailles, and the royal family were brought back to Paris. But Mirabeau also seemed to be making himself indispensable to the king: the Assembly, suspicious of his ambition, vetoed any chance of his becoming a minister.

Mirabeau still saw the king as potentially the best defence against both an aristocratic counter-revolution and popular anarchy. In March 1790 he entered into secret negotiations with the royal family – he was paid, he boasted, to express opinions which had always been his own. Unfortunately, even his considerable political skills could not enable him to retain his popularity with the people and radical revolutionaries, while counselling Louis to support the moderate Constitution. He died a hero and was accorded a state funeral and burial in the Panthéon; but the discovery in 1792 of his secret correspondence with the king completed the ruin of his reputation among the revolutionaries.

While appearing to give way to the National Assembly, Louis XVI took steps to rally royalist forces and called the duc de Broglie, an ultra-reactionary, to be maréchal of the king's forces.

Monsieur: I need beside me someone of whose loyalty I can be sure, someone capable of commanding my troops. I will not disguise from you the fact that the situation is near to a crisis, but I am counting on your zeal and your attachment to me. I beg you to come straight to Versailles, as soon as you are able.

The memoirs of Bailly, at this stage president of the National Assembly, highlight the military threat Broglie's forces posed to the assembly.

THE court soon regretted having so easily agreed to the merger of the three estates into the National Assembly. The aims of the assembly were known. What they had done indicated what they intended to do: a new constitution, the object of unanimous approval backed up by total commitment, would provide the means to remedy all abuses.

The court was aware that the nobility and the upper clergy would snatch at any chance to disband an assembly which was planning their downfall; but they needed forces capable of holding Paris in check, of breaking up the assembly, and forcing acceptance of the declaration of 22 June.

Soon, however, thirty regiments were marching on Paris. The pretext was the maintenance of public order: the true purpose was the dissolution of the assembly.

Necker was too involved in the continuance of the assembly to be sympathetic to the court's attitude; he was unpopular with the king and hated by the queen, the princes (the king's brothers) and the powerful Polignac faction – only the people and the assembly were on his side.

Continuous problems delayed the troops' arrival in Paris: no supplies were forthcoming; money could only be obtained with the greatest difficulty.

The duc de Broglie, in command of the Ile-de-France province, set up his headquarters in the palace of Versailles with a brilliant staff. No commander had ever enjoyed such wide powers; everything was put under his command, even the royal bodyguards; and with the common interest in mind, all concern for corporate or individual interest vanished.

The growing crisis seemed inextricably linked with politically manipulated economic shortages, as even the royalist newspaper *L'Ami du Roi* later reported.

THE nearer 14 July came, the greater became the shortage of food. The crowd, besieging every baker's shop, received a parsimonious distribution of bread, always with warnings about possible shortages next day. Fears were redoubled by the complaints of people who had spent the whole day waiting at the baker's door without receiving anything.

There was frequent bloodshed; food was snatched from the hand as people came to blows; workshops were deserted; workmen and craftsmen wasted their time in quarrelling, in trying to get hold of even small amounts of food and, by losing working time in queuing, found themselves unable to pay for the next day's supply.

This bread, moreover, seized with such effort, was far from being of good quality: it was generally blackish, earthy and sour. Swallowing it scratched the throat, and digesting it caused stomach pains.

At the Ecole Militaire and other grain stores I saw flour of terrible quality: disgusting-smelling yellow mounds which produced such rock-hard lumps of bread that it could only be divided up with assiduous use of an axe.

As for myself, discouraged by my lack of success in obtaining this unappetizing bread, and disgusted at the bread available even in hostelries, I completely gave up this item of food. In the evening I went to the Caveau café, where fortunately they had thought to keep for me two of the small bread rolls known as *flûtes*: this was the only bread I had eaten for a whole week.

As I was forced at the height of the shortage to go to Versailles for a short visit, I was curious to see what sort of bread was being eaten at court, or served at the ministers' and deputies' tables. Nowhere could I find even rye bread: everywhere I saw only beautiful bread, of the finest and most delicate quality it was served in great abundance and delivered by the bakers themselves.

THE CHRISTIAN'S, SCHOLAR'S, AND FARMER'S MAGAZINE, (Elizabethtown, N.J.), *April and May, 1789*

London, Feb. 11. The French government have ordered one hundred hand mills to be erected in Paris for grinding flour, to prevent in future any scarcity proceeding from severe frost.

Hunger

In 1790 the National Assembly estimated that one French person in ten was poor. Historians now think that the proportion was nearer one in five, or even one in three. In the short term, the number of the poor depended on the state of the harvest and beliefs about it. If the harvest failed, soaring prices meant that many urban artisans and peasants who leased small plots of land were as vulnerable to shortage of food as were the very young or the very old. In bad years, like 1769, 1776, 1783 or 1789 itself, poverty spread far beyond the most vulnerable core of the destitute.

It was largely a result of the vagaries of the agricultural cycle. The size of the harvest determined the quantity of corn available for seed, the surplus left for sale, the prevailing level of rents and the amount of income available to landowners to spend on manufactured goods. Increases in the price of bread led to reductions in expenditure on non-essential goods and therefore urban unemployment.

Yet the size of the harvest did not, in itself, set the boundary between subsistence and starvation. Dearth, rather than famine, was the usual outcome of harvest failures and tended to be most acute in the late spring and early summer, when prices were governed as much by rumours about the forthcoming harvest as by what had happened the previous year. Agriculture was immensely varied, but was integrated into increasingly interdependent regional markets. The great cereal-producing regions of the Lauraguais near Toulouse, and the Beauce, the Brie and the Ile de France around Paris, supplied corn to more market towns and cities than many other less fertile or less intensively cultivated agricultural areas. The cost of transporting corn differed throughout the kingdom, and higher prices could be made in some important markets, affecting those elsewhere, regardless of the quantity supplied. The price of corn was also determined by what wholesalers and retailers could afford to pay.

The massive price increases of 1788-9 occurred at a time when many sections of the population were vulnerable to the effects of dearth. As corn prices rose, the cost of a 4lb loaf of bread in Paris rose from 8 or 9 *sous* to 14 or 15 *sous* in February 1789, and remained at that level until after the fall of the Bastille. There were similar increases in almost every other urban centre. The effects of the price rises were reinforced by government disarray and the cumulative effects of the rise in rents since the 1750s, a series of livestock epidemics, a sharp fall in the price of wine (and therefore of the income of many wine producers) and a disastrous silk harvest in 1787.

The spectacular surge in prices in the spring of 1789 was as much a result of panic induced by the spectre of hunger, as by the failure of the harvest.

French agricultural prices (1731–1789)

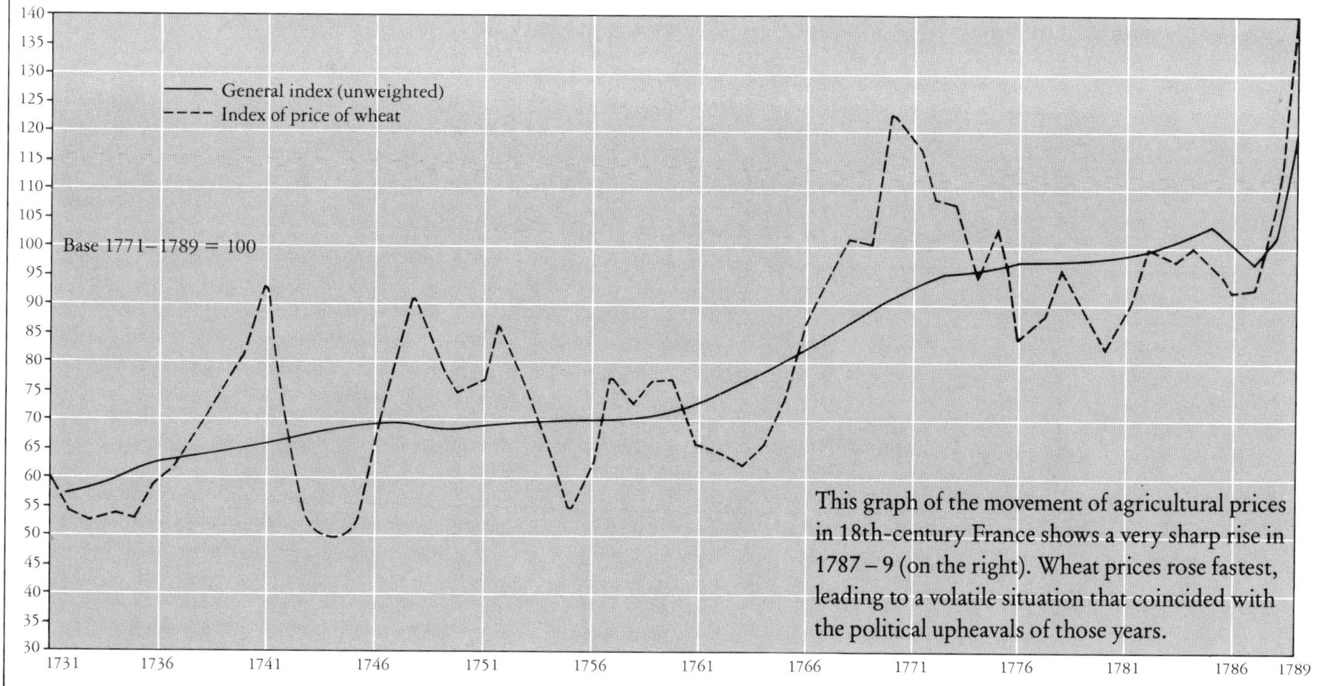

This graph of the movement of agricultural prices in 18th-century France shows a very sharp rise in 1787 – 9 (on the right). Wheat prices rose fastest, leading to a volatile situation that coincided with the political upheavals of those years.

The dismissal on 11 July of the king's popular principal minister Necker is recounted by his daughter, the writer Mme de Staël. It seemed to clear the way for a royal *coup d'état* aimed against the National Assembly, and was the prelude to the events of 14 July.

M. NECKER, my father, continued to visit the king every day; but he was never told anything of importance. This silence towards the principal minister was very disturbing, at a time when foreign troops were seen arriving from all parts and were stationed around Paris and Versailles. Every night my father told us in confidence that he expected to be arrested the next day; but that the danger to which the king was exposed was so great that he made it a rule to seem unconcerned.

At three o'clock in the afternoon of 11 July, M. Necker received a letter from the king; it ordered him to leave Paris and France itself, adding only that he should conceal his departure from everyone. Baron de Breteuil's opinion had been that M. Necker ought to be arrested, as his dismissal was sure to cause a riot. 'I guarantee,' said the king, 'that he will strictly abide by the discretion I will require of him.' M. Necker was touched by the trust this showed, even though it accompanied an order sending him into exile.

Two days after his departure, when his fall from power became known, all the theatres were closed as if for a public disaster. The whole of Paris took up arms.

Necker's reply to the king's letter of dismissal emphasizes his loyalty.

11 JULY 1789. Sire, Your Majesty is losing his most tenderly devoted and honest servant. Please have fond memories of me – I hope you would allow me to justify myself if you have any doubts. I have never feared slander. Sire, I lay before you these feelings which are engraved on my heart. I am leaving alone, without passing through Paris or talking to anyone.

I ask Your Majesty to be similarly discreet.

Necker

The young writer and journalist Camille Desmoulins, writing to his father on 15 July, here describes how he led the call to arms in Paris following Necker's dismissal.

Dearest father,

I can now write to you. How things have changed over the last three days! Sunday last, Paris was aghast at the dismissal of M. Necker; no one would take up arms in spite of my efforts to galvanize people into action. About three o'clock I went to the Palais-Royal; I was deploring our lack of courage to a group of people when three young men came by, holding hands and shouting Aux armes! *(To arms!). I joined them, my enthusiasm quite obvious; I was surrounded and pressed to climb up on a table: there were immediately six thousand people around me;*

I was bursting with hundreds of ideas, and spoke without thought: 'Aux armes!' I cried, 'Aux armes! Let us all wear cockades.' I grabbed a ribbon and pinned it to my hat. My action spread like wildfire! Sound of the tumult reached the camp; the Cravates, the Swiss, the Dragoons, the Royal-Allemand all arrived. The prince Lambesc, heading the latter, entered the Tuileries on horseback. He personally cut down an unarmed Garde Français with his sword, and knocked over women and children. The crowd became wild with anger. And then there was but a single cry across Paris: Aux armes!

The duc de Liancourt tried to impart the seriousness of the situation to Louis XVI.

IT is said that on 12 July, the duc de Liancourt having gone to Versailles to report to the king on the disturbances in Paris, was asked by him: 'So, this is a revolt?' to which the duke replied, 'No Sire, this is a revolution!'

The radical newspaper *Les Révolutions de Paris* describes the organization of defence in the capital as the threat grew of military intervention by the king.

THIS morning, 13 July, at 9 o'clock, the tocsin was rung to assemble the bourgeoisie. Citizens of all ranks and ages able to carry arms answered the call and reported to their districts.

Calm has returned to the capital tonight; except for a few arrests made by the *garde bourgeoise*.

One victory was reported, which may astonish our children: it is the fall of the Bastille, in about four hours. This glorious day must be a surprise for our enemies, and heralds the triumph at last of justice and liberty. Tonight, the whole city will be illuminated.

Necker

JACQUES NECKER was born in Geneva in 1732. He was sent to Paris as an apprentice banker, and soon acquired an enormous fortune. He retired in 1772 to devote himself to public service and entered the government of Louis XVI four years later, in October 1776. In June of the following year he was appointed Director-General of Finances. He soon established a European-wide reputation as an administrator of genius by financing French involvement in the American War of Independence without further burden to the taxpayer.

In his 'Account presented to the king' (*Compte-rendu au roi*), in January 1781, Necker explained the rationale behind his policies. 'Public credit', he wrote, 'consists of nothing more than prudence, order, and good faith.' He particularly stressed the importance of bringing the royal finances out of the council chamber into public view; the *Compte-rendu* was the first account to be published. Conservatives loyal to the absolute monarchy, however, were appalled at such indiscretion, and managed to bring about Necker's resignation in May 1781.

Necker had fallen into disgrace with the king, but not with the general public, who were profoundly dismayed at his departure from office. During 1788, with the government facing bankruptcy and mounting public hostility and with the Estates General already promised for the following year, the court and the queen persuaded the king to recall Necker to his former position. He entered his second ministry on 25 August 1788.

Necker lived up to the public's expectations by successfully managing the financial crisis and the accompanying food shortages, caused by a drastic crop failure that summer. But the political crisis was of a different order. Necker's vision of what should come out of the Estates General was the transformation of absolute monarchy into a limited monarchy on the lines of British government; a national representative assembly would share legislative power with the king, who would be left with complete executive power. He tried valiantly to steer events in this direction.

This goal was probably what a great many educated and responsible deputies, from all three estates, envisaged when the Estates General met on 5 May 1789. However, the Third Estate came to be dominated by the 'patriots', who declared the supremacy of a national legislative body over all other authorities, including the king's. Necker's attempts to find a compromise on the question of voting by order or by head in the Estates General failed, and on 17 June the Third Estate declared itself the National Assembly, sole representative of the French nation. When Louis XVI, under the influence of those who wanted to crush the revolution by force, dismissed Necker on 11 July and stationed troops around Paris, he ignited the popular explosion of 14 July.

After the fall of the Bastille both the king and the National Assembly begged Necker to return to the government. He did so without hesitation, although he realized that the political landscape had fundamentally altered. The king's attempt at force had come to nothing, and it was now a question of whether even a moderate ministry could govern a country in the throes of spreading anarchy and popular violence. A financial crisis loomed – the collapse of public order had reduced the government's revenue by half – and the subsistence crisis mounted as the transport of grain was interrupted.

Necker hoped to establish a working partnership between his ministry and the National Assembly, but the latter was convulsed by a struggle between the 'anglophiles', who still wanted a limited monarchy, and the 'patriots'. On 5 and 6 October – the October Days – the hopes of the moderates were dashed: the National Assembly was forced to move from Versailles to Paris with the royal family, and came under the influence of the Parisian democracy.

During the first eight months of 1790, Necker struggled to restore royal authority and tried to restrain the use of paper money (*assignats*), which, he held, would only worsen the financial crisis. On 2 September, defeated and with extreme bitterness, he submitted his resignation and went into exile.

The British ambassador in Paris, Lord Dorset, in a dispatch to the Foreign Office, surveys the main events of the revolutionary day – or *journée* – of Tuesday 14 July 1789. It highlights the importance of the new bourgeois militia, or *garde bourgeoise*, formed by Parisian property-owners to resist the royal army at Paris's gates and to maintain order.

16 JULY 1789. I wrote to Your Grace on the 12th inst. by a messenger extraordinary to inform you of the removal of M. Necker from his majesty's councils. I have now to lay before Your Grace an account of the general revolt of 14 July, with the extraordinary circumstances attending it, that has been the immediate consequence of that step.

On Sunday evening 12 July all the troops left the capital, and the populace remained unmolested masters of everything. Much to their credit, however, uncontrolled as they now were, no material mischief was done; their whole attention being confined to the burning of some of the customs barriers that ring Paris. Very early on Monday morning the St-Lazare monastery was forced, in which, besides a considerable quantity of corn, were found arms and ammunition.

Now a general consternation was seen throughout the town: all shops were shut; all public and private works at a standstill and scarcely a person to be seen in the streets excepting the garde bourgeoise, *a temporary police for the protection of private property.*

In the morning of Tuesday 14 July the Hospital of Invalids [the veterans' retirement home], was summonsed to surrender, and was taken possession of after a very slight resistance. All the cannon, small arms and ammunition found therein were immediately seized upon, and everyone who chose to arm himself was supplied with what was necessary. The cannon were disposed of in different parts of the town.

In the evening a large detachment with two pieces of cannon went to the Bastille to demand the ammunition that was there, the garde bourgeoise *not being then sufficiently provided. A flag of truce was sent on before and was answered from within, notwithstanding which, the governor (the marquis de Launey), contrary to all precedent, fired upon the people and killed several. This proceeding so enraged the populace that they rushed to the very gates with a determination to force their way through if possible.*

The governor agreed to let in a certain number of them on condition that they should not commit any violence. These terms being acceded to, a detachment of about forty in number advanced and were admitted; but the drawbridge was immediately drawn up again and the whole party instantly massacred.

This breach of honour, aggravated by so glaring an act of inhumanity, excited a spirit of revenge and tumult such as might naturally be expected: the two pieces of cannon were immediately placed against the gate and very soon made a breach which, with the disaffection that as is supposed prevailed within, produced a sudden surrender of that fortress.

M. de Launey, the principal gunner, the tailor, and two old veterans from the Invalides who had been noticed as being more active than the rest, were seized and carried to the Town Hall [Hôtel de Ville].

After a very summary trial before the tribunal there, the inferior objects were put to death and M. de Launey had also his head cut off at the Place de Grève, but with circumstances of barbarity too shocking to relate.

Besides the above mentioned, prévôt des marchands, *M. de Flesselles, who the day before was unanimously called to preside at the assembly at the Hôtel de Ville, was immediately shot with a pistol. His head was cut off, which, with M. de Launey's and the tailor's hand, all placed upon pikes, was exhibited at the Palais-Royal and afterwards in several of the neighbouring streets.*

In the course of the same evening the whole of the Garde Française *joined the bourgeoisie with all their cannon, arms and ammunition. The regiments that were encamped in the Champ-de-Mars, by an order from government, left the ground at 2 o'clock yesterday morning, 15 July, and fell back to Sèvres, outside Paris, leaving all their camp equipage behind them. The magazines of powder and corn at the Ecole Militaire were immediately taken possession of and a* garde bourgeoise *appointed to protect them.*

Upon searching the Bastille not more than four or five prisoners were found, of whom none had been there any length of time, except an Englishman who calls himself Major White, and who had been confined in a dungeon upwards of 30 years; the unhappy man seemed to have nearly lost the use of his intellects and could express himself but very ill; his beard was at least a yard long.

Thus, my lord, the greatest Revolution that we know anything of has been effected with, comparatively speaking – if the magnitude of the event is considered – the loss of very few lives: from this moment we may consider France as a free country; the king a very limited monarch, and the nobility as reduced to a level with the rest of the nation.

The Bastille

ALTHOUGH the name of the Bastille evokes dark images of despotism and unjust imprisonment, in reality it was a great deal pleasanter than most ordinary prisons. Throughout the 18th century there were never more than 40 inmates, most of them serving short sentences. On 14 July 1789, when the Bastille was stormed, there were only half a dozen prisoners, two of whom were manifestly insane.

Originally built in the 14th century to guard one of the principal entrances to Paris, by the 18th century the Bastille served only as a prison – mainly for political and aristocratic prisoners who could not be thrust into the crowded gaols with common criminals – and occasionally as a store for arms. Earlier in the century, Protestants, and subsequently Jansenists, had been incarcerated because of their opposition to the government's religious policy. The fortress also accommodated printers, booksellers and authors who produced works that the authorities considered seditious. Voltaire was imprisoned there twice: first in 1717, when he was suspected of writing verses accusing the Régent of incest, and again in 1726. Later prisoners included contributors to the *Encyclopédie*, Marmontel, the abbé Morellet and Diderot, and the lawyer and journalist Linguet. Author of a periodical banned in 1776 for its outspoken criticism of the government, Linguet continued to publish from London and, on his return to Paris, was imprisoned in the Bastille. Soon after his release he wrote his best-selling *Mémoires sur la Bastille*, whose revelations of his supposed sufferings made his reputation and also added to that of the fortress.

Closely associated with the Bastille were the infamous *lettres de cachet*, warrants signed by the king for the arrest and indefinite detention without trial of a named person; the *cachet* was the wax seal attached to them. This form of arbitrary arrest became the focus for opposition to absolutism during the second half of the 18th century, although its use was in fact in decline under Louis XVI, and political figures were by no means the most common targets of these warrants. The royal government's authority was based on respect for patriarchal dominance, and it was particularly responsive when a family requested the imprisonment of a member whose activities displeased and risked dishonouring them. Mirabeau and the marquis de Sade were both incarcerated in the Bastille for this reason.

Towards the end of the 18th century the Bastille was widely seen as a dark, mysterious dungeon where, at the whim of the king or his ministers, people might disappear for ever and undergo terrible sufferings. A central part of the myth, and an indication of its potency, was the story of a prisoner supposedly forced to wear an iron mask to conceal his identity even from his guards – the sufferings of this Man in the Iron Mask were given wide publicity by Voltaire. Archives of the Bastille reveal that there was indeed a masked prisoner from 1698 until 1703, when he died. The mask was of velvet, and he was well treated.

The legend of the Bastille was given further ►

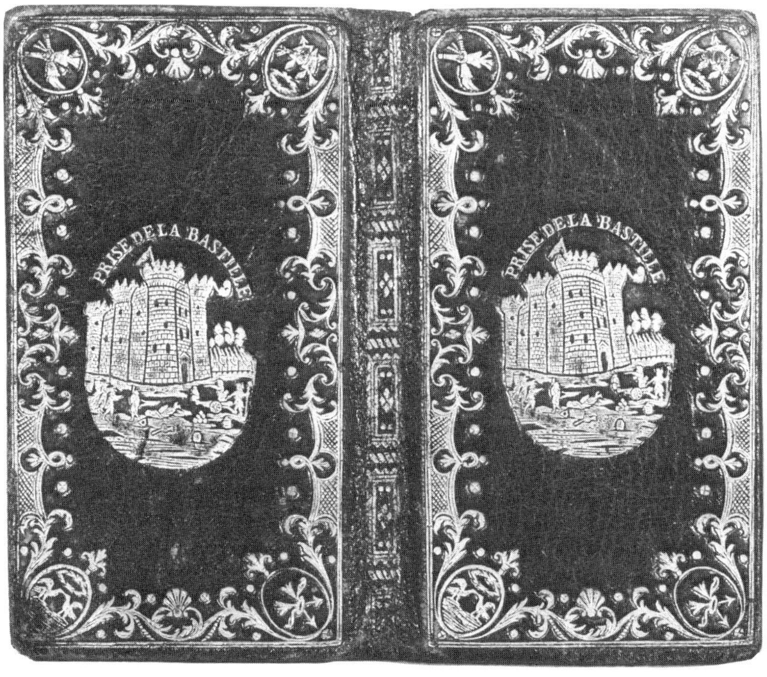

LEFT A commemorative book binding. Long after the Bastille had been demolished its effigy was paraded in Revolutionary festivals.

LEFT A button commemorating the taking of the Bastille.

impetus by Latude, a crook who, in 1749, sent Mme de Pompadour, Louis XV's mistress, a letter warning her that there was a plot to kill her with a letter-bomb. At the same time he sent, anonymously, a packet that supposedly contained gunpowder. His writing was identified, and he was imprisoned in the Bastille. His spectacular escape in 1756 was followed by recapture. Later released but reimprisoned for fraud, he spent a total of 35 years in prison.

ICI ÉTAIT L'ENTRÉE DE L'AVANT COUR
DE LA BASTILLE
PAR LAQUELLE LES ASSAILLANTS
PÉNÉTRÈRENT
DANS LA FORTERESSE
LE 14 JUILLET 1789.

ABOVE The plaque in the Place de la Bastille marking the site of the forecourt of the prison, where the besiegers first broke into the fortress on the historic date, 14 July. The ground plan of the razed fortress is still marked in the cobbles of the Place de la Bastille, now occupied by a column commemorating the 1830 Revolution.

RIGHT After the taking of the Bastille, the crowd seized de Launey, the governor of the prison. He was summarily butchered despite the efforts of the bourgeois militia to protect him; a foretaste of events to come. Rumours of a royal plot to suppress the National Assembly's supporters in Paris and Versailles drove the crowd to act.

The first man to climb on to the tower of the Bastille gives an account of his *journée* of 14 July.

MY name is J. B. Humbert, and I am a native of Langres, working and living in Paris, at M. Belliard's, watchmaker to the king, rue du Hurepoix.

I went to the district of St-André-des-Arts on Monday morning 13 July with the rest of the citizens, and patrolled the streets with them all that day and night, armed with swords, the district having no firearms or only a few.

Overcome with weariness and lack of food and sleep, I left the district at six in the morning. I learned during the course of the morning that arms for the various districts were being distributed at the Invalides. I promptly went back to inform the garde bourgeoise *of St-André-des-Arts.*

We reached the Invalides at about two o'clock. I followed the crowd, to get to the cellar where the arms were kept. On the staircase leading to the cellar, seeing a man armed with two muskets, I took one from him.

Armed with my gun I then set off for my own district. As I learned on the way that they were handing out powder at the Hôtel de Ville I hurried thither, and was given about a quarter of a pound, but they gave me no shot, syaing that they had none.

As I left the Hôtel de Ville I heard someone say that the Bastille was being besieged. My regret at having no shot prompted an idea which I immediately carried out, namely to buy some small nails, which I got from the grocer's at the Coin du Roi, Place de Grève. There I prepared and greased my gun and immediately set off for the Bastille, loading my gun as I went.

It was about half-past three. The first bridge had been lowered, and the chains cut; but the portcullis barred the way; people were trying to bring in some cannon which had previously been dismantled.

I crossed over by the small bridge and from the further side helped to bring in the two guns. When they had been set up on their gun-carriages again, everybody with one accord drew up in rows of five or six, and I found myself in the front rank. The cannon were then levelled: the bronze gun at the large drawbridge and a small iron one, inlaid with silver, at the small bridge.

It was decided to start the attack with musket fire. We each fired half a dozen shots. Then a paper was thrust through an oval gap a few inches across; we ceased fire; one of us went to fetch a plank which was laid on the parapet to enable us to go and collect the paper. One man started out along it, but just as he was about to take the paper, he was killed by a shot and fell into the moat. Another man, carrying a flag, immediately dropped his flag and went to fetch the paper, which was then read out loudly and clearly, so that everyone could hear.

This message, which offered capitulation, proving unsatisfactory, we decided to fire the gun; everyone stood aside to let the cannon-ball pass.

Just as we were about to fire, the small drawbridge was lowered; it was promptly filled by a crowd of people, of whom I was the tenth. We found the gate behind the drawbridge closed: after a couple of minutes an invalide *[veteran] came to open it, and asked what we wanted: Give up the Bastille, I replied, as did everyone else: then he let us in. My first concern was to call for the bridge to be lowered; this was done.*

Then I entered the main courtyard (I was about eighth or tenth). I happened to glance at a staircase on my left, and I saw three citizens who had gone up five or six steps and were hurrying down again.

I immediately rushed over to the staircase to help the citizens, whom I assumed to have been driven back. I rapidly climbed up to the keep, without noticing that nobody was following me; I reached the top of the stairs without meeting anyone, either. In the keep I found a Swiss soldier squatting down with his back to me; I aimed my rifle at him, shouting: lay down your arms; he turned round in surprise, and laid down his weapons, saying: 'Comrade, don't kill me, I'm for the Third Estate and I will defend you to the last drop of my blood; you know I'm obliged to do my job; but I haven't fired.'

Immediately afterwards I went to the cannon that stood just above the drawbridge of the Bastille, in order to push it off its gun-carriage and render it unusable. But as I stood for this purpose with my shoulder under the mouth of the cannon, someone in the vicinity fired at me, and the bullet pierced my coat and waistcoat and wounded me in the neck; I fell down senseless. When I recovered from my swoon I found myself very weak and decided to go downstairs; people made way for me on seeing my blood and my wound.

On the way to the Bastille kitchens I met an army surgeon, who urged me to show him my wound; when he had examined the place, he told me I had a bullet in my neck which he could not extract by himself, and persuaded me to go to a hospital to get it seen to.

On my way there I met somebody who had just been to the Minimes monastery to have a sprained wrist attended to. He immediately took me to the Minimes, where they readily attended to my wound. No bullet was found in it.

The conquerors of the Bastille

ON 14 July 1789, thousands of people marched upon the fortress of the Bastille, which, after a generation of campaign for legal reform, had come to symbolize all that was hateful with an absolutist regime that allowed the king to imprison his subjects without trial and dismiss his ministers at will.

The fall of the Bastille was precipitated by news on 12 July 1789 of the king's dismissal of Necker. On the same night, weapons were seized from gunsmiths' shops and a general quest for more started. Crowds burned down the ring of customs barriers around the city, and were joined by the armed forces garrisoned there, the Garde Française. On the morning of 13 July a permanent committee was established to govern Paris and ordered the mobilization of property-owners to form a civic militia, the *garde bourgeoise.* The quest for arms continued and, after a successful raid on the Hôtel des Invalides on the morning of 14 July, the crowds turned upon the Bastille. A delegation from the municipality tried unsuccessfully to persuade its governor to surrender the munitions it was rumoured to contain. Finally two detachments of the Garde Française, supported by several hundred armed civilians, fought their way into the building.

Nearly a hundred people were killed during the fighting. Of the many thousands of survivors, over 650 were officially recognized by the National Assembly as 'conquerors of the Bastille' for the part that they had played in the fall of the fortress. Sixty were soldiers, a further fifteen were cavalrymen, but the great majority were drawn from the ordinary civilian population of Paris. Almost all, however, had taken part in the events of 14 July as members of the recently mobilized *garde bourgeoise*. Only one woman was formally recognized as a *vainqueuse de la Bastille.* Most of the conquerors lived near the Bastille, three-quarters of them in the Faubourg St-Antoine, immediately to the east, and many were involved in the furnishing trades, the mainstay of the suburb's economy. Joiners, cabinet-makers, locksmiths, shoemakers, sculptors and representatives of a further two dozen trades made up more than two-thirds of the crowd that marched on the Bastille.

The 'conquerors of the Bastille' occupied a special place in the public ceremonies held to mark the anniversary of 1789 on 14 July 1790, and the date has been celebrated ever since.

ABOVE Cannon outside the Invalides. Similar weapons seized from the pensioners guarding the veterans' hospital armed the large civilian contingent which accompanied the militia forces attacking the Bastille on 14 July. As well as sheltering old soldiers, the Invalides also served as an arsenal.

LEFT A primitive but contemporary representation of the taking of the Bastille. Most of the civilian attackers came from the Faubourg St-Antoine to the east, not only the closest district but also one of the poorest.

The visit which Louis XVI made to Paris on 17 July seemed formally to endorse the events of 14 July and set the seal on the king's acceptance of the Revolution, notably when he agreed to wear the tricolore cockade, which merged the monarch's emblematic white with the heraldic red and blue of the city of Paris.

THE king set out at about eleven o'clock, in a very simple carriage and accompanied only by a captain of the guard and two staff officers; they were escorted by no more than ten bodyguards and some of the National Guard, while many of the common people went ahead, with women of the roughest kind bearing branches of trees in their hands and cockades in their hair.

The king went very slowly so that the people and the militia could keep up with him.

At the Chaillot gates, the king trembled when he saw that the new buildings at the barrier had been burnt down in the disturbances. But a much more striking spectacle awaited him, in the form of the two unbroken triple ranks of armed citizens lining his entire route.

M. Bailly and the Parisian municipal council met him at the gates to present him with the keys of the city; at the Pont-Neuf he was greeted with a salvo from the cannons placed there.

First the people shouted: 'Vive la Nation!' *then* 'Vive la Nation et l'Assemblée Nationale!' *and finally they shouted* 'Vive le Roi et la Nation!'

The king crossed the city in the midst of a great crowd of people who had flocked in from all sides to see him pass. The Paris municipal councillors received him at the Hôtel de Ville to the sound of drums and a military band, and general acclaim. Yet when he entered it was not without some disquiet. According to some of the popular rumours, the Parisians did not intend to let him leave again, and would insist on him bringing the Assembly into their midst. He was presented with a red, white and blue cockade like those of the citizens.

Bailly spoke on the king's behalf, and said that His Majesty was mindful of nothing except the love of his people. The king himself was moved, and did not speak. He returned to Versailles in great good spirits.

A letter from the abbé Barbotin, a clerical deputy in the National Assembly, indicates the major problem of government in late July and early August 1789.

31 JULY. Everything in the Versailles area seems calm, but all the neighbouring provinces are still in a state of turmoil. It appears that the Estates General have emboldened everyone, and that no one is answerable any longer to anyone else.

Everywhere there is looting, destruction, damage, fire; public funds are stolen: so that the kingdom is being despoiled and brought to within a hair's breadth of its downfall. This has only happened since the scattering of our enemies at court.

I think that all these disturbances are organized by people who are paid agitators, for strangers or foreigners have been noticed in all the riots. But why are peaceful men so stupid that they listen to them and follow them?

As Bailly showed in his memoirs, rumour and anxiety tended to be the mobilizing forces in the 'Great Fear', which led on to social revolution in the countryside.

THE areas around Paris swarmed with threatening brigands looting everything. We heard about this through deputations from villages in a state of alarm. M. de Lafayette, commander of the National Guard, was instructed to send them help. The reports were found to be entirely without foundation.

I recall that at about this time a man whose name I knew but have now forgotten came to tell me that there was an army of brigands near Mont-Rouge on the outskirts of Paris, and that when in that area he had been forced to turn back and return to Paris. On checking it was found that there was no such gang.

What is extraordinary is that these rumours and fears of brigands were spreading across the whole kingdom; and at the same time it was also being said that the corn was being cut down before it was ripe. There was no truth in this.

Rumours of conspiracy and crime, reports of disasters, sprang up everywhere, both by word of mouth and in writing. Terror reigned in the provinces; townsfolk and peasants abandoned their work and rushed to take up arms. It seemed that fear was spread to provoke disorder, so that disorder would bring anarchy, and anarchy would bring tyranny.

GENTLEMEN AND LADIES' TOWN AND COUNTRY MAGAZINE (Boston), *February 1789 – August 1790*

(from a letter dated 21 October)
The provinces, it is also said, are all arising; and what is the most dreadful circumstance, in different interest. The approach of thousands to the capital is daily expected, and there is no other probability than that this Christmas will be spent throughout the country in domestic bloodshed.

The nation, the king and the law

Two grave threats to the emerging Revolution led to the creation of a National Guard in Paris in July 1789. Firstly, despite his apparent capitulation to the National Assembly on 27 June, Louis XVI had ordered an unprecedented build-up of royal troops, including a large number of Swiss and German regiments, in and around the capital – a clear preliminary to the forcible dissolution of the assembly. Secondly, Necker's dismissal on 11 July had set off a wave of mass violence that included the seizure of weapons and attacks on property.

To combat both dangers, the bourgeois electors of Paris, who had assumed municipal authority after selecting their representatives to the Estates General in May, met at the Hôtel de Ville and ordered the establishment of a bourgeois militia (*garde bourgeoise*) of 48,000 men from the city's sixty districts.

Although some members of the force soon began to police Paris, it was weeks, even months, before the new National Guard was fully organized. On 15 July a permanent committee of the electors named the marquis de Lafayette commander, an appointment later confirmed by the king and the Parisian districts. Regulations approved in August called for six 'divisions' of infantry, each consisting of ten battalions, one per district.

Long before these rules could be implemented, the new force's limitations and functions were defined. On 10 August 1789 the assembly decreed that all officers of the National Guard had to take an oath of fidelity to the nation, the king and the law, and to swear that they would never employ their men against citizens except on the order of civil officials.

The next month the entire Paris National Guard paraded to the cathedral of Notre-Dame, where the archbishop blessed their flags and officers took the new oath.

This ceremony was repeated in most regions of France during the following months, for few institutions of the Revolution spread so rapidly, so widely, and so spontaneously; within less than a year two and a half million men were enrolled.

The diffusion of the National Guard highlights the fact that the revolution of 1789 was not exclusively Parisian.

The movement also involved the towns and cities of provincial France, where the old ruling élites were overthrown and new elected administrations installed in response to two powerful stimulants: news of insurrection in Paris, and pressure from hungry demonstrators, on the very doorsteps of the local town halls (*hôtels de ville*).

Local populations had already been politicized by the drawing up of lists of grievances (*cahiers de doléances*), and by the elections of local deputies to the Estates General in Versailles – the first step in many cities in the ousting of traditional élites. The revolt of the cities was most violent in the west: the Breton town of Rennes was convulsed by three days of fighting. In the east, the old town council of Strasbourg was removed by force, and its council building destroyed. In Troyes, the mayor was assassinated.

Sometimes, as in Rouen or Dijon, a committee, formed from the political élite which had emerged from the Third Estate at the time of the local elections to the Estates General, was established to take over administration, without yet obliterating the old authorities.

The formation of a National Guard was characteristic of the urban rebellion, as the triumphant bourgeoisie searched for reliable coercive weapons to cement and enforce its success. These emerged out of the often archaic bourgeois militias, which stepped into the vacuum caused by the breakdown of order.

ABOVE Members of the National Guard in the company of other citizens, armed to defend 'Liberty or Death'.

It seems also, and with some justification, that there was a deliberate intention, through widespread fear, to induce everyone in the countryside and in the towns to take to arms.

Who was responsible for this concerted action? Who provided the necessary funds to bribe agents and transport them everywhere to organize these events? It is a mystery, which perhaps the future will solve.

The steward of the Norman estates of the duc de Montmorency reported instances of popular revolt to his master; this was usually aimed against the nobility, who seemed to be behind the Great Fear.

Montmartin, 2 August 1789. Sir, In order to avoid alarming you, I have not until now mentioned the fears which have been distressing me for too long; but now I think it would be unwise to leave you any longer in ignorance of them. There is brigandry and pillage on all sides. The populace blames the nobility of the kingdom for the high cost of grain and is enraged against them.

Reasoning is of no avail: this unrestrained populace is deaf to all but its anger, and throughout all our province the peasantry are in such a state of revolt that they are ready to commit any crime: indeed in this very parish, convinced that the royalist baron de Breteuil and his family are at the château, they talk openly about setting fire to it.

You will realize, Sir, that in such circumstances I am taking all possible care.

As I was about to end my letter I learned that about three hundred brigands from all areas, together with the vassals of the marquise de Longaunay, have taken away the deeds of taxes and rents from the manor, and demolished its dovecote; they then gave them a receipt of removal signed in the name of the Nation.

The burning of feudal land records – as noted here by a local notary from Glanes, in Savoy – was one of the most typical and effective acts of peasant revolt.

We need no longer be so alarmed over those gangs of thieves which we feared would descend on us. They are simply peasants who are seizing their land deeds from the châteaux, and burning them if they meet with resistance. People have the same idea in Savoy. To achieve peace the nobility must reduce their demands.

The letter from Périgny, an administrative official in Paris, to the marquis de Romé highlights the extent and the variety of peasant insurrection in France.

Paris, 13 August 1789. Sir, the flames are sweeping through Anjou and Maine. The comte de Laurencin read out to us yesterday the terrible events suffered by Madame his sister at two châteaux in Dauphiné: papers burnt, the châteaux pillaged, and roofs removed if they were not burnt. They were not even left with the means of gathering and securing their harvest.

At the end of her letter, M. de Laurencin's sister says that she is in despair because she was not killed by the first shot which reached her room; she has been hounded through the two châteaux and then to a friend's house, and with her was her young and beautiful unmarried daughter. The two of them, with her husband, were pursued for thirty-five hours without respite.

The monks at Cluny were more clever and more fortunate. The inhabitants of that small town have become so attached to them, through their good deeds and the renunciation of their rights and dues, that, under the leadership of one of the monks, the townsfolk wiped out the whole gang of marauders.

The citizens of Cluny hid themselves, well armed, in the abbey, they concealed two cannon in a shed facing the main road into the town. The brigands had thought to take the abbey and the townsfolk by surprise; the inhabitants let them all come in, closed the gates of the town while at the same instant they uncovered the two cannon loaded with shot, and all fired at the same time. Not a single outlaw escaped. They were all killed or taken off to the royal prisons.

They were found to be carrying printed papers 'On the king's orders'. These documents encouraged the burning of abbeys and châteaux, on the pretence that the nobles and abbots hoarded supplies of grain and poisoned wells, and intended to reduce the people, the king's subjects, to the direst misery.

In Alsace the inhabitants destroyed the superb forests at Bitche and Hagueneau, destroyed the fine glass-making establishments at Baccarat, and the king's own magnificent ironworks. They are at work now in the forest of St-Germain, cutting down the finest trees.

It is impossible to be sure now, and for the immediate future, where to live in France, or who can preserve their wealth.

The king is in a state of despondency and in reply to complaints, says that there is nothing he can do.

I remain yours most sincerely, Périgny

The Great Fear: the peasant revolution

EVERY year, particularly during the critical months of April to July, when one year's harvest had almost run out and the following year's crop was still in the ground, rumours added to an already tense situation as prices rose, cereals circulated between different markets and officials tried to keep order. Attempts by royal officials to control price fluctuations by buying up large quantities of corn for resale at inflated prices often led to rumours of government-inspired famine plots.

The Great Fear of the summer of 1789 owed much to this attitude. It was also the result of widespread suspicion of the migrant labourers, paupers, beggars, smugglers and criminals who supplied rural France with much of its seasonal agricultural labour and, at the same time, posed a threat to order and a massive claim on charitable institutions.

These long-standing popular anxieties were compounded by the deepening political crisis which enveloped the kingdom after the Estates General assembled at Versailles in May 1789. Local administrations were paralysed and informally constituted committees, established during the elections to the Estates General, took political control. Public order collapsed in many regions, as to price-fixing riots were added scores of local insurrections. As news of Necker's dismissal on 11 July and the disturbances in Paris spread, suspicion of court intrigue and fear of the itinerant poor combined in a rumour that originated in half a dozen widely separate localities and circulated widely over most of France between 20 July and 5 August 1789. This was the Great Fear.

At its core was the belief that an army of court-inspired brigands was about to destroy the harvest, ransack property and starve the people into political submission, forcing the self-proclaimed National Assembly to capitulate to the nobility. Sightings of the imaginary brigands (often agricultural labourers in search of work) caused local populations to take to arms and self-defence developed into movements whose main objective was to destroy seigneurial titles and papers.

BELOW Part of the provincial disturbances that made up the Great Fear: the sacking of Strasbourg's Hôtel de Ville.

On the night of 4 August, following several weeks of anxiety caused by news of peasant risings throughout France, the National Assembly made sweeping reforms which were represented as ending the feudal regime. Bailly's account of the session stresses the revolutionary character of the measures.

DURING the evening a proposed proclamation was read out to end the looting and burning of châteaux, and to order the payment of taxes and of rents and dues which no one wished to pay any more.

This proclamation was the cause of an impressive debate and of a scene which was truly magnificent, enthralling and unforgettable. It was noted that the refusal to pay dues and the burning of deeds derived from the hatred of the feudal regime and the burdens which it imposed on country people.

Vicomte de Noailles proposed the motion on this occasion. He declared that, at the same time that the assembly proclaimed fiscal equality, it should also decree that seigneurial labour services and personal servitude would be abolished without indemnity, and that feudal rights could be redeemed if desired by those who were liable.

M. Cotin proposed the abolition of seigneurial courts; the bishop of Chartres added the abolition of hunting rights, and recognition of the right which every landowner should have to kill game on his own land. Priests proposed to give up whatever fees they received for their services. These may not have been the greatest sacrifices, but they had the effect of stimulating greater ones.

La Rochefoucauld spoke in favour of the abolition of serfdom. Several barons from Languedoc and some other people sacrificed their baronies.

All the deputies then voted, offered or promised to relinquish all privileges of the state, province, or city. M. Fréteau offered to sacrifice the rights and privileges still preserved for the magistrature.

Never before have so many bodies and individuals voted such sacrifices at one time, in such generous terms and with such unanimity. This has been a night for destruction and for public happiness.

We may view this moment as the dawn of a new revolution, when all the burdens weighing on the people were abolished and France was truly reborn.

The feudal regime which had oppressed the people for centuries was demolished at a stroke and in an instant. The National Assembly achieved more for the people in a few hours than the wisest and most enlightened nations had done for many centuries.

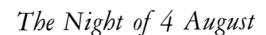

The Night of 4 August

THE Great Fear transformed open insurrection into revolution. As peasant uprisings broke out all over France between mid-July and early August 1789, notably in Normandy, Flanders, Alsace, Burgundy, Dauphiné and the Languedoc, villagers almost invariably singled out the owners of seigneurial rights as their principal victims. Papers were burned; nobles or their agents were forced publicly to renounce their titles to real or honorific seigneurial dues; large amounts of food and wine were consumed at the expense of local landlords or their officials.

Many members of the National Assembly welcomed the destruction of these privileges as necessary to national regeneration. But continued unrest threatened the already precarious state of public finances and, if the insurrections grew, the assembly might be forced to rely on the court and the royal army to restore public order. By early August it was clear that a solution had to be found, and public order restored.

The debate on the night of 4 August was the outcome of this situation. Its initial purpose was to issue a proclamation calling for calm and establishing the principle of tax equality, thereby ending the privileges and immunities enjoyed by nobles, the clergy and townspeople, and which were denied to the inhabitants of the countryside. The session of the National Assembly was carefully prepared by members of the Breton Club.

On Tuesday, 4 August 1789, the general session of the National Assembly opened at 8 p.m. The draft proclamation calling for a restoration of public order was read. As soon as it had been heard, the duc de Noailles stood up to speak. He pointed out that order would only be restored if the people had an interest in maintaining it. And he proposed that the assembly should introduce a proclamation declaring that everyone was liable to taxation in proportion to income, that feudal dues could be ended by village communities compensating seigneurs for their losses and that feudal servitude would be abolished. He was followed by the duc d'Aiguillon. Speeches by two commoners, Le Guen de Kerangal and Dupont de Nemours, set the tone for the following six hours. Layer after layer of privilege was stripped from the edifice of the established political order. Speakers vied with one another, sometimes maliciously, sometimes enthusiastically, to abolish the feudal regime that had governed people's lives for so long.

What was abolished on the night of 4 August was both more and less than 'feudalism'. Vestiges of

ABOVE A symbolic representation of the events of 4 August: the Three Estates and the common man demolishing the trappings of feudalism.

BELOW The session of the National Assembly on the night of 4 August, which developed into the wholesale abolition of feudal institutions.

personal servitude derived from medieval serfdom were eliminated at once. So too were many of the legal privileges attached to the ownership of seigneurial domains, such as the right to hold a seigneurial court. And 'feudalism' was extended to encompass the purchase of offices in the royal judicial and administrative systems and, finally, to the clerical tithe. However, members recognized that income from office or clerical vocation, and many seigneurial dues, were a form of property – and property they respected.

Thus on 11 August, when the assembly finally ratified the decisions taken the previous week, it made a distinction between feudal dues derived from serfdom, which were alleged to be grounded in coercion and were abolished outright, and other seigneurial dues (quitrents, for example) allegedly based on free contractual agreement. The latter were viewed as forms of property, and those possessing them were entitled to commute them to rents. This emphasis on property rights meant that the outcome of 4 August was less spectacular than the night itself.

The account of the night of 4 August by the marquis de Ferrières is altogether more jaundiced and regretful. But he too was clear on the revolutionary significance of the measures introduced.

THE deputies were standing, all mingled together, in the centre of the chamber, agitating and talking all at once. Those of the former Third Estate tried, by feigned enthusiasm and thunderous applause at every new sacrifice, to maintain the excitement. The assembly looked like a gang of drunken men in a shop full of delicate furniture, breaking and smashing at will everything that came to hand. Lally-Tolendal, a passive witness of all these excesses, passed a note to Le Chapelier, the president, saying, 'They have all lost control, close the session.'

Immediately a multitude of voices cried out that since individuals had given up their rights and privileges, justice required provinces and cities to make the equal sacrifice of the privileges and rights which weighed on the greater portion of the kingdom and rendered the tax burdens shockingly disproportionate. A feeling of hatred, a blind wish for vengeance rather than love of the general good, appeared to be the motive force.

Soon the ancient French constitution, crumbling noisily under redoubled blows from this gang of wild men, was seen with astonishment to consist of nothing but a shapeless mound of ruins and fragments!

The *Ami du peuple* of the radical journalist Jean-Paul Marat was one of the most extreme newspapers of this period. In this article, of 21 September 1789, Marat sees the abolition of feudalism as inspired by fear rather than altruism.

NO doubt the repeated acts of justice and benevolence, dictated by humanity and love of our country which was keen to manifest itself, must result in the spectators' highest admiration; and with these acts of generosity vying to surpass each other, enthusiasm must border on enchantment.

Was that really so? We must not deny virtue; but we must not be taken in. If it is indeed goodwill which dictated such sacrifices, it must be agreed that it has taken a long time to be heard.

What! It is by the light of the flames of their burning châteaux that they have discovered that greatness of heart which renounces the privilege of keeping in irons men who have taken up arms to regain their liberty!

At the sight of the torture of depredators, defrauders, supporters of tyranny, they generously yield up seigneurial tithes and demand nothing from these unfortunates who have scarcely enough to live on!

The reforms of the night of 4 August were consecrated in a decree of the National Assembly on 11 August.

DECREE OF THE NATIONAL ASSEMBLY
11 AUGUST 1789

THE National Assembly abolishes the feudal system in its entirety. It decrees that feudal rights and duties relating to mortmain or to personal servitude are abolished without compensation; all others are declared capable of being redeemed, the price and manner of redemption to be fixed by the National Assembly.

Exclusive rights over pigeon houses and dovecotes are abolished. Pigeons will be enclosed for set periods by the community; during this time they will be considered as game, and everyone will have the right to kill them on their land.

The exclusive right of hunting and open warrens is likewise abolished. All hunting rights, even royal, and all private hunting restrictions, under whatever regulation, are also abolished.

All seigneurial justice is suppressed without indemnity.

Tithes of all kinds, and dues which may be in place of tithes, in the possession of secular and recognized institutions, and other religious and military bodies, are abolished.

The purchase of judicial and municipal office is suppressed as from this moment. Justice will be rendered without payment.

Fiscal privileges are permanently abolished. Payments will be made by all citizens and on all property in the same manner and by the same method.

All special privileges of provinces, principalities, regions, cities and communities are irrevocably abolished.

All citizens, without distinction regarding birth, are admissible to all employment and advancement, whether ecclesiastical, civil or military, and no useful profession will involve loss of status.

No pluralism of benefices will be allowed.

Accounts of pensions, favours and salaries will

be put before the National Assembly, who, together with the king, will act to suppress those which are undeserved, and reduce those which are excessive.

The National Assembly ordains that in memory of the great and important proceedings which have recently been undertaken for the happiness of France, a medal will be struck, and that a thanksgiving Te Deum will be sung in all the parishes and churches of the kingdom.

The National Assembly solemnly proclaims King Louis XVI 'Restorer of French Liberty'.

The National Assembly will go in a body to the king to present to His Majesty the decree which it has ordained, to pay homage to him of its most respectful gratitude, and to request that the Te Deum be sung in his chapel in his presence.

The National Assembly agreed to compose a statement of the rights of man which would represent the basis of the new constitution. In his journal, Duquesnoy marked the stages of the composition of the Declaration of the Rights of Man and of the Citizen, which would be decreed on 26 August 1789 and which remains one of the most significant political statements in modern history.

18 August 1789. We are going to start work on this declaration of rights; unfortunately, it gives too much scope to vague metaphysical ideas. But one is struck dumb on hearing a M. Crénières state boldly that the American Declaration of Rights is the most inept that has ever been offered mankind.

19 August 1789. There was a debate this morning as to which proposed declaration should be adopted as a basis for discussion.

I have suggested to the department to which I belong that Rousseau's Social Contract *should be printed at the head of the constitution.*

24 August 1789. There remain only two or three more articles to be drawn up; they will probably be finished on Wednesday 26 August; at least we must hope so and, in truth, it is high time to turn to more practical and immediately useful tasks.

27 August 1789. The declaration of rights is finally drawn up, and although there have been proposals to add several more articles to it, the assembly has decreed that it will consider them only when the new constitution is completed.

Declaration of the Rights of Man and of the Citizen

All men have an invincible inclination for the pursuit of happiness; it is in order to attain it by unity of effort that they have formed societies and established governments. Every government must therefore have public happiness as its goal.

In consequence of this indisputable truth, the government exists for the benefit of those who are governed, and not of those who govern; no public function may be regarded as the property of those who exercise it.

Nature has made all men free and equal; social distinctions must therefore be founded on common necessity.

To be happy, man must be entirely free to exercise all his physical and moral faculties.

The duty of each individual consists in respecting the rights of others.

The government, in order to achieve general happiness, must therefore protect rights and prescribe duties. It must not place any limits on the free exercise of human faculties. It must, above all, guarantee inalienable rights which belong to all men, such as personal liberty, property, security, the protection of honour and life, free expression of thought, and resistance to oppression.

It is by means of laws which are clear, precise and uniform for all citizens that rights should be assured.

Citizens may not be subject to any laws other than those to which they have freely consented.

To prevent despotism and ensure the rule of law, the legislative, executive and judicial powers must be separate. Their union in the same hands would put those who hold them above all law, and would enable them to substitute for it their own will.

All individuals must have access to the law.

Punishment shall not be arbitrary but must be determined by law, and must be absolutely identical for all citizens, whatever their rank or fortune.

Every member of society who is entitled to protection by the state should contribute to its prosperity and share its costs in proportion to his wealth; and no one may claim favour or exemption, whatever his rank or his employment.

No man should suffer for his religious beliefs.

Freedom of the press is the strongest support of public freedom. It should be sustained by law, while ensuring the proper means of punishing those who abuse it by spreading seditious statements or libel.

The countryside rejoiced at the decree of 4–11 August and indulged in attacks on game, whose hunting had formerly been a seigneurial monopoly. An extract from comte Beugnot's memoirs shows a countryside where deference seems to have been destroyed.

ON publication of the decrees of 4 August the National Guard at Montigny, strengthened by all the local patriots, descended in a flood on the barony of Choiseul and in three or four days ruthlessly wiped out all the hares and the partridges which had been there for so long, spared by the tender heart of my father-in-law.

The ponds were fished, the dovecote in the courtyard of the château was shot at and the pigeons killed. These fine fellows went so far in their insolence as to approach my father-in-law, offering to sell him some of his own fish, as they had too much, and his own pigeons, as they did not know what to do with them. These patriotic celebrations did not upset me; I was kept busy restraining my father-in-law, from whom we had wisely removed anything which in his rage he might use as a weapon.

By the early autumn, when the harvest had been gathered in, the economic crisis eased in many rural areas, but the same was not true of many towns. The marquis de Ferrières, in his memoirs, shows the escalation of political and economic grievances.

THE scarcity and price of grain increased dramatically; bakeries were besieged; people gathered there, and political agents mix with the crowds. A great many workmen, obliged to wait a whole day to obtain a four-pound loaf, left in despair.

There were also attempts to frighten them over the quality of grain used. Men were paid to go into the merchants' grain stores, steal the rotting flour put to one side as not to be sold, and take it out into the streets of Paris, showing it to the populace and telling them that this was the rotten grain which was used to make their bread.

Yet there had been an abundant harvest; it was the beginning of October; throughout all the provinces there was new corn to eat. This artificial shortage spread daily, instead of diminishing. Every party conspired to maintain it, for all hoped for an insurrection. To these manœuvrings, which alone were enough to arouse the people, were added rumours of civil war and counter-revolutionary plans.

THE TIMES (London), *7 August 1789*

We again repeat that the renewed violence of the people will in the end destroy that liberty they are intended to support, and go farther to open the eyes of the nation to its true interest than all the violent speeches of patriotic declaimers.

Bailly's memoirs recount the infamous banquet of the Flanders regiment held at Versailles, which gave rise to the revolutionary *journées* of 5 and 6 October.

3 OCTOBER. Today the king's bodyguards gave a magnificent feast in the opera house at the palace of Versailles. The guests were the officers of the Flanders regiment, the Montmorency dragoons, the Swiss guards, the Swiss regiments, the Cent-Suisses regiment, and others including a few officers of the Versailles National Guard.

During the meal there were toasts to the health of the king, the queen, the dauphin, and all the royal family. A toast to the nation had been suggested and, according to some, was omitted on purpose; according to many of the party, it was expressly rejected by the royal bodyguards who were present.

When the king returned from hunting he was brought to see the spectacle which was described to him as being very lively.

The queen, holding her son by the hand, stepped forward to the entrance of the hall, which immediately rang with applause and acclaim. All the guests, drawn swords in hand, drank to the health of the august persons whom they were honoured to receive in their midst. The royal visitors accepted this homage and withdrew.

From this moment on the banquet degenerated into an orgy. Everyone's mind became heated with the astonishing profusion of wine of all kinds. Someone sounded the Charge; the opera boxes were scaled. Finally, in the midst of highly indecent suggestions, someone dared to insult the national tricolore cockade and toasted the white cockade which had been displayed by, amongst others, several captains of the Versailles National Guard.

The *cour de marbre* – the central courtyard of the palace – then became witness to the most scandalous disorder. Royal bodyguards and officers spewed out terrible curses against the National Assembly.

Peaceful citizens were bewildered by such tumult and excess; Versailles remained uneasy until the revellers were finally reduced to total inaction through fatigue and drunkenness.

The rights of man

ON 26 August 1789, the National Assembly passed the Declaration of the Rights of Man and of the Citizen. It presented to the world a summary of the Revolution's ideals and principles and justified the destruction of a government based upon absolutism and privilege, and the establishment of a new regime based upon the inalienable rights of individuals, political equality and liberty. The Declaration became the preamble to the Constitution of 1791. Translated into practically every major language, it has been referred to either directly or indirectly by nearly every major revolutionary movement since 1789 and is the basis of the constitutional foundations of many countries, including France's Fifth Republic.

Many ideas for the Declaration arose out of the Enlightenment, but perhaps the most important influence was John Locke's *Second Treatise of Government*, first published in England in 1690, at the time of the 'Glorious Revolution'. His stress on natural rights, religious toleration, civic equality and the limits of governmental power all find expression in the document. Jean-Jacques Rousseau's *Social Contract* (1762) was also responsible for some of the thinking behind the Declaration, in particular in the articles on law, but he did not share Locke's preoccupation with natural rights, representative government and the crucial importance of private property.

Although the United States Federal Constitution had been written some two years earlier, the two documents cannot be compared. The American Constitution was written after their revolution had been won; the French Declaration at the start of their Revolution, when political stability was not yet in sight. A more appropriate comparison is with the American Declaration of Independence (1776), but even this is essentially a petition of grievances listing the reasons for rebellion against George III. It is limited to a particular struggle at a particular time. In contrast, the French Declaration is full of abstract statements concerning the nature of political societies everywhere and at all times. There is nothing in the American document to suggest that other peoples should follow their example – the logic of the French Declaration is precisely that its general principles were applicable world-wide.

By 1791 the Declaration of the Rights of Man had been transformed from a legislative document into a kind of political manifesto. No one assisted this process more than the Anglo-American pamphleteer Tom Paine, whose *Rights of Man* (1791–2) became one of the best-selling books in English history, and the bible of working-class radicals. He reproduced the document word for word, treating it as a sacred text that ushered in a new epoch of world history.

The first and perhaps most important opponent of the Declaration was King Louis XVI. In a note written to the National Assembly on 4 October 1789 he refused to endorse it because its clauses were too ambiguous, and only sanctioned it under popular pressure in the *journées* of 5–6 October.

Since then, it has been adopted by all kinds of political groups, and has been used both to justify revolution and to suppress it.

ABOVE A National Guard officer takes his oath to the Constitution, placing his hand upon the Declaration of the Rights of Man.

Marat's *L'Ami du peuple*, like other newspapers, alerted the Parisian population to events at Versailles, and proposed violent measures against the possibility of a military coup led by the royal court.

TO the Editor:

Paris, 4 October 1789. Sir, another orgy of revelling amongst the royal bodyguards, officers from the Flanders regiment, a large number of officers from other regiments, and the leaders of the bourgeois militia – an orgy where a noble princess appeared with the heir to the throne, where an anti-patriotic cockade was flourished and where undercover conspiracy was loudly rehearsed – has recently spread alarm through the capital: you have shown yourself worthy of the confidence of all good citizens, we beg you to help us with your advice.

Editor's comments:

It is certain that the orgy took place; it is no less certain that the alarm is general: we have insufficient reliable information to state whether there is indeed a conspiracy. But, even if it were imaginary, no one doubts that, were the enemy at our gates today, he would find us unprepared; such negligence in providing the capital with war supplies of any kind is a real crime against the state.

There is not a moment to lose: all good citizens should arm themselves and meet together, send a substantial detachment to remove all gunpowder from Essonne; each district should withdraw its cannon from the Hôtel de Ville.

In the *journées* of 5 and 6 October, here recounted by Duquesnoy, a massive Parisian march on Versailles almost got out of hand. As a result, Louis XVI gave the sanction he had hitherto withheld to the Declaration of the Rights of Man and to the decrees of 4 and 11 August abolishing feudalism. At the same time, he agreed to move his residence from Versailles to the Tuileries in Paris.

5–6 October 1789. The president of the National Assembly, M. Mounier, announced that a deputation from Paris was demanding admission on pressing business. The news had already spread that ten, twenty, thirty thousand people were coming to Versailles, intent on seizing the king, according to some, seeking to force the assembly to hasten its work, according to others, etc.

Imagine the surprise of many members of the assembly when some twenty fishwives entered, led by a reasonably well-dressed man called Maillard, who spoke on their behalf with great facility and in a well-educated French. The women had come to say that Paris was short of bread; they sought the help and support of the assembly. This action was simple, and justified; it was an important commission, for to be hungry is a terrible distinction.

Following the spokesman's address, the president replied with great goodwill, but became involved in a discussion with the women. They attacked the archbishop of Paris, saying that a miller had received two hundred livres not to grind corn from a priest who was a member of the assembly. They then proceeded to make accusations against all the clergy.

A proposed decree concerning supplies was read out to the women: the king was requested to take the strongest possible action to facilitate the free circulation of grain, etc.

All this took place honourably and peacefully, until some members were unwise and bold enough to leave their places to go and chat with the women, so that their conversations were prejudicial to good order.

However, when M. Mounier left to go to the king and the bishop of Langres took his place as president, the chamber was soon filled with drunken women, who danced, climbed up on to the president's dais and tried to kiss him. Vicomte de Mirabeau (the brother of the great Mirabeau) grabbed the bosoms of the prettiest women, and the most indecent behaviour occurred in the sacred shrine of the representatives of the world's leading nation.

A number of detachments of the Paris National Guard began to arrive, however; they were preceded, followed or generally escorted by a crowd of people who were obviously not part of the militia, ill-clothed and armed with scythes, pitchforks, iron bars, etc. It was not yet known what they intended. M. de Lafayette led them, but he had difficulty in controlling them. There were cannon in front and behind.

At six o'clock in the evening it was learned that they had a grudge against the royal bodyguards, swearing to kill them because they had insulted the national cockade.

Soon the National Guard stood at the doors of the chamber; they took over all the sentry posts round the palace of Versailles and sounded the charge against the mounted royal bodyguards. Some guns were fired, cannon were aimed at the guards' barracks, some of them were seized and wounded, others were brought

Versailles

THE palace of Versailles was very much the home of Louis XVI, who only twice in his life journeyed outside the Paris basin. The great palace, 12 miles (20 km) outside Paris, had started life as Louis XIII's hunting lodge; it was Louis XIV who took the decision to remove the court from the Louvre in Paris. Versailles was steadily extended to become a massive imposing setting for court life, and government, centred on the king and containing some 10,000 people.

The internal planning and decoration that had evolved at Versailles served as a setting for the rituals of court, focusing on the king's state bedchamber, the most important room in the palace, situated next to his council chamber. The state rooms were given an allegorical and mythological dressing of celebratory images and emblems echoing the king's virtues and accomplishments, predominantly using Apollo, Alexander the Great and Hercules as appropriately superlative *alter egos*.

The Hall of Mirrors housed Lebrun's depictions of Louis XIV's most famous victories, and provided a huge parade-ground for the court to disport itself, gossip and exchange elaborate salutations. The king would pass through this lengthy space on his way to chapel, and could be approached by those seeking favours, position or royal approval. The lavishness of the Hall was manifest in the expanse of Venetian glass employed, then an extremely expensive commodity. When necessary, as in the case of the presentation of ambassadors, the Hall doubled as a huge throne-room.

The gardens, laid out by Le Nôtre in the 1660s, extended the regular plan of the interior into radiating avenues, punctuated by grottoes and fountains.

Louis XIV himself had built the château at Marly nearby, and the Grand, the Petit and the porcelain Trianons within the grounds of Versailles, in order to be able to escape from the incessant requirements of his station into a more personal, private domain. These moves away from the grand public spaces of the main body of the château were continued under Louis XV and XVI. Most notorious of all, perhaps, was the toy hamlet constructed to the orders of Marie-Antoinette.

Another example of Marie-Antoinette's influence at Versailles was in the realm of the theatre. Courtly culture was maintained by means of command performances of Parisian stage successes and amateur theatricals, with the queen as impresario and actress.

From the earliest days of the elaboration of the palace and grounds, Versailles had always maintained remarkably open access – when the gates were ordered to be closed in October 1789 to keep out the marchers from Paris, it took several hours to force them shut since, after decades of disuse, they had rusted up in an open position. Throughout, the court offered not only a spectacle of local political significance, but also a visual feast for admirers of the casts of antique sculptures that had been placed in the gardens, the royal picture collection of old masters, the latest trends in interior decoration and fashions in dress – hotly contested by Parisian society. But serious visitors to France sought the best, most stimulating entertainment and new ideas in Paris.

OVERLEAF Counter-revolutionary scenes in the *cour de marbre*, Versailles' central court, led to the events of 5–6 October.

BELOW The Parisian housewives en route to Versailles on 5 October to make their protest to the king and the Assembly.

down from their horses, several fled (it seems that the king had not ordered them to defend themselves). The National Guards of Versailles and Paris joined forces; the Flanders regiment and the dragoons refused to fire on the populace.

The assembly was still in session or, to put it more accurately, still in disorder, deputies mingling with the common women – one of them sitting in the president's seat – when Mounier returned. He called everyone to order.

The king's reply was as follows:

'I declare that I accept purely and simply the declaration of the rights of man and citizen and the articles of the constitution which you have presented to me.'

This response, written and signed by the king, was read to the assembly, and there were loud cries of *'Vive le Roi!'*

The palace of Versailles was in a state of turmoil all night. The queen was threatened, and people were heard to say: 'The only problem is how to share out pieces of the queen.' There was open talk of hanging her, etc. She knew this, was fully aware of the danger she was in, yet did not wish to leave. It is claimed that when the king knelt to beg her to go she replied, 'Sire, my place is at your feet. That is where I ought to die, if it must be that I am to die.' These words may perhaps absolve her from many wrongs. I heard this anecdote from the marquis de Crillon, one of the most truthful men I know.

Others have told me that during the night, when the queen was in bed, she heard a noise in the adjoining rooms – people breaking down the doors to seize the royal guards, who fought back and defended their posts. She jumped out of bed in only a petticoat and took refuge in the king's room. It must be said that she showed at all times the greatest firmness and confidence of outlook, and displayed very great courage.

Ministers gathered round the king; they discussed whether or not he should leave Versailles. Some apparently urged him to do so, no doubt from love of him and fearing the dangers he might face; they did not consider that such an action would put his crown and his life in danger. The next morning, the king had decided to leave Versailles for Paris.

As a letter of the obscure clerical deputy, the curé Pous, observed, the removal of the king to Paris was followed by the decision of the National Assembly henceforth to meet in Paris rather than in Versailles.

Versailles, 6 October 1789. Yesterday and during the night more than fifty thousand armed Parisians arrived, headed by more than forty pieces of cannon and commanded by M. de Lafayette. Some guns were fired.

The gentlemen from Paris wished to take the king and all the royal family back to their city. His Majesty agreed, and at midday the royal procession departed. It will not be coming back. From now on our monarchs will live at the Tuileries. This revolution took less than twenty-four hours.

That is still not the end of it: the National Assembly, hearing of the king's decision, decreed anew that the representatives of the nation cannot be separated from the king; and that therefore the Estates General are to move to Paris, whither we must all go.

Bailly's account of the king's entry into Paris on 6 October highlights the demonstrators' conviction that Louis' presence in Paris would ensure cheaper bread as well as political stability.

THE king arrived in Paris yesterday, at about six o'clock in the evening. Maillard and his retinue of women had appeared in the middle of the morning at the Hôtel de Ville and handed over to the Paris commune the decrees of the National Assembly. Joy had replaced the agitation of the previous day.

As soon as it was certain that the king was coming, a great crowd ran to meet him and formed a double rank from Passy to the Hôtel de Ville.

First to arrive was a large section of the Parisian army, with cannon, and quantities of women and of men armed with pikes, on foot, in carriages, on wagons, on gun-carts.

Then came fifty or sixty wagons of grain and flour, immediately followed by the vehicles bearing the court, surrounded by deputies, civil cavalry, grenadiers and women. The latter were carrying long poplar branches which looked very pretty admidst all the guns and pikes.

They sang vulgar ditties which apparently showed little respect for the queen. Then, with one hand pointing to the flour and the other to the royal family: 'Friends,' they announced to the crowd, 'we will not lack for bread in future, we are bringing you the baker and his wife, and the baker's boy.'

Bailly

JEAN-SYLVAIN BAILLY was one of the most powerful political leaders during the early stages of the Revolution. Head of the Third Estate's Paris delegation at the Estates General in May 1769, first President of the National Assembly established by deputies of the Third Estate on 17 June of that year, and most significantly, mayor of Paris from July 1789 to November 1791, he played a crucial role in the development of France from an absolute to a constitutional monarchy. But when the Revolution became a democratic crusade, he fell out of favour and eventually died during the Terror.

ABOVE Jean-Sylvain Bailly (left) as President of the Constituent Assembly. An honoured figure in 1789, he was one of the many casualties of the Revolution's gradual drift to the Terror.

Bailly grew up in the Louvre, the king's Paris palace, where his father was curator of the royal painting collection. Raised in comfort and security, he received the finest education available. At first he tried his hand at *belles-lettres*, but his efforts at writing eulogies and plays met with little success. He found his niche in the sciences and became one of France's best-known astronomers. By the 1780s he had been admitted to France's three most prestigious academic institutions, the Académie française, the Académie des Belles-Lettres and the Académie des Sciences.

Bailly thought of the National Assembly as a kind of academy, where politicians would be chosen from among the country's most enlightened citizens. These political intellectuals would debate the nation's problems according to the rational criteria established by the *philosophes* of the Enlightenment.

Increasingly, this approach led him to fear the participation of ordinary people, and he soon earned the reputation of an élitist snob who wished to prevent the Revolution from moving towards democracy. Although he supported the liberal and reforming aims of the National Assembly and the Declaration of the Rights of Man, he vigorously opposed the radicals who sought to extend the vote, and the right to hold office, to those who owned no property.

Yet for the two years after July 1789, when he was elected the first mayor of Paris, he spent his energy developing sound municipal institutions for the capital.

The various neighbourhood and city assemblies that had sprung up in Paris during the spring and summer of 1789 provided a platform for the Revolution's most left-wing activists – Danton, Brissot, Marat among others. In 1791 and 1792 they tried to transform France into a democratic republic, but at the time of Bailly's mayoralty they were serving their political apprenticeship. They wanted Paris to be ruled as a democracy, with neighbourhood councils and their representatives dictating policy to the mayor. Bailly became their arch-enemy. He did everything he could to strengthen the office of mayor – and minimize the role of the municipal assembly and neighbourhood councils. When he tried to arrest Danton and Marat in the spring of 1790, the radicals printed libellous tracts that accused him of treason.

In August 1790, Bailly was re-elected with 12,550 out of 14,010 votes cast, easily defeating Danton, who came second with 1460 votes.

In July 1791 he used his authority to declare martial law during a radical demonstration for a democratic republic. When the demonstrators refused to disperse, the troops fired into the crowd, killing some fifty unarmed activists. The radicals called this the Massacre of the Champ-de-Mars, and held Bailly responsible.

In November 1791 Bailly retired from public office and went to live in the countryside, where he settled down to write his memoirs. But he was prevented from living in obscurity. With the fall of the monarchy and the establishment of the First Republic in 1792, Bailly's former enemies became the nation's new leaders. In July 1793 he was arrested for political crimes, including his part in the 'Massacre'. He was found guilty by the Revolutionary Tribunal and was executed on 12 November 1793 by a guillotine specially erected for the purpose on the Champ-de-Mars.

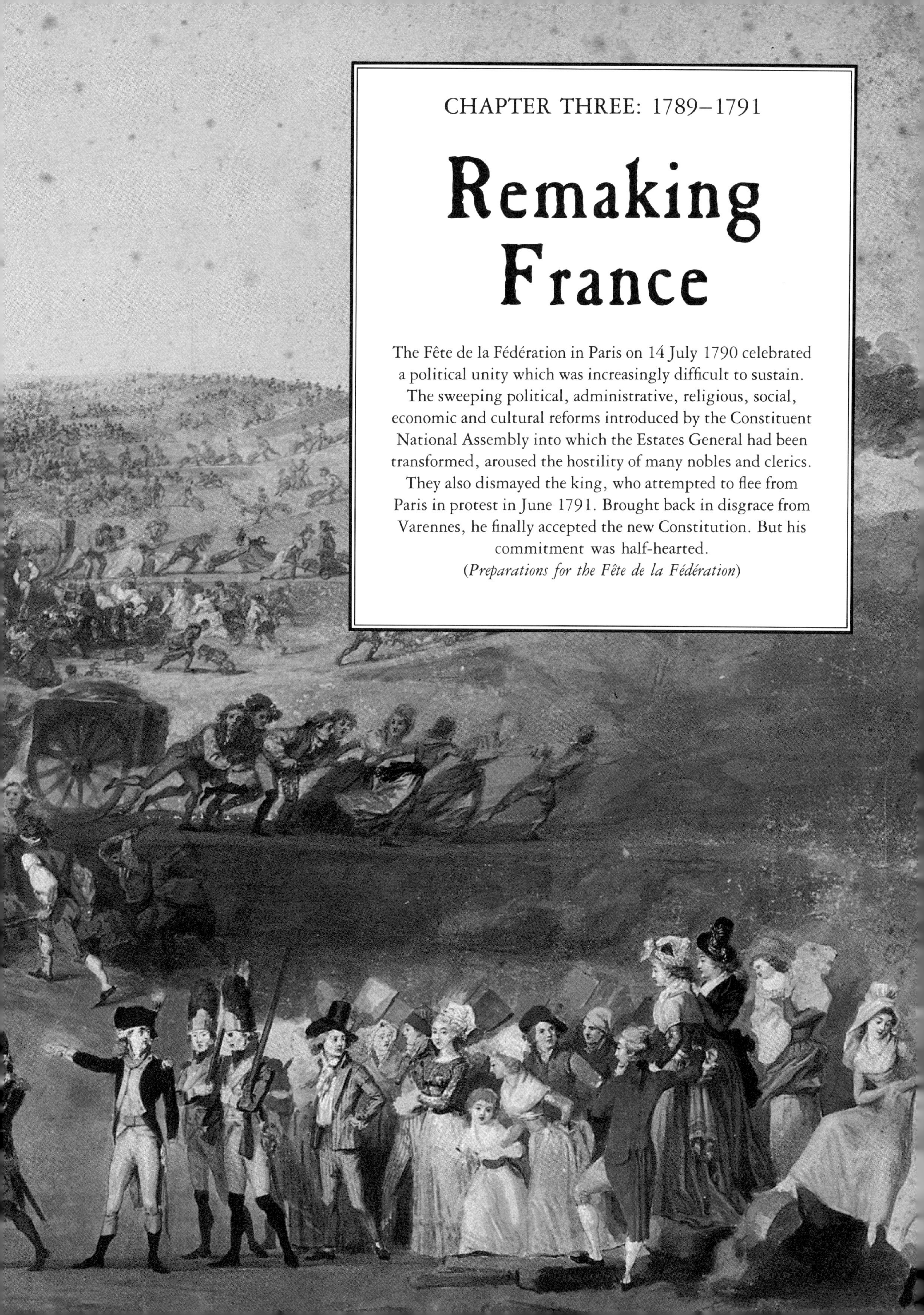

CHAPTER THREE: 1789–1791

Remaking France

The Fête de la Fédération in Paris on 14 July 1790 celebrated a political unity which was increasingly difficult to sustain. The sweeping political, administrative, religious, social, economic and cultural reforms introduced by the Constituent National Assembly into which the Estates General had been transformed, aroused the hostility of many nobles and clerics. They also dismayed the king, who attempted to flee from Paris in protest in June 1791. Brought back in disgrace from Varennes, he finally accepted the new Constitution. But his commitment was half-hearted.

(*Preparations for the Fête de la Fédération*)

ONCE in the Tuileries the king was forced to change his daily routine and find new distractions now that he no longer lived in the palace of Versailles. Following prayers as soon as he rose, he would go downstairs, check the temperature and make a note of it.

Then he received morning greetings from his wife and children. It was a moment which should have been particularly heartening, but was sometimes disturbed by the queen's comments on their situation and the king's own dark thoughts on their future.

These moments sometimes ended with some light-heartedness, more often in expressions of tenderness. Then the king would have breakfast, gaining information from his servant about events outside, the situation, and people's feelings. He would often make use of these reports to contradict his ministers, and even the queen herself. The time between breakfast and Mass was taken up with business affairs, letters, and a little work on his hobby of lock-making.

Hunting was not allowed, and since exercise was necessary for his health, he walked in his rooms until healthy perspiration required him to stop. After Mass he spent some time with his faithful subjects and then returned to his own apartments until it was time to lunch. He ate quickly and with good appetite and drank little, in spite of his reputation for excessive drinking; generally he took less than a bottle of wine, and diluted it with plenty of water. With dessert he took half a glass of liqueur to end the meal.

His afternoon was taken up with reading and playing with his children, particularly the dauphin. In the evening he would go into the salon, or into the billiard-room for a few games with one of those present, often with the queen. He was a poor player, and very much disliked losing: more than once he was known to break a cue.

Although the activities of the National Assembly often distressed him, there were times when he was favourably impressed with some of their laws. One such was the law which divided France into eighty-three departments. He drew up a map for himself showing the new system, indicating those areas which had belonged to one province and were now placed in a department under another name.

Newspapers entertained the Parisians with reports – such as the above – of how Louis XVI tried to keep boredom at bay in his new home in the Tuileries palace.

The new departments

THE *ancien régime* administrative divisions were so confusing that some letters ordering elections for the Estates General were directed either to the wrong *bailliage* (legal district) or to ones that did not exist. These antique judicial divisions, moreover, generally had disputed boundaries, a characteristic shared with the many other overlapping sectors of France's territory. Since judicial areas did not correspond with those for ecclesiastical, military, fiscal or administrative purposes, further confusion and inequity ensued.

The ancient provinces of France played only a small administrative role. But they could obstruct the centralizing and rationalizing plans of ministers bent on uniformity. They drew on deep funds of loyalty, based on history, customs, language. Those like Brittany or Languedoc, which preserved their own assemblies, or estates, were especially proud of their traditions.

The supervisory role of the Intendants, zealous servants of Versailles, was increasingly resented. Provincial consciousness revived. Yet exasperation at the chaos of France's administrative organization also grew. From the 1770s onwards, several reform schemes were introduced, the most promising incorporating provincial assemblies. However, the government was loth to concede much initiative to such bodies.

Inspired by the *cahiers de doléances*, which demanded a simpler, more harmonized administrative system, the National Assembly in 1789 had a unique opportunity to treat France as an 'empty map' on which to trace new, rational boundaries.

Although, in the abstract, geometrical spirit of the Enlightenment, it was suggested that France be carved into rectangles, it was soon decided that existing relationships between the different parts of France should not be brutally broken. Eighty-three departments were created, small enough for people to travel to the capital, or *chef-lieu*, in a day; departments were subdivided into districts composed of communes designed to revive moribund municipal life.

The key was the department. The political unit for elections – which now assumed an unprecedented role in public affairs – the department's own elected administrators supervised public works, communications and education, and allocated the taxes to the districts. The departments' boundaries were also taken for the new dioceses, far fewer in number but much more equal in size and resources, as befitted both Christian and revolutionary *'égalité'*. A criminal tribunal dispensed justice from the capital, with a civil tribunal in each district.

These privileges and perquisites made the choice of a departmental *chef-lieu* a hotly debated issue. The *chef-lieu* was greatly prized, with jobs in administration and a political role permitting favouritism, and rivalry was bitter. Sometimes, in the face of such fierce local feuding, no decision could be made and a *chef-lieu* might commute between towns or be fought over physically. In August 1792 a band of men marched from Marseille to Aix – and returned with the departmental administration.

Despite such troubles, and the draconian centralization of the Terror, the departments survived. The Napoleonic prefects reduced their powers, but their creation was one of the successes of the Revolution.

The National Assembly, as Bailly's memoirs record, attempted to extricate itself from the state's near-bankruptcy by nationalizing church property.

M. de Talleyrand showed that, although the state's normal resources were exhausted, there remained immense resources in the form of church property. It might be worth 150 million livres – i.e. 80 million from tithes, and 70 million from property. Under the proposed scheme, this latter income will immediately be placed in the state's hands.

George Washington, in this letter to the US envoy in Paris, Gouverneur Morris, analyses the obstacles to the resolution of conflicts engendered by the events of 1789.

New York, 13 October 1789. The revolution which has been effected in France is of so wonderful a nature, that the mind can hardly recognize the fact. If it ends as our last accounts to 1 August predict, that nation will be the most powerful and happy in Europe.

But I fear, though it has gone triumphantly through the first paroxysm, it is not the last it has to encounter before matters are finally settled. In a word, the revolution is of too great a magnitude to be effected in so short a space, and with the loss of so little blood. The mortification of the king, the intrigues of the queen, and the discontent of the princes and nobles, will foment divisions in the National Assembly, and they will unquestionably avail themselves of every faux pas *in the formation of the constitution, if they do not give a more open, active opposition.*

Great temperance, firmness, and foresight are necessary. To forbear running from one extreme to another is no easy matter, and should this be the case, rocks and shelves, not visible at present, may wreck the vessel, and give a higher-toned despotism than the one which existed before.

I am, dear Sir, &c.

George Washington.

THE MASSACHUSETTS MAGAZINE (Boston) *February 1791*

The value of the possessions of the clergy in France, is estimated at 180 Millions of pounds sterling. When these enormous sums are paid into the publick Treasury, and when many savings in expenditure shall have been made, France will rise in the scale of Europe as almost a new country, without debts, and without heavy and oppressive taxes.

One revolution looks at another

FOLLOWING the fall of the Bastille, Lafayette sent the key of the fortress to the new president of the United States, George Washington – as, he said, 'a tribute which I owe as a son to my adoptive father, as an aide-de-camp to my general, and as a missionary of liberty to its patriarch'. There was a strong feeling in both countries to identify the French Revolution with its American antecedent. The pleasure of James Madison, leading congressman and future president, at events in France was 'enhanced by the reflection that the light which is chasing darkness and despotism from the Old World is but an emanation from that which has procured and succeeded the establishment of liberty in the new'. Among the eighteen foreigners later made honorary French citizens by the French assembly were Washington, Madison and Secretary of the Treasury Alexander Hamilton.

The news of the Revolution was warmly received in America, whose people recognized the debt they owed France for taking their side during the War of Independence – volunteers like Lafayette joined Washington's army, and the young republic was supported by French military power from 1778. To ties of gratitude could now be added shared political ideas.

However, some observers soon became uneasy: events in France were not following the benign and well-ordered course that they had in America. Washington was apprehensive that 'the tumultuous populace of large cities are ever to be dreaded'. Vice-President John Adams was concerned that the one-chamber assembly adopted by the French did not provide sufficient checks and balances to restrain the excesses of democracy. But such doubts were swamped by a surge of sympathy when France was threatened with invasion by Austria and Prussia in 1792. Even a conservative congressman like John Marshall, a future chief justice, later admitted that he 'sincerely believed human liberty to depend in a great measure on the success of the French Revolution'. Consequently the news of France's victory over the despotic German powers was 'celebrated throughout the country with every demonstration of festivity; and every exertion employed to combine the cause of France with the preservation of American Liberty'.

However, 1793 marked a parting of the ways in American attitudes to the Revolution. Southern plantation owners were becoming alarmed by the steady stream of refugee French planters and their families seeking shelter in the United States from the slave rebellion in the colony of Saint-Domingue. Lafayette's flight from France in 1792 led some to wonder where

LEFT James Madison, fourth president of the United States, was made an honorary French citizen by the National Assembly in 1792.

BELOW Thomas Jefferson, US president and former ambassador in Paris.

the real aims of the Revolution lay. France's attacks on the Low Countries and north Italy in late 1792–early 1793 took some observers by surprise; and still more were horrified by the September massacres of 1792 in Paris, the execution of the king (celebrated by the populace of Philadelphia but mourned in plantation Virginia), and the reign of terror that followed.

Nevertheless, the Revolution still had its strong defenders. Thomas Jefferson protested that 'the liberty of the whole earth was depending on the issue of the contest, and was ever such a prize won with so little innocent blood?' Others were coming to share Alexander Hamilton's view that 'there is no real resemblance between what was the cause of America and what is the cause of France. The difference is no less great than that between Liberty and Licentiousness.'

Alienation of the American ruling classes was increased, and the sympathies of the wider American public almost lost, by a new French envoy's blatant interference in America's internal government in 1793. Edmond Genêt attempted to stir up popular feeling and intimidate Washington's government into allowing France to control America's neutrality in the European war for its own military purposes. The horrified pro-French (but loyal American) Republican party saved itself from losing popularity among the population at large by disavowing Genêt altogether. It became extremely difficult for the United States to maintain its neutrality in the ensuing Anglo-French maritime war. America tended to favour Britain from commercial needs: this angered the French, and relations between the two countries deteriorated into quasi-war, which ended with the formal annulment of their original 1778 alliance in 1800.

The back-bench deputy Adrien Duquesnoy reflected in his diary on the benefits the Revolution had already brought the French people.

16 January 1790. Putting aside priests, nobility, magistrates and financiers, it is clear that all the rest of the kingdom reaps infinite benefits from the revolution. And indeed, amongst those citizens whom I have just listed there are a great number who should judge it advantageous to them, because in truth it is. Thus the clergy of second degree and almost all provincial noblemen, who were recently oppressed by bishops and court nobles, should consider themselves fortunate to be relieved of this aristocracy.

Moreover, anyone who can for an instant put aside all private interest, cannot but bless this revolution. When one thinks of the great abuses of all kinds which burdened this poor kingdom, it seems obvious that only an upheaval of such intensity could achieve such an end.

In any case, one thing is certain – it would be difficult for things to be worse than they were under the former regime.

I often hear people around me asking a very strange question: they enquire, 'What has the assembly been doing for the last six months?' I only know of one reply to this question: 'Look, and observe: clergy and nobility abolished, provincial privileges gone, ecclesiastical property nationalized. Could you have achieved so much in ten years?'

Despite the formal abolition of feudalism on 4–11 August 1789, high levels of tension and violence remained in many regions and, as this debate in the National Assembly reveals, was often focused on symbolic aspects of feudalism such as weather-vanes bearing seigneurial crests.

M. de Foucault: A time has been indicated for the Feudal Committee to make its report on the redemption of feudal rights. It is important for the assembly to deal with this straight away. There is no more time for procrastination. My province, Périgord, is ablaze; landowners are being stripped by the landless...

Foucault then read out three letters.

First letter: 'Armed peasants arrived here, they interrogated me for twenty-four hours, and forced me to renounce rents which had fallen due. If they had only attacked my weather-vanes, I would have kept quiet.'

Second letter: 'M. de Bar's residence has been burned down; he took refuge in Sarlat. A bodyguard, his nephew, was put in prison. Three common prisoners have been released. People talk about pulling down weather-vanes.'

Third letter: 'The Mirandole family were visited by two villages grouped together; they attacked the weather-vanes, the tocsin rings all the time; the people are perpetually drunk.'

M. la Chèze: Such excesses are commonplace in Quercy: six people have been killed there. Things are getting worse and are reaching their peak; there is a general attack on all property.

M. Gourdan: There is only one way to bring back peace and quiet; to work without delay and without hindrance on the constitution.

A new, allegedly humane method of dispensing capital punishment, the guillotine, attracted much interest. The following piece is from *L'Ami du Roi*.

LEGISLATION and the arts are improving every day. Thanks to new discoveries in anatomy, our criminal law is going to acquire new strength and, if philosophy still permits the spilling of human blood, at least the ingenious and gentle way in which it is spilt in future may serve as model for all the world's legislators. It fell to M. Guillotin, a Paris deputy, and as skilled in medicine as in mechanics, to offer the world his plan for a machine for beheading which will spread the glory of the name of France to the very shores of the Bosporus.

This prompt and expeditious system will offer so many advantages over the method favoured by the English!

The grandeur and elegance of the spectacle will attract many more people to the place of execution; more people will be impressed, and the rule of law will be more greatly respected.

This method will make it possible for the criminal to approach his death boldly, he will be thus enabled to face up to the blade of eternity which he will see suspended above his head.

One great problem which has arisen concerns the name which shall be given to this instrument. Should the language be enriched by the adoption of the name of its inventor? Those who favour this notion have had no difficulty in offering the sweet and charming name of 'Guillotine'.

The guillotine

THE guillotine is a symbol of violence and death, an enduring image of the French Revolution; yet its use from 1792 onwards was the culmination of demands by humanitarians and legal reformers throughout the *ancien régime*.

Previously, the same crime had carried different punishments according to the social status of the criminal: a noble convicted of treason was publicly beheaded, but the lower orders were not permitted this relatively honourable and certainly less painful death. Similarly, there was no uniform method of execution for other capital crimes. Heretics and blasphemers could be burned alive, minor theft punished by hanging and, in the case of highway robbery, by breaking the criminal's bones with an iron bar and leaving him tied to a wheel to die. To many contemporaries, penalties like these were one of the most objectionable features of monarchical government.

By the 1780s the monarchy seemed ready to accept some of the criticisms voiced by the penal reformers, and judicial torture was gradually abolished. This impetus was continued under the Revolution. Although few argued for the abolition of capital punishment, reformers viewed the debates on the new penal code, completed in 1791, as a golden opportunity to put the principles of humanity, rationality and uniformity in administering the death penalty into practice. In 1789 the Parisian deputy Joseph-Ignace Guillotin, a well-known doctor, proposed uniform punishment for those guilty of capital crimes, and suggested using a new machine which, he said, 'would separate the head from the body in less time than it takes to wink'.

ABOVE The guillotine, nicknamed 'the national razor', was conceived as an efficient and humane machine for decapitation.

On 5 June 1791, the provision for a uniform death penalty by decapitation was included in the new penal code. The following April, the surgeon Antoine Louis began to test Guillotin's machine; he experimented on large animals like sheep and calves, as well as on human corpses from the public poorhouse at Bicêtre. Louis was not only concerned to produce an efficient, humane machine for decapitation. He was also investigating the possibility that the decapitated head might live on in full consciousness after its separation from the body.

The new machine, known as the 'Louison' or 'Louisette' after Dr Louis, was erected in accordance with his design of 'two uprights, a foot apart, with grooves down which ran a well-tempered blade, heavy enough to fall rapidly and give a decided blow to the victim, who is to be lying flat on his stomach with his head across a block of wood immediately below the blade'. It was used in Paris for the first time on 25 April 1792, to execute a forger named Pelletier. Initially set up on the traditional public execution site of the Place de Grève, it was re-erected on 21 August on the Place du Carrousel, where it remained for nine months except when it was moved to what is now the Place de la Concorde, for the execution of Louis XVI on 21 January 1793. The guillotine returned to the Place de la Concorde from 10 May 1793 to 8 June 1794; after that it stood on the Place du Trône.

Members of the Sanson family worked the machine. They had provided the public executioners of the *ancien régime*, and the dynasty continued in this office until the mid-19th century. In Paris, 2690 victims were guillotined during the Terror.

The regulations of the Paris Jacobin Club – first known as the Society of Friends of the Constitution – in early 1790 placed great store on the importance of publicity and civic education in political discussion.

THE Society will be dedicated to the spreading of truth, the defence of freedom and the constitution, and its methods will be as honourable as its objectives; openness will be the guarantor of all its initiatives.

Fidelity to the constitution and devotion to its defence, respect and submission to the powers it establishes, these will be the first laws imposed on any wishing to be admitted to these Societies.

Qualifications for entry will above all be the love of equality and that deep feeling for the rights of man which is evident in instinctive devotion to the protection of the weak and oppressed.

The new political awareness reached down into the world of shopkeepers and artisans, as this sardonic account of a visit to the cobbler reveals. Written in early 1790, the letter was from the aristocratic Mme de Cressonnier to her friend the baron de Blaisel.

Rejoice, my dear baron. Hurrah, hurrah for liberty! My cobbler, one of the best known in his district, said to me just now: 'Well then, Madame, you must be pleased?' – 'And, why's that, my dear Sir?' – 'Well, Madame, everything is going well, and the king has just declared himself the leader of the Revolution.' – 'That's fine, if that's what you want; but before I rejoice, I need to see business pick up again, and money reappear, and have my pensions paid, and then I will shout with the wildest' – 'But, Madame, we must light up and rejoice, everything is wonderful.' 'Many families are reduced to living on charity as a result of these changes. But all this, you say, is nothing compared with the king declaring himself the first bourgeois of the kingdom! That's fine by me. It brings us together, and if my son were handsome he could hope to marry the king's daughter.' – 'And why not,' said the cobbler, 'I certainly hope that my son will one day be a marshal of France. Am I not the major in my National Guard battalion?'

You see, my dear baron, the madness which is turning the heads of all these fine fellows! It is ridiculous. Anyway, in spite of everything, I must be gay, rejoice and shout myself hoarse with 'Hurrah, hurrah for the Nation, the law, the king' – and kiss you with all my heart, which is infinitely more pleasant.

The Jacobin clubs

IN the absence of official parties, political clubs were essential to the organization of the Revolution. They set up speakers and issues for debates in the assembly and supported election candidates. They were also centres of information, political education and philanthropic work. Many Parisian clubs, like the Jacobins, Cordeliers and Feuillants, took their names from the premises of the religious order where they first met.

The Jacobins were formed from the Breton Club, a group of deputies who met in Versailles during 1789 to discuss questions about to come before the National Assembly and work towards a constitution; the membership then numbered about 400, and its official name was the Society of the Friends of the Constitution. After the October Days the club moved to Paris, with the court and the assembly, and its members became known as the Jacobins. In May 1790, Lafayette formed a breakaway group, the Société de 1789, to promote his personal and political ambitions.

Dominant in the Paris Jacobin Club down to mid-1791 was the triumvirate of Barnave, Adrien Duport and Alexandre de Lameth, who followed a liberal, constitutional monarchist line. At the time of the king's flight to Varennes, the triumvirate left the Jacobins to form the Feuillant Club, and from that time the Jacobins became associated with increasingly radical and republican views.

The Jacobins started as a well-organized debating club, which charged an entrance fee and a substantial annual subscription. Orators would re-read their speeches there. Originally the preserve of deputies, liberal aristocrats and well-to-do bourgeois, it gradually opened its doors to a more democratic membership of artisans and small shopkeepers.

A network of equally democratic clubs sprang up in the provinces. In Strasbourg the club's 300 members in early 1791 were mainly merchants, manufacturers, professional men and army officers. Women were not usually eligible for membership, and allowed in only as spectators, which did not prevent them from participating in the debates. After the king's flight to Varennes, provincial members also became more radical, and the Strasbourg club, together with that of Montpellier, called for a republic.

There were about 5500 Jacobin clubs. The earliest network outside Paris was formed in the south-west, and the Mediterranean Midi, where members sometimes took over the premises, and rituals, of religious lay confraternities. In some areas there was continuity with *ancien régime* masonic lodges. In 1791,

Jacobin clubs were solidly implanted in central France as well, and large numbers were established in the north between 1793 and 1794. The greatest concentration, however, was in the south-east: in the Var, 92 per cent of communes had a Jacobin club by 1794.

They circulated national news: the Marseille club published its own newspaper as well as pamphlets and brochures. Rallies and processions were organized to celebrate the new revolutionary festivals and to honour the martyrs of the Revolution. They collected funds for widows and orphans bereaved by the revolutionary wars, and promoted their own candidates in local elections. They also acted as employment agencies, giving jobs in local and military administration to people with the right political credentials, and kept a close watch on local authorities, denouncing them if they showed weakness in applying legislation against *émigrés*, refractory priests or other political suspects. During the Terror the Jacobin clubs and their executive committees were increasingly responsible for administrative purges, arresting political suspects, recruitment, food supplies and the observance of the new republican calendar. In large regional centres they were vital to the Revolution. In 1791–2, the Marseille club vigorously opposed the counter-revolutionaries in Arles and Avignon, and the delegation of *fédérés* it sent to Paris in the summer of 1792 was nationally famous for the part it played in the overthrow of the monarchy.

The Jacobin clubs were abolished in the right-wing phase of the Revolution in 1794–5. Although they often promoted narrow, local interests, they were essential grass-roots institutions of the Revolution; their national network introduced French citizens to a new, democratic political life.

BELOW The seat of the Paris Jacobin Club, formerly the monastery of the Dominicans of St James, or 'Jacobins'.

Louis XVI's personal account-book, the *Livre Rouge* or red register, was made public on the orders of the National Assembly in April 1790. It indicated levels of royal expenditure on personal favourites and sinecures under the *ancien régime* which seemed scandalous in the context of state bankruptcy.

ANALYSIS OF THE RED REGISTER

THE total amount entered in the Red Book from 19 May 1774 to 16 August 1789 is 227,983,716 livres, 10 sous, 1 denier.

This sum can be broken down under several headings:

	livres
To the king's brothers	28,364,211
Gifts, gratuities	6, 174,793
Pensions, salaries	2, 221,541
Charity	254,000
Indemnities, advances, loans	15, 254,106
Acquisitions, exchanges	20,868,821
Financial transactions	5, 825,000
Foreign affairs, postal costs	135,804,891
Various expenses	1, 794,600
Personal expenses of the king and queen	11, 423,750
	227,985,716

From late 1789, the government had issued state bonds 'assigned', or secured, on the church lands which had been nationalized on 2 November. In April 1790, these bonds (*assignats*) were accepted as paper money.

THE National Assembly decreed, on 16 and 17 April:

From this current year, ecclesiastical debts will be considered national debts; the public treasury will be responsible for paying interest and capital.

Assignats shall be legal tender throughout the kingdom, and will be accepted as currency in all public and private transactions.

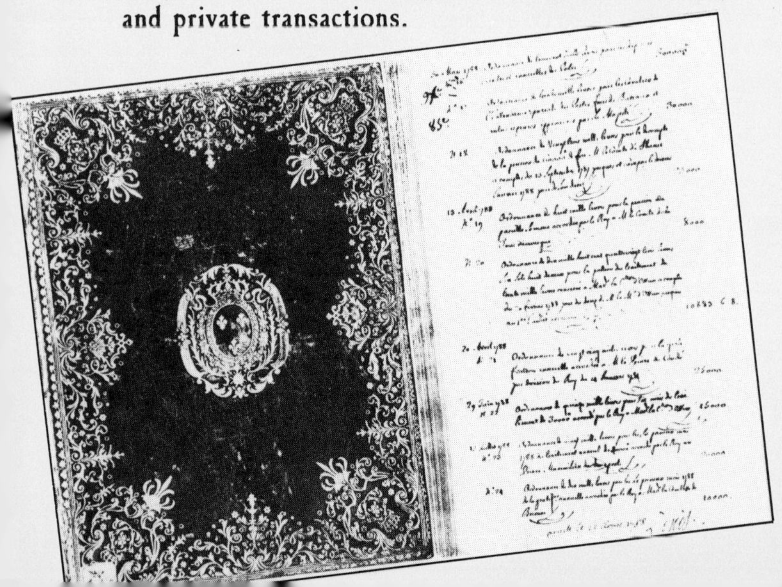

Paper money, secret funds

THE Revolution had been precipitated by impending state bankruptcy, but the financial crisis did not disappear. The government still had to levy taxes to pay the armed forces and the police network, and to care for a population threatened by famine and suffering from unemployment. Revenue fell to half the normal yield, and all attempts to raise loans during August 1789 failed.

Throughout the 18th century it had been argued that church lands, which were held in mortmain and could not be put up for sale, should be secularized and sold on the open market. The National Assembly seized upon this idea as a solution to its financial problems and on 2 November 1789 voted to appropriate the church's vast acres, amounting to between five and ten per cent of France's total land surface.

The money was needed immediately, and therefore had to be turned into liquid assets as quickly as possible. On 19 December the assembly decided to sell impounded land worth 400 million livres and create bonds yielding five per cent interest. These would be sold to the public and be redeemable in five years; holders would have priority in purchasing land offered for sale. The bonds, called *'billets d'achat'* were soon known as *'assignats'*.

By April 1790 little of the land had been sold, and an alarmed National Assembly converted the bonds into money, like banknotes, and made them legal tender. The final step towards a monetary system based entirely on paper notes was taken in September 1790, when the National Assembly backed a motion by Mirabeau and declared that the value of *assignats* in circulation would be increased to 800 million livres and that they would lose their interest-bearing quality. The new paper money was made available in units as small as five livres, and often replaced silver coins. In a little over two years, by January 1793, more than three billion livres of paper currency had been printed. The runaway inflation that resulted created a social crisis which led on into a political crisis. Although the Terror kept the problem within bounds, with the overthrow of the Jacobins on 9 Thermidor (27 July) 1794 controls were abandoned and prices rocketed. Within seven years of its creation the *assignat* was not worth the paper it was printed on, and on 4 February 1797 the Directory returned to a metallic standard.

Another aspect of the financial uncertainty engendered by the Revolution was the furore created in early 1790 by the publication of the so-called 'Red Register' or *Livre Rouge*. It purported to show how great quantities of taxpayers' money had gone into the

pockets of the royal family and their favourites. The evidence came from secret royal authorizations – *ordonnances de comptant* – which were normally withheld from public scrutiny.

This episode revealed the extreme sensitivity of public opinion to the supposed extravagance of the royal court. Marie-Antoinette's lavish expenditure had been widely publicized – she loved fine clothes and entertainment, and gave generously to close friends – and the king's flamboyant younger brother, the comte d'Artois, attracted attention by his spectacular gambling losses and enormous debts. Although Louis himself was anything but a wastrel – he listened to finance ministers who urged a policy of economy – he was unable to control those around him who were.

In comparison to the debt created by frequent wars, the sums spent by the court were trifling. But wars could be justified as having been undertaken in the national interest: wasteful spending by the court could not. Resentment against such former extravagance was amplified by the financial problems the revolutionaries found impossible to avoid.

ABOVE Courtly extravagance before the Revolution: the illumination of the Belvedere at the Petit-Trianon, 1781.

OPPOSITE The *Livre Rouge*, so-called for its rich red leather binding.

BELOW An *assignat*, bonds which soon became paper money

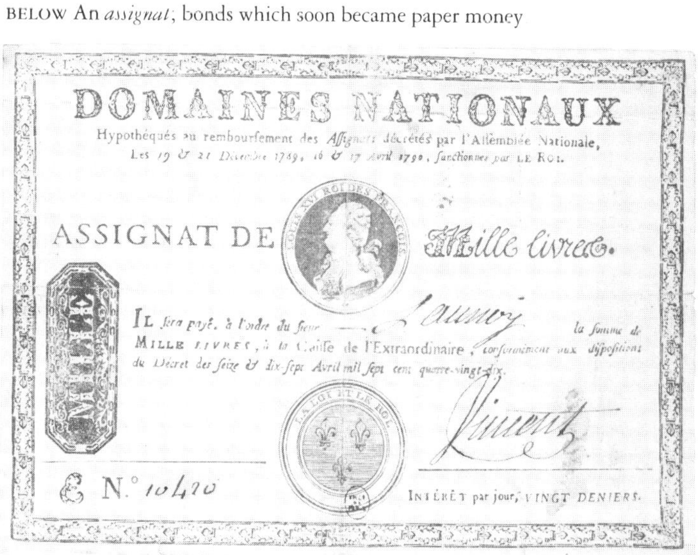

The social consequences of the use of *assignats* as money were predicted with some accuracy by the royalist newspaper *L'Ami du Roi*.

IF the new *assignats* can circulate in the same way as coinage, if they are used in trade, above all if they are unwisely issued for small amounts, their effect will inevitably be to overwhelm the coinage, raise the price of goods, and bring about the complete ruin of trade. The *assignats* will become negotiable; they will pass from hand to hand, they will infest the whole of France, like swarms of harmful insects ravaging and devastating an immense country, and no one will want to buy from anyone else.

The appearance of Burke's *Reflections on the Revolution in France* in England started a rightward drift in European opinion on the Revolution. But in France, the Prussian baron Anacharsis Clootz, speaking from the bar of the National Assembly, requested that foreigners be allowed to join with Frenchmen on the great day of national celebration, the Fête de la Fédération, planned for the first anniversary of the fall of the Bastille. This report is from the *Moniteur*.

19 JUNE 1790. *Baron Clootz:* Gentlemen, the imposing sheaves of flags from all over the French Empire which will be unfurled in the Champ-de-Mars on 14 July will mark a celebration not only for the French, but for the whole human race.

We too have given birth to an inspired idea, and would dare to suggest it should add to the great national day. A number of foreigners from all nations on earth wish to gather in the centre of the Champ-de-Mars, and flourish the cap of liberty as a token of their unhappy fellow-citizens' fast approaching deliverance.

You have truly recognized, gentlemen, that sovereignty dwells in the people; but the people are everywhere under the yoke of dictators, who claim sovereignty in spite of your principles.

What a lesson is there for despotism! and what consolation for unhappy nations, when they learn that the leading nation of Europe, assembling beneath its flags, heralded the happiness of France, the Old World and the New.

This speech was interrupted several times by the assembly's applause.

A Turk spoke next. He spoke French with such difficulty that we were unable to follow what he said.

Edmund Burke

'I BELIEVE in the Honorable Edmund Burke, who reflected on the French Revolution', ran the second item of 'The aristocrat's creed', a fictional piece printed in a Gainsborough newspaper, the *Country Spectator*, in its issue of 6 November 1792. Edmund Burke, born in 1729, was a prominent member of the Whig opposition in Britain, who had been a leading critic of George III's alleged tyrannical aspirations and a supporter of the cause of American liberty. He was one of the first leading political commentators outside France to criticize the infant French Revolution and its possible implications for other countries.

In contrast to the general welcome given in Britain to the events of 1789, Burke described France, in September of that year, as 'a country where the people, along with their political servitude, have thrown off the yoke of laws and morals'. In November he argued that France was 'a country undone; and irretrievable for a very long course of time. I see many inconveniences, not only to Europe at large, but to this country in particular from the total political extinction of a great civilized nation in the heart of this our Western system'.

A year later, on 1 November 1790, he published a major attack on the Revolution and its British supporters, *Reflections on the Revolution in France and on the proceedings of certain societies in London relative to that*

ABOVE A contemporary English cartoon typifying the attitude towards the French Revolution which Burke promulgated.

event. Over 17,000 copies had been printed by the end of the year and the book was widely discussed and quoted in the press. A French translation appeared on 29 November and by June 1791, French demand alone had been sufficient to require ten reprints. The book was praised by George III, who said publicly at court, 'I know that there is no man who calls himself a gentleman that must not think himself obliged to you, for you have supported the cause of the gentlemen'; but it was savagely criticized by supporters of the Revolution.

Burke's essential thesis was that the Revolution was dangerous because it sought to destroy, rather than improve, past institutions and traditions. He condemned the 'barbarous philosophy' which he claimed motivated the revolutionaries: 'all the pleasing illusions, which made power gentle and obedience liberal, are to be dissolved by this new conquering empire of light and reason. On this scheme of things, a king is but a man.' Burke warned that it would lead to a more violent and autocratic state: 'the usurpation which, in order to subvert ancient institutions, has destroyed ancient principles, will hold power by arts similar to those by which it has acquired it. Plots and assassinations will be anticipated by preventive murder and preventive confiscation. Kings will be tyrants from policy, when subjects are rebels from principle. When ancient opinions and rules of life are taken away, the loss cannot possibly be estimated. From that moment we have no compass to govern us.'

Burke tried to turn the Whigs against the Revolution, and in his *Appeal from the New to the Old Whigs*, dated 1791, argued that his views, as expressed in the *Reflections*, were consistent with his support of the English 'Glorious Revolution' of 1688. Burke also developed close links with the *émigrés*. By the autumn of 1791 he was equating the constitutional monarchists with the Jacobins, and arguing that Britain must prepare for war.

The ministry of William Pitt the Younger refused to support the counter-revolutionary crusade and remained neutral when the revolutionary wars began in 1792. However, Burke's works played a significant role in increasing British distrust of French developments and in exacerbating France's suspicion of British intentions.

By linking British reformers and radicals with French revolutionaries, he sought to discredit the former – and with considerable success. In a parliamentary debate in December 1792 he claimed that an order had been placed at Birmingham for 3000 daggers, threw what he claimed to be a specimen on the floor of the House and declared, 'This is what you are to gain by an alliance with France.' Once war had broken out between Britain and France, Burke tried to turn a struggle that arose essentially from opposing interests in the Low Countries into an ideological conflict. He was only partially successful, but his writings sustained the notion of a crusade against atheism and rebellion. He was the leading spokesman for the cause of European counter-revolutionaries; his *Reflections on the Revolution in France* was their credo and their catechism.

The abolition of noble status by the decree of 19 June 1790 was part of the move to establish civic equality.

THE National Assembly decrees that hereditary titles are abolished henceforward and for ever in France; and that in consequence the titles of marquis, knight, squire, count, viscount, messire, prince, baron, noble, duke, and all other similar titles, shall not be taken by any person, nor given to any person; that no one may dress his domestic staff in livery, nor possess coats-of-arms; that the title of Monseigneur shall not be granted to any body or any individual, similarly with titles of Excellence, Highness, Eminence.

The marquis de Ferrières placed responsibility for the abolition of noble titles on liberal aristocrats, drawn from the ranks of the Paris Jacobins.

I won't go into details of Saturday's [19 June] session. This was a frenzy, but a frenzy prepared by the Jacobin Club. It was people like the Lameth brothers, Lafayette, Lepeletier proposed the decree and had it passed. Thus it is from the nobility itself that its greatest enemies have arisen.

THE CHRISTIAN'S, SCHOLAR'S, AND FARMER'S MAGAZINE (Elizabethtown, N.J.), *June and July 1790*

The key of the French Bastille has been sent over by the marquis de Lafayette to Mr Payne, an American; in order to be transmitted by him to General Washington, as a glorious token of triumphant liberty over despotic oppression.

For several months prior to 14 July 1790, the National Assembly had planned a great national celebration, to be held on the Champ-de-Mars in Paris. The Fête de la Fédération was to be attended by *fédérés* – National Guardsmen and other delegates – from each of the 83 departments. This record of part of the festivities is from a letter of a *fédéré* from eastern France.

TWO days before the Fête de la Fédération, the fédérés *were ordered to gather in the afternoon in the Champs-Elysées for inspection by the king. Torrential rain brought a change of orders, and they marched through the hall before the king, the queen and their family. Instead of wearing dark blue, my department adopted sky-blue uniforms, with red lapels and facings and white lining and buttons; this gave an unusual effect which caught the queen's eye.*

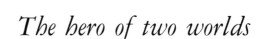

The hero of two worlds

BY the beginning of 1790 the marquis de Lafayette (Marie Joseph Paul Yves Roch Gilbert du Motier) seemed destined to occupy a central position in the French Revolution, as it was claimed he had in America's. His family's wealth and his wife's connections had enabled him in the spring of 1777, at the age of twenty, to buy a ship and sail to America, despite Louis XVI's wish to keep French aid to the American rebels surreptitious. Although only a captain in the regiment owned by his in-laws, the powerful Noailles family, Lafayette received a commission as a general in the American army, and his gallantry and charm endeared him to George Washington who became his patron and protector.

Although Lafayette's original motive for supporting the American struggle seems to have been desire for glory and revenge after France's humiliating defeat in the Seven Years War (1756–63), he later identified himself – and, more importantly, was widely associated – with the general cause of 'liberty'. As the dramatic events of the late 1780s in France approached revolution, Lafayette figured prominently among upper-class liberals. Like other court aristocrats and veterans of the American Revolution, he was a member of the radical caucus the Society of Thirty; and his election as a deputy of the nobility of Riom to the Estates General in March 1789 ensured the continuation of his political influence.

During the second half of 1789 he helped draft the Declaration of the Rights of Man, was appointed commander of the National Guard on 15 July, helped to negotiate a suspensive veto – that is, the right of the monarch to block the implementation of legislation for anything between two and five years – for the king; and he was instrumental in moderating and containing the violence of the *journées* of 5–6 October.

Nevertheless, 1790 was the 'year of Lafayette'; in particular, on the first anniversary of the fall of the Bastille, Lafayette's National Guard played the central role in the Fête de la Fédération in Paris. Only six weeks later his attitude towards the army mutiny at Nancy shattered the illusion of national fraternity. Lafayette's enthusiastic endorsement of the marquis de Bouillé's repression of the uprising satisfied the proponents of law and order, but alarmed the radicals.

His fall from power was more rapid than his rise. At the outbreak of war with Austria in April 1792, Lafayette was given command of one of France's three field armies. But the first battles resulted in French defeats, setbacks which further undermined Louis'

ABOVE Lafayette at the Fête de la Fédération, taking his oath to the Constitution. Talleyrand, bishop of Autun, is on the right.

position. When a Paris crowd invaded the Tuileries on 20 June in an attempt to intimidate the king, Lafayette returned to Paris, where he tried to persuade the National Assembly to repress all radical elements. He was unsuccessful. When the monarchy was overthrown on 10 August 1792, Lafayette despaired of the Revolution and attempted to turn his army against Paris. He failed in this, fled, and on 19 August was captured by the Prussians; he was imprisoned until 1797.

I was marching at the head of the first squad. We were halted for some two minutes right in front of the king. The queen leaned forward, pulled gently at the skirts of my jacket, and said, 'Monsieur, which province are you from?' – 'From that one where your forebears were rulers,' I replied, lowering my sabre. 'What! You are . . . ?' – 'Your loyal subjects from Lorraine,' and I spoke honestly. She thanked me with a slight bow and a look which I see still, so deeply did it pierce me; and, leaning towards the king, she told him, 'These are your faithful subjects from Lorraine.' The king nodded in greeting, and as we marched on I saw no more.

Well! These few words, this look which none of my comrades missed, moved us so much that we would have done anything those two unhappy persons might have demanded of us at that instant. I am only quoting this personal encounter in order to demonstrate how easy it would have been for the king to have at his disposal some eighty thousand men gathered together in Paris who, like myself, were seeing the king for the first time.

While France celebrated national unity, one of the main causes of discord throughout the 1790s was coming to a head. The Civil Constitution of the Clergy, passed on 19 July 1790, reorganized the French church. According to the radical newspaper *Les Révolutions de Paris*, any opposition to the decree could only come from vested interests.

THE REIGN OF THE PRIESTS HAS PASSED

THE reign of the priests has passed; and the more efforts they make to shore up the tottering remains of ecclesiastical power, the sooner will they hasten its collapse.

The National Assembly, in debating the Civil Constitution of the Clergy, has declared that each department will form a single diocese. It has established the election of bishops and curés, and committed this election to the same body that nominates the members of the departments and districts.

If the clergy were less concerned with their past glory and wealth, if they did not wish to foment civil war at any possible price, they would no longer resist the lawful will of the nation. We would not see the majority of the bishops of France, together with the curés, crying out that the Catholic religion is lost because they have been denied a display of wealth that is both insolent and absolutely opposed to the principles and spirit of the Gospel.

Fête de la Fédération

In May 1790 the districts of Paris decided to celebrate the first anniversary of the Fall of the Bastille on 14 July 1789 and formally to identify Paris as the centre of political events. The idea was greeted with enthusiasm throughout the provinces and, after much nationwide discussion, it was agreed that representatives of the National Guard would swear allegiance to the Nation, the Law and the Crown; mass would be said by Talleyrand, bishop of Autun, and a Te Deum sung; and the banners of the 83 departments of France would be blessed. Both royalists and patriots had reservations about inviting large numbers of provincial militia to Paris, but in the end they posed no threat.

To provide a setting for the ceremony, a vast amphitheatre was excavated on the Champs-de-Mars between the Ecole Militaire and the Seine. Gangs of

municipal labourers worked long hours, but the time available before 14 July was too short and the task was only completed in time thanks to the spontaneous participation of Parisians from all walks of life. This collaborative effort quickly became enshrined in revolutionary memory: the more the political consensus fragmented, and the more fractious the conflicts between groups became, the more the Fête de la Fédération was savoured as a moment of unanimity and happy fraternity. This interpretation was embraced throughout the country: it seemed to consecrate the success of the Revolution, its finest hour – and it diverted attention from internal conflicts.

The festival itself, although hampered by heavy rain, was a cross between a military parade and a religious rally. The active participants, the National Guard, paraded through Paris to the Champ-de-Mars, crossing a pontoon bridge to pass through a huge temporary triumphal arch with figurative bas-reliefs and mottoes extolling constitutional monarchy and celebrating the new era of freedom. The Guard formed up within the shallow amphitheatre, around a central raised altar. The royal family looked on from the south, while spectators ringed the arena to witness the event. National Guardsmen held the centre stage, led by Lafayette, their commander-in-chief; Talleyrand was the other leading participant. The fusion of patriotism and religious vows was entirely typical of the early Revolution, before the Civil Constitution of the Clergy obliged French men and women to choose between allegiance to the state or to the pope. In contrast to later festivals – when the state tried to take over and incorporate piety – at this moment church and state were in harmony.

BELOW The Champ-de-Mars during the Fête de la Fédération. The National Guard are drawn up in the amphitheatre, with the main altar in the centre and the triumphal arch to the right.

The bishops rise up against the election of priests and bishops. But do they not know that almost all the bishops of the early church were elected by the people? And how can the bishops resist the institution of popular elections, when they are the ones who have calmly watched ecclesiastical offices distributed and sold in the most infamous fashion by unworthy courtesans, by valets and prostitutes?

Ministers of the altar, be more sincere in your protests. It is not the changing of the ecclesiastical rule that rouses you against the new constitution: you miss your scandalous wealth, your soft and sensuous life, so little suited to the successors of the apostles. Surrender with good grace. Submit while there is still time, or fear the just severity of a people whom you have for too long trampled underfoot.

Pope Pius VI expressed his disquiet over the Civil Constitution of the Clergy in this missive to Louis XVI dated 7 December 1790.

Our beloved son, we have no doubt of your devotion to the apostolic Roman Catholic church, to the heart of unity, the Holy Seat, to ourselves and to the faith of your glorious ancestors; but we fear that through specious and illusory arguments your love for your people may be led astray and that Your Majesty's ardent wish to see order and peace restored within the kingdom may be abused. We must say to you, with firmness and all our paternal love, that if you give your approval to the decrees concerning the clergy, you will be misleading your people, you will plunge the kingdom into schism and, perhaps, into a cruel war of religion.

The religious issue was one of the reasons behind the royal family's considering fleeing from Paris as a means of re-establishing royal authority. Here Marie-Antoinette alludes to this possibility in a letter to her brother Leopold II of Austria, Holy Roman Emperor. Her allusion to masonic influence on the Revolutionaries was a favourite conservative theme. Mercy, formerly Austrian ambassador in Paris, was a key intermediary in the clandestine plans of the royal family.

17 August 1790. Your letter, my dear brother, overwhelmed me with gratitude and joy. Your friendship is so evident therein that my heart found a moment of happiness.

I must mention to you Count Mercy, the honourable servant of our gracious mother. He looks upon me as his child. You may trust him completely; Prince Kaunitz holds him in high esteem, and the wisdom of his counsel is very valuable to me. I have hidden nothing from him of my feelings concerning our situation, which becomes daily more terrible, and yet I think we must be patient still; but I do not wish to send you all the details in writing: others will give them for me.

Farewell, dear brother. I trust your friendship indeed; in return, please count on all the tender affection of your unhappy sister.

Take good care to keep away from any association with freemasons. You must already have been warned; it is by this route that all the monsters here expect to reach the same goal in all countries. Oh, may God protect my country and you from such misfortunes!

The reactionary baron de Breteuil was accorded plenipotentiary powers by Louis XVI on 20 November 1790 to negotiate secretly on his behalf with foreign courts.

M. de Breteuil, conscious of all your devotion and fidelity, and wishing to give you fresh proof of my confidence, I have chosen to entrust you with the interests of my crown.

Since circumstances do not permit me to give you my instructions on particular topics, nor to maintain a steady correspondence with you, I am sending you this letter giving you full power and authorization vis-à-vis the various powers with whom you may have to deal on my behalf.

You know my wishes, and I trust to your wisdom to use this power as you think necessary for the good of my service. I approve all that you may do to attain my objectives, namely to reinstate my legitimate authority and the happiness of my people.

I pray to God, M. le Baron, that He will protect you.

THE COLUMBIAN MAGAZINE (Philadelphia), *October 1789*

The intelligence from this distracted country appears to be of the utmost consequence. If we may judge from what has been received, much is to be feared from the Emperor of Germany, who it is said has concluded a truce with the Turks; indeed, it is not to be expected that he will remain a tranquil spectator of the degradation of a beloved sister.

Freemasons

IN 1789 there were 35,000 Freemasons and more than 650 masonic lodges in France, under the regulating authority of the Grand Orient Lodge in Paris, which had been established in 1773 with the future duc d'Orléans as Grand Master. The masonic network – the only secular network of associations found throughout France – stood outside the official corporative structure of the *ancien régime*. Freemasonry cut across traditional social boundaries, and included nobles, clergy, soldiers, merchants, professional men and even artisans and shopkeepers.

Freemasonry functioned as a network of social and business contacts, as a body for organizing philanthropic undertakings, and as a forum for discussing Enlightenment ideas. Its symbolism, ritual and legend, especially in its more mystical branches, appealed to the fashionable taste for the esoteric. Above all, it responded to the late 18th-century passion for civilized sociability. The fraternal 'equality' between members was not intended to disrupt the social order. Masonic rules forbade political and religious controversy, and in 1781 Marie-Antoinette had assured her sister that French Freemasonry was simply 'a society of good works and pleasure', whose members' habits led the king to remark that 'people who sing and drink do not conspire'.

Despite the queen's assurances, many Freemasons were active participants in the Revolution; at least two hundred were elected to the Estates General and about a hundred sat in the Convention. Their political views were seldom radical – they tended to withdraw as the Revolution became more left-wing – but masonic habits were an integral part of developing revolutionary political culture. The use of mottoes, like *'liberté, égalité, fraternité'* was derived from Freemasonry, as were many symbols – notably the level, symbolizing equality, and the eye, representing vigilance.

But such influences did not make Freemasonry a revolutionary organization. With moderates like Bailly and Lafayette, and extremists like Couthon and Barère, as members, as well as numerous *émigrés*, including the Grand Orient's administrator, the duc de Montmorency-Luxembourg, and the comte d'Artois, it was a far from homogeneous body. As the Revolution developed, masonic solidarity became increasingly illusory – a lapsed Freemason reminded the Grand Orient in 1792 that Frenchmen had 'more urgent and much more consequential occupations than those of masonry'. Recruitment and lodge attendance declined sharply; by the time of the Terror, French Freemasonry was in almost total eclipse, and it recovered only under Napoleon.

In effect, Freemasonry was a casualty of the Revolution; but in counter-revolutionary myth, because of its secrecy, religious liberalism and egalitarianism, it became its prime mover. For the next hundred years the two were linked in the minds of conservatives.

BELOW Reception of a master mason at a lodge meeting.

The National Assembly tried to impose acceptance of the Civil Constitution of the Clergy by insisting clerics took an oath of allegiance.

27 November 1790. The National Assembly decrees as follows:

The bishops, archbishops and priests are required to take the oath to which they are subject by Article 39 of the decree of 24 July last, on the Civil Constitution of the Clergy; in consequence of which they will swear to watch with care over the faithful of the diocese or parish entrusted to them, to be faithful to the nation, the law and the king, and to uphold with all their power the constitution decreed by the National Assembly and accepted by the king.

The oath will be taken on a Sunday, at the end of Mass.

Those of the said bishops, archbishops, priests, and other ecclesiastical public servants, who are members of the National Assembly, and who currently carry out their duties as deputies there, will take the oath at the National Assembly one week following the day on which the approval of this decree shall have been announced.

This satirical attack on the clerical oath of allegiance appeared in the counter-revolutionary newspaper *L'Ami du Roi* on 22 March 1791.

France in Division

Authorities who condemn the oath demanded of the clergy:	*Partisans of the oath demanded of the clergy:*
The pope and the cardinals	Mirabeau
Thirty bishops in the National Assembly	Two bishops in the National Assembly
Ninety-six other French bishops	Three or four other French bishops
The greater part of the priests from the city of Paris	Fifteen or sixteen priests from the city of Paris, out of fifty-two
All the cathedral and collegiate chapters	Some apostate monks
The Sorbonne, the greater part of the University of Paris, the provincial universities	Academics of the current philosophies
Fifty thousand priests or vicars	Seven to eight thousand priests or vicars – ambitious, troublesome, fanatical, ignorant
All the Catholic churches of Europe, foreign nations, even the Protestants	The emissaries of the Jacobin Club, the propaganda missionaries
Three-quarters of the city of Paris	The Palais-Royal, the hired public
The right wing of the National Assembly, or the élite of the defenders of religion and of the throne	The left wing, and the monstrous assembly of the principal enemies of the Church and of the monarchy, Jews, Protestants, Deists
All the papers, friends of order and of truth	All the newspapers in the pay of the factions, such as the execrable rags of Desmoulins, Brissot, Marat, etc.
All good Frenchmen who love their country, their religion and the happiness of their brothers	All the brigands who burn châteaux, pillage mansions, set up gallows; all the scoundrels who have bathed France in blood, and yet still breathe, thanks to the impunity of their frightful instigators
All worthy and virtuous citizens	All the libertines, cheats, Jews and Protestants
The will of our good king	The most detestable tyranny, which has taken his place, and exercises in his name a most frightful despotism

The Civil Constitution of the Clergy

POLARIZATION between a clerical Right and an anti-clerical Left increased in the assembly with the passage of the Civil Constitution of the Clergy on 12 July 1790. The Civil Constitution was more radical than anything previously suggested. 52 dioceses were suppressed, and the boundaries of the remainder redrawn so that they were identical with civil departments. Parishes were reorganized to take account of population distribution, canonries and other benefices without cure of souls were closed down. Parish priests were to be paid from 1200 livres to 6000 livres depending on their responsibilities. Bishops were obliged to live in their dioceses, and had their incomes slashed to 12,000 livres a year.

Most controversial of all, bishops were to be elected by the departmental assemblies, and parish priests by the district assemblies.

This final provision, inserted at the last minute as the debates grew more heated, caused much heart-searching among the clergy; it allowed all citizens, including non-Catholics, to choose priests, which represented a complete change in church organization. Nevertheless, there was much in the Civil Constitution that appealed to churchmen, especially lower clergy. It offered them decent salaries and good career prospects. Benefices would be granted according to merit and would no longer go to men with good family connections and a talent for intrigue. Discontent came mainly from the upper clergy.

The bishops argued that the legislation affected the church so profoundly, in spiritual as well as temporal matters, that individual clerics could not be expected to give their consent until the whole church had considered it. In practice, this meant waiting for papal approval.

Departments were anxious to fill clerical posts that were already vacant, and the first sales of church lands under the provisions of the law nationalizing church property on 2 November 1789 were due to begin in the autumn. On 27 November 1790 the deputies passed a decree imposing an oath of loyalty to the Civil Constitution on all bishops, parish priests (*curés*) and their assistants (*vicaires*). Those who refused to take it would have to leave their posts. On 26 December Louis XVI sanctioned the decree, a decision he regretted to the end of his life.

The members of the assembly believed that the prelates would eventually come round and swear the oath. They were wrong: only seven bishops did so. It was widely held that the pope would approve the Civil Constitution: in fact, he had already written privately to Louis condemning the legislation. For diplomatic and political reasons the king kept this secret, and Pius VI made his opposition public only in April 1791, when the oath-taking was over.

In the absence of papal guidance, lay deputies, bishops, king and ministers agreed that the curés and vicaires would offer little resistance. They gained much from the Civil Constitution and had supported the Revolution from the start.

In the event, the lower clergy proved divided over the oath. About 55 per cent of clerics swore early in 1791, and became known as the juring or constitutional clergy. A few, perhaps 5 per cent, retracted when the papal condemnation became known. Juring clerics were less common in the towns than in the country and, with the important exception of Paris, the larger the town the fewer the jurors.

The influence of the laity was often crucial, and generally the highest numbers of those who refused to take the oath were in areas of the greatest religious fervour such as Brittany, Alsace, parts of Franche-Comté and Flanders. Conversely, jurors predominated where religious sentiment was less strong – in the centre and south-east for example.

Relations between jurors and non-jurors became increasingly bitter as the hope that the church would sanctify and back the Revolution faded. So too did hopes of national unity: the forces of reaction and counter-revolution could now argue that they fought to defend the church and religion from attack by the revolutionaries.

BELOW Pope Pius VI, from a contemporary print.

The clerical deputy Thomas Lindet, writing to the municipal officials of Bernay, suggested that opposition to the Civil Constitution was orchestrated by the nobles and clergy who wanted the return of their *ancien régime* privileges.

Paris, 5 January 1791. I hoped that example and reason would win over a greater number of members of the National Assembly. With the exception of two bishops, all were determined to refuse the oath, and several priests were persuaded to follow in these erring ways. They put forward modifications and restrictions on the oath, which the assembly would not accept.

The clergy in general is the dupe of the nobility; many poor priests have been duped by the bishops; and the bishops have been duped by their own vanity.

The nobility know full well that it would be vain to try and interest the people in their rights to care for their rabbits, pigeons, deer and hinds, their immunities, privileges, emancipation from taxes, the right to ruin their creditors, and to do everything with impunity.

In March 1791, while Frenchmen awaited the views of the pope on the Civil Constitution of the Clergy, and while the king plotted, the National Assembly went in for metrication.

THE former bishop of Autun [Talleyrand] read out a proposed decree, which was passed as follows:

The National Assembly, aware that, in order to attain uniformity of weights and measures, it is essential to establish a natural and invariable unit of measure, and that the sole means of disseminating this uniformity to foreign countries and leading them to accept the same standard is to choose a unit which is not based on any arbitrary principle nor peculiar to any one nation on earth: has ruled and decreed that it adopts the measure of one-quarter of the earth's meridian as the basis of the new system of measurement; that consequently the work necessary to determine this basis will be put in hand immediately; and that consequently the king will instruct the Academy of Science to nominate commissioners who will undertake the work without delay.

Plans to enable the royal family to escape from Paris reached a new phase in early 1791. In his memoirs, the marquis de Bouillé revealed his own role in the plot.

IN early 1791 the king wrote to me that he hoped to be able to leave Paris in March or April: I was to indicate the route he should take for Montmédy, to let him know my plan and to settle it when I present it to him.

I advised him that from Paris two routes led to the fortress: one through Reims and Stenay, which includes along the way only a few large towns, such as should be avoided; the other passing by Chalons and Ste-Menehould, Varennes, or Verdun, a fortress city which is the more dangerous because its garrison, people and municipality are odious. To avoid that problem he should take the road to Varennes.

At the same time I urged the king to ask Leopold II of Austria to arrange for a body of soldiers to march to the Luxembourg frontier, near Montmédy, to give me a pretext to assemble troops there myself; I would then be ready to provide him with support when he arrived.

Louis XVI's letter to the ultra-reactionary bishop of Clermont on 16 April 1791 revealed his preference for the refractory clerics – that is, those who had refused to take the oath of allegiance to the Civil Constitution of the Clergy.

Can I, or must I, perform my Easter duties in the next fortnight? You know how unfortunate it would be if I gave the appearance of being forced into them. I have never hesitated in remaining at one with Catholic pastors in my own affairs. I am also firmly resolved fully to re-establish the Catholic faith if I recover my power. One priest I have seen thinks these feelings are sufficient, and that I can go ahead with my worship. But you are better placed to know what the church thinks in general, and in the particular circumstances in which we find ourselves. If, on the one hand, this would not scandalize one group, I see, on the other hand, innovators (who are, in truth, not to be counted on) already talking menacingly.

Louis

THE MASSACHUSETTS MAGAZINE (Boston) *January 1791*

The political horizon of our generous ally, appears rather cloudy. The proud genius of ancient nobles, the intrigues of disappointed ecclesiasticals, and a spirit of division among the popular leaders, prognosticate a long train of evils. The eventual triumph of liberty, admits of certainty, although at a later hour than was fondly anticipated some months past. The majesty of the people can find astonishing resources. Happy are the United States who know the dignity of republican virtue.

Talleyrand: renegade or reformer?

As bishop of Autun, in the National Assembly on 10 October 1789, Talleyrand proposed the transfer of church revenues to the state. Most prelates and priests never forgave him for this and other acts of betrayal. In the royalist clubs he was known simply as *le scélérat* – the villain.

Before the Revolution his career in the church had given scant indication that he would take an axe to its institutional life. Charles-Maurice de Talleyrand-Périgord, born in 1754, had impeccable aristocratic credentials and a powerful intelligence, but a deformed foot limited his opportunities and his family chose an ecclesiastical career for him. His uncle was archbishop of Reims (after 1777), and Talleyrand could expect a

ABOVE Talleyrand; apostate bishop, diplomatist and intriguer.

similar prize sooner rather than later. Personal scepticism was no obstacle to success. Between 1780 and 1785 the abbé de Périgord (as he was known before 1788) served as Agent-General of the clergy of France.

In 1788, he was awarded the bishopric of Autun, an assured but overdue promotion; the delay was due to prelates living longer, not the king's disdain for Talleyrand's amorous liaisons or his enjoyment of Parisian salon society (it was Talleyrand who referred to the 'pleasure of living' before the Revolution). Autun saw just enough of its new bishop to be charmed, like most others on first acquaintance. He was easily elected to the Estates-General on 2 April 1789 (having a good chef helped) and left Autun early on Easter Day to avoid displaying his ignorance of the liturgy during Mass in the cathedral.

Caution was the keynote of his conduct in the Estates-General in May/June 1789. Although he went to sit with the Third Estate on 26 June, it is likely that he expected the king to close down the self-proclaimed National Assembly: when a royalist coup failed to materialize, he accepted the logic of the situation and decided, after the Assembly and the king had moved from Versailles to Paris on 5–6 October, to court popularity with the dominant revolutionary faction. This decision, privately and deliberately taken, dictated his public conduct throughout 1789.

Talleyrand's support for successive measures of church reform, culminating in the Civil Constitution of the Clergy, isolated him among episcopal deputies. His constituents repudiated his actions and other prelates shunned his company as he became the revolutionaries' 'pet' bishop. On 14 July 1790 he celebrated an open-air Mass to commemorate the first anniversary of the fall of the Bastille – the Fête de la Fédération – and sported a cope in patriotic red, white and blue. 'For God's sake, don't make me laugh,' he whispered audibly to Lafayette during the consecration (he resigned the see of Autun in January 1791).

As one of just four diocesan bishops to take the oath of the Civil Constitution, he was asked to perform one final service for the revolutionaries before he embraced a wholly secular career: the ordination of the first bishops for the Constitutional Church. Although he derided the notion of apostolic succession, Talleyrand obliged. It was a suitably ironic note on which to end his clerical vocation.

ABOVE A constitutional priest takes the civic oath.

On 18 April 1791, the royal family, in what may well have been a 'dry run' for their planned escape, tried to leave Paris for their palace at nearby St-Cloud.

As the king's sister, Mme Elisabeth, here recounts in a letter to the émigrée Mme de Raigecourt, they were prevented from doing so by a Paris mob, flanked by National Guardsmen, on the grounds that the king should be prevented from receiving Easter communion at St-Cloud from a refractory cleric.

There was a little drama yesterday, dear heart; the king wished to go to St-Cloud but the National Guard did not let him, so much so that we were not able to get past the courtyard gates.

They are trying to force the king to dismiss the priests from his chapel or make them take the Civil Constitution oath, and to attend Easter devotions in his parish. That is the reason for yesterday's rebellion. The trip to St-Cloud was the pretext. The Guard was clearly disobeying Monsieur de Lafayette and all its officers. Luckily there was no harm done.

We are all well. I attended my Easter devotions yesterday, so I am at peace on that score.

Farewell, I have no time to write more; do not worry about us, nothing will come of all this. I embrace you with all my heart.

The king spoke with strength and kindness and gave an excellent account of himself.

Marie-Antoinette, writing to Mercy on 20 April, made it plain that the St-Cloud incident had strengthened the royal family's resolve to leave Paris.

The events which have just occurred give added purpose to our plans. The guard which surrounds us threatens us most. Our very lives are endangered. We must appear to yield in everything until we are able to act, and in any case our very captivity proves that we cannot act of our own free will.

Before taking any action, however, it is essential for us to know if you could arrange, through some pretext, for fifteen thousand men to go to Arlon and Virton, and an equal number to Mons. This is the express desire of M. de Bouillé, as it will provide him with an opportunity to assemble troops and munitions at Montmédy.

Send me an answer quickly on this point. Our situation is horrible; it must come to an end next month. The king wishes it even more than I.

Marie-Antoinette

HEADSTRONG, frivolous and spendthrift, interested only in her circle of favourites and the Habsburg House of Austria, Marie-Antoinette became the natural focus of the gossip and scandal directed against the court and the monarchy, the symbol of its decadence.

Mme Campan, her lady-in-waiting, noted in her memoirs that Marie-Antoinette mocked French courtly etiquette because she had not been taught its significance. She compensated for her disappointing marriage by seeking cheerful company in her hamlet of Trianon, built in the park of the palace of Versailles. She also confided in Mercy, the Austrian ambassador, and wrote freely to her mother in Vienna.

Napoleon considered that the Diamond Necklace Affair of 1785-6 marked the beginning of the Revolution. The Cardinal de Rohan, a member of one of France's most powerfully connected families, was a conceited rake eager to win his way into favour at court. A courtesan, Mme de Lamotte, and an adventurer persuaded him that the queen, who refused to speak to

ABOVE Marie-Antoinette, 'l'Autrichienne', amusing herself on horseback in the opulent days before the Revolution.

him, was in fact in love with him, and wanted him to acquire for her a diamond necklace worth 1,600,000 livres. They provided Rohan with a forged order for the royal jewellers, and arranged a midnight meeting with a chambermaid impersonating the queen. The cardinal collected the necklace and gave it to Mme de Lamotte; it was not seen again. When Boehmer, the royal jeweller, sought further payment, the king was informed. He arrested the cardinal and had him publicly tried. As a peer of the realm the cardinal demanded a trial before the parlement and was acquitted, an outcome which apparently justified assumptions about the queen's immorality and extravagance, and seriously damaged royal honour.

The queen, unlike the king, was a target of popular hatred from early in the Revolution. She was greeted with hostility at the Estates General's opening ceremonies; Louis was cheered. When the mob invaded the Palace of Versailles in the October *journées* of 1789, her chamber was stormed, but she had fled to her husband's room. Marie-Antoinette loathed the revolutionaries, whose ideas and barbarities she could not understand. A resolute woman of feeling, she thought in terms of personal loyalties, and believed the good people had been deliberately deceived. She was reluctant to accept the advice and services of a covert constitutional monarchist like Mirabeau, whom she regarded as a gross demagogue, and she considered

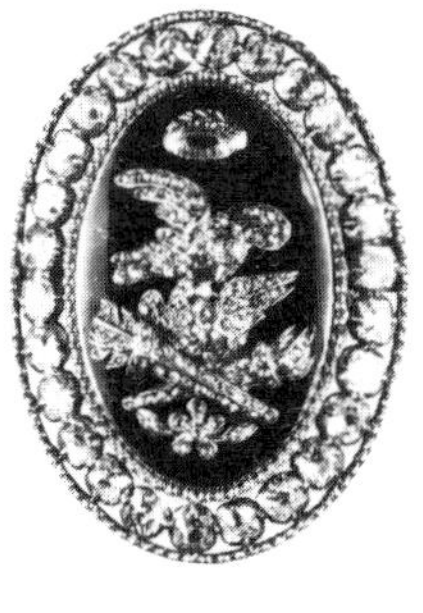

ABOVE The Temple of Love at the Petit-Trianon, the queen's private playground where she fled the cares of state to act out her costly Arcadian fantasies.

LEFT A diamond bracelet clasp belonging to Marie-Antoinette, whose supposed extravagance, earning her the nickname 'Madame Déficit', was underlined in the Diamond Necklace Affair.

Lafayette over-ambitious and untrustworthy, refusing to accept his plan of flight in 1792; ironically, he was thought to be her favourite, or even her lover.

After the flight to Varennes, she cultivated a friendship with Barnave and his Feuillant allies, but did not follow their advice to work with the constitution.

'L'Autrichienne' did intrigue, notably with Fersen, even if there was no 'Austrian Committee' masterminding the counter-revolution from the queen's chamber, as the revolutionaries alleged. By 1792 she was hoping for a war to undermine the Revolution, and when it was declared she gave military information to the enemy.

After the overthrow of the monarchy in the *journée* of 10 August 1792, the king and his family were imprisoned in the Temple, where their affectionate closeness touched the guards. Marie-Antoinette developed a new dignity with which she endured her humiliating trial and execution on 16 October 1793.

The Swede Fersen, confidant and probably the lover of Marie-Antoinette, here writing in code to the Swedish envoy in Paris, was also party to the royal plot.

The situation is becoming so terrible from day to day that it is impossible for the king to bear it any longer, and he has decided to stake his all rather than go on living in the daily degradation to which he is reduced by a seditious rabble. Such a bold step may persuade the still hesitant powers to decide in his favour. He still intends to act at the end of this month.

From the memoirs of the marquis de Bouillé. The route chosen by the king would take him – fatefully – through the town of Varennes.

ON 27 May the king wrote to me that he would leave on 19 June, between midnight and one o'clock; that he would go in an ordinary carriage as far as Bondy, one post stage from Paris, and there take his own carriage which should be awaiting him. One of his bodyguards, appointed to act as courier, should wait there in case the king did not arrive by two o'clock, which would show that he had been unable to leave. This same bodyguard should go straight to Pont-de-Sommevelle to bring me news so that I might look to my own safety.

The king also said that if he were not recognized along the route, and if there were no disturbance amongst the people, then he would travel incognito and would not make use of the escort, which would follow some hours behind.

The day after I received this letter from the king I instructed M. de Choiseul to order his men to be at Varennes on 18 June, with horses ready to serve as relays for the king's carriage.

Fersen's diary records the tense final moments as, on the night of 20–21 June 1791, the royal family slipped quietly out of Paris.

20 June 1791. As the king left he said, 'M. de Fersen, whatever happens to me, I shall not forget all you are doing for me.' The queen was weeping copiously. I left her at six o'clock: she was going out for a walk with her children. There were no special precautions. I went back home to conclude my business.

At 7 o'clock I was at Sullivan's to see if the carriage was there. Came back home. At 8 o'clock I wrote to the queen to change the rendezvous with the chambermaids and make sure that they let me know the exact time through the bodyguards; took the letter; all quiet. At a quarter to nine the guards came to me; they gave me the letter for Mercy. Instructed them; came home, sent my chair; gave them my coachman and horses for their departure. Went to take the carriage. Thought I had lost the letter for Mercy.

At a quarter past ten in the princes' courtyard; at a quarter past eleven the children came out, managed without difficulty. Lafayette came by twice. At a quarter to midnight Mme Elisabeth, then the king, then the queen. Departure at midnight, joined the carriage at the St-Martin gate.

In the passport carried by the royal family on their flight, Marie-Antoinette had taken the alias of the baroness de Korff, the head of the party, while Louis XVI posed as a valet.

IN the king's name, to all civil and military officers responsible for the surveillance and maintenance of public order in the various parts of the kingdom, etc. We instruct and order you to permit passage to Frankfurt to baroness de Korff with her two children, a maid, a manservant, and three domestic staff, without hindrance or causing others to hinder such passage, etc. This passport issued at Paris, 20 June. signed, Louis

---

The king's departure created a political vacuum in Paris: no one knew precisely what was happening. From the memoirs of the National Guard officer Charles Alexandre.

BY about nine o'clock in the morning of 21 June rumours of escape had spread and were confirmed; the entire National Guard, of its own accord, took up arms; at the Tuileries there was extreme turmoil.

The king and his family, who under the protection and advice of the Swedish colonel Fersen, were preparing to escape and leave France, succeeded in tricking their guards and got out of the Tuileries during the night of 20–21 June. How did they manage it? I do not think this is fully known yet.

What is absolutely certain is that the king, the queen, Madame Elisabeth, Madame Royale, the

Fersen: une liaison dangereuse?

THERE is a large and rather fanciful literature concerning the handsome, brooding Swedish nobleman Count Hans Axel von Fersen and his romantic attachment to Marie-Antoinette. One of her most devoted admirers throughout the 1780s, he remained loyal to the royal family after 1789.

Many of his papers still exist, including secret letters between the queen and himself, his correspondence with his father and friends, and his meticulous and rather dry journals, which contain a mixture of detailed

observation, ironical conceit and melancholy. An early entry noted that he was not one born to be happy; a later one wistfully commented on his own striking appearance and how many ladies admired him. He had mistresses, but never married. His morose, aloof character was romanticized in terms of his love for Marie-Antoinette.

Fersen had embarked on the Grand Tour, an important part of the education of a young European aristocrat or gentleman, when he was fifteen. In late 1773, at the age of eighteen, he was presented at the French court; he attended four balls given by Marie-Antoinette and in the New Year they talked together for some time at a masked ball at the opera. When he returned to France in 1778, the queen recognized him as an old friend: evidence, to some observers, that they were in love. Fersen left for the American War of Independence immediately afterwards – a move that has been interpreted as doing the honourable thing and taking a lover's exile. After the war ended in 1781 he spent most of his time in Paris as an agent of the Swedish government and as the commander of a French regiment. Tall, dark, handsome, with somewhat gaunt, sculpted looks, he became an acknowledged favourite of Marie-Antoinette and often went riding with her, sometimes unaccompanied. He may have become her lover.

From the time of the Revolution, Fersen became the Swedish king's special contact with the royal family, and proved to be one of their most faithful friends. As a staunch defender of the old order, he was utterly against the Revolution and his own sovereign, Gustavus III, was determined to intervene to strengthen Louis' position. Fersen influenced the queen against compromising with constitutional monarchists, and made arrangements for the flight from Paris to Varennes. He redesigned the interior of the berlin and acted as coachman for the first part of the journey before leaving the royal party and making his way to Brussels. Despite the eventual failure of his plans, the count had earned the gratitude and esteem of both king and queen for his chivalrous loyalty, courage and friendship. He even gave Louis a loan of more than a million livres, which the princes and émigrés later refused to honour.

Fersen's secret correspondence with the queen dates from the period after the attempted flight. The interpretation of his papers is controversial: there are famous deletions which may, however, refer to state matters. His journals demonstrate that he had a mistress, Mrs Sullivan, at the time: and she may well be the subject of various notes and comments that historians have interpreted as referring to Marie-Antoinette. His letters to the queen never abandoned the correct, respectful forms of address, and show dedication and concern for her and Louis XVI. Marie-Antoinette's are direct and poignant, but discuss state affairs as well as the condition of her family. There is affection, but not intimacy. This could have been habitual discretion, however, and arguments that he could not have been the king's friend and the queen's lover are naïve. Fersen saw the queen for the last time in February 1792, when he undertook a secret mission presenting another Swedish plan of escape.

His diplomatic and political career continued over the next twenty years. On 20 June 1810 he was assaulted and brutally murdered by a mob in Stockholm.

young dauphin, Mme de Tourzel, a lady-in-waiting and three bodyguards – disguised as couriers – managed to meet at an agreed place and to set off, so that when their escape was discovered they were already five or six hours away, and by the time something was done about it they were further away, so one may understand the great difficulty of catching up with them.

The king's departure disconcerted Paris, as reported in the radical newspaper *Les Révolutions de Paris*.

THE streets and public places offered an unusual sort of spectacle. The National Guard was drawn up everywhere in imposing style. It was not the active citizens and royal blue uniforms which were most admired at the gathering; the red cap reappeared and eclipsed the busby. Women competed with men over the guard of the city gates, telling them, 'It was women who brought the king to Paris, it was men who let him escape.' But the men replied, 'Ladies, do not boast so much, that was no great prize you brought us.'

From the correspondence of Fersen, who, after setting the royal family en route on 20–21 June, had himself fled to Belgium.

23 June 1791, midnight.
Sire, All is lost. The king was stopped sixteen leagues from the frontier and brought back to Paris. I am going to see M. Mercy, to take him a letter from the king asking the Emperor to intercede on his behalf. From Brussels I will come to see Your Majesty.
I am, with the deepest respect to Your Majesty,
Your most humble and obedient servant,
Axel Fersen

Arlon, 23 June 1791, midnight.
All is lost, my dear father, and I am in despair. The king was stopped at Varennes, 16 leagues from the frontier. Imagine my distress and pity me. M. de Bouillé, who is here, brought me the news. I am leaving now to take to Count Mercy in Brussels the letter and the orders with which the king entrusted me. I have only time to assure you of my respect and my love.
Axel Fersen

The flight to Varennes

BY the end of 1790 Louis XVI had abandoned his sincere attempt to work within the constitution. His acceptance of the decree against non-juring priests on 26 December 1790 went so much against his conscience that his attitude to the Revolution seemed to change decisively: he resolved to accept the advice to flee Paris. The crucial incident was at Easter 1791, when the mob prevented the royal family from leaving for St-Cloud on 17 April. The situation that morning was ugly, and it was plain that Lafayette could not guarantee the king's safety from the National Guard, let alone the Paris crowd: proof enough that the royal family was effectively captive in the Tuileries palace. The king decided that he should seek refuge in the provinces, preferably in the area commanded by the fervently royalist marquis de Bouillé. Montmédy, a town in Lorraine on the frontier with Luxembourg, was chosen as his destination. Once Louis was there, military action would, it was hoped, be unnecessary. The king planned to generate foreign pressure and rally sufficient forces – both troops and faithful subjects – to induce the revolutionaries to parley. In this way he hoped to impose a moderate outcome on the Revolution.

Marie-Antoinette was the driving force behind the plans. She induced her brother, Leopold II of Austria, to position troops on the frontier to dissuade pursuing revolutionaries. The queen's confidant Count Fersen, who visited the Tuileries daily and brought out letters for foreign destinations, was also a firm believer in the wisdom of flight and was entrusted with the details of the arrangements for leaving Paris. Although two small carriages would have been less conspicuous and more rapid, Louis refused to risk splitting up his family and insisted upon a berlin large enough to hold six passengers. Such a large conveyance was not easy to find – and was far from inconspicuous. Its occupants would be plainly recognizable as aristocrats and so the party assumed the identity of a Russian baroness travelling with her attendants; a passport was obtained by deception. Alterations were made to rooms in the Tuileries so that it was possible to pass unnoticed between the royal apartments and jewellery was sent discreetly to Brussels.

Bouillé's role was crucial: he was to provide detachments of loyal dragoons to ensure the safety of the royal party after they reached Châlons. Louis finally sent him a message giving 20 June as the date of the flight. The royal party managed to reach Châlons by four in the afternoon of 21 June.

But they had arrived two hours later than planned,

ABOVE The royal family's berlin stopped at Varennes.

and the dragoons had left after sending a message to the other detachments that the flight must have been postponed. The berlin pushed on to Ste-Menehould, from where it left for Varennes at eight. An hour later the postmaster at Ste-Menehould, Drouet, received word from Paris via Châlons that the king had left the capital, and set off in pursuit of the suspicious-looking carriage and its occupants. At Varennes the family was stopped and only bloodshed, with its attendant risks, could have prevented recapture. Provence and Fersen reached Brussels safely by a different route. The flight sent shock waves through Paris and profoundly altered the political situation.

Louis had left in the Tuileries a declaration which clearly expressed his views. It had been carefully drawn up over the preceding months by trusted counsellors, and the king made his own amendments to it. The document reveals how seriously Louis misunderstood the Revolution. In essence, he seemed to regard it as the product of plots and factions, and he failed utterly to appreciate the wide basis of popular support it enjoyed, even in the provinces. The declaration seemed to envisage a return to the policies laid out in the ill-fated *séance royale* of 23 June 1789, which even then had been out of date with its emphasis on the division of society into three orders and its refusal to countenance the abolition of feudal privilege.

By June 1791 all this was hopelessly anachronistic. The flight sent shock waves through Paris and profoundly altered the political situation. As the monarch was suspended from his functions, the National Assembly was given the chance to prove that it could govern without a head of state; this was bound to encourage republicanism. The king could expect no help from the royalists, whose extreme views only jeopardized his situation; the émigrés abroad, led by his brothers, were ineffectual.

Too inflexible, and too disenchanted with the Revolution to compromise with any enthusiasm, Louis was destined to play a double game which was doomed to failure. He became depressed and lethargic and no longer seemed to care what happened – he felt that he could only work for the future of his son. By both character and temperament he was unsuited to the exertions required of him in the increasingly complex political arena.

In this letter to his wife, Ferrières records the impact of the king's escape on the National Assembly.

All the deputies gathered in the chamber of the National Assembly, and it must be said to the eternal credit of this same assembly that its affairs were conducted with a wisdom and firmness worthy of the greatest days of the Roman Senate.

When the assembly learned of the excesses intended by the people towards those who appeared to have aided the king's flight, it sent a commission from amongst their number with orders to protect Messieurs de Lafayette and Bailly, and to persuade the people to remain calm. Peace was restored.

Lafayette and Bailly, commander of the National Guard and mayor of Paris respectively, were to ensure the security of the city, to maintain order and protect the citizens' property.

Once these various arrangements had been made, the assembly calmly returned to the order of the day and debated some article of the penal code as coolly as if nothing unusual had happened. At midday M. de La Porte, in charge of the king's civil list, read out a memorandum from the king, written in his own hand, headed: 'Declaration to the French people.' In it the king protested against everything he had been obliged to do, went into a long list of events, and finished by forbidding his ministers from signing any order and the Keeper of the Seals from placing the royal seal on any decree.

The king's flight had been thwarted by the humble postmaster of Ste-Menehould, Jean-Baptiste Drouet. Here Drouet recounts his adventure to an admiring National Assembly.

I am postmaster at Ste-Menehould, a former dragoon of the Condé regiment. On 21 June, at half-past seven in the evening, two carriages and eleven horses relayed at the staging post at Ste-Menehould. I thought I recognized the queen, and on seeing a man at the back of the carriage on the left I was struck by his resemblance to the effigy on the fifty-livre *assignat*. (*Applause.*)

These vehicles were accompanied by a detachment of dragoons and preceded by a detachment of hussars, as if to protect some treasure; this escort confirmed my suspicions. However, fearful of raising false alarms, I let the carriages go on. But when I saw that the dragoons were following on, and that, after requesting horses for Verdun, the vehicles took the road for Varennes instead, I went across country to meet up with them and was first to reach Varennes first. It was eleven o'clock in the evening; it was very dark; everyone was in bed. The coaches stopped in a street as a quarrel arose between the postilions and the local postmaster. The latter wanted to rest and refresh the horses. The king, on the other hand, wanted to press on. Then I said to my comrade, 'Are you a good patriot?' 'Of course.' 'Well then,' I said to him, 'the king is at Varennes, and he must be stopped.' We dismounted and decided that the success of our plan depended on barricading the street and bridge where the king would be passing. (*Applause.*)

Luckily there was a vehicle close by laden with furniture which we brought and overturned, so that it was impossible to get past. (*Applause.*) Then we ran to find the town prosecutor, the mayor, and the commander of the local National Guard, and in less than ten minutes we were a group of eight men of firm purpose. The commander of the National Guard and the town prosecutor went up to the carriage and asked the travellers who they were and where they were going. The queen replied that they were in a hurry; they were requested to show their passport; finally she handed her passport to two guards, who climbed down and came to the inn. This passport bore the name of the baroness de Korff, etc. Some of the people who heard the passport read out said that that should suffice. We disputed this, because the passport was only signed by the king and it should also have been signed by the president of the National Assembly. It was decided that the travellers should not continue their journey until the next day.

Then the king, of his own accord, said: 'I am the king, these are my wife and my children; we beg you to treat us with the regard which the French have always had for their kings.' Immediately the National Guardsmen crowded round, and we saw the hussars arriving with drawn sabres.

The commander of the National Guard then ordered his gunners to line up and fire; they picked up the fuse . . . but I have the honour to report to you that the guns were not loaded.

The commander of the National Guard and the National Guard itself did so well that they disarmed the hussars; and so the king became their prisoner.

Having thus carried out our duty, we returned home in the midst of congratulations from our fellow citizens.

The king's diary of 21–25 June 1791 covers the period of his return from Varennes to Paris.

TUESDAY 21 June. Left Paris at midnight, arrived and stopped at Varennes, in Argonne, at eleven in the evening.
22. Left Varennes at five or six o'clock in the morning, dined at Ste-Menehould, arrived at ten o'clock at Châlons, supped and slept there at the former intendancy.
23. At half-past eleven, Mass was interrupted to hasten our departure; lunched at Châlons, dined at Epernay, met the commissioners from the National Assembly at the port at Binson, arrived at Dormans at eleven o'clock, supped there, slept for three hours in an armchair.
24. Left Dormans at half-past seven, dined at La Ferté-sous-Jouarre, arrived at Meaux at eleven o'clock, supped and slept at the bishop's house.
Saturday 25. Left Meaux at half-past six, arrived in Paris at eight o'clock without stopping.

Fréron's radical newspaper, *L'Orateur du peuple*, noted the humiliation of the royal family as they re-entered Paris on 25 June.

THE king and the queen were in the first vehicle; M. Barnave, the commissioner sent by the National Assembly, with the dauphin between his knees; the queen appeared upset and pretended to weep; the king, according to the account of the National Guards who spoke to the citizens lining the way, had got drunk at Pantin. This was no triumphal procession, it was the prison convoy of the monarchy!

The king, in his statement to the committee established by the National Assembly to cross-examine him, seemed quite unrepentant, presenting the flight to Varennes as a learning experience.

26 June 1791. The reasons for my leaving were the insults and threats profferred against my family and myself on 18 April. Since then provocative writings inciting violence against me and my family have been published, which have remained unpunished; in the circumstances I believed that there could be no security, nor even propriety, for me in Paris.

I therefore wished to leave the city. Since I could not do this openly, I decided to leave by night and without any retinue; I had no intention at any time of leaving the kingdom; I had no agreement to that end, whether with foreign powers, my own relatives, or any of the French subjects who have left the kingdom.

The passport was necessary to facilitate the journey; it was drawn up for a foreign country only because the office of foreign affairs does not issue them for the interior of the kingdom; and indeed, the route indicated for Frankfurt was not even used during the trip.

I realized during the journey that public opinion had decided in favour of the constitution. I did not think it possible to be fully conversant with this public opinion in Paris; but from the views which I gathered personally along my route, I was convinced of the necessity of giving power to the established authorities for the maintenance of public order, and even for the support of the constitution itself.

As soon as I realized the general will, I acted without hesitation, just as I have never hesitated to make a personal sacrifice for the good of my people, which has always been my wish.

I shall happily forget all the troubles which I may have suffered, in order to assure the peace and happiness of the nation.

As Ferrières recorded in this letter to his wife on 27 June, the inclination of the National Assembly towards the king was to forgive and forget, for the sake of the new constitution.

The king's statement is skilful; it is not a justification; but, given the overriding desire of the wise men of the assembly that both monarch and monarchy should be preserved, I trust that everything will be settled satisfactorily. The aristocrats on the right have every intention of doing something thoroughly stupid; they met together on Sunday and talked nonsense as usual.

These poor fools are not satisfied with the king's declaration. Since they still dream of re-establishing the three orders and of a return to the old regime, they do not want the king to side with the new constitution. In fact they rely greatly on foreign powers who will probably make no move following the king's arrest, and who would be promptly driven back if they did attempt to invade France, which would only succeed in making matters worse for the nobility and clergy.

This secret missive from Louis XVI to his émigré brothers on 7 July casts doubts on the sincerity of the king's apparent reconciliation with the Revolution.

I rely entirely on my brothers' feelings of tenderness towards me, their love and attachment for their country, the friendship with sovereign princes, my relatives and allies, and on the honour and generosity of these other sovereigns, to agree on the manner and means to be used in concerting the re-establishment of peace and order in the kingdom. In my absence, I grant all powers to my brothers to negotiate to that end with whomsoever they think fit, and to choose the individuals who will put these political means into effect.

LOUIS

The National Assembly's wish to whitewash the conduct of the king contrasted with the growth of republican feeling on the streets of Paris. As the deputy Thomas Lindet records, however, the popular movement was crushed in the so-called Massacre of the Champ-de-Mars.

18 July 1791. Dear brother, there has been violent opposition to Friday's decree re-establishing the king. For several days various clubs made the most vigorous protests. A general rendezvous at the Champ-de-Mars was arranged. There a petition was signed, demanding that opinions be sought throughout the eighty-three departments on the subject of the king, since the National Assembly is not competent.

Yesterday morning two rascals were found beneath the national altar [set up for the Fête de la Fédération at the Champ-de-Mars]; it was rumoured that they were setting mines to blow it up. Without further investigation they were seized and hanged; the gathering continued, and the collection of signatures.

In the afternoon the National Guard arrived with M. de Lafayette: he was ill-received. He went to the Hôtel de Ville and returned with the red flag, the mayor, infantry, cavalry and cannon.

At the entrance to the Champ-de-Mars canvassers threw stones at the National Guard, who fired and fell upon their attackers with bayonet or sabre in hand. Several people were killed or wounded. They resisted too long, someone shouted, 'Kill Lafayette and the mayor, they are traitors!' People were frightened that the whole Faubourg St-Antoine would rise, but patrols of the National Guard prevented that.

The Champ-de-Mars massacre

GROWING distrust of Louis XVI provoked demands for a republic during 1791, and such calls multiplied when news broke of the royal family's flight on 20 June. The radical press, most conspicuously Marat's *L'Ami du peuple*, called for popular action to depose the king. The authorities, fearful of a new uprising by the people of Paris and supported by most of the sections, placed the National Guard on alert, seized copies of offending newspapers, and ordered numerous arrests. In response the Cordeliers Club and other societies gathered support for a massive demonstration. On 24 June some 30,000 people marched on the National Assembly with a petition demanding a republic, only to be turned back by the National Guard. When the assembly's delegates, Barnave, Pétion and La Tour-Maubourg, brought the royal family back to Paris the following day, the crowd maintained a hostile silence as the carriage rolled past.

The flight exacerbated an already tense situation. After a wave of strikes against falling real wages in the early months of 1791, the municipality had forbidden all workers' associations, a move endorsed at national level by the Le Chapelier Law of 14 June 1791. Only two days later the authorities announced that the charity workshops, which had provided unemployment relief over the hard winter of 1790-1, would be closed. The government considered the men who worked in them – more than 30,000 by June 1791 – a serious threat to public order. On 3 July there was a further announcement: anyone dismissed from the workshops who could not find other work would either have to leave the city or join the army.

These measures were bitterly opposed by the radical press and popular clubs, who linked their protests with demands for a democratic republic. Popular agitation grew and there were renewed calls for a march on the National Assembly, which was flooded with republican petitions. However, the assembly responded favourably to the pro-monarchical exhortations of Barnave. To dismiss the king would destroy much of the assembly's work on the constitution, and would also mean conceding victory to the radicals, who wanted more democratic policies, which might lead to more radical legislation on a variety of fronts. There was also the risk of aggravating the European powers, who were taking an increasingly warlike stance. On 16 July the assembly accordingly decided to reinstate the king and all further discussion on the subject was outlawed.

The Cordeliers Club responded by drawing up its most radical petition to date. It declared the assembly's decision contrary to the will of the people and called for its re-organization. On 17 July, 6000 people flocked to the Champ-de-Mars – the huge field on the edge of Paris where the Fête de la Fédération had been celebrated three days before – to sign this petition. The confrontation that many feared, and some welcomed, was sparked off quite accidentally. As people began to climb on to the platform built for the Fête de la Fédération, on which the petition was placed for signing, two men were discovered underneath. The angry and suspicious crowd dragged them out and summarily hanged them. In response, Bailly and Lafayette marched to disperse the gathering at the head of the National Guard. They carried the red flag, symbolizing the imposition of martial law, and opened fire on the unarmed crowd. Fifty people were killed.

In the aftermath of the 'massacre of the Champ-de-Mars the authorities clamped down on popular political activity; a number of newspapers were banned, there were numerous arrests and Desmoulins, Marat and other prominent radicals went into hiding.

ABOVE The fusillade at the Champ-de-Mars, when demonstrators were shot down by Lafayette's National Guard.

BELOW The Ecole Militaire from the Champ-de-Mars, before which the popular movement was suppressed – for the moment.

The Pillnitz Declaration between Austria and Prussia threatened France with armed intervention on behalf of its monarch.

HIS MAJESTY the emperor and His Majesty the king of Prussia, having heard the wishes and representations of Monsieur [the comte de Provence] and of the comte d'Artois, the king's brothers, declare jointly that they regard the present situation of the king of France as a subject of common interest to all the sovereigns of Europe. They hope that this interest will not fail to be acknowledged by the powers whose help is sought, and that in consequence they will not refuse to employ, in conjunction with their said Majesties, the most effective means relative to their strength to assist the king of France in consolidating, in the fullest liberty, the foundations of a monarchical government suited equally to the rights of kings and the well-being of the French nation.

Therefore, their said Majesties the emperor and the king of Prussia are resolved to act promptly in mutual accord, with the force necessary to bring about the proposed common aim. Meanwhile they will give to their troops appropriate orders to be ready to act.
Pillnitz, 27 August 1791.
Léopold and Frédérick-Guillaume

Louis XVI came to the National Assembly on 13 September to sanction the new constitution which the assembly had passed on 3 September.

GENTLEMEN, I have carefully examined the constitutional act which you have presented for my sanction. I accept it, and I will see that it is implemented. At another time this declaration would have been sufficient; today I owe it to the national interest and to myself to make known the reasons for my conduct.

From the very outset of my reign I wished to reform abuse, and in all acts of government I wished to be guided by public opinion.

Throughout the sequence of events of the revolution my intentions have never varied. When, having reformed the existing institutions, you began to replace them with the first attempts of your undertaking, I did not wait to learn the full content of the constitution before I accepted it. I favoured the establishment of its parts even before it was possible to judge the whole.

Let every man recall the moment when I departed from Paris. The motives which impelled me no longer exist today; you have shown your wish to re-establish order: you have remedied the army's lack of discipline; you have recognized the necessity of suppressing the excesses of the press. The people's will is no longer in doubt for me; I have seen it in evidence both by its support for your courageous action and by its attachment to the maintenance of monarchical government.

I therefore accept the constitution. I undertake to maintain it at home and to defend it from external attack; and to have it executed by all the means which it places in my power.

As the National Assembly broke up to give way to the new Legislative Assembly, the marquis de Ferrières, in a letter to his wife, viewed the future with some optimism.

Paris, 24 September 1791. The king and queen, my dear, appear entirely in favour of the constitution, and they are wise to be so. I hope that all interests will be reconciled; but we must see the new legislature.

Tonight the king and the queen are going to the Opera. **Oedipus at Colonus** *is playing. Last Sunday there were superb illuminations at the Tuileries and the Champs-Elysées. This was presented by the king.*

Next Sunday the city of Paris will take its turn to provide illuminations. The people are delirious. The king and queen are acclaimed the moment they appear; so you see, everything points to a solid new order of affairs.

ST JAMES'S CHRONICLE (London), *21 January 1792*

Let the future form of the French government be what it may, many years must elapse before that country's credit, finances and commerce, are fully restored, even to that degree of prosperity which it had for centuries enjoyed, under an oppressive form of government.

PUBLIC ADVERTISER (London), *23 January 1792*

(France) has before her, as we have repeatedly and invariably stated, the moral certainty of foreign war, of civil commotion, of national bankruptcy, and of general ruin.

The Constitution of 1791

THE clamour for a constitution was almost unanimous in 1789. A constitution was viewed as a panacea which would cure all the ills of a political system which had become corrupt. Reforming ministers such as Turgot in the 1770s had told the monarch that France needed a written constitution to regulate the operation of the state and so ensure that it worked harmoniously.

Many political writers held that France already had a constitution, composed of the inherited customs and usages governing her political and social life. Certain 'fundamental laws' laid down the functions and powers of the monarchy and of important institutions like the parlements. It was widely agreed, however, that laws needed updating, to fit changes in society. The growth of trade and enlightenment called for a recognizably modern, and practical, constitution.

In 1789, one of the first tasks the National Assembly set itself was to draft such a text. It assumed 'constituent power' for, as Sieyès argued, only the nation had a right to give itself a constitution. From 6 July successive committees of the assembly, staffed mainly by lawyers such as Mounier and Target, worked hard to produce such a document. Completed by September 1791, it was prefaced by the Declaration of the Rights of Man, voted in on 26 August 1789, partly as a guide for the constitution makers. Initially regarded as subject to modification, the Declaration soon assumed a 'religious' character and became sacred and inviolate.

BELOW Equality before the Constitution: coal porters and nobles alike submit their feudal insignia to the authorities.

The constitution of 1791 was far from a mere regularization of existing laws and practices, as moderate deputies had first desired. Certainly the monarchy was preserved, with traditional – not to say reactionary – aspects, for example the exclusion of women from the succession. But royal power was carefully circumscribed. Louis became the first 'functionary' of the state.

A permanent legislature, which the king could not dissolve, would make laws. The king was given a suspensive veto over legislation which could postpone ratification for up to five years, though Mirabeau had proposed an absolute, or permanent, veto. The executive power which would implement the laws was headed by the monarch; it was intensely distrusted, because it might provide opportunities for a revival of despotism.

The idea of a legislature with two chambers was rejected. Any upper house would, its opponents thought, be a bastion of aristocracy, defending past abuses and thwarting the nation's general will. It would be divisive, whereas the Nation, and its representation, needed to be one.

This made the constituent power virtually a legal dictatorship. It overrode the separation of powers, advocated by Montesquieu and accepted by most Enlightenment thinkers, and was proclaimed as a defining feature of any true constitution in the Declaration. Future legislatures were given certain executive powers, fixing public expenditure levels and taxation, while the king, head of the executive body, by his veto had a share in making laws.

The chronic weakness of the executive and the unpopularity of the king's ministers, Louis himself felt, made the constitution unworkable. After his escape attempt and capture at Varennes in June 1791, some modifications were made to reinforce his position, but they failed to reassure him and his acceptance, on 14 September, was half-hearted. The constitution, after so much debate and trouble, lasted only eleven months.

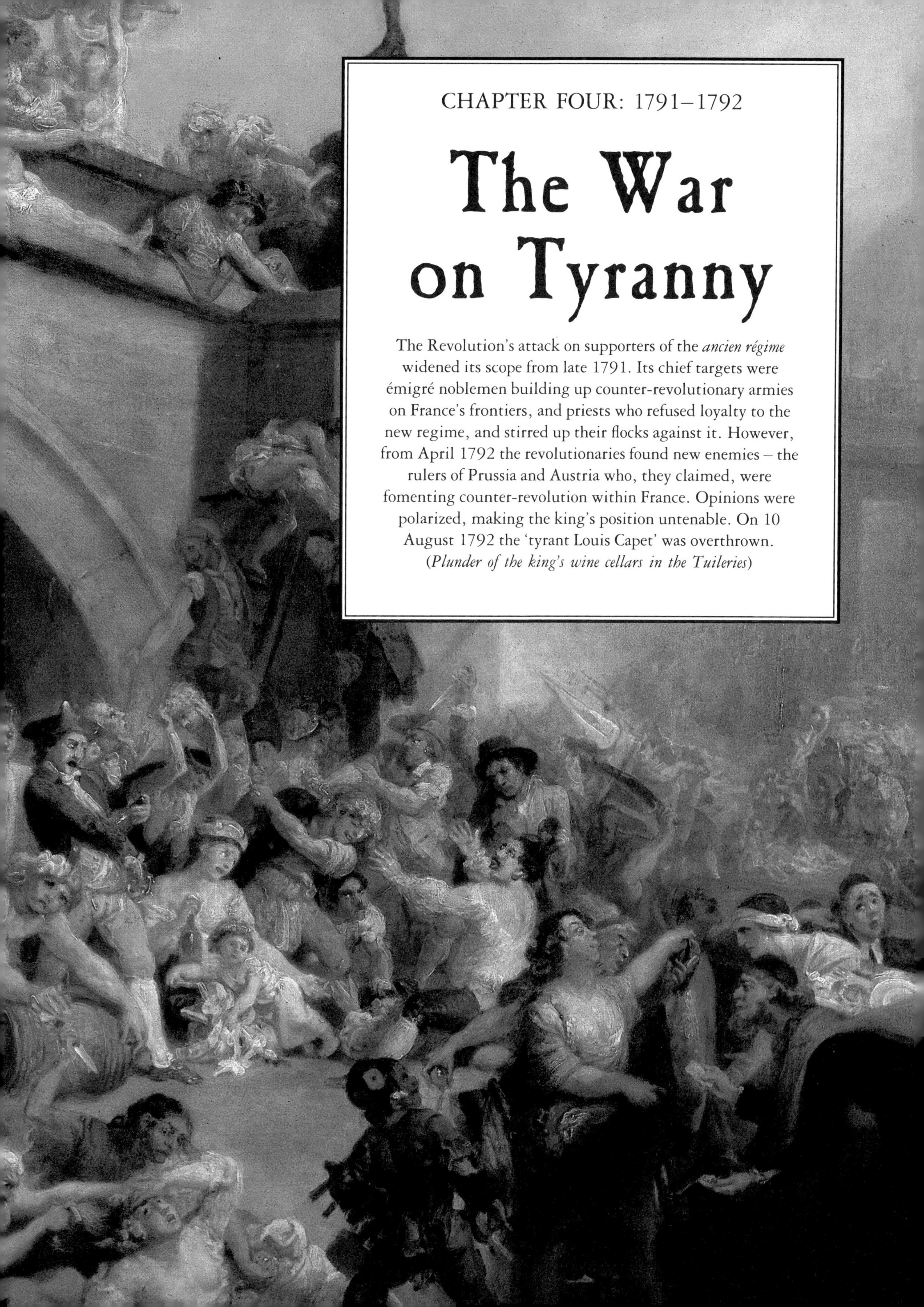

CHAPTER FOUR: 1791–1792

The War on Tyranny

The Revolution's attack on supporters of the *ancien régime* widened its scope from late 1791. Its chief targets were émigré noblemen building up counter-revolutionary armies on France's frontiers, and priests who refused loyalty to the new regime, and stirred up their flocks against it. However, from April 1792 the revolutionaries found new enemies – the rulers of Prussia and Austria who, they claimed, were fomenting counter-revolution within France. Opinions were polarized, making the king's position untenable. On 10 August 1792 the 'tyrant Louis Capet' was overthrown.

(*Plunder of the king's wine cellars in the Tuileries*)

There is nothing to be done with this assembly, it is a gathering of scoundrels, madmen and clods; the few people in it who want order and who are a little less ill-intentioned than the others are not listened to and dare not speak. Moreover, it is discredited even by the people, whom they are trying in every possible way to arouse but who nowadays are only interested in the high cost of bread.

In a secret letter to Fersen, Marie-Antoinette expresses her views on the new Legislative Assembly, voted in to replace the Constituent Assembly in September 1791, under the provisions of the 1791 Constitution. They augured badly for relations with the court.

Louis XVI's attitude to the new Constitution, here reported in the memoirs of Navy Minister Bertrand de Moleville, was hardly inspiring.

AFTER a few general observations on the difficulty and danger of public affairs the king said to me: 'So have you any other objections to make to me?' No, sire, I replied, I wish only to obey and to please Your Majesty; but since I desire to know whether I can be of any service to you, I hope that Your Majesty will deign to tell me your feelings about the new constitution and the line you expect your ministers to take.

'Nothing could be fairer,' said the king, 'this is what I think: I consider the constitution to be far from a masterpiece; I think it has serious faults, and that if I had been allowed to comment, a few beneficial alterations might perhaps have been made. But at this point that is no longer important. I have sworn to uphold it as it stands, and I am determined to do my duty and to abide fully by my oath.

'It is my opinion that carrying out the constitution to the letter is the best way to make the nation aware of the improvements that could be made to it. I have no other plan than that, nor can I have. I certainly will not deviate from it and I do not wish my ministers to follow any other plan.'

As Gaultier de Biauzat, retiring deputy from the Constituent Assembly, noted in this letter to his constituents on 11 October 1791, one of the key problems his successors faced was the threat to the Revolution posed by foreign powers. War was already on the agenda.

The intentions of the various European powers are veiled in uncertainty at the moment: it is established, as you know, that several monarchs have formed a coalition to stir up and support the former French aristocracy against our revolution. Either they must wipe out all the effects of the French Revolution, or they must expect to see this epidemic spread as far as their own lands. The interests of all despots and their nobility are threatened by our revolution: it is to be expected, politically, that they will all come together to destroy it.

'So there will be a war?', you will say. I think so; and, although it would indeed be a terrible thing, I venture to say that I would welcome it, for the following reason: Providence, ever-watchful over our nation, well knows that this evil brood, the aristocrats, would always, in France, be like bad seed growing on good land.

The letters from the Parisian publisher Nicolas Ruault to his brother form an illuminating testimony to the impact of the Revolution in Paris. Here, in late October and early November, he points out that issues of war and peace depend on the émigré nobles based in Coblenz who were forming counter-revolutionary armies, and also on the king himself.

It does not seem to me that your counter-revolutionaries are unreasonable, my dear brother, in drawing conclusions from the king's actions totally different to those of the patriots.

The famous and brilliant acceptance of the constitution by the king cuts little ice with the foreign courts; it is seen as having been dictated by the force of circumstances.

The emigration of the few great nobles still in Paris, since the king's acceptance of the constitution, confirms the worst forecasts. Thirty or so of them who had not put a foot outside France since 1789 left last week for Coblenz, which is the general headquarters for these gentlemen. They came to the Tuileries to bid a public farewell to the king, the queen and Mme Elisabeth, and to take leave of their Majesties; they left for Coblenz openly and in state as if for an acknowledged embassy and mission.

The National Assembly talked of nothing but emigration, emigrants, émigrés, refractory and constitutional priests. It is time that an end was put to these long discussions and that a few useful decrees were produced.

Counter-revolution at Coblenz

FOLLOWING the fall of the Bastille on 14 July 1789, Louis XVI gave in to the National Assembly and to street violence; other members of the royal family thought a stronger stand was required. While the comte de Provence stayed at court, the king's other brother, the comte d'Artois, together with other princes of the blood, Conti, Condé and Bourbon, left France to marshal support and co-ordinate action.

From their headquarters in Turin, Artois sought to implement a three-pronged policy formulated by his protégé, the former finance minister Calonne. First, Louis needed his freedom of action restored. Second, the rulers of Europe's great powers, spearheaded by Bourbon Spain and the monarch's closest ally Austria, should be encouraged to bring pressure to bear on the French government. Finally, royalist supporters in France needed to be encouraged and mobilized.

Artois was informed by the royalist agent François Froment that Languedoc would be ripe for such mobilization. The Revolution had upset the delicate balance between Protestants and Catholics in the region, and the élites of each community were challenging each other for power. Several thousand Catholic National Guards, a minority of whom issued a declaration of 'fidelity to religion and the monarchy', established a camp at the château of Jalès and set up a committee to organize the area's resistance to the Revolution; a network of commanders was served by couriers and safe houses. Agents fanned out over the south-east of France, stimulating royalist organization and agitation.

Artois' plan was to seize Lyon amidst a general rising timed for December 1790. By then the king would have escaped from Paris, and royalist forces would march north to join him in Burgundy. These fantastic schemes were nullified mainly by the revolutionaries' penetration of the royalist conspiracy.

Louis and the queen sought assistance from friendly powers, but short of invasion or military intervention which might lead to civil war, a view that matched the priorities of other European rulers. 'Have these two princes (Artois and Provence) to dinner, yes,' Leopold of Austria told his sister Marie-Antoinette, 'but no troops and no money. They're simply out for revenge and their own personal interests.' The most he would do, even after the royal family's flight and capture at Varennes, was to threaten force.

Nevertheless, this threat, combined with the assembling of émigré armies centred on Coblenz, where both Artois and Provence (following his flight from Paris in June 1791) were based, served to intensify paranoia within France. The princes' actions paradoxically accelerated the destruction of the very institution they claimed they were trying to save.

ABOVE Republican cartoon ridiculing the so-called 'Grand Council' of the *émigrés*.

BELOW Another view of the flight of the French nobility, some to join Calonne on English soil, finger raised (left).

The loyalty of the refractory clergy was an additional problem, as this report of a debate in the Legislative Assembly in November 1791 shows.

Unknown deputy: Here is a message from the administrator of the Maine-et-Loire department: 'The department's problems are so great that incalculable damage will result unless the National Assembly takes prompt and stern measures. Crowds of three to four thousand armed men have gathered in several parts of Maine-et-Loire to indulge in all the excesses which the fever of superstition and fanaticism can produce.

'Pilgrimages and nocturnal processions led by seditious priests have served as the pretexts for these unlawful assemblies. They were easily dispersed while the pilgrims were still armed only with rosaries, but now they carry muskets, scythes and pikes, and have several times held out against the National Guard.

'Everywhere the constitutional priests are being ill-treated, assassinated even at the altar steps. Priests who have not sworn the oath have taken up their office again, and could well finish by bringing about a counter-revolution through civil war.'

M. Goupilleau: The department of the Vendée, next to that of Maine-et-Loire, is perhaps in an even more frightening situation. There are the same troubles, the same unlawful gatherings there too.

A law against the émigrés was passed on 9 November, on whose implementation Louis imposed his veto.

THE National Assembly, considering that the calm and safety of the realm demand that it take prompt and effective measures against those Frenchmen who, in spite of the amnesty, continue to conspire abroad against the French Constitution, decrees that:

French citizens gathered together beyond the kingdom's frontiers are henceforth declared to be suspect of conspiracy against their native land.

If, on 1 January next, 1792, they are still mustered together, they will be declared guilty of conspiracy and as such will be prosecuted and punished by death.

THE TIMES (London), *26 September 1792*

The number of French clergy now in London is estimated at about 900.

The refractory clergy

BY 1791 religion had become a political issue. Attitudes towards the Civil Constitution of the Clergy governed attitudes towards the Revolution itself, and religious divisions were discussed in basic political terms: clerics who swore to the Constitution were patriots, refractory priests who refused were aristocrats. In theory, the refractories were to suffer no greater penalty than loss of office. In practice, the oath was treated as a test of loyalty to the new regime, and clerics who did not swear were regarded as traitors.

The behaviour of many refractories in the aftermath of the oath-taking reinforced this view. A tiny minority denounced the Revolution outright, and came close to calling for a civil war. The overwhelming majority confined themselves to causing trouble for the members of the constitutional clergy who had taken the oath and who were sent to replace them. For example, they locked them out of churches and presbyteries, refused to hand over the parish registers and ornaments, and held rival masses at the same time, depriving them of congregations. Some told parishioners that sacraments performed by a constitutional priest were invalid: marriages would be null and void, and to receive absolution from one was to court damnation.

Laymen were also hostile to the constitutional clergy, especially in northern and western France, where the 'intruder' was jeered at in the streets, his services boycotted, and his house pelted with stones. Some priests were the victims of physical attacks, and on

ABOVE A contemporary inkwell showing a *bonnet rouge* crushing a priest; thus were priesthood and reaction confused.

ABOVE The massacre of patriots at Montauban on 10 May 1790; a symptom of the growing divisions in France. The Catholic royalists attacked the predominantly Protestant patriots.

occasions, demonstrations were so extensive that the National Guard had to be called out to restore order.

It is unclear how far the laity were led by the refractories. Many country people were thoroughly disillusioned with the Revolution by this stage, and little incitement was needed to stir them into action: by showing their hostility to the constitutional priest, the representative of the state church, they voiced their hostility to the Revolution. On the other hand, the refractory clergy were men of influence and authority in the villages, and their example and arguments may well have swayed the people. Whatever the truth of the matter, revolutionaries blamed them for inciting the troubles, and were quick to point out that areas which witnessed the biggest demonstrations of opposition to the government contained most of the clergy who had not taken the oath. Refractories and counter-revolution appeared to go hand in hand.

The refractories were also linked in the minds of the patriots with the forces of reaction outside France – mainly the émigrés. A number of clerics, including most of the *ancien régime* bishops, joined the emigration in 1791, and those who remained behind were assumed to be a 'fifth column', in league with the émigré armies. As fears of an invasion grew, especially in the aftermath of the royal family's abortive flight to Varennes, a number of departments took action.

In the frontier department of the Doubs, a number of priests were interned without trial, and elsewhere they were forbidden to reside in their former parishes. On 29 November 1791 the Legislative Assembly passed a decree declaring refractories to be 'suspects' and liable to expulsion from areas where troubles occurred. The king vetoed the measure, infuriating the patriots who felt he was working to undermine the Revolution. The fact that he vetoed a decree against the émigrés at about the same time only served to link the two rebellious groups more closely. With the outbreak of the war with Austria in April 1792 pressure for severer measures against the refractories grew irresistible. On 26 May the assembly ordered that those denounced by twenty active citizens were liable to deportation. Again the king blocked the measure, but with the fall of the monarchy in August 1792 the decree became operative.

Legislation passed in the summer and autumn of 1792 was even harsher, and refractories were confronted with a terrible choice. Those over sixty or in poor health were liable to be interned, the rest faced voluntary exile or deportation. Refractory priests who wished to remain in France were obliged to go into hiding.

The king's veto on the above law cast doubt on the monarch's good faith, as this extract from the radical newspaper *Les Annales patriotiques* shows.

THE court has at last unmasked itself, by using the Executive Veto on the law against the conspirator émigrés and their guilty leaders.

The National Assembly, faithful to its duty and to the constitution, and convinced by the most positive of evidence that the king's brothers and cousins are armed ready to march against our country, had decided it was time to make the law heard.

The conspirators at court realized that the decree against the émigrés placed the monarchy in a difficult position, by forcing it to break its strange silence.

The so-called Girondin group in the Legislative Assembly – deputies from Bordeaux in the Gironde department such as Vergniaud, plus others such as Brissot, Barbaroux, Isnard – sprang to prominence by their call for war, as in this extract from a speech of Isnard on 20 November.

EVEN if the émigrés are not thinking of attacking us, the very fact that they have assembled in a threatening manner is enough to make it essential that we disperse them by force and put a stop to it all.

The French people will become the most outstanding in the world. As slaves they were bold and daring; could they be timid and weak now that they are free? Always ready to fight for freedom, always ready to die for it, and to disappear entirely from the face of the earth rather than be cast back into chains, that is the nature of the French people. (*Sustained applause.*)

Let us say to Europe that if the French people should draw their swords they will throw the scabbards away and will not go back for them until they are crowned with the laurels of victory; and if, despite their strength and courage, they are overcome while defending freedom, their enemies will reign only over dead men. (*Applause.*) Let us say to Europe that if its ministers engage kings in a war against the people, we will engage the people in a war against kings. (*Applause.*)

Finally, let us say to Europe that ten million French people, fired by freedom, armed with the sword, the pen, reason and eloquence could single-handedly change the face of the world, and make all tyrants tremble on their thrones of clay.

Marie-Antoinette's letter to her secret adviser Barnave on 24 November showed the court's growing pessimism linked to the questions of the émigrés and the refractory clergy.

I am not in any way deceiving myself about all the difficulties and the dangers of our position: everything is against us. The return to France of Provence [the king's brother], which these gentlemen rightly regard as very important for our personal safety and consequently for the monarchy, is causing a thousand problems at the moment. The summons taken out against him, the hateful decree on the émigrés, even though the king used his veto on it – all these things could stop Provence returning.

I won't say any more about the law concerning priests. The matter seems to me to be settled: the king must either veto it or abandon the constitution.

The following decree of 29 November instituting closer controls over the refractory clergy was to be instantly vetoed by the king.

THE National Assembly, having heard the various reports of the civil commissioners sent to the department of the Vendée, and the petitions of a large number of citizens concerning the public disturbances stirred up in several departments of the kingdom by the enemies of public welfare under the pretext of religion, decrees that:

Within a week of the publication of this decree, all members of the clergy will be expected to come forward to swear the civic oath at their respective town halls.

Those members of the clergy who refuse to swear the civic oath or who retract it will, in addition to forfeiting all salaries and pensions, be deemed suspect of rebellion against the law and of ill intent against the country and, as such, will be particularly subject to and recommended for surveillance by the relevant authorities.

As a result, any member of the clergy who has refused to swear the civic oath and who happens to be in a commune where public disturbances occur on religious grounds, may be temporarily exiled from his usual place of abode.

In case of disobedience, the offenders will be taken before the courts, and will be punished by imprisonment.

Louis' secret letter to the king of Prussia on 3 December, couched in the diplomatic language of the *ancien régime*, shows his growing reliance on foreign powers.

Monsieur my brother, I have heard of the interest shown by Your Majesty, not only in my own affairs but in the welfare of my kingdom. Your Majesty's wish to prove this to me, wherever it may benefit the welfare of my people, has moved me deeply. I know I can call on you now, when despite my acceptance of the new constitution, the rebels are openly hatching a plot to destroy what is left of the monarchy.

I have just written to the emperor of Austria, the empress of Russia and to the kings of Spain and Sweden, and have suggested that the best method of stopping the trouble-makers here, and of ensuring that the evil which racks France does not spread to the other European states, is to set up an alliance of all the main European powers, backed up by armed force. I hope these ideas will meet with Your Majesty's approval, and that you will keep them secret; you will understand that circumstances compel me to be as circumspect as possible.

Petitions to the National Assembly such as this one, protesting at Louis' veto on the decree against the refractory, highlighted the links between the clergy and the émigré armies grouping on France's frontiers.

THE refractory priests lead people astray, they disturb the public peace, they abuse the confessional and recruit people for Coblenz! There will be no calm until the law on religious disturbances is put into effect. Peace prevails only in the parishes where the curés have sworn the oath. (Municipality of Dax.)

The philosophical spirit has not made very rapid progress. The refractory priests are making a lot of converts, especially among women and womenish men. (Municipality of Lauzun.)

Two priests have been arrested at Longuyon recruiting for the émigrés. One of them wanted to enlist dragoons from the dauphin's regiment who were on detachment in the frontier village of Malmaison, the other had induced some dragoons of the same regiment to desert and had come to Longwy with the same aim. The gendarmes at Montmédy chased out a refractory priest called Lorin, who was acting the missionary there. At St-Jean, near Morville, a priest named Bouton was evicted in the same way. (Municipality of Longwy.)

Marie-Antoinette's secret notes to Fersen, in early December, show the court's satisfaction that the Girondin call for war was received sympathetically both in the Legislative Assembly and the Jacobin Club.

7 December. Our position has improved somewhat; it appears that all those who call themselves constitutionalists are rallying in force together to oppose the republicans and Jacobins. The Jacobins are committing all the atrocious acts they can, but at the moment they've only got brigands and scoundrels on their side. I say at the moment, because things can change from one day to the next in this country and you never know where you are. It would be wonderful if one day I could show all these good-for-nothings that they never had me fooled.

9 December. I believe that France is going to declare war, not on a power which might have something to put in the field against us – we are too cowardly for that – but against a few German princes. The idiots don't see that if they do this it will help our cause, because once war starts, all the powers will have to become involved to defend their own rights.

Louis was playing a double game, as can be seen from a letter by Robert Lindet, deputy in the Legislative Assembly, to the Jacobin Club in his native Bernay, 16 December 1791.

The king arrived to attend the afternoon session of the National Assembly yesterday: he was received in profound silence. He read a well-written speech, and announced that he had high hopes of the Holy Roman Emperor, that all the other nations had replied to his demands as regards the émigrés in a satisfactory way, that he is going to enforce respect for the French nation's power and liberty, and restore it to a position of influence in Europe, and that he is conscious of the wrong done to him.

He finished by saying: I feel deeply how fine it is to be king of a free people. His speech was several times interrupted by loud applause.

The king left to the applause of the assembly and the public galleries.

This letter from Gouverneur Morris, U.S. envoy in Paris, to President George Washington in January 1792, pointed out how widespread was the call for war.

The situation of France's finances is such that every considerate person sees the impossibility of going on in the present way; and as a change of system, after so many pompous declamations, is not a little dangerous among a people so wild and ungoverned, it has appeared to them that a war would furnish some plausible pretext for measures of a very decisive nature.

Others again suppose that, in case of a war, there will be such a leaning from the king towards his brothers, from the queen towards the Holy Roman Emperor, from the nobility (the very few) who remain, towards the mass of their brethren who have left the kingdom, that the people may be prevailed on to banish them all together, and to set up a federal republic.

Lastly the aristocrats, most of them poor, and all of them proud, hope that, supported by foreign armies, they shall be able to return victorious and re-establish that species of despotism most suited to their own cupidity. It happens therefore that the whole nation, though with different views, are desirous of war.

Robespierre, virtually alone among prominent politicians, spoke out against the call for war at the Jacobin Club in January 1792.

SHALL we make war or shall we make peace? Shall we attack our enemies or shall we wait for them at home?

Certainly, I am in favour of a war undertaken for the purpose of spreading the rule of liberty, and I too could abandon myself to the pleasure of extolling in advance all its wonders. But I wonder if the war which will be fought will be the one which all this enthusiasm promises us, and I wonder who is proposing it, how, in what circumstances and why? Could the court propose a measure as drastic as war without that being part of its plan?

THE TIMES (London), *28 September 1792*

Robespierre was bred a butcher, which may, in some measure, account for the tranquility of feeling with which he has brought such numbers to the block. No man has better talents to be the leader of a mob than this.

Robespierre 'The Incorruptible'

MAXIMILIEN Robespierre was born in 1758, into a family of lawyers from the Pas-de-Calais, in northern France. He was the eldest of five children, only three of whom survived infancy: Maximilien, his sister Charlotte and his brother Augustin, who also was active in the Revolution. His mother died in childbirth, and his father left home, leaving Maximilien a virtual orphan, with full responsibility for the family.

A pupil at the Oratorian college in his home town of Arras, he subsequently won a scholarship to the select Collège Louis-le-Grand in Paris, where he became a friend of Camille Desmoulins, one of the Revolution's greatest propagandists. Unlike his school friend, who took up journalism in Paris, Robespierre returned to practise law in Arras, after being called to the bar in 1781.

Robespierre immediately identified himself with local supporters of the Enlightenment, and in a celebrated case during 1783 successfully defended a local savant, de Vissery, against a court order to dismantle a strange new invention – a lightning conductor. He rose quickly to become president of the Arras Academy, was elected to the literary society of the Rosati, and submitted essays on political and legal subjects to competitions held by provincial academies. Serious and scrupulous, with an intellectual clarity that would hold parliamentary audiences and a coldness which made him a difficult friend, he never married. In 1789, he was elected to the Third Estate, one of eight deputies from the Artois region; he had by now become an ardent disciple of Jean-Jacques Rousseau's theories of the general will, and a staunch democrat.

He often spoke in the National Assembly, was a member of the Jacobin Club at its inception, and was elected its president in April 1790. In line with his democratic views, he opposed the royal veto on legislation, and attacked the property qualifications imposed on voters and would-be deputies under the 1791 constitution. He demanded that the National Guard should also be open to all citizens, regardless of their status or wealth, and in May 1790 he proposed an unsuccessful motion to allow priests to marry. A supporter of the annexation of papal Avignon, he also defended the rights of Protestants, Jews and the black slaves of the West Indian colonies. On 18 May 1791 he successfully carried a motion that deputies should be ineligible for re-election to the Legislative Assembly – a 'Rousseauist' measure to prevent the perpetuation of parliamentary factions and self-interested, professional politicians.

ABOVE Robespierre, dressed with characteristic neatness.

Robespierre remained active in the Jacobin Club, and lived on his salary as public prosecutor of the Paris criminal court. He attacked the Girondins' attempts in the new Legislative Assembly to lead France into an aggressive war, and argued that the Revolution's enemies had yet to be defeated at home: military aggression would only play into the hands of Lafayette and the court. He distrusted Lafayette, at that time commander of the Parisian National Guard, whom he suspected of planning a military dictatorship. Generally, his espousal of radical causes like these, long before most leading revolutionaries accepted them, made him the enemy of the totalitarianism with which his name is frequently, but mistakenly, associated.

After the king's flight to Varennes, Robespierre unsuccessfully demanded his trial. It was his hatred of royal intrigue and refusal to compromise with the court that gave rise to his reputation for incorruptibility. Although he played no personal part in the Revolution of 10 August 1792, in which the king was deposed, he was immediately elected a member of the Insurrectionary Commune – the provisional city government in Paris which co-ordinated the overthrow of the monarchy – by the section des Piques. He was now a leading personality of the left, with a sense of high moral duty.

Robespierre had no sense of humour, and has often been labelled a self-righteous prig. Nevertheless, he was immensely popular. Women he had never met wrote to offer him marriage, or to request a lock of his hair. No other French revolutionary figure inspired this kind of personal devotion.

The political crisis was exacerbated by a new wave of popular discontent. High prices for colonial produce led to riots in Paris in January and February 1792, here reported in Brissot's *Le Patriote français*.

SATURDAY 21 January. Yesterday the people of the Faubourg St-Marceau broke into a shop belonging, it is said, to M. Dandré, and the sugar they seized was sold at 21 *sous* the pound. Everyone who took any, paid for it faithfully!

During the night the prison of La Force caught fire and was severely damaged. Although a large area of the prison was destroyed by flames, not a single prisoner escaped. A member of the clergy has been accused of starting the fire.

Artisans and shopkeepers from the Faubourg St-Antoine – who would later form the *sans-culottes* movement – protested at the bar of the Legislative Assembly on 26 January against the sugar riots, and called for more determined action against the enemies of state.

THE citizens of the Faubourg St-Antoine leave it to the women, the elderly and the children to shout for sugar. The men of 14 July do not fight for bonbons. Our wild and savage nature responds only to liberty and the sword. Let the conspirators, the hoarders, the enemies of order know that while their hired brigands are inciting the people to attacks on property, we are calmly forging the pikes which will exterminate them, the scoundrels! So let those who disturb the peace tremble: the people's patience is wearing thin!

In March 1792, Louis replaced his ministers with men linked to the Girondin party in the Legislative Assembly. Most prominent in this 'patriot ministry' was Roland de la Platière; the following letter is from his wife to the deputy Bancal des Issarts.

23 March 1792. I want to be the first to tell you who our new ministers are:
Foreign Affairs: M. Dumouriez. War: M. de Grave. Navy: M. Lacoste. Taxes: M. Clavière. Justice: M. Garnier (he has refused). (There's a lot of talk of appointing you in his place.) Interior: M. Roland.

It seems that harmony will rule in the government and will bind to it the sounder section of the National Assembly.

The Revolution in the colonies

IN 1789, France was a major colonial and maritime power. It possessed fishing bases off Newfoundland, trading bases in India and Africa, a small South American settlement at Cayenne – and a chain of colonies in the West Indies that included Saint-Domingue (modern-day Haiti), the pearl of all European overseas territories, which produced over two-fifths of the world's sugar and more than half its coffee. Saint-Domingue's trade was greater than that of the entire United States and all Britain's rich Caribbean colonies combined.

The thriving West Indian colonies were disrupted and eventually destroyed by the Revolution, which released pent-up tensions within the disciplined and rigidly organized ranks of colonial society. In a struggle which initially mirrored the conflict in France, the élite – white planters and land-owners – attempted to wrest power from the royal governors. This led other white merchants and tradesmen to demand political equality with their social superiors, which stimulated Saint-Domingue's 55,000 mixed-blood mulattos to press for civic equality with the 55,000 whites.

In Paris the National Assembly vacillated, torn between two powerful pressure groups. The 'Friends of the Blacks' (*Amis des Noirs*) advocated more humanitarian treatment of negroes, the gradual abolition of the slave trade and, at some future date, emancipation of the 594,000 slaves who kept the West Indian economy going; and they found powerful spokesmen in Brissot, the Rolands and Robespierre. On the other side, proprietors and traders formed the Massiac Club (so-called after their meeting place, the Hôtel de Massiac) to defend their economic interests and found a strong spokesman in Barnave.

In March 1790 the assembly gave the colonies permission to set up their own representative bodies, but, although it established property qualifications, it was silent about colour. The mulattos of Saint-Domingue, refused participation in the island's administration, rose in revolt in December of that year and their leader, Ogé, was captured and executed. However, they were never fully suppressed and the assembly's attempted compromise in May 1791, which enfranchised West Indian coloureds born of free parents, satisfied neither side.

The situation became more complex as these disputes among the free population raised the slaves' expectations of freedom. In August 1791 they rebelled in the northern province of Saint-Domingue: 2000 whites and over 10,000 slaves died, and the area was devastated. The following month, the Massiac Club persuaded the National Assembly to renounce the May decree and leave the regulation of race relations to the white settlers – a move that united mulattos and slaves in a running 'bush war', which continued into 1792.

ABOVE Barnave, the slave-owners' voice in the Assembly.

LEFT The blacks of Saint-Domingue had to struggle to retain the freedom which the Republic conferred on them in 1793.

In April 1792 the 'Friends of the Blacks' won the upper hand in Paris and the assembly granted full equality to mulattos and free negroes. Commissioners and troops embarked for Saint-Domingue to enforce the law and order was tentatively re-established in the summer of 1792 – only to break down a few months later when the monarchy was abolished. Royalists in Saint-Domingue staged a coup against the revolutionary administration, but were unsuccessful. In addition there were pro-royalist revolts in Martinique and Guadeloupe. Many white planters and proprietors were asking for British support even before open war broke out between France and Britain in 1793.

In consequence, even before a blockade by the British navy cut off trade between the colonies and France, the situation was verging on chaos. Revolution and the revolutionary wars combined to shatter the colonial economy on which much of France's commercial prosperity in the 18th century had been based.

Lafayette kept his former comrade in the American War of Independence, George Washington, informed about French politics.

March 1792. There have been changes in the government. The king has chosen his council of ministers from among the members of the most extreme section of the popular party, i.e. from the Jacobin Club, which is a kind of Jesuitical institution, more fitted to making people desert our cause than to attracting new converts. Nevertheless, since these new ministers are not in any way suspect, they might perhaps stand a chance of re-establishing order. They say they are going to work hard at it.

The National Assembly is not very well informed. The king lags behind events in his day-to-day conduct of affairs, although from time to time he acts really well. Anyway, we'll manage, and the success of the revolution cannot be in any doubt.

It was at this time that one of the most enduring symbols of the Revolution, the red cap of liberty or *bonnet rouge*, was popularized. Nicolas Ruault remarked on this in March 1792, in his correspondence.

*Paris, 20 March 1792. On Wednesday the 15th of this month we saw a peculiar sight at the Jacobin Club: some members came in wearing red caps (*bonnets rouges*) and were warmly applauded. At the next session the president, Thuriot, the secretaries, the speakers at the rostrum and more than three hundred members all appeared wearing red woollen caps. The next day red bonnets were everywhere – in the streets, in the squares, in the gardens and even at the theatre.*

This latest novelty seems very odd; for my part I have not worn one nor do I intend to, since it seems the height of vulgarity and is totally unnecessary. Only about half of society is dressing this way. It is to be feared, if this continues, that the bonnet rouge *will be the cause of a schism between those who wear it and those who don't. Many quarrels and disagreements between men have stemmed from equally trivial causes.*

We hear from Strasbourg that the bonnet rouge *is worn by all the* Friends of the constitution *(the Jacobins). The craze has probably come from there, for the Parisians are imitators rather than initiators. Anyway, the* bonnet rouge *is set to become the headgear of all French patriots, the obligatory headgear of three-quarters of the population.*

The aristocratic marquis de Romé, in a letter to his friend de Salaberry, former magistrate at Blois, saw the sinister side of the phenomenon.

The bonnets rouges *are making trouble everywhere. Yesterday an abbé was walking in the Palais-Royal. A gang of these* bonnets *appears and tries to force him to take a cap. He refuses. The gang insists. He makes the mistake of spitting on the bonnet. This acts as a signal for a fight. These people, bare-arsed but with bonnets, throw themselves on him, tear off all his clothes and when he's completely naked they start to lash his shoulders harshly with their sticks. The sticks in question are thick hawthorn cudgels like the ones porters carry, with a thong which goes round the wrist. If the National Guard hadn't come up at the double that would have been the end of the abbé, who is said to be a good fellow, very much a constitutionalist and normally very good-natured.*

This recruiting advertisement for the émigré armies appeared in the royalist newspaper *L'Ami du Roi* before war broke out.

I have the honour to ask you to announce the formation of the company of Soissonnais under the command of the prince de Condé, so that some of our comrades who are still in France may join together on the field of honour. The headquarters of the prince de Condé are at Benheim, three leagues from Worms and five from Mannheim.

The moment is approaching for the destruction of the hydra which has been devouring France.

Your very humble and obedient servant de Bonnefond, still a captain in the true regiment of the Soissonnais.

Marie-Antoinette, writing to Fersen on 19 April, saw the forthcoming conflict as a war of revenge.

19 April 1792. The ministers and the Jacobins are making the king declare war tomorrow on Austria. The ministers are hoping that this move will frighten the Austrians and that within three weeks we will be negotiating. God forbid that should happen: may we at last be avenged for all the outrages we have suffered from this country!

The bonnet rouge

IN the early days of the Revolution the liberty cap – inspired by the *pileus* with which enfranchised Roman slaves covered their heads – was held aloft at ceremonies and rituals and hoisted on poles and liberty trees as a symbol of the new age in human freedom.

The caps came in a variety of shapes and colours, and could be made from cotton, silk, wool – even cashmere, revealing an 'aristocracy of dress' beneath an apparently egalitarian symbol. Although they became popular as headgear, they were at first worn only by speakers at meetings of political clubs and on other public occasions; the familiar *bonnet rouge* did not become fashionable until the summer of 1792, when it was associated with the Jacobin Club and popular politics. The king's willingness to wear one after the invasion of the Tuileries palace on 20 June elevated the common man's woollen cap to the status of a national patriotic symbol. It was an essential part of *sans-culotte* imagery during 1793–4, and was later enshrined in 19th-century myths of the Revolution.

The *bonnet rouge* was often worn with the tricolour cockade. The latter originated in July 1789, supposedly at the instigation of the journalist Camille Desmoulins, as a badge for revolutionaries faced with the threat of royal troops. Red and blue were the colours of Paris, white that of the Bourbons, Louis' family name: together they symbolized national unity – king and people joining forces in the Revolution – and soon became fashionable as ribbons tied round hats and bonnets, and in embroidered waistcoats. Variations included green cockades for followers of the comte d'Artois, and all-white ones for royalists.

The rumour that the royal guards were allegedly insulting and trampling on the red, blue and white cockade provoked the women of Paris to march on Versailles in October 1789. In 1790 it was made illegal to wear any other combination of colours.

BELOW One of the many types of objects used for revolutionary propaganda; a watch face with the *bonnet rouge* held aloft.

BELOW A 'patriotic' chair; *bonnets rouges* crown the back legs, which imitate fasces, and a tricolour seat.

On 20 April, the assembly declared war on 'the king of Bohemia and Hungary' – that is, the Holy Roman Emperor Leopold II of Austria, the queen's brother. A letter from the Girondin deputy Barbaroux to the municipal officials in his native Marseille, 21 April, emphasized the need for greater internal surveillance.

War has been declared. It was midday yesterday when the king came to propose it and in the evening the legislative body agreed to it unanimously. At the moment we are only declaring war on the king of Bohemia and Hungary, that is, the Austrian house, but it is very certain that we will also have to fight the king of Prussia and a few other equally delirious powers.

I have no doubt that the zeal of the French, their honour and patriotism, the entirely justifiable enticements which will be used to open the eyes of the foreign soldiers at long last, and the general anxiety of the peoples – all these will lead to victory for us on the frontier. But our enemies in the interior might stir up trouble: it is essential that they be watched and kept under police scrutiny so that their least actions are known and so that they cannot undertake anything against the state.

The memoirs of the radical deputy Choudieu described the émigré armies who threatened France from a Jacobin perspective.

AFTER the capture of the Bastille the comte d'Artois gave the signal for emigration, along with his two sons.

Emigration became a sort of fashion. It was smart to go on a trip to Coblenz, which, it was said, should be shorter in duration than a pilgrimage to Mecca or to Notre-Dame-de-Lorette. Our women of fashion themselves encouraged this new sort of crusade, and sent distaffs to those who were putting off going. An organizing committee set itself up in Coblenz and sent off letters summoning all former comrades who were lagging behind. The invitations were soon followed by threats if the addressee did not hurry to join up under the flag of the counter-revolution.

These new-style crusaders believed that the sword would be enough to restore everything to its former order. They would have been much more dangerous forming groups at home, but the court was so blind that even the queen and the courtiers who surrounded Louis XVI were in favour of the emigration of the nobility.

Yet émigré soldiers found life not always to their taste, as this letter from the marquis de Vibraye shows.

It is said that we are going to settle in the neighbourhood of Coblenz, in billets, as we were here. You have no idea of the discomfort suffered by these poor nobles since our departure from Worms and the patience, courage and gaiety with which they have put up with it in the hope of doing something. There have been no complaints, no regrets; in truth it is a phenomenon which history will one day, I hope, record with respect.

To give you an idea of the way we have been living since we've been in this country, I will just tell you that out of 1580 nobles, half have no sheets and have to sleep in their shirts and boots and the other half have two bundles of straw: those are the beds. And as many as 15 to 20 of them sleep together in a peasant bedroom, the floor of which often consists only of very damp earth.

The memoirs of the writer Chateaubriand, who served in the émigré armies in 1792, give a good idea of military life.

THE princes' army was composed of nobles, grouped according to province and serving in the rank and file. At the very end of its days the nobility was going back to its roots, and to the roots of the monarchy, like an old man regressing to his childhood. In addition there were brigades of émigré officers from various regiments, who had also gone back to being ordinary soldiers.

The nobles of my province made up seven companies and there was an eighth, composed of young men of the Third Estate. The iron-grey uniform of the latter distinguished them from the seven others, who wore royal blue with ermine flashes. Men united in the same cause and exposed to the same dangers perpetuated their political inequality through these hateful distinctions. The true heroes were the plebeian soldiers: their sacrifice was not motivated by self-interest.

We had some tents, but we lacked everything else. Our German-made muskets, weapons other people had rejected, were horribly heavy, broke our backs, and were often not in any condition to fire. I went through the whole campaign with one of these muskets and its hammer would never strike.

Emigré armies

THE establishment and growth of émigré armies were closely tied to the emigration of officers from the regular army. Although civilians joined these units and enlisted men followed their commanders, the dominant element in these forces was the court aristocracy, who led the infantry and cavalry regiments. They were the first to leave, followed to a lesser extent by artillery and engineer officers. Younger men left their posts earlier and in greater numbers than older ones, many of whom had a sense of commitment to their profession or career and stayed with their troops. Of those who did go during the first three years of the Revolution, a substantial majority, perhaps three-quarters, served in the émigré armies.

The first and smallest émigré army, the 'Black Legion', was created in Baden in September 1790 by the vicomte de Mirabeau – Mirabeau's younger brother, nicknamed *Tonneau* or 'cask' for his physical appearance and fondness for wine. Like its arrogant and irascible commander, who died of apoplexy two years later, this unit had a brief and stormy existence. Between 1791 and 1792 the bulk of the royalist forces were assembled: the army of the princes led by the comtes de Provence and d'Artois, the king's brothers, which absorbed the remnants of Mirabeau's band and became the largest of these groups, with headquarters at Coblenz; the army of the prince de Condé, which proved to be the most durable, and the army of the duc de Bourbon. All reached their peak strength by the summer of 1792, after which the number of military émigrés declined substantially.

The armies were hampered by a severe shortage of funds. The subsidies provided by the courts of Spain, Austria, Prussia and Russia, as well as by lesser princes, proved inadequate. Consequently, the émigrés borrowed heavily, restored the sale of commissions, took menial positions, and even, in some instances, resorted to pillage – some 200 émigrés were dismissed for looting during the winter of 1791–2. The situation was exacerbated by nobles who refused to serve in any capacity other than as officers. The lack of rank-and-file soldiers resulted in 'companies of gentlemen', bands of officers who often took the names of the regiments they had left. However, they expected to be paid at their previous levels, an attitude that was only too typical of the generally haughty, frivolous, insolent and often irresponsible behaviour which undermined their effectiveness as a fighting force and antagonized their host nations.

The émigrés' fundamental problem was their failure to appreciate the situation in their homeland. This misunderstanding was painfully evident in the advice to the duke of Brunswick, commander-in-chief of the Austro-Prussian armies. They drafted the threatening manifesto issued by the duke on 25 July 1792, which, far from intimidating the people of Paris, strengthened their resolve and helped to precipitate the overthrow of the monarchy a fortnight later. They also petitioned Brunswick to allow them to form the spearhead of the allied invasion force, promising that they would have the full support of the peasantry and rally loyal regiments of the line army. Although the duke had little confidence in their claims, he felt duty bound to accept the émigrés' participation.

Their contribution to the invasion of France in the late summer of 1792 was worse than the most pessimistic predictions. They failed to accomplish even the simplest of missions, for example the capture of Thionville. Far from attracting popular support, they intensified peasant resistance and national patriotism. They refused to accept orders; at one point Brunswick was forced to put the prince de Condé under arrest for insubordination. They also provided a scapegoat for the allied military failures in the autumn of 1792. The emperor, Francis II, ordered their dissolution.

Although they had mustered between 20,000 and 25,000 troops in July and August 1792, by the end of that year only Condé's army of less than 5000 survived intact. The émigré armies were no longer an independent military force.

BELOW Part of the combined émigré/Austro-Prussian invasion force bombarding Lille in 1792.

Usually an army is made up of soldiers of more or less the same age, the same height and the same strength. Ours was very different: it was a jumbled collection of grown men, elderly men and boys come down from their dovecotes.

This feudal levy presented a last image of a dying world. I saw elderly noblemen, stern-looking, grey-haired, their coats torn, their bags on their backs and their muskets slung across their shoulders, dragging themselves along with a stick. All the men in this poor troop were making war entirely at their own expense while at home the decrees being promulgated were stripping them of everything they had and were throwing our wives and mothers into prison.

France's armies looked shaky once battle was joined. An early engagement on the northern front led to panic among the troops and the murder of their own commander, Dillon. The *Moniteur* recorded the event.

THE troops under M. Dillon were routed and chased into Lille in the most horrific circumstances, half of the men and horses killed and wounded on the road.

The verbal report of an officer to the commanding officer, M. Rochambeau, estimates the losses at between 260 and 500 men dead or wounded.

It seems that M. Dillon, who had matched his belief in the constitution with his ardour in its service, was killed near the town which should have protected his retreat, and that he died at the hands of the men for and with whom he had just been fighting. (*The assembly shook with indignation.*)

The revolutionary cause was not helped by Marie-Antoinette passing secret military intelligence to the enemy, as in this coded letter to Fersen on 5 June 1792.

There are orders for Luckner's army to attack at once; he is against it but the ministry insists. The troops are short of everything and are in very great disorder.

THE PUBLIC ADVERTISER (London), *20 February 1792*

. . . from the general movement of troops on the Continent, and the frequent insurrections in the provinces of France, we cannot alter our opinion that a counter revolution will yet be effected.

The army in 1792

THE royal army was bound up in the course of the Revolution from its very beginnings. During 1787 and 1788 noble officers had refused obedience and resigned their commissions rather than enforce orders to repress the judges of the parlements at Rennes and Grenoble. An important factor in the success of Parisian revolutionaries in July 1789 was the unreliability of many of the regular troops in the city, and their defection to the insurgents in mid-1789 set the pattern for developments in the armed forces: growing insubordination in the ranks, strengthening hostility on the part of the officers towards the new regime, and increasing conflict between officers and men.

Inevitably these divisions came to be expressed in political terms. Troops gave patriotism as their motive for insubordination, a claim legitimized by the amnesty extended to them by the government in the summer of 1789. At the same time, officers, alarmed by the collapse of discipline, blamed the new system. Between March and August 1790 there was a rash of mutinies, most notably at Nancy, where there was bitter fighting and severe repression of both the mutinous soldiers and the civilians who had supported them, including the local National Guard and the city's Jacobin Club. Although these conflicts were often sparked off by purely military grievances, such as the officers' abuse of

authority, and the rights of off-duty soldiers, they were increasingly presented as struggles between 'patriot' soldiers and their 'aristocratic' commanders.

However, most officers remained at their posts, until Louis' flight to Varennes in June 1791, when the king's arrest and suspension cut what they felt to be the last ties with the government. Thousands resigned, deserted and emigrated; by the end of the year well over half of those serving in 1789 had left the service. A hopeless cycle had been established: the mass exodus of officers for political reasons increased the troops' distrust of those who remained. This created further insubordination, which led more officers, encouraged by comrades who had already gone, to decamp.

The military and civil authorities were seriously worried by these defections, particularly when the danger of foreign war intensified in late 1791 and early 1792. All three military commanders – Rochambeau, Luckner and Lafayette – were convinced that their forces were totally unprepared for action. Following the declaration of war with Austria on 20 April 1792, the first combat engagements confirmed the most dire predictions. When the French advance against Tournai in the Austrian Netherlands was routed on 29 April, the troops panicked, cried betrayal and poured back into Lille, where they murdered their commander, General Dillon. By the end of May, all three field commanders were counselling immediate peace.

The military situation in the summer of 1792 was dismal. These early defeats were followed by the advance of invading armies into France and the position was further aggravated by a new wave of officer emigration. There was also talk of treason at the highest levels – rumours that were sometimes well founded; certainly Marie-Antoinette secretly divulged military plans to the enemy. The overthrow of the monarchy on 10 August and Lafayette's subsequent attempt to turn his army on Paris exacerbated the crisis. But there were encouraging signs. The men who replaced the émigrés were non-commissioned officers with extensive military experience, who had a common bond with their men, and whose careers were directly linked to the success of the Revolution. Also, there was a substantial influx of recruits into the regular army between 1791 and 1792 who brought with them an enthusiasm and patriotism which would not shame the national volunteers.

ABOVE A volunteer embraces his family before his departure. The portrait behind him shows a family martial tradition.

LEFT The less glamorous reality. In the summer of 1792 the French army was dispirited and riven by rumours of treachery.

The correspondence of the royalist Fougeret gives a striking picture of the state of Paris in mid-1792.

It is rumoured that some of our army is in revolt against its leaders and ready to disband. Should such a misfortune occur, villages and small towns will be pillaged by bands of soldiers who will have no other means of existence.

Vital foodstuffs are rising to exorbitant prices. In Paris, meat costs 12 sous *for households which buy a lot, but small households are having to pay 13 or 14* sous *a pound and mutton is 18. Bakers' assistants are demanding a pay rise, and all the workers are following their example. However unfortunate this may be where the other trades are concerned the consequences* vis-à-vis *the bakers are serious and it is feared that the price of bread will rise.*

Policing and security are non-existent. People commit robbery and murder in the middle of Paris as if they were in the depths of a forest, and after 9 o'clock in the evening the outlying areas are death-traps.

Wine, wood, vegetables, everything is going up in price and becoming prohibitively expensive. Meanwhile, it's virtually impossible to get your hands on your income. The interest owing from state bonds is not being paid out. Bankruptcies are common and the interest rate on the assignats *is getting higher every day, because they are so risky to invest.*

It seems that within two or three weeks we can expect our poor France to be invaded in horrific fashion: from Spain in the south, from Piedmont and Savoy, Switzerland and part of Germany in the east, and in the north from Prussia, the German frontier states, the Holy Roman Empire, Holland, Russia, etc. It is said that England is getting ready to fight us as well. To pit against these three hundred thousand men, we have a few wretched troops still in a state of rebellion, undisciplined, apparently short of everything they need, and with entire regiments continually going over to the émigrés who must, because of this, have more than thirty thousand armed men.

Feeling threatened, Louis began to take precautions: he gave the following instructions to his secret envoy to the courts of Europe, the Swiss journalist Mallet du Pan, June 1792.

The king begs and exhorts his brothers and French émigrés not to let the current conflict take on the character of a war fought between two foreign powers through any hostile or offensive participation on their part. Such conduct would provoke civil war, would endanger the lives of the king and his family, would mean the overthrow of the throne and the massacre of the royalists, would rally to the Jacobins all the revolutionaries who have broken away from them – and who continue to break away daily – would revive the excitement which is tending to die down at the moment and would stiffen an opposition which will buckle at the first reverses.

Point out to the courts of Vienna and Berlin the usefulness of a proclamation common to the states who have allied together for the war, and the importance of drafting this proclamation in such a way as to split the Jacobins from the rest of the nation, to reassure those who are likely to come back to our cause or who, although not wanting the current constitution, want to see an end to corrupt practices and would prefer the liberal rule of a monarch whose authority is limited by law.

In a letter to his brother Joseph at Ajaccio, Napoleon Bonaparte, then a junior officer stationed in Paris, described the popular demonstration on 20 June which ended in the invasion of the Tuileries palace.

M. de Lafayette has written to the National Assembly denouncing the Jacobins. His letter is very strongly expressed; many people think it is forged. M. de Lafayette, the majority of officers in the army, all honest men, the ministers and the Parisian administration are on one side; on the other are most of the assembly, the Jacobins and the people.

The Jacobins are fools; they have no common sense. The day before yesterday the assembly was petitioned by seven or eight thousand men carrying pikes, axes, swords, guns and sharp sticks, who then went on to the king. The Tuileries gardens were shut and guarded by 15,000 National Guards. The people smashed the gates, got into the palace, set cannon up against the king's apartment and offered him a choice between two cockades, a white one and a tricolour one. Choose whether you rule here or in Coblenz, they said. The king reacted well and chose the red cap, as did the queen and the royal prince. Then they drank with the prince and stayed in the palace for four hours.

I am sending you a copy of the Cabinet of Fashions *for Paoletta.*

This anonymous account of the *journée* of 20 June 1792 was given in the Jacobin Club.

I have just come from the Tuileries where, at a window, I saw the king wearing a red cap on his head. The people expressed the wish that I should speak to him in their name. He was sitting on a slightly raised seat with three or four National Guards and a few deputies at his side. The people had entered this apartment in considerable numbers, shouting: 'Down with the veto! ratify the decrees! long live the nation!'

The king was wearing the cap of liberty on his head and was drinking, from a bottle, to the health of the nation. He was unable to make himself heard and several times he rang a little bell to get them to listen. When he finally got their attention he told them that he was in favour of the constitution and swore to uphold it.

The people shouted that it wasn't true, that he had already deceived them and would do so again, and then they went on: 'Down with the veto! ratify the decrees! bring back the patriot ministers! long live the nation!' So I went up to the king.

'Sire,' I said, your enemies aren't in Paris, they're at Coblenz and it is time you realized that however much you would like to go and join them. The people, on the other hand, only want to see you happily going along with the constitution, and if you did this in good faith they would love you even more because, I repeat, they want to love you.

'The people are completely behind the Revolution, they want the constitution to work, they want you to ratify the decrees, they want you to recall ministers in whom they have confidence. Yes, we will stick to the constitution, but it has to work; we will lay down our lives, if necessary, to defend it, but if we fall, we will drag you down with us.'

The king opened his mouth, gaped at me wide-eyed, then replied that he would always remain faithful to the constitution. 'You are still deceiving us, Sire,' I said, 'but you had better watch out.'

The people were still shouting that it was pointless, that he had cheated us, and repeating their refrain: 'Down with the veto! ratify the decrees! long live the nation!' Several nobles, with little ivory sticks covered in fleurs-de-lis, were very politely saying, 'Respect the law.' At last, by dint of repeated civility, the people began to realize that the king wanted time to think and that there were lots of other citizens who wanted their turn to see him. The ones I was with left, and I with them.

The decree of 11 July 1792 declaring 'the country in danger' (*la patrie en danger*), allowed the authorities to assume emergency powers in the face of the war threat.

LARGE numbers of troops are marching on our frontiers. All those who hate liberty are taking up arms against our constitution.

Citizens, the country is in danger.

May those who have the honour of being the first to march in defence of that which is dearest to them never forget that they are Frenchmen and free, that their fellow-citizens in their homes are upholding the security of the individual and of property, that the magistrates of the people are ever watchful, that with the calm courage of true strength everyone is waiting for the signal from the law to act, and the country will be saved.

As the memoirs of Bertrand de Moleville record, in mid-July, just as the king's position was worsening, Girondin deputies led by Vergniaud approached Louis XVI to see if they could negotiate the reappointment of the 'patriot ministry' led by their friend Roland, which had been dismissed the previous month.

AT this time the Girondins exercised a very strong influence over the assembly and the Jacobins. Amongst the leaders of this faction were Vergniaud, Guadet and Gensonné. These deputies in a letter to the king, stated that the people's dissatisfaction was on the point of exploding in the most terrible manner, and that it would take very little to trigger off a far more widespread and violent uprising than the one of 20 June. They predicted that this would take place during the next fortnight, and that as a result the king would, at the very least, be deposed.

The only way of avoiding this catastrophe would be to recall Roland, Servan and Clavière to the government, within the week. If the king gave his word that he would do that they would swear on their lives to stop the uprising.

THE MASSACHUSETTS MAGAZINE (Boston), *April 1792*

A few days ago, an American back woodsman, presented himself at the bar of the National Assembly, and informed that he had made a discovery which might be a substitute for soap, and would save France 80 millions of livres annually. He was received with politeness.

Louis' reply to Vergniaud loftily rejected the Girondin olive branch.

THE king has no intention of neglecting the question of the choice of ministers.

The declaration of war was entirely the work of so-called patriot ministers.

He had previously tried everything possible to prevent the alliance of powers and that the only means now of getting the armies to withdraw from our frontiers were very general ones.

Since his acceptance of the constitution he has observed its laws scrupulously but that many people were now working against it.

This republican petition from Angers, read out in the National Assembly on 23 July, revealed the swell of republican feeling developing within France.

LEGISLATORS, Louis XVI has betrayed the nation, the law and his oaths. The people are sovereign over him, and you are their representatives. Pronounce his downfall and France will be saved. There follow ten pages of signatures. (*Applause from the galleries, long murmuring in the assembly.*)

In his letters, Ruault describes how, under the provisions of the decree on *la patrie en danger*, the assembly established a camp of National Guardsmen, or *fédérés*, at Soissons, to defend Paris.

Paris, 27 July 1792. Quite a number of National Guardsmen have arrived here in the last few days since the Fête de la Fédération of 14 July, and you must have a good idea why: for the most part they are old soldiers with fierce moustaches. Some of them have also gone off to the camp at Soissons, and to the frontiers.

The National Assembly, which can see the storm coming, is at a loss to know which side to take. Should it dethrone the king in order to prevent terrible things from happening? But then it would immediately have to organize a new executive authority. Whom would it appoint? It is impossible to offer the crown to any prince. Who would want to wear it at the moment?

'Formez vos bataillons'

FEDERATIONS – spontaneous festivals of national unity, celebrating civic and moral virtues – had been popular from the start of the Revolution. Distinctively military, they culminated in the Fête de la Fédération, the national ceremony on the Champ-de-Mars in Paris on 14 July 1790, which prominently featured the National Guard and the royal army. Revolutionary ideals were reinforced: the celebrations in Paris included the singing of the egalitarian *Ça ira*. The rash of mutinies that erupted in military units during the following weeks was commonly blamed on exposure to revolutionary propaganda.

The 1790 festival commemorated the fall of the Bastille, and was expected to be the first in a series of annual celebrations of that event. However, the king's attempted flight on 20 June 1791 and his subsequent suspension from power precluded any such holiday in Paris that year, although there were festivities in the provinces. In 1792, when the third anniversary of the fall of the Bastille approached, the military situation had deteriorated rapidly following the declaration of war on 20 April, and suspicion of monarchical intrigue had increased. The Legislative Assembly was forced to take drastic action and, in the last week of May, dissolved

the king's Constitutional Guard and summoned 20,000 volunteers from the National Guard to defend the capital.

Louis vetoed these measures, together with the assembly's proposal to deport all refractory clergy denounced by twenty or more citizens. However, the National Guardsmen, or *fédérés*, had already begun their march to Paris from all over France, and the assembly outmanœuvred the royal veto by authorizing them to attend the federation ceremony scheduled for 14 July.

After the popular demonstration and invasion of the Tuileries on 20 June 1792, the king reluctantly agreed to 20,000 *fédérés*, on condition they be stationed at Soissons, more than 100 kilometres from the city. Within a week of this decision, on 3 July, the first battalions of volunteers began to arrive in the capital, just as the declaration of '*la patrie en danger*' established a formal state of emergency.

On their arrival in Paris the *fédérés*, most of whom were staunch revolutionaries, made contact with local democratic groups, the Jacobin Club, the sections and the *sans-culottes* themselves; they also set up a central committee to co-ordinate their activities. These armed bands were not slow to make their presence felt. On 17 July they participated in a petition to suspend the king and to purge all aristocrats from public office. Two days later the electoral assemblies of the Paris sections went into permanent session, and admitted 'passive' citizens to their deliberations; on 30 July the city's National Guard was similarly opened to Parisians who were excluded from voting. All these democratic changes met with the approval of the *fédérés*, who continued to pour into Paris. On 25 July a detachment arrived from Brest, in the department of the Finistère, and on 30 July came the Marseille contingent, by far the most renowned of all the *fédérés*. They had already established a reputation for patriotism by repressing counter-revolution in the Midi, and now answered the appeal of their fellow-townsman in Paris, Charles-Jean-Marie Barbaroux, who had called for 'six hundred men who know how to die'.

They entered the city to the strains of the newly composed 'War Song of the Army of the Rhine', soon to be called the 'Marseillaise' in their honour; its potency bolstered the revolutionary spirit and encouraged anti-monarchical sentiment. Four days later the Brunswick manifesto, issued by the allied commander, threatening Paris with 'military execution and total overthrow' if the royal family was harmed, was published in Paris, to the outrage of patriots. The elements of the uprising of 10 August were in place.

LEFT The patriotic oath at the Fête de la Fédération: the starting point for the *fédéré* movement. The National Guardsmen seen here went back to their provinces imbued with revolutionary propaganda; and returned in 1792 to tip the balance of opinion in Paris against the monarchy.

> THE PUBLIC ADVERTISER (London), *27 February 1792*
>
> The Southern Provinces of France exhibit scenes the most wretched. Anarchy is prevalent throughout them, and, whatever may be said to the contrary, the affairs of that once flourishing country have now evidently fallen into a state of the most extreme wretchedness and ruin.

In his memoirs, Chaumette describes the arrival of the *fédérés* delegation from Marseille at the end of July. This was particularly important as the Marseillais were renowned republicans, and would play a major part in the overthrow of the king in the *journée* of 10 August.

THE good Marseillais *fédérés* arrived in Paris on 30 July. The arrival of the Marseillais was the signal for great rejoicing by the patriots, who had been oppressed for so long. All the most faithful friends of liberty rushed to see them march past. It seemed as if this battalion, famous for its exploits in the south of France, was bringing with it the lightning which was going to strike tyranny dead. I can almost see them still, with their tanned, soldierly faces, marching in tight formation, responding to our welcome with cries of *Vive la liberté!*

For the whole length of their march, the Marseillais made the streets of Paris ring with the song which has become so dear to all French people: *Allons, enfants de la patrie*, etc.

The newspaper *La Chronique du Roi* evoked the birth of the 'Marseillaise'.

IN all the theatres at the moment you hear people asking for the song: *Allons, enfants de la patrie!* The words are by M. Rouget de Lisle, a captain in the engineering corps, garrisoned at Huningue. The tune was composed by Allemand for one of our armies, and is both moving and warlike.

The song came with the *fédérés* from Marseille, where it was all the rage. They sing it very harmoniously, and when they get to the bit where they wave their hats and swords in the air and all shout together, *Aux armes, citoyens!*, it really sends a shiver down the spine. These latter-day bards have spread this martial air in all the villages they passed through, and in this way have inspired the rural areas with civic and warlike feelings. They often sing it at the Palais-Royal, sometimes during shows in the interval between the two plays.

The Marseillaise

STRASBOURG, not Marseille, first heard 'La Marseillaise'. This stirring martial music first aroused the enthusiasm of French men and women on 25 April 1792, in what was then a frontier town in the week-old war with Germany and Austria. Originally known as the 'War Song of the Army of the Rhine', it was written by Rouget de Lisle, an army engineer, and sung by Dietrich, mayor of Strasbourg, in his fine tenor voice.

An amateur composer and poet, and author of a 'Hymn to Liberty', Rouget de Lisle was inspired by the songs which expressed the people's determination to defend the Revolution. The rough music of the *Carmagnole*, with words threatening death and destruction to all, including the king and queen, who blocked the people's advance was an example. The *Ça ira* achieved an electrifying effect through its reiterative refrain 'Ça ira' – equality would reign at last. Such songs were not for the faint-hearted or the uncommitted.

The 'Marseillaise' was influenced by the works of the composer Gossec in its use of large choirs and wind instruments, which made so profound an impression at open-air festivals, and also by the sprightly marches written for the National Guard. Above all, it was a call to arms. Carried from Strasbourg to the Midi, it was brought to Paris by the Marseillais *fédérés* – the 'six hundred men who know how to die' – who stormed the Tuileries on 10 August 1792. In every village on the long, hot journey from Marseille to the capital, *Aux armes, citoyens!* had resounded as the Marseillais waved their hats and brandished their swords in terrifying unison.

From the Paris insurrection – and from the streets and theatres of provincial France – the 'Marseillaise' passed to the army. Sung at Valmy on 20 September 1792 in celebration of France's victory over Prussia, it became 'the music of the clash of swords and the roar of cannons', accompanying French troops on their campaigns across Europe. Carnot, the member of the great Committee for Public Safety of 1793–4 with responsibility for military organization, boasted that it added a hundred thousand soldiers to the nation's armies.

The 'Marseillaise' was adopted as France's official anthem in 1795, after the Terror, despite strong competition from *Le Réveil du Peuple* (The Re-awakening of the People), a counter-revolutionary song against extremist Jacobins. Napoleon, mistrustful of popular fervour, allowed it to fall into disuse, and the

ABOVE A songsheet of the 'Marseillaise'; with singing troops.

Bourbons banned it when they returned to the throne in 1815.

During the revolutionary upheavals of 1830, 1848 and 1870–1 the 'Marseillaise' reappeared as a symbol of republicanism, a conception represented by Delacroix's famous painting *Liberty singing the Marseillaise on the barricades and calling the people to the battle of July (1830)*. It was 1879 before the 'Marseillaise' became France's national anthem, as a pledge to the permanence of the republic and its values.

The situation of the royal family, virtual prisoners in the Tuileries, looked increasingly ominous, as Marie-Antoinette made clear in this letter written in invisible ink to Fersen on 1 August 1792.

Obviously, the king's life has been in danger for a long time, as well as that of the queen. The arrival of about 600 Marseillais and of a number of other delegates from all the Jacobin clubs adds considerably to our worries, which are, alas, all too well founded. All kinds of precautions are being taken for Their Majesties' safety, but assassins prowl continually around the Tuileries. The people are being stirred up.

Some of the National Guard are badly disposed towards us and the rest are weak and cowardly. Our only resistance against the scoundrels lies in the few people who are ready to protect the royal family literally with their lives, and in the regiment of Swiss Guards.

The provisions of the Brunswick Manifesto, drafted by the émigrés in the names of the rulers of Austria and Prussia, and issued on 25 July 1792 by the duke of Brunswick, supreme Allied commander, differed markedly from those urged by Louis in his letter to the king of Prussia on 3 December 1791.

THE city of Paris, and all its inhabitants without exception, will be expected to submit immediately to the king's authority, to allow him full and complete freedom, and to ensure that he and all the members of the royal family are given the inviolability and respect which natural and human laws demand that subjects accord their sovereigns.

Their imperial and royal majesties make personally responsible for all events, on pain of trial in a military court and death without hope of pardon, all members of the National Assembly, of the department, district, municipality and National Guard of Paris, the magistrates and all other persons in authority. Their aforesaid majesties also declare that if the Tuileries palace should be broken into or attacked, that if the least violence, the least outrage is done to their majesties King Louis XVI, Queen Marie-Antoinette and the royal family, if immediate steps are not taken to ensure their safety, preservation and freedom, they will exact exemplary and eternally memorable revenge, handing over the city of Paris to military execution and total overthrow, and handing over the insurgents guilty of the attacks to be punished as they deserve.

The royalist Raclet wrote on 3 August that far from intimidating the Parisians, the Brunswick Manifesto seemed to fuel the call for the overthrow of the king. The popular movement was channelled within the 48 sections, or neighbourhood assemblies, of the capital, and bolstered by the *fédérés*.

We are witnessing the greatest events one could ever see. We are threatened by everything that is most sinister. Tomorrow, perhaps civil war will break out. Yesterday, several deputies, then the mayor, Pétion, speaking for the 48 sections of Paris, followed by the wicked Marseillais fédérés, *who had been allowed into the National Assembly, demanded that the king be dethroned on the spot, and the current ruling dynasty totally excluded from the succession. When one deputy tried to come to the monarch's defence a* fédéré *threatened him with his sword: he shut up and the president wisely adjourned the session.*

There are quite a number of honest people in the National Guard and they will be joined by the king's faithful subjects, who seem well inclined to lay down their lives rather than allow the consummation of this abomination. Therefore the deputies will be trembling with fear if they do pronounce this decree. But, unfortunately, the rabble will support them and will use it as a pretext to cut other citizens' throats and loot their houses.

The royal council of ministers, when it met on 7 August, seemed to have no idea how best to avoid the impending storm, as Théodore de Lameth, a moderate royalist, recorded in his memoirs.

THE court, justifiably alarmed, wavered between a thousand different plans which were no sooner conceived than abandoned. This was how d'Abancourt put it to the royal council on 7 August in the queen's presence: 'Unfortunately it is impossible to deny that we are verging on total subversion, and that our only hope of safety lies in measures so drastic that they would carry terror into the ranks of those who are overthrowing social order and the throne, which no authority has attempted to suppress.

'I propose that we arrest Robespierre, Danton, Marat, Panis, Sergent and Santerre, not individually at their homes, but publicly, at a Jacobin meeting.'

One member of the council replied, somewhat ironically: 'This is an excellent plan; but who will carry it out?'

The Brunswick manifesto

ALTHOUGH the proclamation issued on 25 July 1792, as the allied army set out to invade France, is known as the Brunswick manifesto, the duke was not responsible for its contents. The ablest Prussian general of his day, he had not been consulted about the policy of invasion, operational planning was left to King Frederick-William II of Prussia, his army was below strength and he disliked the other allied contingents, particularly the Austrians, who were Prussia's traditional rivals. He regarded the pretensions of the émigrés as beneath contempt, and their fighting capacity as nil. However, he put his name to the proclamation, in the drawing up of which he had had no say.

The manifesto declared that the allied objectives were to end anarchy, defend throne and altar, restore the king to liberty and allow him to exercise his legitimate authority once again. French people were urged to return to the path of reason, justice, order and peace. The manifesto denied any intent to take conquests or meddle in France's internal government, except to free the king to gather such an assembly as he judged proper and ensure his subjects' welfare according to his promises.

These assurances, however, were accompanied by a long string of threats: against National Guards who failed to keep the peace or who resisted the Allies; against regular soldiers who did not submit to the king; against all civil authorities who did not maintain order; against civilians who resisted the invading army; and, above all, against Paris.

The manifesto concluded by offering 'mildness and moderation' to well-disposed subjects and force 'against those only who shall be guilty of resistance or of the manifest evil intention'. However, the list of the guilty had been drawn dangerously wide and, when rumours of the manifesto reached Paris on 28 July, followed by its publication on 1 August, the crown's supporters were aghast. Mathieu Dumas called it fratricide by the king's brothers, while a correspondent of the Swiss journalist Mallet du Pan declared that people laughed at it. The American ambassador ironically interpreted the manifesto as meaning: 'Be all against me for I am opposed to you all, and make a good resistance for there is no longer any hope.' Brunswick considered it 'unfortunate' and confessed that 'I shall repent it to the last day of my life. What would I not give never to have signed it!'

Though not the sole cause of the overthrow of the king on 10 August, it helped activists to persuade doubters. The contents of the moderate constitutional-royalist version of the proclamation had been discussed in Paris for a fortnight before the actual document appeared – perhaps broadcast in the hope of stopping the impending revolution – and although the king quickly disclaimed the Brunswick manifesto, there were enough similarities to the earlier reports to indicate royal collusion with the invaders. On 9 August, a British observer noted that great pains were being taken by radical journalists and sectional activists to prove royal involvement, and the manifesto soon became a major weapon in the arsenal of those advocating a final break with the crown.

ABOVE The duke of Brunswick, the Allies' supreme commander.

RIGHT The Republican response: *sans-culottes* dance the *Carmagnole* round a liberty tree as Allied troops flee in the background.

On the *journée* of 10 August 1792, a massive popular insurrection in Paris overthrew the monarchy. The Swedish ambassador in Paris here recounts the upshot of the day's events, in a letter to Fersen, 11 August.

No words can describe the horror of yesterday. All Paris heard the firing at the Tuileries without knowing that the royal family was at the assembly. It is estimated that the people massacred 700 of the Swiss Guards and that they in their turn shot and killed about 600, 200 of whom were Marseillais who, with the fédérés, *were the moving force behind everything.*

Last night all the Swiss officers still at Courbevoie were taken to the Abbaye prison. All those who were in Paris were killed, and at this very moment they are flooding the underground passages of the Tuileries in the supposition that there may still be some of them there. After 7 o'clock in the evening you might have thought it was a day of public rejoicing, you could hear singing everywhere and the inns were full.

The king and the royal family are safe for the time being. Nobody thought it possible yesterday, today there is hope. For the moment the king has been divested of all his functions. The National Assembly has taken him and the royal family under its protection. You will see the details in the papers.

The Marseillais deputy Barbaroux's account, written to the municipality of Marseille on 11 August, outlined the National Assembly's response to the *journée*.

While the fighting was taking place at the Tuileries and in the streets, the National Assembly was pronouncing highly important decrees.

It provisionally suspended the king, until the nation should reach a decision on the matter through a National Convention, which is to be convoked forthwith. While the king and his family remain hostage, the assembly has dissolved the government. Its conduct will be subject to a more detailed examination, and new ministers have been named. They are: Roland as minister of the interior, Servan as minister of war, Clavière at the ministry of taxes, Monge (the Naval Inspector) at the navy, Danton at justice and Lebrun at foreign affairs.

The assembly also decreed that there would no longer be active and passive citizens.

It sent commissioners to the army.

It voted pensions for the widows and children of the patriots killed at the Tuileries.

It decreed that the statues of kings set up in public places should be pulled down.

It ordered that a camp of twenty thousand fédérés *should be established in Paris, thus solving a problem which had been giving us much concern, that of settling and paying our Marseillais, or at least those of them who want to stay here.*

The overthrow of the king coincided with a worsening of the military situation when the Allied armies poured deep into French territory, as Choudieu's memoirs recall.

BY that time the Prussians had crossed the border.

On 20 August, Longwy was surrounded and cut off, on the 21st the town was bombarded and on the 24th it surrendered.

On 30 August, the enemy army appeared before Verdun.

On 1 September, a messenger from Verdun brought us a letter from the council appointed to supervise the town's defence, dated 31 August and addressed to the National Assembly.

During the night of 1–2 September a new messenger reached me from Verdun, a young volunteer from the Maine-et-Loire battalion who had managed to get through the Prussian lines thanks to a strong horse. His brief was to give a detailed verbal account to the military committee and to the ministers of the critical situation in which Verdun found itself.

It was as a result of the decisions made at this committee that Danton, acting minister of justice, came with me to the assembly, where he displayed all his force and energy.

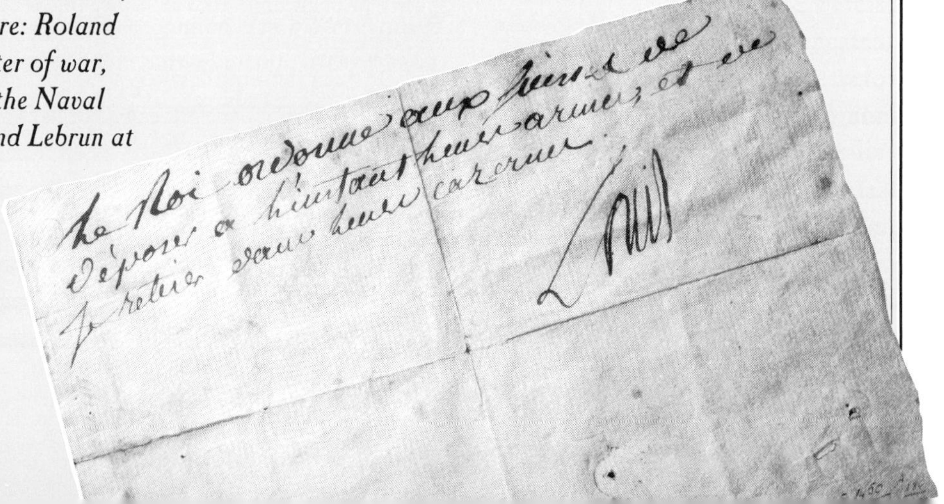
Le Roi ordonne aux Suisses de
déposer à l'instant leurs armes et de
se retirer dans leurs casernes.
Louis

RIGHT Louis XVI's last order, instructing the Swiss Guards to cease fire; surrendering the Tuileries to the attackers.

10 August 1792: the overthrow of the monarchy

ALTHOUGH Louis XVI became 'king of the French' under the 1791 constitution – a constitutional monarch as opposed to the absolute 'king of France' – he had never really reconciled himself to the new order; his discomfort with the revolutionary regime became obvious with his abortive flight to Varennes on 20–1 June 1791. This brought the first manifestation of republicanism in Paris, although most deputies in the National Assembly, like citizens in the provinces, were anxious to maintain a limited monarchy. The outbreak of war in the spring of 1792 precipitated the king's downfall; Louis' passivity in face of danger from abroad inevitably cast him in the role of traitor.

The king and the court had supported the declaration of war on Austria in the hope that defeat for the revolutionaries would restore the aristocracy's fortunes. As the disorganized French armies retreated in the summer of 1792, popular opinion pointed to monarchical treachery as the cause. The king's role as a scapegoat was confirmed when his 'patriotic' Girondin ministry led by Roland proposed measures to tackle the military crisis. Louis refused to sanction a permanent camp in Paris for the 20,000 National Guards, or *fédérés*, who were coming to the capital to celebrate the Fête de la Fédération but who would also be able to defend the city against the advancing allied armies. Then, on 13 June, he sacked the ministers responsible for the plan and publicly announced that he was vetoing it. A week later he was assailed by hundreds of demonstrators, who burst into the Tuileries palace demanding reinstatement of the Girondin ministers and implementation of emergency legislation to face the invasion threat. Louis was obliged to drink to the health of the nation and don the red cap of liberty.

The *journée* of 20 June 1792 was spontaneous, and citizens from the sections, or neighbourhoods, of the capital escaped punishment. However, the immediate effect of their intervention was to provoke a royalist reaction, chiefly in the provinces but even in Paris, where a petition was circulated seeking the arrest of ringleaders of the *journée*. Pétion, the mayor of Paris, was suspended from office for failing to prevent the incident and, with General Lafayette back in the city urging support for a counter-revolutionary coup, the *journée* seemed to have backfired. However, the assembly pressed ahead with the establishment of a *fédéré* camp, while the Girondins demanded that the king declare himself unequivocally in favour of the Revolution.

A fresh insurrection was in preparation from mid-July onwards. Although it occurred in Paris, the provincial volunteers marching to the capital made a vital contribution. Some *fédérés* were already seeking the abolition of monarchy, court and constitution, demands quickly taken up by the Parisian sections, which were now meeting in permanent session and summoning all citizens to defend the country. Middle-class control of the capital had been surrendered to the radical bourgeois and their *sans-culottes* allies. On 31 July, as news from the front worsened, the Mauconseil section withdrew its allegiance from Louis, a gesture which received support from all over the city. On 9 August the Legislative Assembly rejected an ultimatum for the king's deposition.

Early on the morning of 10 August a new revolutionary municipal council of radicals and activists, the so-called Insurrectionary Commune, replaced the Parisian municipality and called upon National Guards from the sections to join with *fédérés* in an assault on the Tuileries. Louis had fled to safety in the assembly, but a bloody battle ensued at the palace: some 800 of the king's men and 400 insurgents were killed. The assembly was invaded and the frightened deputies were forced to dethrone the king, endorse the new government of Paris and prepare for the election of a new, republican assembly – the Convention, which would draw up a new constitution. A rump of the existing assembly remained, and the executive was formally in the hands of a council of ministers, including Danton and Girondins like Roland. But the Paris commune had assumed an overwhelming influence over events.

ABOVE The gates of the Tuileries gardens today.

OVERLEAF A mixed force of Paris *sectionnaires* and *fédérés* from Brest and Marseilles stormed the palace on 10 August.

Danton's speech in the National Assembly on 2 September, calling for *de l'audace, encore de l'audace et toujours de l'audace*, is one of the classics of revolutionary oratory. It rallied Paris against the military threat as Verdun, the last fortress on the Prussian road to Paris, fell under siege.

M. Danton, minister of justice: **It is very satisfactory, gentlemen, for the ministers of the free people to be able to announce to them that the country will be saved. All France is roused, all France is on the move, all France is burning with the desire to fight.**

You know that Verdun is by no means in the hands of our enemies yet.

You know that the garrison has sworn to kill the first person to suggest surrender. Some of our people are going to proceed to the frontier, others are going to dig entrenchments, a third group, with its pikes, will defend the interior of our towns. Paris is going to back up this huge effort: the commissionaries of the Paris Commune are going to issue a solemn proclamation inviting citizens to arm themselves and march in defence of the country.

Now is the moment, gentlemen, for the National Assembly to become a true council of war. We ask that anyone who refuses to serve in person or to take up arms should be punished by death.

We ask that an organizing body be set up to coordinate citizens' movements and we ask that messengers be sent to all the departments to notify them of the decrees which you have issued.

The tocsin that we are going to sound is no alarm bell, it is the signal for the charge against the enemies of the fatherland. (*Applause.*) To vanquish them, gentlemen, we must show daring, more daring, and again daring; and France will be saved. (*Renewed applause.*)

> THE TIMES (London), *6 September 1792*
>
> The conduct of the Duke of Brunswick's army has been very commendable and highly exemplary for its humanity, which gives a direct contradiction to those horrid reports of brutality, which the Jacobin Cabal in this country have had the shameless impudence to invent and circulate.

The following letter, written by an unknown middle-class Parisian housewife to her husband, evokes both the heroic and the sordid aspects of Parisian resistance to the war threat.

Oh, my friend! I take shelter in your arms, to pour out a stream of tears. These tears are shed for the fate of our unhappy brother patriots, cut down by Prussian swords. Verdun is besieged by the Allies and can only hold out for two days.

The joy of our ferocious aristocrats contrasts with our profound sorrow. Listen and tremble: the alarm cannon booms around midday, the tocsin rings, the call to arms sounds out. People come and go in the streets. Everything has been in a state of acute crisis; the municipality's moving proclamations attracted the people's attention and touched their hearts: 'Fly to the aid of your brothers! To arms! To arms!' Everyone is running and hurrying around. Forty thousand men are leaving tonight to descend on the Prussians, whether at Verdun or before, if the enemy are advancing.

At the height of the war crisis, a rumour began that aristocratic prisoners were plotting to break out and attack Paris from within. From 2 to 6 September thousands of prisoners were massacred by vigilante gangs with the tacit support of Parisian sections' militants. In this letter to his brother, the abbé de Bologne, chaplain of the Parisian prison and poorhouse at Bicêtre, recounts his experiences of these days.

People were frightened out of their wits by the capture of Longwy, and the municipal officers rode around on horseback trying to reassure them. At the same time, to ward off fears of pillage, it was decided to massacre all convicted prisoners; this was done, or at least begun.

This went on in the capital for two days. Amongst the dead were almost two hundred refractory priests, who had been locked up in prisons in the Carmes and the Cardinal Lemoine seminary. Then, at Bicêtre, we witnessed the arrival of a troop of about three thousand men, armed to the teeth. The day and night of this butchery were hard to bear, so awful were they. The administrator of the hospital, a detestable and detested man, was the first to die; two hundred prisoners suffered the same fate. A few rash words nearly cost the Mother Superior, a former religious servant from the hospital, her life. Finally, after a great deal of searching through cellars and other places, the men decided to go away, having been here for three days. I am congratulating myself for having escaped the butchery, and several people have complimented me on it. I do not know whether I will be as lucky in the future.

I have the honour to be, with respect and gratitude . . .

Danton

'THE tocsin that we are going to sound is no alarm bell, it is the signal for the charge against the enemies of the fatherland. To vanquish them, gentlemen, we must show daring, more daring, and again daring; and France will be saved.' These words were spoken by Georges-Jacques Danton, minister of justice, on 2 September 1792, as Verdun, the last fortress protecting the capital, fell to the advancing Prussian army. With Paris in acute danger, his words heralded a new spirit of defiance.

Danton was born in 1759 at Arcis-sur-Aube in the Champagne region. His father died when he was three and he was educated at the Oratorian college in nearby Troyes, where he was an able, though not outstanding, pupil. From there he went to Paris to study law, and in 1787 married a Parisian girl, Gabrielle Charpentier. With the help of her dowry he bought a law practice in the Cordeliers district, on the left bank of the Seine, and settled down to the comfortable life of a lawyer.

However, during the summer of 1789 he deserted law for politics. By 1790 he was president of the Cordeliers district political assembly, and later in the summer, when the Cordeliers club was founded, he was one of its leading and most popular members. He worked with fellow-radicals, including the journalists Jean-Paul Marat and Camille Desmoulins, and attracted a team of loyal and ardent supporters.

Although Danton was elected to the departmental council of Paris in January 1791, his honesty was already doubted. He had always lived well beyond his means and had few scruples about accepting political bribes, not least from the king's wealthy and ambitious cousin, the duc d'Orléans. At the time of the flight to Varennes in June 1791, Danton called for Louis' abdication in favour of his son, the future Louis XVII, with Orléans acting as regent. However, few politicians trusted the duke, and popular feeling favoured a republic. Danton distanced himself from republican sentiment and, the day before the massacre of the Champ-de-Mars in July 1791, left for a short visit to Arcis-sur-Aube and England.

He returned to Paris in time for the elections to the new Legislative Assembly, but failed to win a seat. Only in the following January did he obtain another political position, this time on the municipal council. By now the question of war with Austria was dominating political life, and Danton supported Robespierre's opposition to armed conflict. On 11 August, with his popularity at its peak, he was elected minister of justice in the provisional government that

preceded the meeting of the Convention, a difficult post as all his fellow-ministers were from the Girondin faction, whom he had often criticized. However, his massive energy and determination soon triumphed, and he emerged as the effective head of government. He raised more volunteers for the army and accelerated the arrest of political suspects, but when popular support for his policies overflowed into violence on 2 September, with the notorious September massacres, Danton could do little other than turn a blind eye.

For the next eighteen months he was a leading, but controversial, political figure. Elected to the Convention, he continued to concentrate on the war effort and was an early member of the Committee of Public Safety created in April 1793 to co-ordinate the war effort. However, his attempts to negotiate a peaceful end to the war met with suspicion, and in July 1793 he was removed from the committee. From now on his political fortunes declined. Doubts about his honesty and that of many of his friends resurfaced, and his old energy began to flag. In the spring of 1794 the Committee of Public Safety, fearing that he might emerge as the leader of an opposition group, decided to eliminate him. After a blatantly rigged trial, Danton was guillotined on 6 April 1794: the voice of 'daring' was silenced, and with it much of the raw dynamism of the Revolution.

The September Massacres, said to have been organized by Marat, Danton and Robespierre, tarnished Madame Roland's view of the Revolution, as she wrote to Bancal des Issarts.

5 September 1792. We are under the knife of Robespierre and Marat; they are doing all they can to stir the people up and turn them against the National Assembly and the council of ministers. They have set up a star chamber, they have a little army which they bribe with what they found or stole from the Tuileries and elsewhere, or with what Danton gives them – he being the secret leader of this horde.

9 September. My friend Danton controls everything; Robespierre is his puppet. Marat holds his torch and his dagger: this wild tribune reigns – at the moment we are merely oppressed, but waiting for the time when we become his victims.

If you knew the awful details of the killing expeditions! Women brutally raped before being torn to pieces by these tigers, guts cut out and worn as ribbons, human flesh eaten dripping with blood! . . .

You know my enthusiasm for the Revolution: well, I am ashamed of it! Its reputation is tarnished by these scoundrels, it is becoming hideous! In a week from now . . . who knows what will have happened? It is degrading to stay here, but it is forbidden to leave Paris; we are being shut in so that we can have our throats cut at their convenience. Adieu: if it is too late for us, save the rest of France from the crimes of these madmen.

THE TIMES (London), *10 September 1792*

Are these 'the Rights of Man'? Is this the LIBERTY of Human Nature? The most savage four footed tyrants that range the unexplored deserts of Africa, in point of tenderness, rise superior to these two-legged Parisian animals.

The French armies distributed propaganda sheets in French and German to Allied footsoldiers.

INVITATION FROM THE FRENCH GOVERNMENT TO THE PRUSSIAN AND AUSTRIAN SOLDIERS TO LEAVE THEIR STANDARDS AND SETTLE IN FRANCE

FRIENDS and brothers! You are being forced to risk your lives fighting a nation which maintains that men are equals and brothers. Kings and nobles do not want men to know that they are brothers and equals.

The rulers of Austria and Prussia thought that King Louis XVI and the nobles still had a lot of supporters in France, but they were wrong. The treachery and conspiracies of the nobles and of the superstitious and miserly priests have been discovered, and the guilty ones have been killed or are awaiting punishment.

The French nation wishes to end the war without delay. It wishes to spare men's precious blood. This is why it offers all soldiers in the enemy armies the happiness of living in France as free men. This, friends and brothers, is the fate France offers you. Compare it with the one you have been bemoaning for so long, and make your choice.

This kind of propaganda seems to have had an effect, to judge by a letter home from a young Prussian footsoldier.

I talked with people from Lorraine on several occasions and I was happy to learn that in all respects they owed a lot to the Revolution. They told me that the crushing taxes which formerly hung over them had been abolished, that they could now think, work, help each other freely and enjoy life and the fruits of their labour in peace, and put a little money aside; that all the different sales taxes had been abolished, their fields were no longer destroyed by game animals, in short they were now aware of being men, rather than slaves at the mercy of the nobles and priests.

Demoralization among the émigré troops accompanying the Allied advance is described in a letter by a footsoldier in the émigré army, captured in early September and later read out in the National Assembly.

We are beginning to be weary of this war, the way it's going. We have to fight front-line troops, none of whom deserts, national volunteers who put up a strong resistance, and armed peasants who either fire on us or murder anyone they find alone.

Since we arrived in France it has poured with rain every day. In addition we are starving. We are finding it unbelievably difficult to ensure the men get bread. There is often no meat. Our shoes and top-coats have rotted and our men are starting to fall ill. The villages are deserted and provide neither vegetables nor eau de vie nor flour. I don't know what will become of us.

The September massacres

THE fall of the monarchy on 10 August 1792 left a profound ambiguity about the legitimate source of government. The confusion was more acute in the capital, where two bodies supposedly represented the 'popular will': the Legislative Assembly, reduced to less than half its original size after the exodus of the conservative deputies, and the Paris Commune, larger and far more radical than before. The assembly's authority was greatly weakened after its announcement that there would be elections for a new legislature, the Convention, which would draw up another constitution, and the Commune, supported by Robespierre and other prominent Jacobins, used thinly veiled threats to force it to set up a special tribunal to try the former defenders of the king. At the same time it rounded up suspects and imposed press censorship.

On 26 August, breaking upon this confusion of authority and mutual distrust, there was bad news of the war. The fortress of Longwy had fallen to the Prussians on 2 September; Verdun, the last major defence between the invader and the capital, was about to capitulate. The Commune called all patriots to arms, and thousands of volunteers came forward to defend the Revolution. Their imminent departure from the capital provoked further concern about the crowded prisons, now full of counter-revolutionary suspects who might threaten a city deprived of so many of its defenders. Rumours spread that these prisoners were plotting to escape, avenge themselves on the helpless population and hand the city over to the Prussians.

Marat, now a powerful figure on the Commune, called for the conspirators to be killed, and on 2 September armed bands began visiting the prisons, starting with those where refractory priests were held, and killed many of the inmates. The massacres continued for five days; improvised courts tried the prisoners for counter-revolutionary intent in a travesty of justice, and executed more than a thousand men and women; a slightly larger number were released.

The killers were ordinary members of the sections, who believed they were carrying out an essential duty. They demanded, and received, payment for the time they had put in. Marat and the other members of the Commune's Committee of Surveillance, established to suppress counter-revolutionary activity, were instrumental in starting the murders, and neither they nor the Commune as a whole did anything to prevent their continuing. Many Parisians thought they were necessary, and some welcomed the opportunity to be rid of opponents. In the midst of the massacres,

ABOVE La Salpêtrière; scene of some of the worst massacres.

Robespierre and Billaud-Varenne, both of whom later became members of the Committee of Public Safety, tried to have Girondin leaders including Roland and Brissot arrested and sent to prison. Danton, then Minister of Justice, was also thought to have connived in the massacres. But in fact he annulled a warrant issued by the Surveillance Committee for the arrest of Roland, Minister of the Interior – an action which was later used against him at his own trial.

The massacres cast their shadow over the first meetings of the National Convention from 20 September 1792. Most of the deputies were from the provinces and many were suspicious of Parisian politics and shocked by what they had heard of the killings. The majority rallied to the Girondins, who did not forget that their opponents had tried to arrest their leaders during the massacres, and who maintained an ardent hatred of the Jacobin leaders – Robespierre, Marat, even Danton – and their *sans-culotte* supporters. The Convention was deeply divided even before it met, and its debates frequently degenerated into mutual recriminations.

In the longer term the *septembriseurs* became central to counter-revolutionary mythology, and henceforth royalists, moderates, and most foreign opinion regarded the Jacobins and the Parisian *sans-culottes* as bloodthirsty savages.

The French commander Dumouriez reported to the National Assembly the lifting of the crisis. The armies of the new French Republic were set to advance.

THE army which the confidence of the nation entrusted to my leadership has deserved well of its country. At Valmy, in the forest of the Argonne, the handful of liberty's soldiers put up an impressive resistance for two weeks against this formidable army. In despair, the enemy attempted an attack which has added a victory to the military career of my colleague and friend General Kellermann.

Our soldiers were badly clothed, they had no straw to sleep on, no blankets, they sometimes went two days without bread. I never once saw them complain; from the songs and the joy you might have taken this terrible camp for one of the pleasure camps where kings paraded regiments for the amusement of their mistresses and children. The hope of victory sustained the soldiers of liberty.

The tiredness and hardship they have suffered have been rewarded. The enemy has succumbed to the season, misery and illness. Its formidable army is in flight, its numbers halved. Kellermann is chasing it with more than forty thousand men; I am marching to the aid of the north with a similar number.

The great German writer Goethe's reflections on his experiences at Valmy proved prophetic.

SO the day ended; the French were halted and their general, Kellermann, too, stood at ease. Our people were withdrawn from the firing line and it was as though no engagement had taken place.

Consternation spread amongst our army. Only that morning they had been confident of giving the French a sound beating; indeed, I myself had been attracted to join this dangerous expedition by my unconditional trust in an army such as this, and in the duke of Brunswick; but now everyone was silent, not even exchanging glances, or spoke only to utter curses. As nightfall approached we unconsciously drew into a circle, without even being able to light a fire; most of us stood in silence, few spoke, and all felt numb and unable to understand what had happened.

Finally I was asked for my opinion, for I had earlier cheered the group with brief remarks. Now I said: 'This is the beginning of a new epoch in history, and you can claim to have witnessed it.'

Valmy: the birth of a new epoch

IN September 1792 the future of the Revolution seemed precarious. Internal opposition gathered in western and south-eastern France. Lafayette, disillusioned with events in Paris, defected to the enemy after an unsuccessful attempt to turn his army on the capital. Suspicion focused on the other commanders as the fortresses of Longwy and Verdun fell to Brunswick's advancing army, which now threatened Paris, where the invasion threat triggered off the notorious September massacres.

Before Lafayette's defection the Army of the North, which had been under his command, was transferred to General Dumouriez, who moved it southward on 1 September and sent a portion of it, known as the Army of the Ardennes, to the Argonne to block the allied invasion force. This plan was frustrated when, owing to confusion, the pass at Croix-aux-Bois was left unguarded and taken by Clerfayt, Brunswick's subordinate, on 12 September. Meanwhile, General Kellermann led the Army of the Centre from Metz to join forces with Dumouriez and halt Brunswick's advance against Paris. A number of minor engagements

ABOVE Goethe. Travelling with the Prussian forces, he saw the battle and dubbed it the beginning of a new epoch.

ABOVE The field of Valmy, seen from the mill around which Dumouriez and Kellermann had disposed their artillery.

took place during the following days. The most disturbing from a French point of view was on 16 September near Montcheutin, when nearly 10,000 of Dumouriez's men, faced with some 1500 Prussian cavalry, panicked and fled, claiming betrayal by their officers. Although Dumouriez managed to rally them, such an experience hardly inspired confidence.

The French armies met together on 19 September near Valmy, and the next day the Prussian forces confronted Kellermann's army, which had taken up battle positions, while Dumouriez's exhausted troops served as reserves. The battle, which lasted from 7 in the morning until 8 in the evening, pitted more than 50,000 French troops with 40 pieces of artillery against nearly 35,000 Prussians and 58 cannon. In many respects what followed was a classic 18th-century engagement. There was a great deal of manœuvering, little hand-to-hand combat, light casualties – approximately 300 Prussians and fewer than 200 French – and the army occupying the battlefield at day's end was counted the victor. On the other hand, Valmy was a harbinger of future warfare, in the use of massed artillery – the deciding factor – by the victorious French, the revolutionary slogans and songs which increased commitment and raised morale, and the employment of large numbers of citizen-soldiers.

Goethe said that the battle of Valmy marked 'a new epoch'. Although most of the French cavalry and artillery were composed of regular troops, 31 of the 75 battalions of French infantry were drawn from 'national volunteers', called up during the previous fifteen months. Beyond this, even the ranks of the line regiments contained a large proportion of recent recruits, half of whom had enlisted since 1789 and a quarter of whom had less than a year's service. Their similar backgrounds explain why regulars joined volunteers in singing the revolutionary song *Ça ira*, and why both responded enthusiastically to the hard-bitten veteran Kellermann when he raised a tricolour cockade on his sabre, shouting *Vive la Nation!* War and ideology had become one.

Valmy provided the first evidence that the French army had recovered from the substantial losses and bitter divisions that had plagued it since 1789. It showed that regulars and volunteers could serve effectively together. And it restored a much-needed confidence to the army and the civil authorities backing it. Ten days after the battle, Brunswick began to retreat toward the frontier. If the Prussians had won, an unobstructed route to the French capital would have been open to them. There can be little doubt that Valmy saved not only Paris, but probably the Revolution and possibly France itself.

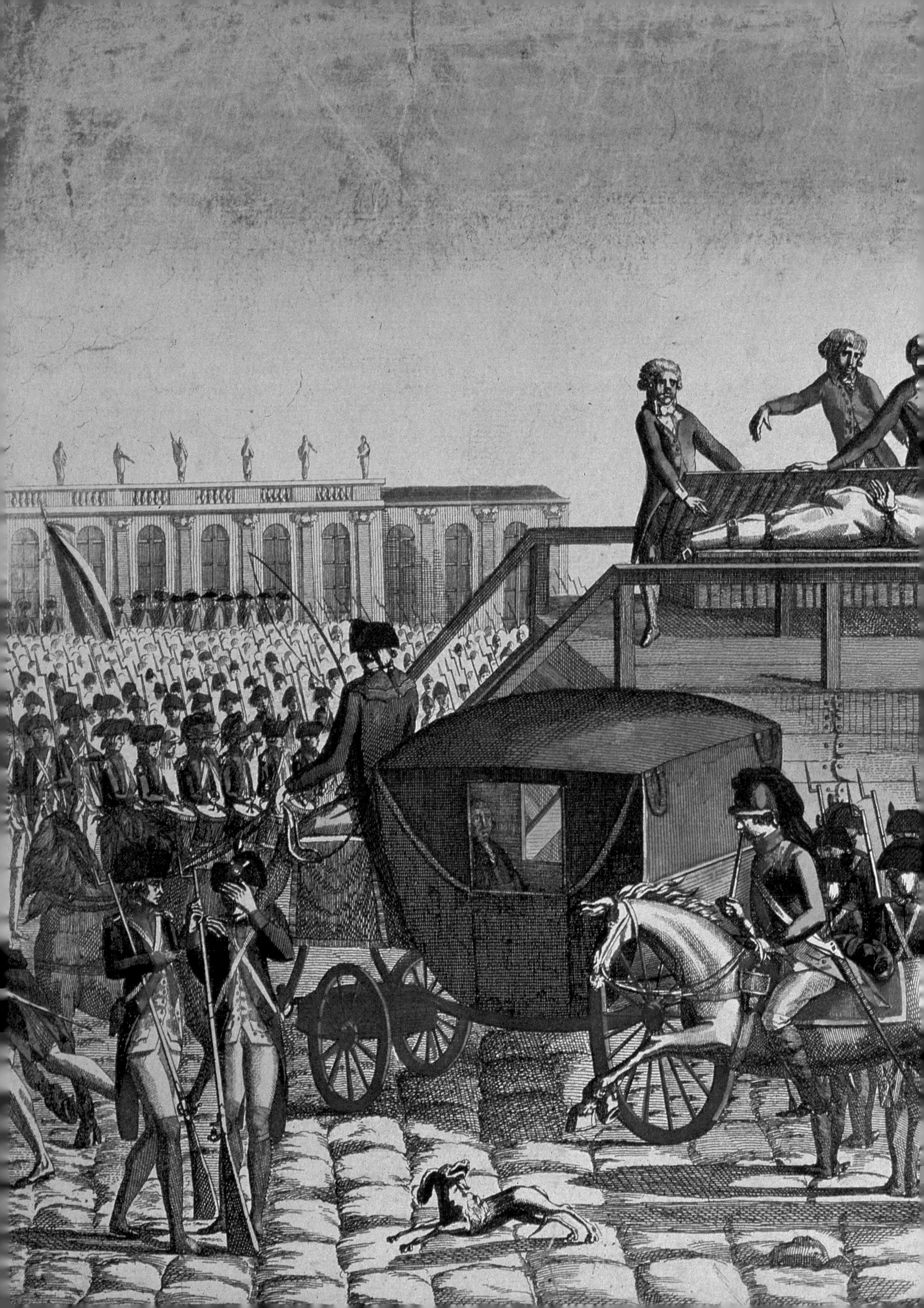

CHAPTER FIVE: 1792–1794

The Terror

The execution of Louis XVI by guillotine on 21 January 1793 led to most European states joining the war against France. The Terror was a response to the internal conflicts and the foreign pressures which threatened to stifle the infant republic. Perhaps 40,000 Frenchmen and women died at its hands, guillotined or shot, sometimes for offences as apparently insignificant as wearing a royalist cockade. Well over twice that number died in the main theatres of civil war, notably in the west. And the impact on French society as a whole affected the daily lives of millions.

(*Louis XVI's death*)

L'ABBÉ GRÉGOIRE; Certainly none of us will ever suggest that France should keep its disastrous race of kings; we know too well that all dynasties are nothing but rapacious cannibals, consuming nothing but human flesh. Those who love freedom may rest assured: this talisman will be destroyed, its magical properties will dazzle men no longer. I therefore demand that by solemn law you order the abolition of royalty.

The entire assembly rose to its feet spontaneously, and unanimously supported l'abbé Grégoire's proposal.

'The National Convention decrees the abolition of the monarchy in France.'

The shouts of delight and cries of 'Vive la nation!' from all the onlookers lasted for several minutes.

The National Convention, the new assembly which had been elected by universal manhood suffrage, replaced the Legislative Assembly on 21 September 1792 and on the same day supported l'abbé Grégoire's motion formally abolishing the monarchy. The proclamation of the Republic, as Barère recorded in his memoirs, seemed both inevitable and unpremeditated.

THIS was a matter more of inspiration than deliberation: it was accepted unanimously, without any apparent division into party, group or faction. The decree was passed without discussion or debate, on a simple motion unsupported by any exposition of the underlying motives. A Republic which had been unforeseen by the naturally subservient had become a necessity for free men. The deep and keenly felt passion for liberty which led to the 1789 revolution, the need for fresh assurances, and the indignation stirred up by the events of 10 August – the unpremeditated creation of the Republic was a product of all these factors.

The English radical Thomas Paine, famous in France for his refutation of Burke, *The Rights of Man*, was made an honorary French citizen and then elected to the Convention. In this letter to the new assembly, he formally accepted both honours.

Paris, 25 September, First Year of the Republic.
Fellow Citizens!
I receive, with affectionate gratitude, the honour which the late National Assembly has conferred on me, by adopting me a Citizen of France; and the additional honour of being elected by my fellow-citizens a Member of the National Convention.

Let us now look forward calmly and with confidence, and success is certain. It is no longer the paltry cause of kings, or of this or of that individual, that calls France and her armies into action. It is the great cause of all. It is the establishment of a new era, that shall blot despotism from the earth, and fix, on the lasting principles of peace and citizenship, the great Republic of Man.

The scene that now opens itself to France extends far beyond the boundaries of her own dominions. Every nation is becoming her ally, and every court has become her enemy. It is now the cause of all nations, against the cause of all courts.
Your Fellow Citizen, Thomas Paine.

BELOW The Convention's decree abolishing the monarchy.

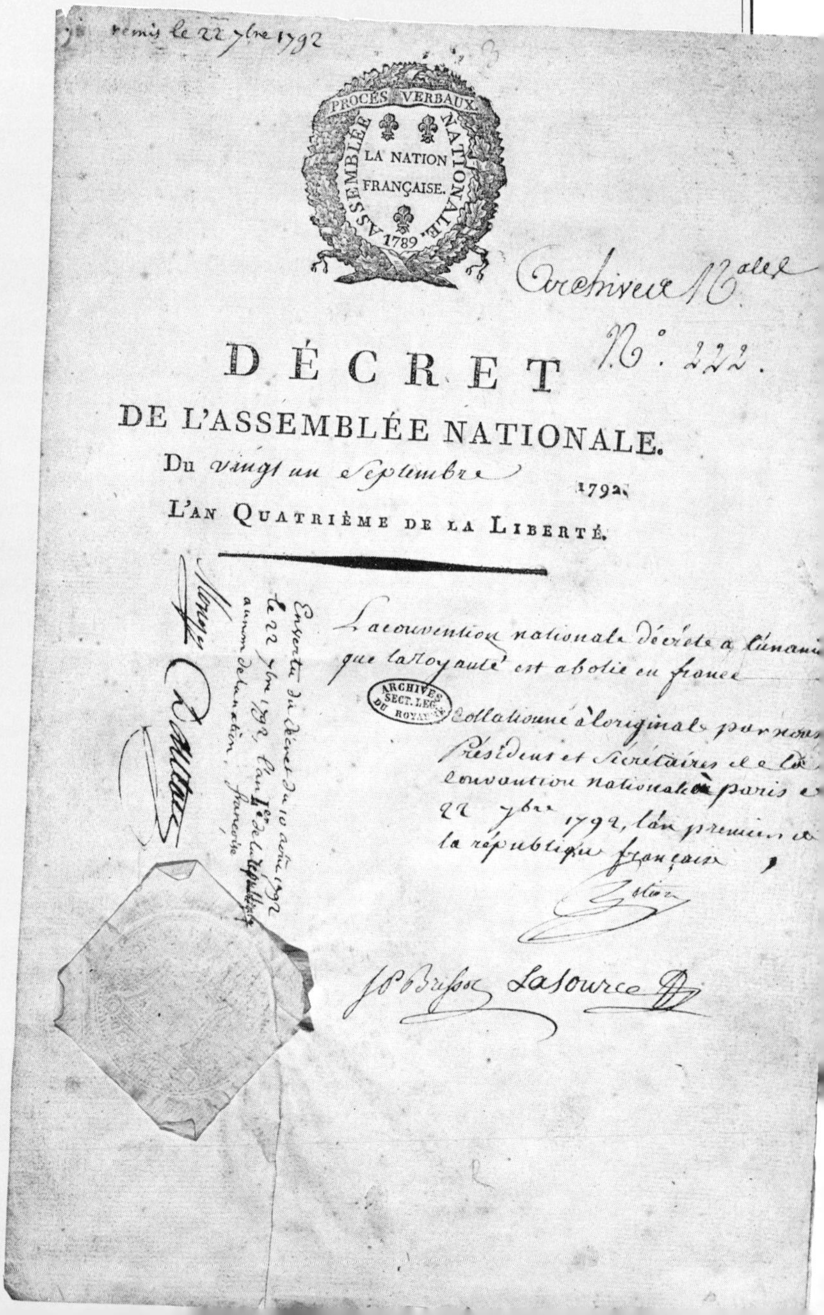
remis le 22 7bre 1792

PROCÈS VERBAUX
ASSEMBLÉE NATIONALE
LA NATION FRANÇAISE.
1789

N°. 222.

DÉCRET
DE L'ASSEMBLÉE NATIONALE.
Du vingt un Septembre 1792.
L'AN QUATRIÈME DE LA LIBERTÉ.

La convention nationale décrete a l'unanimité que la Royauté est abolie en france

Collationné à l'original par nous Président et Secrétaires de la convention nationale à paris le 22 7bre 1792, l'an premier de la république française

Lasource

Tom Paine and Revolutionary France

THOMAS Paine was probably the world's first professional revolutionary. Born in 1737, the son of an English staymaker, he grew up in a middle-class Quaker home. After a few years following his father's trade, he looked for other work. This was not a success and after two marriages, the second ending in separation, he sailed for America in late 1774.

Less than eighteen months after his arrival he became a household name when his political pamphlet *Common Sense* became an instant bestseller, and the American Revolution's most important piece of propaganda. Copies were distributed free to the patriot soldiers. Paine's work, a major influence on the Declaration of Independence, attacked both monarchy and aristocracy as useless, and argued that America ought to be a free and independent republic.

Paine viewed the French Revolution as perpetuating the ideals of the American Revolution – ideals which he expected to help reform his own British government. He hoped that liberal Whig politicians such as Edmund Burke – who had supported Paine and the American cause – would use events in France to push for political reform in England. When Burke published a savage attack on the French Revolution in 1790, Paine picked up his pen to present a defence of Paris.

The Rights of Man was published in two parts, the first in February 1791, the second a year later. Although it makes a strong case against Burke, each part was written under different political circumstances, and each reflects slightly different political ideas. In Part I, Paine defended Louis XVI on the grounds that he was the legitimate king of France's new constitutional monarchy – a far cry from the stridently republican position of *Common Sense*. However, by the time Part II was published, Louis had tried to flee France, and was no longer co-operating with the Revolution. Part I, therefore, advocates a liberal constitutional monarchy, while Part II makes it clear that the only legitimate form of government is a democratic republic. In addition, the last half of Part II focuses on dramatic and original programmes that presage 20th-century social welfare: a progressive income tax to support old age pension insurance, unemployment benefit, a negative tax for the poor, and state education for all children.

Paine's pamphlet sold over 200,000 copies, making him the century's best-selling political author, and his fame was such that on 26 August 1792 the Legislative Assembly accorded him, along with 17 others including Jeremy Bentham, William Wilberforce, Schiller and George Washington, honorary French citizenship for 'courageously maintaining the cause of freedom'.

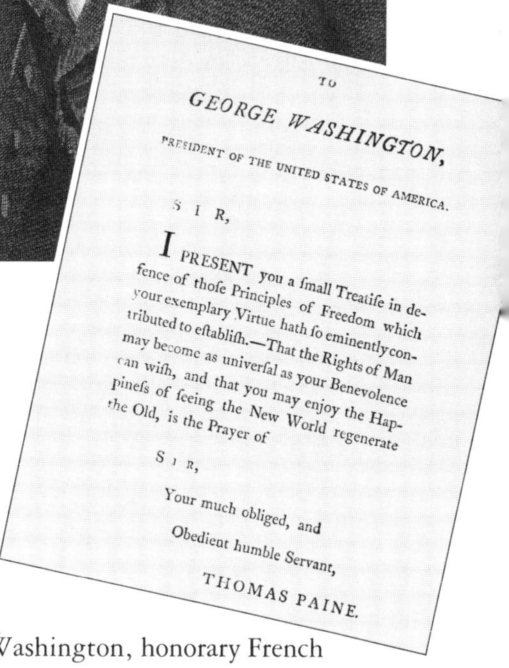
TO

GEORGE WASHINGTON,

PRESIDENT OF THE UNITED STATES OF AMERICA.

SIR,

I PRESENT you a fmall Treatife in defence of thofe Principles of Freedom which your exemplary Virtue hath fo eminently contributed to eftablifh.—That the Rights of Man may become as univerfal as your Benevolence can wifh, and that you may enjoy the Happinefs of feeing the New World regenerate the Old, is the Prayer of

SIR,

Your much obliged, and

Obedient humble Servant,

THOMAS PAINE.

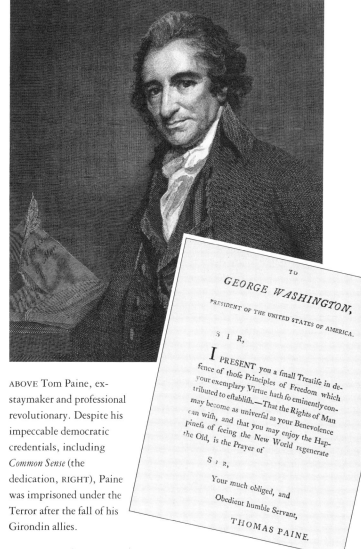

ABOVE Tom Paine, ex-staymaker and professional revolutionary. Despite his impeccable democratic credentials, including *Common Sense* (the dedication, RIGHT), Paine was imprisoned under the Terror after the fall of his Girondin allies.

The following month, three departments elected him to the Convention: he chose to sit for the Pas-de-Calais. In the chamber he was generally identified as a Girondin, although his contribution was limited by the fact that he spoke no French. When he voted in writing on the king's fate, he urged that Louis be imprisoned until the end of the war, and then banished from France for life. His attendance in the Convention became increasingly infrequent, especially after his Girondin friends were purged on 2 June 1793.

Thomas Paine was arrested in December, but escaped the guillotine and was released after the fall of Robespierre. Although he occasionally reappeared on the French political scene he was a spent force. He returned to the United States in 1802 and died there in 1809.

The Scottish physician John Moore, visiting Paris, wrote home describing the change in mores the declaration of the Republic appeared to have wrought.

There is in Paris at present a great affectation of that plainness in dress, and simplicity of expression, which are supposed to belong to republicans. I have sometimes been in the company, since I came last to Paris, of a young man belonging to one of the first families in France who, contrary to the wishes and example of his relations, is a violent democrat. He came into my box last night at the playhouse; he was in boots, his hair cropped, and his whole dress slovenly; on this being taken notice of, he said that he was accustoming himself to appear like a republican. It reminded me of a lady who, being reproached with having a very ugly man for her lover, said, 'It is in order to get used to the ugliness of my husband.'

People are saying 'tu', or thou, to each other. They have substituted the name Citizen for Monsieur, when talking to or of any person; but more frequently, particularly in the National Assembly, they simply use the name, as Buzot, Guadet, Vergniaud. It has even been proposed in some of the newspapers that the custom of taking off the hat and bowing the head should be abolished, as remains of the ancient slavery, and unbecoming the independent spirit of free men; instead of which they are desired, on meeting their acquaintance in the street, to place their right hand on their heart as a sign of cordiality.

David, the celebrated painter, who is a member of the Convention and a zealous republican, has sketched some designs for a republican dress, which he seems eager to have introduced.

The *bonnet rouge* was back in fashion, and somewhat mocked by Ruault in one of his letters to his brother.

Paris, 28 October 1792. I invite you to come and look at Paris now that it is republican, to count the cannon shots fired on the Tuileries that famous 10th of August, to see the palace's magnificent colonnades riddled with gunfire. You will find changes too in Parisian customs and dress: the red cap of liberty is back in favour. All the Jacobins are wearing it – apart from Robespierre; it would disturb his carefully curled and powdered locks. I follow Robespierre's example, even though I don't have my hair curled over my ears. I consider that a red, or white, or grey, cap is only suited to those who have laboured to build the Revolution.

A Revolutionary fashion

DURING the Revolution trends in fashion inspired by the Enlightenment in the 1770s and 1780s – long before the fall of the Bastille – developed and were modified, leading to a freedom and democratization of dress which was indeed revolutionary.

ABOVE David's design for a republican citizen's costume.

By 1790 women had largely abandoned paniers (skirt hoops) and most of the padding that built out their rumps. A simple loose-waisted gown in white muslin or other light fabric was the most fashionable garment, and flatter, natural curls replaced the elaborate, towering coiffures of the *ancien régime*.

Men wore plain, close-fitting suits regardless of class – or occasion. These fashions owed much to England, where polite society was dominated by the landed gentry, whose concern with rural, domestic pursuits had encouraged the development of more practical, country-inspired clothing as early as the 1750s.

In the 1780s, for ordinary day wear, the French man of fashion also adopted a plain frock or riding coat, short waistcoat and high leather boots, in imitation of his English counterpart. 'A l'anglaise' became synonymous with chic.

ABOVE Philippe d'Orléans and his son dressed *à l'anglaise*.

After the overthrow of the monarchy in 1792 court dress was suppressed until Bonaparte's rise to power. Hair powder was left off soon after 1790. Although Robespierre never dropped the fashion, powdered wigs came to be regarded as symbols of the aristocracy and powdering in general was viewed as anti-social: flour could be used to feed the people.

Simplicity in dress became an expression of progressive politics, and erstwhile reactionaries tempered what they wore with a judicious sobriety. The use of the national colours added a contemporary note: patriots devised blue suits trimmed with red and white, and wore coat-buttons decorated with patriotic devices.

In 1793 the Committee of Public Safety invited David, painter and propagandist of the Revolution, to recommend improvements to the national dress, to make it more appropriate to republicanism and the character of the Revolution.

He suggested uniforms based on classical tunics and togas for all state officials and citizens, but despite the enthusiasm of a few fellow artists, the costume remained a political fancy.

The relief and release after the Reign of Terror resulted in a short period of wild eccentricity in the way young people dressed.

In Paris, the carefully negligent air of the Englishman's country dress developed into deliberate scruffiness, and 'sick humour' prevailed.

A red ribbon around the throat or a 'ceinture à la Victime' were too funny for words, as was hair cropped to resemble the shorn heads of those condemned to the guillotine. Women's dress began to reflect the contemporary taste for the antique, already evident in architecture and interior decoration. Their bodies were revealed in a manner unknown for centuries and, for a short time, they enjoyed a freedom of movement which was in perfect harmony with the prevailing moral freedom.

The first major issue members of the Convention had to confront was the fate of Louis XVI. This account of the life of the royal family in the Temple prison at the opening of the National Convention is by Cléry, the king's valet-de-chambre.

THE king usually rose at 6 o'clock in the morning. He shaved himself, I did his hair and dressed him. He then immediately retired to his study. Since this room was very small, the guard remained in the bedroom, with the door ajar so that the king was always within his sight. His Majesty knelt and prayed for 5 to 6 minutes, and then read until 9 o'clock. During this time, after having cleaned his room and set the table for breakfast, I went down to the queen's apartment; she would open the door only when I arrived, to prevent the guard from entering the room. I would dress the young prince, do the queen's hair, and perform the same service for the Princess Royal and Mme Elisabeth in their rooms. At 9 o'clock, the queen, her children and Mme Elisabeth went up to the king's room for breakfast.

At 10 o'clock the king and his family would go down to the queen's apartments and spend the day there. The king, who had taken his son's education in charge, would make him recite passages from Corneille and Racine and give him geography lessons, making him practise colouring in maps. The king was showing him the new geography of France. Meanwhile the queen instructed her daughter. These various lessons lasted until 11 o'clock. The rest of the morning was spent sewing, knitting or doing tapestry. At midday the three princesses went to Mme Elisabeth's room to remove their morning clothes: no guards went in with them.

At 1 o'clock, if the weather was good, the royal family went out into the garden accompanied by four municipal guards officers and one legion chief of the National Guard. I was allowed to join them on these outings; I would play with the young prince – ball, quoits, running races or other games. At 2 o'clock we returned to the tower in the Temple prison for lunch, which I served.

After the meal, the royal family went to the queen's apartments, where their majesties usually played a game of piquet or backgammon. At 4 o'clock, the king would rest for a while, the princesses around him, each with a book in her hands: a profound silence reigned during the king's rest.

At the end of the day, the royal family would sit around a table; the queen read aloud from history books or other books selected to either inform or amuse her children. Often, by chance, situations were described which bore a close resemblance to their own and this would give rise to painful thoughts.

At 9 o'clock the king had his own supper, after which he would go up to the queen's apartments for a short while, bid her and his sister goodnight, and embrace his children. Then he returned to his apartment and retired to his study, where he read until midnight. The queen and the princesses retired to their own rooms.

Mailhe, reporting to the National Convention in the name of the Legislation Committee in November 1792, won assent for the following points concerning the king's trial.

5 NOVEMBER 1792.

Louis XVI is to be brought to trial;
He is to be tried by the National Convention;
Three commissioners from the Convention will be responsible for gathering all items, information and evidence relevant to Louis XVI's alleged crimes;
The commissioners will draw up the detailed statement of the crimes of which Louis XVI will stand accused;
The National Convention will name the day on which Louis XVI is to appear before it.

Thibaudeau, one of the deputies of the unaligned Plain, recorded in his memoirs how the discovery of the *armoire de fer* in the Tuileries palace containing secret royal correspondence made matters look even bleaker for the king.

THE discovery of the *armoire de fer*, an iron chest hidden in the thickness of a substantial wall in the Tuileries palace, helped to hasten the sentencing of Louis XVI. Some of the items found in it were used against him at his trial; others revealed the treachery of some deputies who, while displaying the greatest enthusiasm for national freedom, were accepting gold to obtain its enslavement.

All these items were published and distributed. The Minister of the Interior, Monsieur Roland, was asked to make public the contents of the chest.

The armoire de fer – skeletons in the cupboard

THE *armoire de fer* caused controversy from the moment its existence was disclosed by Gamain, a locksmith who claimed to have installed it at Louis XVI's request in May 1792. An opportunist, he waited until the king's fall was inevitable and then, in November 1792, took his story to Heurtier, Inspector-General of National Buildings. Heurtier made Gamain repeat his account to the Minister of the Interior, Roland, and the three men set off for the Tuileries palace where Gamain removed a wooden panel in the wall to reveal an iron plate. Inside the iron chest (*armoire de fer*) that it covered were bundles of papers.

Roland immediately informed the Convention of the discovery, commented on its probable significance and called for a Commission to catalogue the papers, which, it was widely assumed, would incriminate the king and prove that he had betrayed the nation. But the harmonious opening of the Convention had given way to factional struggle between the increasingly moderate Girondins and more radical Montagnards, and Roland unwittingly played right into the hands of his enemies.

As Girondin Minister of the Interior he should have been careful to authenticate the opening of the *armoire de fer*. As it was, the only witnesses were Gamain and Heurtier, one an informer and the other Roland's protégé. The minister's Montagnard opponents claimed that he had examined the documents beforehand and removed material that incriminated his political allies, perhaps even inserting false evidence against Montagnard leaders. Montagnard deputies took up these accusations and asked why he had dealt with the matter personally rather than referring it to the existing committees investigating the Tuileries. Although Roland had taken the documents directly to the Convention, he had no real defence against such attacks, and when the relatively harmless nature of the papers emerged the Montagnards were able to insinuate that he might have removed documents in order to protect the king.

This episode was peculiarly damaging to the Girondin ministry at a time when it was already under suspicion of trying to delay a judgement in the king's trial, and it was instrumental in discrediting Roland. The affair undoubtedly persuaded him to retire from politics – he resigned on 22 January 1793, the day after the king's execution. The *armoire de fer* also played a vital role in the factional struggle at the heart of the Revolution over the winter of 1792-3, lending support to the Montagnards' accusations that the Girondins were politically dishonest.

The Commission appointed to catalogue the *armoire de fer* papers was expected to prove Louis' guilt in time for his trial in December. However, the documents were of little use and, although some were used in evidence against the king, the *armoire* itself was hardly mentioned. Although it had contained papers which Louis hoped to preserve, it yielded no systematic record of his anti-revolutionary activities. The *armoire* was an archive in which the king kept details of the royal household as well as reports on royal policy during the Revolution. Some documents discredited figures like Mirabeau, Dumouriez and Lafayette, but the archive as a whole was not as useful to the prosecution as had been expected.

The *armoire de fer*'s main value to the Jacobins was as propaganda to discredit the king at a time when public opinion was divided over his fate. Its contents and what they said about his attitude to the Revolution were less important than the symbolic use that could be made of images of secrecy and deception. Popular prints reinforced this view of guilt by association.

For the king's enemies, the *armoire de fer* – in spite of its insignificant contents – could not have been discovered at a better time.

BELOW Engraving of the opening of the *armoire de fer*. The skeleton is that of Mirabeau, one of the people discredited by the chest's contents, holding a bag of gold and a crown.

Louis' trial in the Convention began on 12 December, as M. de Kolly, a royalist in Paris, wrote to his wife.

Paris, Wednesday, 12 December 1792.

My dear Fanny, I anticipated yesterday as a day much to be feared, because the former king was being taken to the National Convention; I was afraid that it would be a truly lethal occasion.

In the event everything went off very peacefully.

The people watched unemotionally as Louis Capet was transferred and interrogated as a criminal. He had great difficulty in accepting this, and had to be threatened with being dragged before the Convention; and he had to be almost torn from the arms of his wife, his sister and his children.

At half past six he was brought back to the Temple prison: this seems to imply that matters will take longer than expected, particularly as his replies yield little to incriminate him.

Louis stonewalled or played the injured innocent through most of his cross-examination in the Convention, as these extracts show.

INTERROGATION of Louis Capet.
The President: The French nation accuses you, Louis, of a multitude of crimes to establish your tyranny, thereby destroying liberty. On 20 June 1789 you attacked the sovereignty of the people by suspending their representatives' assembly and by the use of troops to remove them from their session. You made an army march against the citizens of Paris, and you only withdrew this army when the capture of the Bastille indicated that the people were victorious, and the massacres at the Tuileries speak out against you. What have you to say in reply?
Louis: I was responsible for the movement of troops at that time, but I never intended any bloodshed.
The President: At the Fête de la Fédération of 14 July 1790 you swore an oath to the constitution which you have not kept. Soon thereafter you tried to corrupt the will of the people. What have you to say in reply?
Louis: I do not remember what happened at the time; but it all took place before I accepted the constitution.
The President: On 14 September 1791 you pretended to accept the constitution; your speech proclaimed your intention of upholding it, yet you were working for its overthrow even before it was complete: a treaty had been drawn up at Pillnitz on 24 July between Leopold of Austria and Frederick-William of Prussia, who

The trial of Louis XVI

THE problem of what to do with Louis XVI rested on the question of whether the king of France could be tried. There was no right answer. The constitution of 1791 protected the monarch from any penalty worse than dethronement, and no court in the land had legitimate jurisdiction over him. Yet Robespierre's argument that a trial was unnecessary was generally rejected: Louis could not be condemned unheard. With no other alternative before them, the Convention took on the role of a court. In most respects this was contrary to accepted judicial principles; but it was expedient, and there seemed no other viable course.

Louis' defence centred on his rights under the constitution and the illegality of the institution trying him. Constitutionally his case was unassailable – provided only he could convince the deputies that he had honestly intended to become a constitutional monarch. The evasiveness of many of his replies under cross-examination did not inspire confidence that he

had so intended. By ordinary standards his trial was illegal, as the defence ably argued; but the Convention had absolute powers, and this changed the terms of the discussion. It was inconceivable that the king could be allowed to commit treason with impunity. If deputies found him guilty, the legal penalty was death, and the only way of averting this was to place politics above justice. To allow Louis to live would undermine the principle of revolutionary justice, but relieve the consciences of those who doubted the Convention's right to act as a court.

Paris was hostile to the king and the issues of the trial were avidly discussed in clubs and sections, who brought pressure to bear on the Convention. From late December the Girondins urged a nation-wide referendum, to shift responsibility and remove any suspicion of Parisian intimidation. Most deputies rejected this *appel au peuple*, since it seemed likely to promote civil war.

For the participants the trial was traumatic and dangerous. In the venomous debates in the Convention the right classed all Parisians as *septembriseurs*, radical supporters of street violence, and all those favouring regicide as tainted by bloodlust. Those in favour of executing the king accused their opponents of royalism, a deadly insult to men whose true concern was Parisian extremism or who were opposed in principle to capital punishment, as Robespierre had been in the past. All the deputies knew they were risking their lives; the anti-regicides remembered the September massacres, the regicides feared royalist vengeance. Yet few abstained from voting, and changes of direction continued until the end of the debate. At the first vote, the 693 deputies present unanimously voted Louis guilty and the call for a referendum was rejected by 424 to 283. The death penalty was carried 387 to 334. Seventy-two deputies asked for a reprieve, but an extra vote saw their demand rejected by 380 to 310. On each occasion deputies answered individually to their names. The process spread over five days. On 21 January 1793, Louis was driven through troop-lined streets to the guillotine.

Ultimately, the debate over the referendum, which represented an attempt to overrule the demands of the radicals in Paris, proved more important politically than the king's death: the Girondins failed to recognize its potential dangers and widened the breach with the capital by consistently equating Parisian politicians with the September massacres, rather than with the sacrifices of the overthrow of the monarchy on 10 August. Supporters of the referendum became targets of the *sans-culottes*.

In the Convention, the defeat of the referendum was a disaster for the Girondins, who never reasserted their claim to leadership. Although it was increasingly likely that *sans-culottes* would see the Girondins as counter-revolutionaries, the Convention would not tolerate outside interference with its membership. This impasse was a legacy of January 1793.

OPPOSITE A portrait of Louis XVI imprisoned in the Temple.

BELOW Souvenirs of the royal family's captivity in the Temple, including the king's shaving bowl.

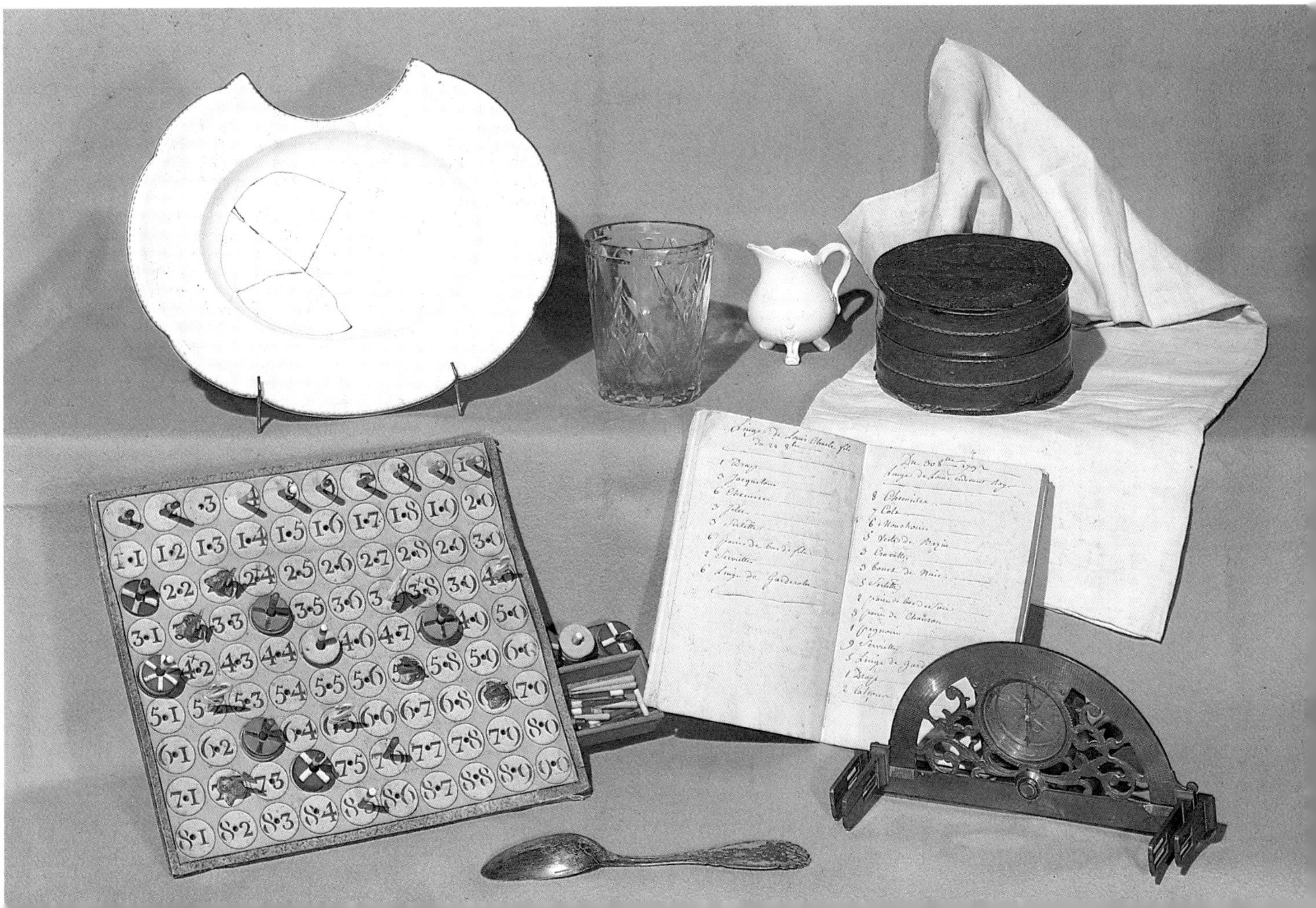

undertook to restore absolute monarchy in France; you said nothing of this treaty until it became known throughout Europe. What have you to say in reply?
Louis: I made it known as soon as it came to my knowledge; apart from that, everything concerning this matter is constitutionally the concern of the ministers.
The President: Your brothers are enemies of the state and have rallied emigrants to their banners; they have raised regiments, taken out loans and contracted alliances in your name; you did not repudiate them until you were absolutely certain that you could in no way interfere with their plans.
Louis: I repudiated all my brothers' activities, as instructed by the constitution, as soon as I knew of them.
The President: In Paris you had secret groups to undertake operations which would help your counter-revolutionary plans. What have you to say in reply?
Louis: I have no knowledge whatever of such plans: the idea of counter-revolution never entered my head.
The President: You were responsible for the shedding of French blood on 10 August 1792. What have you to say in reply?
Louis: No, Sir, it was not I.
The President: Did you have an iron chest built in the Tuileries palace, and did you hide papers in it?
Louis: I have no knowledge of it.

After unanimously voting the king's guilt, the Convention went on to sentence him. The Girondins favoured a referendum on the issue, or to delay the final decision on the matter; the Montagnards wanted immediate execution; the moderates of the Plain wavered. The decision was an individual one, however, and the statement each deputy had to make before his peers remains one of the most dramatic moments of the Revolution.

VERGNIAUD (Gironde – Girondin): I voted that the decree or verdict of the National Convention should be put to the people for approval. The National Convention decided otherwise. I obey; my conscience is clear. It is now a matter of ruling on Louis' punishment. The law says death, but as I utter this terrible word I fear for the fate of my country, the dangers which threaten even freedom, and all the blood which may be shed.
Guadet (Gironde – Girondin): Louis is guilty of conspiring against liberty and the general security of the state. I have only to look at the penal code to see the death penalty there; but I demand the Convention's permission to consider whether the verdict should be carried out immediately, or delayed. I vote, provisionally, for death.
Gensonné (Gironde – Girondin): I vote for the application of the penalty for conspiracy. But so as to prove to Europe and the entire world that we are not the passive tools of one faction, I vote that you command the Ministry of Justice to bring the murderers of 2 September 1792 to justice.
Lacaze (Gironde – Girondin): Citizens, Louis has spilt much blood; but will not this war which he has brought upon us shed much more? Should we not use Louis' life to prevent it? From the depths of my conscience I vote for imprisonment until there is peace, and until such time as the foreign powers have recognized the republic; and then for exile.
Garrau (Gironde – Montagnard): Citizens, Louis is convicted of conspiracy against national safety. The statute book shows the death penalty for all conspirators; I vote for death.
Cambon (Hérault – Montagnard): The will of the whole French nation is perfectly clear: to abolish all privilege. Today I am to pass judgement on one of the privileged who has been convicted of treason, and I would consider myself guilty under national justice if I restricted myself to deportation. I vote for death.
Cambacérès (Hérault – Plain): In my opinion the National Convention should decree that Louis has incurred the penalties for conspiracy, but it should suspend execution of the decree until the cessation of hostilities. Until that time he should remain in prison; if the enemies of the republic should invade French territory, the decree should be carried out.
Lanjuinais (Ille-et-Vilaine – Girondin): As an individual I would vote for the death of Louis; but as legislator, mindful only of the nation's welfare and the interests of freedom, I vote for imprisonment until the restoration of peace, and then for exile, under pain of death if he should return to France.
Amar (Isère – Montagnard): Louis has been found guilty of assault on the general security of the nation, and of conspiring against freedom; his existence is odious, his death is necessary to consolidate a Revolution to which he will always be opposed. I am resolved for his death.
Dartigoëyte (Landes – Montagnard): As a judge, I must avenge the blood of citizens spilt by the orders of the tyrant; as a statesman, I must do what seems in the best interests of the republic: I myself fear the

return of tyranny if Louis lives. I vote for his immediate death.
Chabot (Loire – Montagnard): I vote for death because Louis was, and still is, a tyrant, and because he may act as such again. I vote for death.
Fouché (Loire-Inférieure – Montagnard): Death.
Jean-Bon Saint-André (Lot – Montagnard): Any nation which has sought freedom has achieved it only through the death of tyrants. I vote for death.
Drouet (Marne – Montagnard): Louis has conspired against the state. He opened the gates of the kingdom to our enemies. I condemn him to death.
Anacharsis Cloots (Oise – Montagnard): Louis is guilty of *lèse-majesté*. How should his crimes be punished? In the name of humanity I answer, death.
Robespierre (Paris – Montagnard) (from a long speech): I am no lover of long speeches on obvious matters; they augur ill for freedom. I vote for death.
Danton (Paris – Montagnard): One must never compromise with tyrants. One can only strike at kings through the head; nothing can be expected from European kings except by force of arms. I vote for the death of the tyrant.
Billaud-Varennes (Paris – Montagnard): Death within twenty-four hours.
Marat (Paris – Montagnard): From my profound conviction that Louis is the principal protagonist behind the spilling of so much blood on 10 August, and all the killing which has disfigured France since the Revolution, I vote for the tyrant's death within twenty-four hours.
Legendre (Paris – Montagnard): Since the Revolution I have devoted myself to hunting down tyrants. I vote for death. I respect the opinion of my colleagues who have voted for a different penalty, through political considerations. It is this same policy which makes me vote for death.
David (Paris – Montagnard): Death.
Philippe Egalité (formerly the duc d'Orléans) (Paris – Montagnard): In my conviction that all those who have attacked the sovereignty of the people deserve death, I vote for death.
Thomas Paine (Pas-de-Calais – Gironde): I vote that Louis be imprisoned until the end of the war, and exiled for life thereafter.
Barère (Hautes-Pyrénées – Montagnard): The law proclaims death, and I am here as a servant of the law.
Creuzé-Latouche (Vienne – Plain): It seems unfortunate to me that those who create the law are able to command a man's death. I vote for prison until peace and then exile.
Thibaudeau (Vienne – Plain): I vote for death.
Jean Debry (Aisne – Montagnard): Until the very moment when I stepped up to this desk I was in doubt; my unease is coming to an end. You have made me a judge, I have consulted the law, the inexorable law tells me Death: I speak for the law, for death.
Saint-Just (Aisne – Montagnard): Since Louis XVI was the enemy of his people and their freedom and their happiness, I vote for death.
Lakanal (Ariège – Plain): A true republican needs few words. The motives for my decision are here (gesturing with his hand towards his heart); I vote for death.
Brissot (Eure-et-Loir – Girondin) (from a long speech): I vote for death, the sentence to be suspended until the constitution has been ratified by the people.

Voting in the Convention on the king's sentence.

16-17 JANUARY : What penalty should be suffered by Louis, former king of the French?

361: death
26: death, but with consideration for a reprieve
288: imprisonment, detention, banishment
28: absent

19 January: Should there be a reprieve in carrying out the verdict on Louis Capet?

310: yes
380: no

The formal verdict was pronounced on 20 January 1793.

THE National Convention declares Louis Capet, last king of the French, guilty of conspiracy against national liberty and of assault against national security.

The National Convention decrees that Louis Capet must suffer the death penalty.

THE MASSACHUSETTS MAGAZINE (Boston) *February 1793*

In the letter which Mr. Paine has addressed to the people of France, he visibly inclines towards mercy, which he supplicated for the unfortunate Monarch; but his opinion and wishes will have little weight with an enraged democracy.

The Irish priest abbé Edgeworth, Louis' confessor, recorded the king's last hours.

DAWN was breaking, and already the drums beat the alert throughout Paris. From 7 to 8 o'clock, many people under various pretexts knocked on the door of the king's study where I was closeted with him, and each time I trembled lest it be the last; but the king would rise without emotion, go to the door and calmly answer those who came to interrupt him.

Finally someone knocked at the door for the last time: it was Santerre and his troop. The king opened the door again and was informed that the time had come for him to face death. 'I am busy,' he told them with authority; 'wait for me there, I shall be with you in a while.' As he said this, he closed the door and threw himself at my feet. 'The end has come,' he said. 'Father, give me your final blessing, and pray God to uphold me to the end.'

Soon he rose and, leaving his study, went towards the group standing in the middle of the bedroom. Their faces reflecting complete confidence, they were all still wearing their hats. The king noticing this, asked for his own to be brought to him.

'Is there a member of the Commune among you?' he asked. 'I wish to entrust him with delivering this document.' This was his Will, which someone came forward and took from the king. 'I wish to commend to the Commune my valet Cléry, whose services I cannot praise enough. Be sure that he is given my watch and all my effects here, as well as those in the keeping of the Commune; I also wish that, as a sign of my gratitude for his loyalty, he should enter the queen's, my wife's, service.' (The king used both those words.) The king then said firmly, 'Let us go.'

THE MASSACHUSETTS MAGAZINE (Boston) *April 1793*

The last will of Louis XVI breathes an unaffected air of humility and contribution, which misfortunes alone can effect. The sentiments it contains are worthy of the Christian and the man of sentiment.

The minutes of the Convention on 21 January, as news was brought of the execution of the monarch.

21 JANUARY 1793. The Executive Council addressed to the National Convention an affidavit describing the execution of Louis Capet.

The assembly continued with its routine business.

The royalist Bernard's account of the execution of Louis XVI

Paris, 23 January 1793, Wednesday morning. My dearest mother, I commend to you the spirit of the lamented Louis XVI. He lost his life on Monday, at half past ten in the morning, and to the very last he maintained the greatest possible courage.

He wished to speak to the people from the scaffold, but was interrupted by a drum-roll and was seized by the executioners, who were following their orders, and who pushed him straight under the fatal blade. He was able to speak only these words, in a very strong voice: 'I forgive my enemies; I trust that my death will be for the happiness of my people, but I grieve for France and I fear that she may suffer the anger of the Lord.'

The king took off his coat himself at the foot of the scaffold, and when someone sought to help him he said cheerfully, 'I do not need any help.' He also refused help to climb on to the scaffold, and went up with a firm, brisk step. The executioner wanted to cut his hair; he refused, saying that it was not necessary. But on the scaffold the executioner tied his hands behind his back (this was when the king spoke to the people), and then cut his hair.

After his death his body and head were immediately taken to the parish cemetery and thrown into a pit fifteen feet deep, where they were consumed by quicklime. And so there remains nothing of this unhappy prince except the memory of his virtues and of his misfortune.

Bernard

RIGHT The king's last moments, which he met with a fortitude that contrasted favourably with his previous inadequacy.

Following a diplomatic crisis caused by France's occupation of the Low Countries, and heightened by the execution of Louis XVI, on 1 February 1793, France declared war on Britain and the Netherlands. Within a few months, the Republic would be at war with virtually the whole of Europe.

THE National Convention declares, in the name of the French nation, that in view of multifarious acts of hostility and aggression, the republic of France is at war with the king of England and the stadtholder of the United Provinces [the Netherlands].

In England, the war against republican France took on the character of a crusade in defence of the British constitution. From a speech made in the House of Commons by the Prime Minister, William Pitt, on 11 March 1793.

MANY are the motives which have induced us to enter into the war. I have heard of wars of honour. On the present occasion, whatever can raise the feelings, or animate the exertions of a people, concur to prompt us to the contest: the contempt which the French have shown for a neutrality, on our part most strictly observed; the violations of their solemn and plighted faith; their presumptuous attempts to interfere in the government of this country, and to arm our subjects against ourselves; to vilify a monarch, the object of our gratitude, reverence and affection; and to separate the court from the people, by representing them as influenced by different motives, and acting from different interests. After provocation so wanton, so often repeated, and so highly aggravated, does not this become, on our part, a war of honour, a war necessary to assert the spirit of the nation and the dignity of the British name?

I have heard of wars undertaken for the general security of Europe; was it ever so threatened as by the progress of the French arms?

I have heard of wars for the defence of the Protestant religion: our enemies in this instance are equally the enemies of all religion – and desirous to propagate, everywhere, by the force of their arms, that system of infidelity which they avow in their principles.

I have heard of wars undertaken in defence of the lawful succession; but now we fight in defence of our hereditary monarchy. We are at war with those who would destroy the whole fabric of our constitution.

> THE TIMES (London), *26 January 1793*
>
> The present moment is of all others the most favourable for DECLARING WAR against FRANCE. It has been perhaps a matter of sound policy to delay this declaration to the present moment; and we will venture to say, that no war was ever undertaken with the more general concurrence of the people, than that in which we are about to engage.

To face up to the armies of *ancien régime* Europe, the Convention of 24 February decreed the so-called *levée des 300,000 hommes*.

THE National Convention calls for three hundred thousand men to join the forces of the Republic as soon as possible.

The military call-up triggered off resistance, especially in western France, where civil war was soon raging in the department of the Vendée. This account, written by a peasant on 21 March, brings out the religious element in popular resistance which was soon prominent.

GENTLEMEN and brothers. The inhabitants of Thouaré-sur-Loire may have taken up arms, but only because they were forced to it. On Monday the 11th of this month the rebel bands began to assemble. The inhabitants had no intention of revolting because they are too peaceful for such an enterprise. The young men simply wanted to hold an assembly to agree not to send men to the national army. They were all gathered together on the Nantes road when they heard the news that a troop of the National Guard was on its way from Nantes: imagining that they were coming to seize them by force and since practically none was armed, they all rushed about, seized weapons wherever they could find them and gathered at Mauves, where unfortunately there was bloodshed. But since then the parish has been pretty quiet.

In addition, the decree on religious freedom is one of the principles of the revolt, because the people consider that to give them priests whom they do not want is a denial of freedom. Everyone is demanding the return of the non-juring priests, and the people are offering to pay them. This demand comes from the ordinary citizens and aristocrats alike – they all wish for agreement and perfect harmony. If this had been done more swiftly there would have been no revolt, and plenty of volunteers.

William Pitt and the First Coalition

WILLIAM Pitt tried to distance Britain from the French Revolution. When war broke out between France and Austria in April 1792 he declared neutrality; as late as 6 November, Lord Grenville, his Foreign Secretary, told the ambassador to Britain's Dutch ally that 'this country and Holland ought to remain quiet as long as it is possible to do so.' On the same day, however, the French, under the command of General Dumouriez, won the battle of Jemappes and soon overran the Austrian Netherlands (Belgium); Britain was forced off the fence. A fundamental clash of interests developed between revolutionary France's desire to expand towards the Rhine, its natural defensive frontier, and the British fear that this would provide her with a launching-point from which to extend her influence over western Europe. When the French government refused to give ground, Pitt and Grenville regarded war as inevitable. To put France in the wrong, they provoked her into declaring war on Britain, which she did on 1 February 1793.

Although some people in Britain regarded the conflict as a horrible mistake – Charles Fox bitterly attacked an alliance with continental despots against the cause of liberty – the vast majority felt that France had become anarchic, and was seeking to extend that anarchy all across Europe.

Britain entered the war to find France's opponents shaken by their 1792 reverses and in disarray. Pitt set out to bring them together and, in the words of his Minister of War, Henry Dundas, 'to bring down every Power on earth to assist them against France'. In the course of 1793, Pitt and Grenville negotiated the basis of the First Coalition against France. To their alliance with Holland they added agreements with Russia (March), Piedmont (April), Spain (May), Naples and Prussia (July), Austria (August) and Portugal (September). The signatories pledged that they would not make peace until France had restored to their original owners all the territories she had gained, and promised naval support for a vigorous maritime blockade of France.

Pitt declared that his aim in waging war was 'indemnity for the past and security for the future'. Britain hoped to secure a permanent maritime advantage over France by seizing its East and West Indian possessions; it was prepared to support its allies' territorial acquisitions from mainland France; and it sought to defeat the belligerent French Republic by military invasion while encouraging royalist insurrection from within.

ABOVE William Pitt, architect of European opposition to France.

Internal subversion of the Revolution by the agents of Pitt and Coburg (leader of the largest allied army) became a major republican fear, and 'Pitt's gold' was believed to be the mainstay of the counter-revolution. However, although British subsidies helped sustain the war effort, the amounts were smaller than the revolutionaries believed and little reached the royalists until 1795, when Britain made its greatest effort to precipitate monarchist uprisings.

Conflict between the British and Jacobin governments became a war to the death: as Grenville bluntly stated in 1794, 'the existence of the two systems of government is fairly at stake, and it is perfect blindness not to see that in the establishment of the French Republic is included the overthrow of all the other governments of Europe'. Safe behind its Channel moat, Britain became France's most persistent opponent and the focus of European resistance to the Revolution.

The Convention endeavoured to overcome resistance to its demands for soldiers by sending out deputies into the departments to galvanize the war effort with this decree on the *représentants en mission*, 9 March 1793.

THE National Convention, believing that in a free country each citizen owes his duty wholly to the welfare of the republic, decrees as follows:
Commissioners from among the membership of the National Convention will go without delay to the various departments of the Republic to instruct their fellow-citizens of the fresh dangers which threaten the nation, and to assemble sufficient forces to disperse the enemy.

The Commissioners are authorized to take whatever measures they may consider necessary to make up immediately the contingents set by the Decree of 300,000 men of 24 February and even to seek out where necessary all citizens capable of bearing arms, in whatever style seems most suitable to them.

The Commissioners will have the right to take whatever measures may seem necessary to restore order in any case of disturbance, to suspend temporarily and even to arrest any whom they consider suspect, and to make use of armed force if necessary.

Decree of 10 March 1793 organizing a Revolutionary Tribunal for counter-revolutionary offences.

'Let us embody terror,' Danton had said in the debate on the above decree, 'so as to prevent the people from doing so.'

THE National Convention decrees as follows:
There will be established in Paris a special criminal tribunal concerned with all counter-revolutionary activities and with all assaults on the liberty, equality, unity and indivisibility of the Republic.

The special criminal tribunal will also be responsible for all matters pertaining to the internal and external security of the State, and any form of plotting which seeks to restore the monarchy or to set up any other kind of authority hostile to the nation's liberty, equality and sovereignty, no matter whether those accused may be civil or military officials or ordinary citizens.

The tribunal will consist of a jury and five judges. Their duty will be to direct the proceedings and apply the law when the jury has come to its decision on the matter.

The *comités de surveillance* established on 21 March by the following decree were watch committees with extensive policing powers.

WISHING to endow the people's magistrates with all means possible to discover and prevent evil, the Convention decrees as follows:
Each commune of the Republic shall set up a committee composed of twelve citizens.

The members of this committee may not be chosen from members of the church or former nobility, or from former seigneurs of the locality or agents of such seigneurs. The committee shall be responsible for receiving for its district the registration of all foreigners currently living in the commune, or who may arrive there.

There were far more executions during the Terror under the law of 29 March – enabling armed rebels to be shot within 24 hours – than guillotinings decreed by the Revolutionary Tribunal. This law, which was introduced by Cambacérès, a deputy of the Plain, was used especially in areas of civil war such as the Vendée.

YOUR Committee is here to propose a decree concerning the rebellions which are erupting in various departments of the Republic. This proposal contains some severe measures. I merely point out that circumstances are pressing, and you will be aware that circumstances almost always dictate decisions.

All those who are denounced for taking part in the counter-revolutionary revolts or riots which have broken out, or which may break out in the future, in the course of recruitment in the various departments of the republic, and those who have adopted the white cockade or any other emblem of rebellion, are outside the law.

If they are taken or arrested with weapons in hand, they will within twenty-four hours be handed over to criminal judgement, and put to death once their deeds have been confirmed by a military commission.

Priests, former nobles, former seigneurs, agents and servants of all such people, foreigners, those who were employed by the former government, or those who have instigated or supported any of the rebels, the leaders, instigators and those convicted of murder, arson and pillage, will suffer the death penalty.

The Revolutionary Tribunal

THE Revolutionary Tribunal of Paris, established on 10 March 1793, was intended to prevent massacres like those of September 1792. Composed of five judges, a jury of twelve and a public prosecutor – the notorious Fouquier-Tinville – it had wide jurisdiction over men and women suspected of opposing the Revolution. Many suspects were referred to it by the National Convention, which controlled appointments to the Tribunal, and the Committee of Public Safety became increasingly involved in political cases, putting pressure on Fouquier-Tinville and taking up measures to speed up convictions.

The Committee of General Security provided the Tribunal with an abundant supply of suspects thanks to the work of surveillance committees (*comités de surveillance*) in the departments; *représentants en mission* also co-operated, often in conjunction with the local surveillance committees.

There were frequent complaints at the Tribunal's slowness, and irate orators often called for a specific number of heads per day. Plans to speed up the system were instituted by the law of 5 September 1793, passed as a result of a massive demonstration by the sections, which called for rapid and exemplary punishment of nobles, priests, rich speculators, hoarders and the like. The number of judges was increased to sixteen and jurors to sixty; artisans were well represented.

At first the Tribunal followed a formalized legal procedure, which only broke down during major political trials. A preliminary interrogation, the *acte d'accusation*, took place, then evidence was sought out and scrutinized, witnesses were heard and any relevant background data on the accused submitted.

When the Law of 22 Prairial II (10 June 1794) on revolutionary justice was passed, it abolished counsel for the defence and allowed conviction on patriotic intuition rather than any evidence.

In Paris, a total of 2750 were sentenced to death by the Tribunal from the first death sentence on 15 April 1793 to the last on 6 May 1795. However, although the nobility, clergy and higher ranks of the bourgeoisie suffered out of proportion to their number in the population, the Tribunal was far from being an agent of class extermination. Almost the same number – some 2250 – were acquitted.

In the provinces, where relatively slow revolutionary tribunals were often replaced by ruthless commissions, generally staffed by outsiders operating under the eye of *représentants en mission* seeking a reputation for zeal, it is estimated that 35,000–40,000 were killed during the winter of 1793-4.

BELOW Marie-Antoinette was one of the Revolutionary Tribunal's victims.

Faced with civil war in the west and foreign war on all fronts, the republic's future looked grim in late March and early April 1793, when the army's principal commander, Dumouriez, lost the battle of Neerwinden, was obliged to evacuate Belgium and then defected to the enemy. Thibaudeau's memoirs put his flight in context.

AFTER Dumouriez had shared in the first successes of the republican armies and negotiated the retreat of the Prussians, he returned to Paris and was welcomed there with enthusiasm, receiving Robespierre's warmest greetings at the Jacobin Club.

Back with the army once again, he won the battle of Jemmapes and conquered Belgium. Dumouriez then showed great temper, entered into open conflict with his agents, and bitterly denounced the War Ministry and the Treasury commissioners. He returned to Paris on the pretext of seeing to the needs of his army, but in reality in order to judge for himself what support he might find for his own purposes. There he found almost everyone ill-disposed towards him and soon left again, reopened his campaign, seized Holland, and was defeated at Neerwinden on 18 March.

Dumouriez's treachery led the Convention, on 6 April, to introduce an executive committee to direct the war effort, the Committee of Public Safety. From now to the fall of Robespierre in July 1794, the Revolutionary Government which implemented the Terror would be directed by this Committee, whose members were drawn from the Convention and which, in its early days, was dominated by Danton.

THE National Convention decrees:

There will be established a Committee of Public Safety, made up of nine members of the Convention.

This Committee will deliberate in secret. It will be charged with overseeing and speeding up the work of administration entrusted to the council of ministers.

In cases of urgent need, it is authorized to undertake measures of domestic and foreign defence, and decrees signed by a majority of its members in consultation, which must not be less than two-thirds of the total, shall be carried out without delay.

The Committee will prepare each week a general written report on its operations and on the state of the Republic.

The Committee of Public Safety

ON 5 April 1793, General Dumouriez, supreme commander of French forces on the northern front, defected to the enemy. The following day, stunned by this occurrence, the Convention instituted a new committee, the Committee of Public Safety, to oversee the war effort. The new committee would remain at the heart of revolutionary government throughout the reign of Terror.

Charles-François Dumouriez was from an aristocratic family with strong military traditions and a new career of foreign adventure beckoned him when the Revolution broke out. In 1790 he was a French adviser to the Belgian rebellion against Austria. In Paris he allied himself with the Girondin deputies, was promoted general, and in March 1792, briefly became foreign minister. Clandestinely, he also received secret funds from the court.

ABOVE The Committee of Public Safety in session.

In November 1792 he led the Army of the North into Belgium following his victory at the battle of Jemappes. However, he was suspected of corrupt dealings with private army suppliers, and revolutionaries resented his accommodating attitude towards the Belgian clergy: he protected them from property confiscations, while at the same time borrowing money from them. In March 1793, he was defeated by the Austrians at Neerwinden, and after this disaster opened negotiations with the enemy.

When two government commissioners arrived to investigate Dumouriez's activities, he arrested them. The Austrians gave him an armistice, which would

RIGHT Collot d'Herbois, who became one of the Committee's most radical members.

LEFT General Dumouriez, whose treachery led to the creation of the Committee of Public Safety.

allow him to lead his army in a military coup on Paris – a plan similar to that of his predecessor Lafayette. The army, however, refused to follow its defeated and royalist general and on 5 April, Dumouriez defected to the Austrians, a move which weakened morale and threatened to paralyse the war effort.

This treachery fatally compromised the Girondins in the National Convention who were closely associated with him, and as a result none were elected in April 1793 to the new Committee of Public Safety.

The Committee assumed many ministerial functions, but it was not a dictator. It was dependent on the support of the Convention, which renewed its powers every month during the Terror by a majority vote, and only gradually assumed the identity which made it the embodiment of the Revolution in action in 1793-4.

The 'great' Committee of Public Safety, dominant at the height of the Terror in 1793-4, had twelve members, eight of them lawyers, and all except Collot d'Herbois and Hérault de Séchelles, provincials. One, Jean-Bon Saint-André, was a Protestant. Not all members were present at any one time. Several, like Couthon in Lyon and Saint-Just in Alsace, were absent for long periods, on missions to the provinces or to the army. Neither Saint-André nor Prieur de la Marne played central roles, and Hérault was arrested in March 1794. The others worked through months of political tension to save the Revolution from foreign invasion and civil war. They often deliberated round the clock, writing, eating and sleeping where they sat, at the Committee's distinctive long green table.

Robespierre, who had been elected to the Committee on 27 July 1793, shared collective responsibility with his eleven colleagues, but his speciality was the ideology behind the Jacobin Terror, supported by the Cult of the Supreme Being, and leading towards the Republic of Virtue. His closest colleagues were Couthon, permanently confined to a wheelchair, who proposed the Law of 22 Prairial II (10 June 1794) on revolutionary justice, and Saint-Just, who was entrusted with the report leading to the arrest of the Dantonists in March 1794.

However, the Committee's main task was to mobilize the economy and organize the war effort. The vital administration of recruitment, munitions and other military supplies was the particular concern of Robert Lindet, Prieur de la Côte d'Or and Carnot, whose success in this period made him a national hero as the 'organizer of victory'.

Bertrand Barère usually represented the Committee on the floor of the Convention, where he was always its most popular member. Billaud-Varenne had chief responsibility for supervising the *représentants en mission* in the provinces.

The Committee was not always unanimous: Billaud and Collot were its most radical members, closest to the aspirations of the Paris popular movement. Carnot and Lindet were moderates – Lindet refused to sign the decree of Danton's execution – and Carnot and Saint-Just often quarrelled over military questions. Nevertheless, the dedicated collective work of the 'Twelve Who Ruled' ensured the Revolution's survival during its most desperate months.

Most of the emergency war legislation of the spring of 1793 had been introduced on the initiative of the Montagnards. The Girondins found the Revolution shifting too far to the left, and became increasingly critical of the Montagnards in the assembly and the support they drew from the Parisian popular movement (sections, clubs, etc.) outside it. As the Montagnard deputy Baudot noted in his memoirs, the Girondins were increasingly overtaken by events.

THE Girondins wanted to halt the revolution with the bourgeoisie in power, but at that time it was both impossible and impolitic. There was open war on the frontiers, and civil war threatened; the foreign forces could only be repulsed by the masses who had therefore to be roused to support the Revolution. The Mountain alone truly understood its mission, which was primarily to prevent foreign invasion, and it made use of the only means which could achieve success in such an enterprise. It felt constrained by the circumstances, and dared to proclaim this: the Girondins either did not recognize the fact or did not wish to undergo the consequences. 'They are lawyers, fine speakers and skilled in procedure,' said Danton, 'but they have never picked up anything greater than a pen or an usher's rod.'

The Girondins were tribunes without popular support. They were foolish enough, at a time when all the masses were aroused, to declare war unto death on the Mountain, who understood and spoke for the interests of these same masses.

Many Girondin deputies stirred up opposition to the Montagnards and the Paris popular movement in their home constituencies. From a letter by the Girondin Lanjuinais to the electors of the Ille-et-Vilaine department, written in April 1793.

It is not to us that you should direct your reproaches concerning the scandalous debates in the Convention, but to those who have created this scandal, to those who advocate murder and pillage, who draw up lists of proscription against the people's representatives, who applaud them, who endorse them more or less openly, who provoke the dissolution of the Convention through the most absurd slanders, who do not want work to continue on the Constitution, who utter or repeat all the anti-freedom remarks of such men as Marat, Robespierre and their friends.

The Convention of 1792

THE 1792 elections were held during the harvest and at the height of a crisis in the war with Austria. The introduction of manhood suffrage – men over 21 now had the right to vote – did not result in a massive turnout (after all, France was at war), but voters were enthusiastic, and there was certainly no royalist backlash as some had feared. Supporters of the king were allowed to vote, except in Paris, but they had little effect: the Convention was solidly republican.

Less than ten per cent of the deputies were new to public life. The fact that the Legislative Assembly was widely credited with the overthrow of the king attracted many votes to members of that assembly who had sat on the left: most were returned to the Convention. Pétion, mayor of Paris, and Robespierre were among 83 who had been members of the Constituent Assembly. For the rest, a wide range of local and judicial officials and activists came, like earlier deputies, largely from professional backgrounds; 47 per cent were lawyers. There were also 55 clergy, and the butcher Legendre, the woolcarder Armonville, the armaments worker Noel Pointe, the gravedigger Montegut and the corsetmaker Viguy had seats alongside eight marquises and the king's cousin Philippe Egalité, the former duc d'Orléans.

Parisian voters rejected Brissot, Condorcet and Kersaint in favour of a delegation in which 20 out of 24 deputies, including Robespierre, Danton and Marat, were linked with the Commune and Parisian radical politics.

ABOVE Brissot, the leader of the Girondin faction, which eventually lost the struggle to dominate the Convention.

In the Convention, the Parisian contingent and the Jacobin Club became the core of a wider association known as the Montagnards, or the Mountain, because its delegates occupied the highest seats in the Convention's chamber. The groups clustering round Brissot, elected by the Eure-et-Loir, Vergniaud and the Rolands, were known as the 'Gironde' (Vergniaud's department). There were 250-300 Montagnards, about 180 Girondins (sixty or so loosely linked friends, plus those who supported them) and, finally, 250-300 deputies of 'the Plain' who avoided involvement in factional disputes. Formal party organization was unknown, and patterns took time to develop.

The Montagnards included some radicals, but in social background and attitudes they were very similar to the Girondins. The quarrel between the two groups, whatever its origins, was political. The leading Girondins bitterly distrusted the Commune (during the massacres, Brissot and Roland had felt their own lives threatened), and were convinced that there were plans for a Paris-based dictatorship, which could only be countered by provincial-based support for the Convention. Most Montagnards disliked Parisian claims to be 'pure' revolutionaries, though some sympathized with the *sans-culottes*, but they all believed that the Republic would be seriously endangered by provincial counter-revolution, and were prepared to buy off the Parisians, if necessary, to avoid this.

In 1792–early 1793, most deputies wanted to ignore personal brawls between (for example) Louvet and Robespierre, but none wanted the Convention bullied by *sans-culottes*; Paris needed discipline. Unfortunately, the Girondins showed little judgement. During the king's trial, a Girondin proposal to balance Parisian influence by holding a referendum on the sentence was torpedoed when Vergniaud's July letter to the king, revealing the Girondin deputy's attempt to negotiate his way to a ministerial appointment, became known. The deputies involved were not seriously accused of royalism – Thuriot said scornfully, 'They wanted to be ministers!' – but their reputation never recovered from the inference that ambition might corrupt their political judgement. In the autumn of 1792, however, they had ample opportunity to promote their views. Roland, still Minister of the Interior, used official funds to support the anti-Parisian Girondin press, and his ministerial circulars were Girondin in tone. In the departments, the hostile Girondin view of 'Paris' and the situation in the Convention circulated more widely than any Montagnard publication. This may help to explain the widespread 'Federalist' reaction in the provinces to the expulsion of the Girondin deputies from the Convention in June 1793.

ABOVE Revolutionary wallpaper symbolizing the Mountain, surmounted by the Rights of Man, smiting France's enemies.
BELOW Madame Roland, wife of the Girondin leader and an active Girondin herself; she died in the Terror.

THE ST. JAMES'S CHRONICLE (London), *1–3 January 1793*

Private letters from Bilbao, of the 15th of December, inform us that the French Jacobins had attempted to introduce weapons of assassination into Spain.

A vessel from France arrived there, laden with a great number of chests, which the Captain declared were full of scythes to be used in the woods. One of these chests having slipt from some of the people, who were unloading them, broke by its fall, and a quantity of others, where instead of scythes, they found sabres, poignards, and every species of destructive instruments, many of which, being made in a strange manner, terrified the spectators. The officers of the Police immediately put the Captain of the vessel into irons, as well as the Merchant to whom this singular cargo was addressed, and they seized the whole.

The following letter was written on 5 May 1793 by the leading Girondin deputy, Vergniaud, to his electors in the department of the Gironde, based at Bordeaux.

I am awaiting my enemies, and I am certain I will make them blanch. It is said that they are likely to come today or tomorrow, seeking to quench their thirst in the blood of the National Convention.

Be prepared; if I am forced to it I will appeal to you from the rostrum to come and defend us, if there is time, and avenge freedom by exterminating the tyrants. If we cease to exist, Bordeaux can save the Republic. And indeed! how we have worked for four years, what sacrifices we have made, what iniquity suffered; shall France have shed so much blood only to fall prey to a few brigands, to bend the knee to the most shameful tyranny which ever oppressed any nation?

Men of the Gironde, there is no time to lose.

I send you fraternal greetings,

VERGNIAUD

Newspapers like the radical journalist Hébert's *Le Père Duchesne* increasingly equated the Girondins with royalists, and called on the radical elements in the Paris sections – the famous *sans-culottes* – to take action against them.

LE PERE DUCHESNE'S great denunciation addressed to all *sans-culottes* in all departments, concerning plotting by the Brissotins, Girondins, Rolandins, Buzotins, Pétionists, seeking to achieve the murder of the brave Montagnards, Jacobins, and the Paris Commune, so as to kill off freedom and restore the monarchy.

'Our armies are giving the Republic's enemies the boot all over the place. It's in the Convention now, yes indeed, d—— it, it's among the people's representatives that you will find the focus of counter-revolution. The accomplices of Capet and Dumouriez are moving heaven and earth to stir up civil war and arm the citizens from the departments against Paris.

'The Brissotins insult the Montagnards, in Paris they are recruiting an army of errand-boys and little shop assistants to chase away the *sans-culottes* in the sections: the sugar traders from Rouen, from Bordeaux, from Marseilles, are drawing up petitions.

'My fine *sans-culottes*, your enemies are only bold because you stand there with your arms folded; wake up, d—— it; stir yourselves and you will find them at your feet. Disarm all those b——s who piss ice-water in a heatwave and who want no part in the Revolution. The poison of moderation is more dangerous than Austrian weapons. Strike while the iron's hot. If you slumber even a short while more you can expect to wake up to bloody slavery, f—— it.'

The threats against Paris – which recalled those made in the Brunswick declaration of July 1792 – uttered on 25 May 1793 by the Girondin Isnard, in his temporary role of president of the Assembly, further soured relations between the two sides.

FRANCE has placed in Paris the seat of national representation; Paris must respect this. If ever the Convention was brought low ... (loud murmuring from the extreme left – applause from the opposite side. Several voices from the party on the left: 'That is not an answer') ...

The President: If any of these repeated insurrections resulted in an attack on national representation, I swear to you in the name of the whole of France ... ('No, no' – cries from the extreme left; the rest of the assembly rises together, and all members shout: 'Yes, speak in the name of France') ...

The President: I swear to you in the name of the whole of France, Paris will be wiped out ... (violent mutterings from the extreme left drown the voice of the president.

All members of the opposite party: 'Yes, the whole of France would take shattering vengeance for such an attack').

Le Père Duchesne

For three and a half years, between 1790 and 1794, Jacques René Hébert published a small, scruffy newspaper called *Le Père Duchesne*, named after a fictional fairground figure who smoked a pipe and talked common sense to ordinary people. Less a newspaper than a monologue on current political issues, it was written in the earthy style of Parisian street talk, and littered with bad language. This familiar style made it extremely popular with artisans and *sans-culottes*; for them Hébert really was the Père Duchesne.

The son of a master goldsmith, Hébert was born in 1757 at Alençon in Normandy and received a good education. In his late teens he fell in love with a local widow twice his age – who also had another lover, a well-known doctor. When Hébert attacked him in print his rival sued for libel and was awarded hefty damages. In despair Hébert fled to Paris, where he spent several years before the Revolution in poverty, working as a clerk and ticket seller for theatres.

He started to write political pamphlets when the revolution broke out, and after their initial success he teamed up with a printer, Tremblay, to produce *Le Père Duchesne* in September 1790. He was not the first to use the fairground personality for the title of a newspaper, but he was the most successful, because of his technique of incorporating popular slang, picked up during his years of poverty.

At first his political views were moderate. He deferred to Lafayette and Mirabeau, and was a keen admirer of 'that good old devil' the king. However, in the spring of 1791 he became a member of the radical Cordeliers Club and of his local section, Bonne-Nouvelle. His views became more extreme. He attacked Lafayette, and campaigned vigorously for a republic after the king's flight to Varennes in the summer of 1791. Over the next year his criticism of both Louis and Marie-Antoinette became more strident, and after 10 August, he was elected to the Paris Commune.

He took advantage of this new arena to oppose the Girondin faction, and in mid-May 1793 called for a popular uprising to bar them from the Convention. He was arrested by the Commission of Twelve, but his popularity was so great that the *sans-culottes* secured his release within three days. The Girondins were subsequently removed from the Convention, and Hébert became a loyal follower of the Mountain, the radical group within the Convention. But after Marat's death in July 1793 his views became increasingly extreme. He accused the Committee of Public Safety of not doing enough to defeat counter-revolution and help the poor, and on 5 September organized a *sans-culotte* invasion of the Convention to bring down food prices. He engineered the Law of Suspects and supported the dechristianization campaign of the winter of 1793-4, both means of intensifying the impact of the Terror.

Le Père Duchesne was now the most widely read newspaper in France, and Hébert an influential speaker at both the Jacobin and Cordelier clubs. However, his extremism soon worried the Committee of Public Safety, and involved him in bitter conflict with the moderates, led by Danton. In March 1794, when he called for an uprising to get rid of them, the Committee decided to act. He was arrested on the night of 12-13 March, sent before the Revolutionary Tribunal and guillotined within a week. With Hébert's death all criticism of the Committee came to an abrupt end, as did *Le Père Duchesne*. The *sans-culottes* in Paris were stunned by his disappearance. Four months later, when Robespierre was arrested by the Convention, few of them were prepared to rally to his support: his death was *Le Père Duchesne*'s revenge.

ABOVE The last session of the Cordeliers Club, which Hébert pushed far to the Left and which closed after his arrest.

Je suis le véritable pere Duchesne, foutre:

LA MINE ÉVENTÉE,

OU

La Grande Colere

DU

PERE DUCHESNE,

A la découverte d'un nouveau projet de contre-révolution, annoncé pour le 25 Août.

LE plus difficile à écorcher, c'est la ...
le proverb...

RIGHT *Le Père Duchesne*, France's most popular radical newspaper because of Hébert's style, with its slang and obscenities.

Marat: Step down from the chair, President, you are acting like a coward. You are dishonouring the assembly.
The President: Soon people would search the banks of the Seine to see if Paris had ever existed ... (murmurs from the party on the left, applause opposite) ...
The President: The sword of justice which is still dripping with the blood of the tyrant is ready to strike at the head of anyone who may dare to raise himself above national representation. (Applause from the party on the right.)

Ruault's correspondence reveals growing distrust for the motives of the Girondins. The decision of the Convention to establish a 'Commission of Twelve', packed with Girondins, to investigate the threat posed by the Paris popular movement, triggered off popular insurrection.

Paris, 16 May 1793. The conspiracy against the popular clubs, especially against the Paris Jacobin Club, goes on growing.

The Gironde faction pursues them relentlessly; for their part the Jacobins make war, but it is an implacable war against these Girondins who would like, so it is said, to divide France into little republics which would federalize together. It is to this end that the Girondins want to eliminate the popular clubs which buzz around together like a swarm of bees and who make up a formidable body against this federalist spirit. If the republic is to bring good in its train, it is to the popular clubs that we will owe it.

Paris, 23 May 1793. Everything I see, everything I hear, makes me believe that the Jacobins must destroy or be destroyed, must conquer or be conquered, within a very few days.

30 May 1793. The Girondins are pursuing their plan to eliminate the Jacobins. On the 21st they found out how to set up a Committee in the Convention called The Twelve, to hunt down the authors of I don't know what ideas held against them in the sections and in the popular clubs of men and women.

They set to work on the 26th; they arranged for the night-time arrest of a great many patriots whose ideas were contrary to their own, and sent them to the Abbaye prison. No royalist or person suspected of unpatriotic behaviour was taken under their orders.

Jean-Paul Marat

MARAT was famous for his talent as a journalist, and notorious for his belief in violent solutions to political problems.

As editor of *L'Ami du peuple* (the friend of the people) he attacked the National Assembly for its failure to carry out radical reforms, for not abolishing feudalism entirely, and for not making France totally democratic. He accused the Paris municipal authorities of deliberately starving the poor, and condemned Bailly and Lafayette as agents of counter-revolution. He called for power to be given to a dictator, preferably himself, and for opponents of the Revolution to be executed in their thousands.

These ideas attracted many readers among radicals in Paris, but people in the provinces regarded him as dangerous, eccentric and mad. Government officials took a similar line and there were many attempts to arrest and prosecute him. Marat usually went underground and published his papers from hiding.

In mid-August 1792 he was co-opted on to the Paris Commune. In mid-September he was elected to the National Convention by Paris, and was immediately attacked by the Girondins because of his role in encouraging the massacres earlier in the month. He revelled in the controversy, voted for the king's execution and denounced the high food prices caused by hoarders and speculators. In April 1793 he called for armed intervention to remove the Girondins from power in the Convention. Arrested and sent for trial before the Revolutionary Tribunal, he was acquitted. Two months later the Girondins were arrested, with Marat's approval, and the Montagnards took control of the chamber.

Marat's influence was at its peak. However, opponents of the Revolution were increasingly hostile to him. One was Charlotte Corday, who believed that only Marat's death would end the Revolution. She travelled to Paris, obtained an interview with him on 13 July and, while he was taking a medicinal bath to relieve his painful eczema, stabbed him in the chest.

Marat's pierced heart was hung from the ceiling of the Cordelier Club in Paris as an object of almost religious veneration, and his body was placed in the Panthéon, the mausoleum for national heroes. However, in little more than a year the winds of political fortune had changed: his body was removed from its resting-place, dragged through the streets and thrown into a common grave.

RIGHT David's famous painting of the dead Marat as martyr.

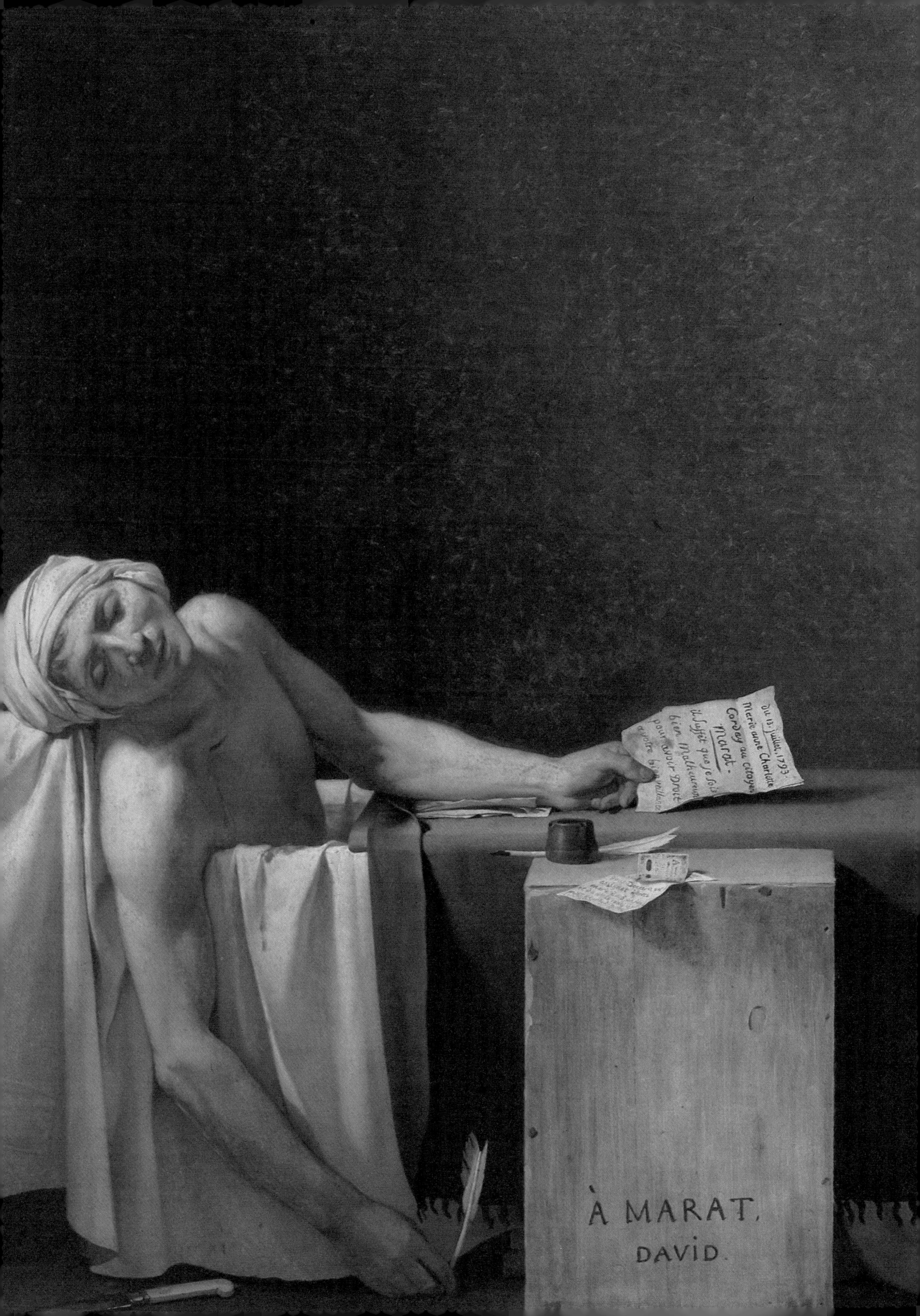
À MARAT,
DAVID.

Two popular demonstrations by the Paris sections, on 31 May and 2 June, left deputies in the Convention little choice but to accede to the sections' demands for the arrest of 32 notorious Girondins. The Montagnard deputy Robert Lindet, in a letter to his electors in the department of the Eure, gave an account of – and a justification for these two *journées*.

On 31 May a large deputation from all the forty-eight sections of Paris came to pronounce a solemn denunciation against the Commission of Twelve, and the twenty-two members who had previously been denounced; the deputation demanded that they be handed over to the Revolutionary Tribunal.

The Commission of Twelve was suppressed. The Committee of Public Safety was made responsible for seeking out the authors of the plots denounced by the various Paris deputations, and report on them.

On 1 June a deputation from the department of Paris and the Commune demanded a decree accusing the twenty-two deputies. After discussion the petition was sent on to the Committee of Public Safety. Next day the National Convention decreed the arrest of thirty-two of its members.

The *journées* accelerated the increasingly violent course of the Terror, as recorded in the memoirs of the moderate deputy Thibaudeau.

THE Terror began on 31 May 1793 and ended on 9 Thermidor, 27 July 1794. Of that terrible period we should say, as the Chancellor L'Hospital said of the, Saint Bartholomew's Day massacre: '*Excidat illa dies.*'

In a despotic state the leader, the courtiers, certain classes and certain individuals at least, are safe from the terror which they inspire. They are the gods who launch the thunderbolts without fear of being struck down by them. In France under the reign of the Terror no one was spared, it hung above every head and struck impartially, arbitrary and swift as the blade of Death. The Convention as well as the people supplied their share of its victims.

Nothing could have been less systematic than the Terror: its development, despite its rapidity, was only gradual; people were drawn into it little by little, and followed it without knowing where they were going; they went on advancing because they dared not turn back, and there was no visible way out.

31 May-2 June 1793

IN May 1793 the simmering hostility between *sans-culottes* and Girondins exploded in a Parisian *journée* which for the first time threatened to divide Paris from the rest of revolutionary France.

Since the king's trial in January, mutual mistrust had increased steadily. A *sans-culotte* attack on Girondin printing presses in March arose from anger at the anti-Parisian propaganda they disseminated. The *sans-culottes* saw those campaigning for a nation-wide referendum on Louis' fate as virtual counter-revolutionaries, and there were demands that well-known Girondins be removed from the Convention. The impeachment of Marat, who was not allowed to defend himself before the Convention, did nothing to calm the situation, but instead showed the ruthlessness of Girondin methods. For their part, the Girondins were repelled by Parisian extremism, and afraid of mob violence. Convinced that a coup against the Convention threatened, they saw Montagnards who were serving as enthusiastic *représentants en mission* as potential agents for a Parisian dictatorship, and issued appropriate warnings.

After Marat's trial, the radical Montagnards dominated the Convention's debates, controlled its policies – and disagreed with the Girondins on many questions. They were usually backed by a majority of deputies on key issues, but bickering between *sans-culottes* and Girondins was nevertheless dangerous. First, with revolt in the Vendée and disaster on the frontiers, the Republic had never needed unity more; whatever the defects of some deputies *en mission*, they represented the Convention, not Paris, and to attack their authority was to invite counter-revolution. Second, if the Convention would not control the Girondins' sniping at Paris, the *sans-culottes* might turn against the whole legislature, with incalculable results. Yet firm control of the Girondins was impossible. The Convention's deputies were independent.

By May there were Girondin suggestions that the Convention's replacement deputies (the *suppléants*) take over, meeting somewhere, perhaps in Bourges, where they would be safe from Parisian interference. Then the Girondin Isnard threatened Paris with total destruction. Finally, the Girondins moved to resolve the conflict: they planned to undercut Parisian 'conspiracy' by arresting leading *sans-culotte* politicans, and to destroy the machinery of *sans-culotte* power by setting a constitutional limit of 50,000 on the population of any commune. The Convention would probably have rejected the provocative constitutional clause, but concern over the Paris Commune's

ABOVE The deputies file out of the Convention to show their independence from the *sans-culottes* threatening them.

behaviour allowed a Girondin-dominated Commission of Twelve to look into its activities. The *sans-culotte* leaders Hébert and Varlet were arrested – an action which caused the long-awaited Parisian conspiracy to become a reality. A newly-formed Central Revolutionary Committee called the *sans-culottes* on to the streets. The customs clerk Hanriot was appointed their commander, and the Convention was surrounded.

From 31 May to 2 June there was a stalemate. The deputies stood their ground – at one stage they solemnly filed out and back between armed demonstrators, to show their 'freedom' – but really had little choice. On 2 June, 29 Girondin deputies and two ministers were put under house arrest and the danger of an attack on the Convention was averted.

The Committee of Public Safety, led by Danton and elected before the rising, tried to contain its consequences. Protests from nearly 100 deputies at this outrage to France's representatives were backed by 60 departments. Lyon, Toulon, Marseille and Bordeaux rose in revolt, and a dozen of the arrested Girondins fled to Caen in Normandy to organize rebellion there. A democratic constitution, issued on 24 June for implementation after the end of the war with the Allies, persuaded most of the departments to accept the situation. No such way out was open to the Girondin rebels. On 8 July, after a damning speech by the young radical Saint-Just, newly elected to the Committee of Public Safety, they were outlawed.

The 1793 revolts had little effect on the Girondin cause, which had failed to rouse much popular support, but, innocent or guilty, the Girondins themselves suffered because of them. After another Parisian rising in September, 75 moderate deputies who had protested about the events of 2 June were imprisoned, and on 31 October an ill-assorted batch of alleged Girondins were executed. Deaths continued for months: Roland committed suicide, Chambon was lynched, Guadet executed and Condorcet died in prison. By July 1794 nearly two-thirds of the most prominent Girondin deputies were dead.

It was the opposition of enemies of the Revolution, at home and abroad, which gradually brought about the Terror by giving birth to excessive patriotism. It started amongst the upper classes with heated and violent speeches, and ended among the lower classes in atrocities.

When the Third Estate abolished privileges, it took the place of the aristocracy in the eyes of the people; and after the people had waged war on them – the defenders of their rights – it sought in its own midst obscure victims to nourish the Terror, just as slaves who, having broken their chains and wiped out their tyrants and their liberators, then massacre one another, drunk with blood and blinded by their own victories.

In his private notebook, written just after the expulsion of the Girondins, Robespierre reveals his awareness of the need to win popular support for the Revolution by radical policies. He was elected to the Committee of Public Safety in July 1793, and remained until July 1794 its most dominant figure.

There must be a single will.

It must be either republican or royalist.

If it is to be republican, there must be republican ministers, republican newspapers, republican deputies, a republican government.

Foreign wars are a deadly sickness (a deadly plague), while the body politic is sick with revolution and the division of wills.

The internal dangers derive from the bourgeoisie; to overcome the bourgeoisie we must rally the people.

Everything was poised, on the one hand, to place the people beneath the yoke of the bourgeoisie, and, on the other, to bring the defenders of the Republic to their death on the scaffold.

The present insurrection must continue until those measures essential for the safety of the Republic have been taken.

The people must ally themselves to the Convention and the Convention must make use of the people.

The sans-culottes *must be paid and must remain in the cities.*

They must be provided with weapons, must be incited to anger, and must be enlightened.

We must encourage enthusiasm for the republic by all possible means.

Who were the *sans-culottes* who had contrived to purge the Convention of its moderate wing? A radical pamphlet attempted to give an answer.

A *sans-culotte*, you devils? This is a creature who always goes on foot, who does not own millions of livres, as you would all like to do, owns no châteaux, has no servants to do his bidding, and who lives very simply with his wife and children, if he has any, on the fourth or fifth floor.

He is useful, for he knows how to work in the fields, or in a smithy or sawmill, how to use a file, how to cover a roof, make his own clogs – and how to pour out his blood to the last drop for the good of the republic. And since he is at work, one many be sure not to see his face in the fashionable Chartres café, nor in the low bars where there is conspiring and gambling, nor in the literary salons.

In the evening he goes to his section meeting, without powder or scent or boots, not with any hope of being noticed by the women citizens on the benches, but in order to lend all his strength to sound motions, and to crush any which arise from the odious faction of so-called statesmen. Apart from that, a *sans-culotte* always has an edge on his blade: to trim the ears of ill-wishers. Sometimes he marches with his pike; but at the first sound of the drum you may see him setting off for the Vendée, for the army of the Alps or of the North.

THE MASSACHUSETTS MAGAZINE (Boston), *February 1791*

Among the wonders produced by the French Revolution, few would have dared to hope that a race of Amazons would have sprung up, to astonish the world with their martial deeds. That is, however, actually the case; the women of the small town of Guine are at this moment formed into a regiment, and call themselves the National Guard of Guine.

The popular movement had a radical feminist wing. From a pamphlet entitled *Les lettres bougrement patriotiques de la Mère Duchesne*.

THERE'S something to talk about, d—— it. In the old days when we wanted to speak out, we were made to shut our mouths and told politely that we reasoned like women – a bit like b—— animals. B—— me! it's all different now, we women have got important since the Revolution. By God! freedom has given us wings! Today we fly like eagles. I may be ignorant and uneducated, but I can still hold my own in politics.

The sans-culottes

AFTER the overthrow of the monarchy on 10 August 1792, the word *sans-culotte* was associated with the artisans and small retailers who took part in the sectional assemblies and popular societies of revolutionary Paris. The term referred to men who before 1789 wore ordinary trousers, rather than the knee-breeches and stockings of the upper classes. It evoked the industry, manual dexterity and material independence of working people, virtues which were seen as the basis of civil rights and political entitlements.

The word originally had very different – theatrical – connotations; in the Parisian boulevard theatre a *sans-culotte* was a man, often a tutor or writer, who found himself in compromising circumstances with a young woman whose welfare or education he was responsible for. The word was also used in a similar way by royalist pamphleteers in 1790 and 1791 to ridicule many leading figures in the Parisian Jacobin Club.

The meaning began to change in the weeks leading up to the Legislative Assembly elections in September 1791. Some electors, headed by a future member of the Convention, Dubois-Crancé, formed a pressure group to promote their candidates in the name of the wider constituency of the capital's artisans and shopkeepers. By the summer of 1792 the term had come to symbolize the political aspirations of Parisian artisans and shopkeepers.

The vehicles of *sans-culotte* politics were the 48 sections created as electoral assemblies for the Paris Commune in May 1790, which since that time had remained permanent meeting places. They were legitimized by the Legislative Assembly's decision, in July 1792, to allow them to continue in permanent session; this capitulation to popular pressure was the moment at which power passed decisively into the hands of the *sans-culottes*. Between the summer of 1792 and the spring of 1794 no one could command political support in Paris without securing their support; and campaigns over prices, the character of the republic and the prosecution of the war reflected their concerns.

Although no more than several hundred people attended each meeting of the sectional assemblies, they were drawn from a broad cross-section of the Parisian trades: two-thirds of the 1361 individuals who held office in the sections between September 1793 and July 1794 were artisans or shopkeepers. Despite wide differences in wealth, most were young enough – between 25 and 45 in 1794 – to have avoided compromising associations with the old regime, but mature enough to have established themselves in the neighbourhoods where they lived.

As the Convention and its committees tightened their grasp upon Parisian politics, the autonomy of the sections and therefore the power of the *sans-culottes* was gradually eroded, and they were finally eliminated as an effective political force by the Law of 14 Frimaire Year II (4 December 1793), and the trial of Hébert and of the leaders of the Paris Commune in April 1794.

ABOVE The mayor of Rouen menaced by *sans-culottes*, who were often active outside Paris, taking the Revolution to the country.

LEFT The *Carmagnole*, a *sans-culotte* anthem, on a plate.

A popular club, the Society of Revolutionary Republican Women, addressing the Convention from the bar of the house, used the same kinds of radical arguments in favour of social justice and political radicalism as their male counterparts.

CITIZEN Legislators, we have come to demand the implementation of constitutional laws. We did not accept the constitution in order for anarchy and the rule of plotters to be extended indefinitely.

Show us, by stripping bare the nobility, that they have no defenders amongst you. Make haste especially to prove to the whole of France, with positive results, that we have not loudly rallied the representatives of a great people from all corners of the Republic simply to play out a pathetic scene on the Champ de Mars.

Ah, you legislators! Is this how you dupe the People? Is this the Equality which was to be the foundation of their happiness? Is this the reward for the wrongs which they have suffered so patiently? You must render justice to them by dismissing all the guilty administrators; by creating special tribunals in sufficient number so that when the citizens set off to defend the frontiers they can say to themselves: I know my wife and children are safe; I have seen all the conspirators at home perish under the sword of the Law.

> THE TIMES (London), *23 July 1793*
>
> We have been so fortunate as to obtain the PARIS gazettes down to the 18th inst. They announce that MARAT has been assassinated by a WOMAN, who has since confessed, that she thought she had done the best act of her life, by ridding the world of such a monster.

The murder of Marat, the 'friend of the people', on 17 July raised the political temperature. In this letter, his murderess, the young Charlotte Corday, requested an interview with him . . .

Paris, 12 July, Year 2 of the Republic. Citizen, I have just arrived from Caen; your love for the nation leads me to believe that you will be pleased to learn of the distressing events in that part of the Republic. I will call upon you at about one o'clock. I beg you to be so kind as to receive me and grant me a brief interview, and I will give you an opportunity to perform a great service for France.
I am, etc., Charlotte Corday

Revolutionary heroines

CHARLOTTE Corday was guillotined on 17 July 1793, dressed in the long red robe of a condemned traitor. She was totally self-possessed; the execution itself was a necessary part of her purpose. In her own eyes she was blameless since her motives were patriotic. During her trial she answered calmly:

'What led you to assassinate Marat?'

'His crimes.'

'What did you expect to achieve?'

'Peace. Now that he is dead, peace will return to my country.'

Although she came from an ancient titled family, the Cordays d'Amont, and her brothers served in the émigré army, Charlotte Corday was no royalist, a factor played down by those who later adopted her as a heroine. She was a republican, and her ideal republic was modelled on ancient Rome, which she imagined to have been full of 'austere virtue, sublime devotion, heroic actions'. Reading Rousseau and the *philosophes* had taught her that the 'frivolous French' needed to be reborn.

1789 had been the start of this process, but by 1792 France was threatened by invasion and civil war. In Caen, as elsewhere in the provinces, much of the blame for internal unrest was pinned on the Paris Commune. Girondin newspapers vilified the monsters who led the 'seditious minority', Hébert, in the persona of the vulgar 'Père Duchesne', and Marat, the chief *septembriseur*. Attempts to contain the excesses of both men only prompted an armed attack on the Convention and the arrest of 29 Girondin deputies.

The purge of 2 June galvanized the 'Federalist Revolt' throughout the country, stirring dozens of departments and cities, including Caen, into open opposition against the over-mighty Paris. It was against this background that Charlotte Corday decided that by one heroic act she could save France from the 'anarchist leader'. On 9 July she left for Paris.

Marat was ill at home, and it was the evening of 13 July before Charlotte could see him, offering 'vital secrets' from Caen. After 15 minutes' talk she stabbed him with a kitchen knife which she had bought early that day. 'As the avenging knife falls,' she had written the day before, 'the Mountain will tremble.' In the event, Marat's martyrdom, combined with the misfiring of the federalist insurrections, rendered the victory of the radical Mountain more complete.

In many ways, Charlotte Corday's contribution to the Revolution contrasts with other female involvement. Women from artisan and lower-middle-class families,

who were prepared to agitate over economic and political matters, were prominent in riots and mass movements, and had been from the very beginning of the Revolution.

As small traders, family managers and often sole providers, they also took the lead, consistently and frequently, in small-scale actions, denouncing rising prices and forcing shopkeepers to adhere to government price-fixing on essential products like grain, soap, and salt.

As conditions worsened, economic issues were increasingly politicized by middle-class activists such as Pauline Léon and the actress Claire Lacombe, who pointed out the conflict between the economic differences in French society and the Revolution's promises of political and legal equality. The Society of Revolutionary Republican Women which they founded in May 1793, and which favoured egalitarian policies, became the object of suspicion of the Committees of Public Safety and General Security, which closed it down in October 1793.

The militant middle-class women of the Revolution failed in their major aim of winning political equality with men. Denied the right to vote, their sole political advance in those years had been in matters of divorce and inheritance granted by the new regime's law codes.

There was less in the Revolution for women than for men, and this may be one factor behind Charlotte Corday's fateful action.

ABOVE A contemporary cartoon showing a horrified Robespierre discovering Charlotte Corday with the body of Marat.

BELOW The Jacobin *tricoteuses*, lowest class of women radicals, who met to applaud radical motions in the Jacobin Club.

On 23 August 1793, the Convention decreed the *levée en masse* – mass conscription – to combat internal counter-revolution and the allied armies on the frontier.

THE National Convention decrees that:
All French citizens are subject to permanent requisition to serve in the armed forces.

Young men will be sent on active service; married men will make weapons and transport supplies; women will make tents and uniforms and work in the hospitals; children will tear up old linen for bandages, old people will be taken to public places to stir up the courage of the combatants, hatred for kings, and republican unity.

Publicly owned housing will be converted into barracks and public buildings into weapons workshops, and the soil of cellars will be utilized in the extraction of saltpetre.

Firearms will be reserved exclusively for those who are to face the enemy; interior forces will use shotguns or weapons other than firearms.

The Committee of Public Safety is to be responsible for organizing without delay the special manufacture of weapons of all kinds suitable for the condition and energies of the French nation. It is therefore authorized to set up all establishments, factories, studios and workshops which may be considered necessary to carry out this work.

The levy will be general; unmarried men or widowers without children, between the ages of 18 and 25, will go first; they will report at once to their local headquarters, where they will practise the use of arms daily while awaiting their marching orders.

Armed royalism was temporarily triumphant in the Vendée in the early summer of 1793. A government official sent to the Vendée reported back to the Convention on the frightening extent of the rebellion.

It is impossible to calculate the number of rebels; it is almost equal to the population of the region, for they are forcing everyone to march. Their armies consist of about twenty to twenty-five thousand men. For the greater part they are armed with pitchforks, spikes, cudgels, etc. They have about a hundred cannon, though no assault guns. They often lack gunpowder, and you will be angry to learn that our very own volunteers have been selling cartridges to them so as to be able to buy butter and eggs and other campaign supplies.

The guerilla style of warfare adopted by the Vendéan rebels was difficult to defeat, for reasons outlined in this account by a state official.

THE rebel army never stayed together for more than three or four days. Once the battle was won or lost, nothing would keep the peasants together and they went off back home. Only the leaders remained, together with a few hundred deserters or foreigners who had no families to return to; but as soon as another venture was planned the army quickly took shape again.

Messages were sent round all the parishes, the tocsin was rung; all the peasants flocked in. Each soldier brought his own bread, and in addition the generals took care to have a supply baked. Meat was distributed to the troops. Corn and cattle necessary for supplies were requisitioned by the generals, and care was taken to have this expense borne by the nobles, great landowners and émigrés' estates; but it was not always necessary to make requisitions; people were anxious to contribute voluntarily; villages subscribed to the cost of sending wagons of bread to meet the army as it passed; peasant women knelt saying the rosary along the route, offering supplies to the soldiers.

No one ever said to the soldiers: 'Right turn, left turn.' They were told, 'Go towards that house, towards that big tree,' and then the attack began. The peasants hardly ever failed to say their prayers before launching an attack, and they almost all crossed themselves each time they were about to fire.

A rebel peasant's view of fighting in the Vendée.

Our army consisted of peasants like myself, wearing smocks or rough coats, armed with shotguns, pistols, muskets, often with tools – scythes, cudgels, axes, knives, and roasting spits. It was organized by parish and district under the orders of an individual leader.

We would march straight to the enemy, and having knelt to receive our priests' blessing, we would open fire at point-blank range, no doubt rather irregular, but well sustained and well aimed. As soon as we saw the republican gunners about to open fire we would fling ourselves flat on the ground. When the shot had passed without hitting us we would get up and rush on the gun batteries like lightning so as to seize them before they had time to reload the guns.

Rebels in the west

By February 1793 the young French Republic was at war with most of Europe and threatened with imminent invasion on all her land and sea frontiers. To resist the allied armies of the First Coalition, the Convention decreed on 24 February 1793 that 300,000 men should be conscripted into the army.

The draft was resisted almost everywhere, but nowhere with such bitterness or determination as in western France, most notably in the area centred on the Vendée department. The Vendéans were the single most important internal enemy the Revolution ever faced, and their rising was the largest and most militarily impressive in France's history.

Contrary to a persistent myth, the peasantry had not benefited universally from the Revolution's reforms. For a large proportion of country people taxes were higher in 1790 – and much higher after war was declared in 1792 – than they had been under the *ancien régime*, and the market value of their produce had plummeted.

In addition, many people were alienated by the Revolution's policy towards the Catholic church. The 1790 Civil Constitution of the Clergy was very unpopular in many areas. In parts of the Vendée it was almost totally defied: many parish priests refused to take the oath of loyalty, and their congregations tended to support them and to reject the constitutional priests sent to replace them.

The Vendée was the first region in which economic and religious discontents coalesced into organized and effective counter-revolution. There were hundreds of often bloody confrontations, notably over the ecclesiastical issue, throughout 1791 and 1792. By the time the Convention decreed the levy of 300,000 men, the Vendéans had concluded that they would rather fight the revolutionaries at home than the foreign enemy on the frontiers. Local republicans, constitutional priests, landowners and their servants were their chief targets, as were regional administrators, often themselves landlords, who were held responsible for every evil from high taxes to conscription.

Nobles and commoners shared the leadership in their army, sometimes uneasily, and military resources were extraordinarily poor. Few of the troops had any training, specialized arms like calvalry and artillery were rare, communications among the various commanders were lamentable and hospital services rudimentary. None the less, the exceptional bravery of this peasant army, with its intimate knowledge of the terrain, often overwhelmed the republicans.

By early April 1793 the Vendéans had created a council of the Royal and Catholic Army and began to make forays against small towns and departmental capitals. However, they failed to take Nantes at the end of June and then, on 17 October, lost a major battle at Cholet. This setback forced perhaps 100,000 of them to cross the Loire, but their attempt to join up with the British fleet at Granville in Normandy failed and the retreating army was destroyed at Savenay, near the Loire estuary, on 23 December. Thousands drowned in the bogs trying to escape, an equal number were stuffed into the makeshift prisons at Nantes.

Devastating repression followed. Carrier, the Jacobin *représentant en mission* at Nantes, was responsible for packing the prisoners into old boats and sinking them in the Loire; many others were shot without trial. Meanwhile, General Turreau's 'infernal columns' criss-crossed the area, burning and destroying all they could. The great war of the Vendée ended in a deluge of peasant blood.

BELOW The battle of Cholet, a decisive defeat for the Vendéans.

> THE MORNING POST (London), *7 January 1794*
>
> The repeated success of the Republicans has struck with dismay all their domestic enemies. The Loyalists in Brittany separated into small bodies, to make their escape, if possible; but this was prevented by the vigilance of the *sans-culottes*, and thousands of them of course have fallen victim to their late desperate enterprise.

Sans-culotte agitation, increased by the continuing economic crisis, almost spilled into open insurrection during massive popular demonstrations in Paris on 4 and 5 September. The Convention bowed to the popular demand – here voiced by Chaumette, a leading figure in the Parisian municipality – for a semi-regular people's army (*armée révolutionnaire*) to diffuse the Terror nationwide.

PATRIOTS from all departments, and the people of Paris in particular, have shown great patience so far; now all that is over, now is the day of justice. As legislators you should know that the huge rally of citizens yesterday and this morning, outside and within the Hôtel de Ville, had only one object: Food, and the power of the law to make it available!

We are therefore charged to demand that you form a people's army. This army must immediately set up its centre in Paris; in every department it goes through it must enrol all men who want a united and indivisible Republic; and it must be followed by an incorruptible and formidable tribunal, equipped with the instrument of death that will put an end to both the schemes and the lives of plotters.

Addressing the Convention in the name of the Committee of Public Safety, the Montagnard deputy Bertrand Barère declared that the *journées* of 4 and 5 September made Terror 'the order of the day', and accelerated the introduction of radical legislation.

FOR several days now, everything has pointed to royalist stirrings in Paris, but organized and controlled by a people's army, giving meaning at last to the slogan 'Terror will be the Order of the Day.'

This is how to do away instantly with both royalists and moderates, and the restless counter-revolutionary scum. The royalists want blood; well, they shall have the blood of the conspirators, the likes of Brissot and Marie-Antoinette. It will be an operation for special Revolutionary tribunals.

The Law of Suspects decreed on 17 September 1793 was the basis of the policing operations of the Terror, and gave wide-ranging powers to local *comités de surveillance*, or 'revolutionary committees'.

IMMEDIATELY following the publication of this decree, all suspects within republican territory, and who are still at liberty, shall be arrested.

The following shall be considered suspect: first, those who, by their conduct, association, speech or writings, have shown themselves in favour of tyranny or federalism, and hostile to freedom; second, those who are unable to prove their means of existence and the execution of their civil duties; third, those who have been refused a certificate of civic loyalty; fourth, any public officials who have been suspended or stripped of their powers by the National Convention or its commissioners and not reinstated; fifth, those former members of the nobility, including husbands, wives, fathers, mothers, sons or daughters, brothers or sisters, and émigré agents, who have not demonstrated their constant devotion to the Revolution; sixth, those who emigrated between 1 July 1789 and 8 April 1792.

The Surveillance Committees established in accordance with the law of 21 March last are responsible for drawing up lists of suspects, with issuing warrants of arrest against them, and with placing their papers under seal.

A Revolutionary Calendar was decreed in the Convention on 5 October. The Conventionnels felt they had inaugurated a new epoch in human history by declaring the Republic.

THE REVOLUTIONARY CALENDAR

The first year of the French Republic began at midnight on 22 September 1792 and ended at midnight on the night of 21-22 September 1793.

The year is divided into twelve equal months of thirty days each, to be followed by five days to make up the full ordinary year which will not be part of any month. They will be known as days 'additional'.

Each month is divided into three equal parts of 10 days each, called *décades*, which are distinguished by being known at first, second and third.

Every four years on Revolution Day there will be Republican Games in memory of the French Revolution.

The nation in arms

On 21 February 1793 the Convention decreed the *amalgame*, the integration of all line and volunteer units, which had previously maintained their own distinct organization, recruitment policies, promotion procedures, pay scales, and even uniforms, into one armed force which would standardize all of these. It was expected that this amalgamation would fuse the patriotic commitment of the volunteers with the professional competence of the regulars to create a more enthusiastic and efficient army.

Three days later, the Convention ordered a levy of 300,000 men to fill the ranks of the "demi-brigades" (consisting of one regular and two volunteer battalions each), the basic units of the new army. All unmarried, childless French males between eighteen and forty years of age were eligible, and every department was required to supply a number of recruits in proportion to its population. In all, approximately half of the 300,000 men were raised before the *levée en masse* (23 August 1793) established new procedures for mobilization.

The Law of 23 August put all human and material resources of the nation at the disposal of the government for the war, and initiated an age of total warfare. All inhabitants, even those who did not enjoy the rights of citizenship – women and children – were expected to contribute. All items were liable to requisitioning, from grain to gold – church bells were melted for cannon and religious vessels for coinage.

Nevertheless the Convention, under the leadership of the Committee of Public Safety, in which Lazare Carnot was the mobilizing military genius, was able to harness the energies of the nation for war on an unprecedented scale. By mid-1794 well over a million men were enrolled in the armies of the Republic.

The armies played an important part in internal policing as well as external security. They were deployed in the Vendée, for example, as well as in the sieges of Lyon and Toulon. In their internal role, however, their efforts were supplemented by the so-called *armées révolutionnaires*, or 'people's armies'.

These were citizen militias formed in many localities by patriot authorities in April and May 1793 to combat the tide of counter-revolution.

The Parisian *armée*, created in September 1793, was by far the largest of its kind, with 7200 men from similar *sans-culotte* backgrounds. Its bureaucracy was large and complex, a mixture of soldiers, civil servants and radical politicians, from which the Hébertist Charles-Philippe Ronsin emerged as military commander.

The real work of the Parisian *armée*, like that of the numerous departmental *armées*, was to gather food supplies from a reluctant, potentially counter-revolutionary countryside. But the citizen-soldiers also indulged their passion for dechristianization at the expense of parish churches, mingling the townsman's traditional contempt for the peasant with the levelling doctrines found in Hébert's newspaper *Le Père Duchesne*.

The rank and file saw themselves as a political élite, chosen for their unswerving loyalty to the Revolution. They sought confrontation with its enemies – and they found it. The peasantry fought back, in defence of their crops and their religion. The Montagnard leadership soon realized that the *armées* made more trouble than they were worth. Their very existence – to say nothing of their Hébertist persuasion – threatened not only peasants, Federalists and assorted counter-revolutionaries, but also the core of the Revolutionary Government.

The victory of Robespierre and the Mountain in early 1794 led to a return to centralized government through the enforcement of the Law of Revolutionary Government of 14 Frimaire (4 December 1793), and the *armées*, the antithesis of tight government control from the capital, were soon neutralized by the Committee of Public Safety. However, they had contributed in their way to the military successes of 1794, and were an important aspect of the 'nation in arms'.

ABOVE A volunteer's return from the wars.

Now that Terror was 'the order of the day', political trials became frequent. The Revolutionary Tribunal's accusation in the trial of Marie-Antoinette, a forgotten figure in the Temple prison, that the queen had committed incest with her infant son clearly backfired, as Helen Maria Williams, an English woman on close terms with the Girondins, recalled in her memoirs.

FOR a long time the Jacobins had demanded the trial of Marie-Antoinette, whose existence, they declared, endangered that of the republic. She was accordingly arraigned for having committed a series of crimes which, in the language of the indictment, comprehended not merely counter-revolutionary projects, but all the enormities of the Messalinas, Brunehauts, Frédégondes and Medicis. A curious account of the evidence in support of these charges, and the effect which her behaviour produced upon Robespierre, is given by Vilate, a young man of the Revolutionary Tribunal. The scene passed during the trial at a tavern near the Tuileries, where Vilate was invited to dine with Robespierre, Barère and Saint-Just.

'Seated around the table,' he says, 'in a close and retired room, they asked me to give them some leading features of the evidence on the trial of the Austrian. I did not forget that expostulation of insulted nature when Hébert, accusing Marie-Antoinette of having committed the most shocking crime, she turned with dignity towards the audience and said, "I appeal to the conscience and feelings of every mother present, to declare if there be one amongst you who does not shudder at the idea of such horrors." Robespierre, struck with this answer as by an electrical stroke, broke his plate with his fork. "That blockhead Hébert!" cried he, "as if it were not enough that she was really a Messalina, he must make her an Agrippina also, and furnish her with the triumph of exciting the sympathy of the public in her last moments."'

Marie-Antoinette made no defence, and called no witnesses, alleging that no positive fact had been produced against her. She had preserved a uniform behaviour during the whole of her trial, except when a starting tear accompanied her answer to Hébert.

She was condemned about four in the morning (16 October 1793), and heard her sentence with composure. But her firmness forsook her on the way from the court to her dungeon. She burst into tears; as if ashamed of this weakness, she observed to her guards that though she wept at that moment, they should see her go to the scaffold without shedding a tear.

On her way to execution, where she was taken after the accustomed manner in a cart, with her hands tied behind her, she paid little attention to the priest who attended her. She reached the place of execution about noon, and when she turned her eyes towards the palace, she became visibly agitated. She ascended the scaffold with precipitation, and her head was in a moment held up to the people by the executioner.

THE TIMES (London), *23 October 1793*

Thus then has MARIE ANTOINETTE, the unfortunate Queen of France, been brought to the block, and thereby terminated a miserable existence. The descendants of the Caesars, condemned by sanguinary judges, has perished under the hands of a hangman.

The last letter of Marie-Antoinette, written to her sister-in-law, Mme Elisabeth.

This 16 October, half-past four in the morning.

It is to you, my sister, that I write for the last time. I have just been condemned, not to a shameful death – it is such only for criminals – but to go and join your brother. Innocent like him, I hope to show the same steadfastness as he in these last moments. I am calm, as one is when one's conscience is clear.

I deeply regret leaving my poor children; you know that I lived only for them, and you, my good, loving sister, you who have by your friendship sacrificed everything to be with us. What a position I leave you in!

Marie-Antoinette

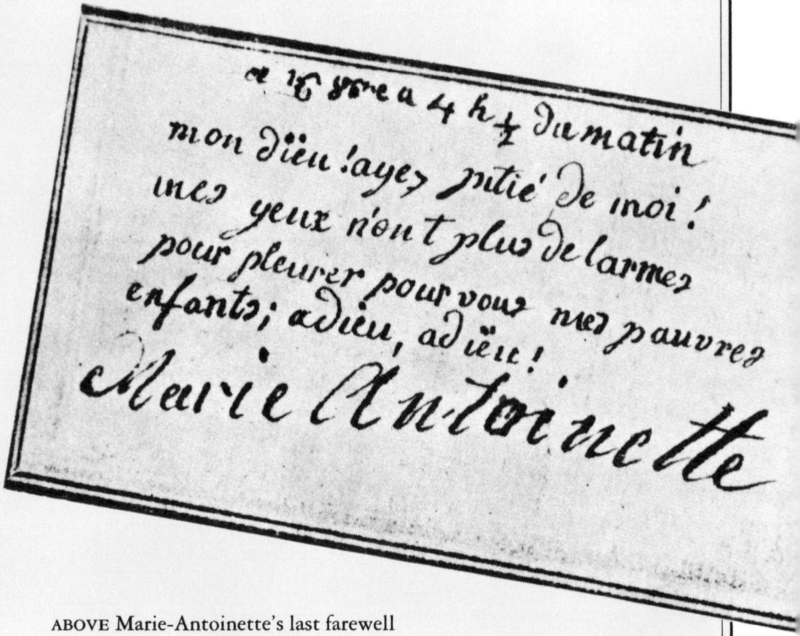
ce 16 8bre a 4 h ½ du matin
mon dieu! ayez pitié de moi!
mes yeux n'ont plus de larmes
pour pleurer pour vous mes pauvres
enfants; adieu, adieu!
Marie Antoinette

ABOVE Marie-Antoinette's last farewell to her children, written in her prayer book.

The trial and execution of Marie-Antoinette

THE gaunt, pathetic figure of Marie-Antoinette, dressed in a plain white shift, her neck shaven for the blade, her wrists tied tight behind her back, seated impassively on a plank of wood in the back of a cart bearing her to the scaffold on 16 October 1793 was captured with savage realism in Jacques-Louis David's famous sketch. Her appearance stirred astonishment and emotion in the crowd who jostled to see her from behind the two ranks of soldiers who lined every inch of the way along her route. The greyness of her hair was not new – she had started to go white after losing her eldest son in June 1789 – but its colour and condition in a woman still only 37 was a cruel contrast with her erstwhile ostentation and glamour.

The queen's stoic calm was impressive: she even apologised to her executioner – Henri Sanson, son of the man who had executed her husband – when she accidentally stepped on his foot as she moved forward to be strapped to the plank beneath the blade of the guillotine. Such dignity, such presence contrasted with the frivolity of the former queen, whose insouciance and arrogance had been legendary. Although she had never recommended that the people eat cake if they could not afford bread, this was the kind of myth that clung to 'Madame Déficit', 'Madame Veto', 'l'Autrichienne'.

Such legends made it difficult for the National Convention to forget about Marie-Antoinette or consign her to life imprisonment or exile. Since the death of 'Louis the Shortened', she had been kept in austere, humble surroundings in the Temple prison. In early July her eldest son was removed from her; her captors disliked the way she treated the child as monarch, allowing him to be served first at meals and observing other forms of archaic court ritual. On 2 August, she was moved from the Temple to solitary confinement in a cell in the grim Conciergerie prison on the Ile de la Cité, an antechamber to the scaffold.

On 3 October the Convention decided to refer her to the Revolutionary Tribunal, largely because of a vicious propaganda campaign orchestrated by Hébert's *Le Père Duchesne*.

The trial of 'Widow Capet' was one of many political trials in the autumn of 1793. 31 Girondin deputies were executed on 31 October: 'Philippe-Egalité' (the former duc d'Orléans) on 6 November, Madame Roland three days later and Bailly on 12 November. Marie-Antoinette's conviction, on 15 October, was essentially on the counts of treasonably aiding and abetting foreign powers and conspiring to foment civil war within France. Although she was guilty on both charges, public prosecutor Fouquier-Tinville had few material proofs at his disposal and he had to rely on character witnesses. It was stated, for example, that Marie-Antoinette's counter-revolutionary intentions were shown by her giving drink to her Swiss Guards before the *journée* of 10 August 1792.

More spectacularly, Hébert, who was called as a witness, raised the question of the queen's allegedly incestuous relationship with her son. Louis had seemingly been tricked by Simon his tutor into claiming that he had been encouraged to masturbate by his mother; that he had frequently slept in the same bed in the Temple prison with the queen and with Madame Elisabeth; and that the two had encouraged the same 'pernicious practice' which had on at least one occasion led to him copulating with his mother (from which he had derived a hernia). This act, it was claimed, 'did not spring from pleasure but from a political wish to enervate the physique of the child'.

The execution followed the verdict within hours. The executioner displayed Marie-Antoinette's head to the crowd before dumping it between the legs of the corpse, which was despatched to an unmarked grave. In 1815, Chateaubriand identified the queen's skull by the set of the jawbone, which he had glimpsed in a smile at Versailles in happier days.

ABOVE Marie-Antoinette's head is held up to the crowd.

The Federalist Revolt lingered on in a number of major cities. In Toulon, the Federalist rebels handed over the French Mediterranean fleet at anchor in the harbour to the British navy, in collaboration with a Spanish fleet. In September, the joint allied commanders had issued the following propagandizing proclamation.

PROCLAMATION. From the most honourable Samuel, Lord Hood, Vice-Admiral and Commander-in-Chief of His Britannic Majesty's squadron in the Mediterranean, etc. etc. etc.;

And His Excellency Don Juan de Langara, Vice-Admiral and Commander-in-Chief of His Catholic Majesty's squadron, etc. etc. etc.:

To the officers, petty officers, soldiers of the French army in the southern provinces of France.

For four years you have been dragged through a revolution which has made you the prey of seditious men, has plunged you into all the horrors of civil and foreign war, and which has finally brought you to the brink of the abyss.

You know from bitter experience the state to which these seditious men have brought you since the assassination of your legitimate sovereign. The evils are reaching a peak and we are coming to deliver you from them, not in a spirit of conquest, as you have been told by your leaders, but to re-establish good order, to restore you to happiness, and to put Louis XVII on the throne.

The good people of Toulon have accepted with gratitude the aid that we are bringing them. They know that the flags flying the national colours everywhere, the power which we exercise, we hold only in trust, that we receive into our forces all those French soldiers who have submitted to the better cause, and that all will be restored in its entirety to Louis XVII as soon as peace and good order are irrevocably restored.

Your food supplies are uncertain, those we offer you are assured and abundant; you are running every risk, we guarantee you all means of welfare. So stop being the instruments of intrigue for a handful of conspirators, and serve your king who is henceforward your sole source of peace and happiness.

We are granting amnesty and forgiveness to all soldiers who will immediately quit the banners of anarchy and come to join all faithful Frenchmen in sustaining the cause and rights of Louis XVII.

Delivered at Toulon, 4 September 1793, the first year of the reign of Louis XVII.

Signed: Hood, Langara.

In October, following a siege which had lasted several months, Federalist Lyon fell to the republican armies. The Convention at once issued the following decree.

UPON presentation of the Committee of Public Safety the National Convention will nominate a special commission, with five members, to administer military punishment without delay on the Lyon counter-revolutionaries.

All inhabitants of Lyon will be disarmed.

The city of Lyon will be destroyed; all the dwellings of wealthy individuals will be demolished; there will remain only the houses of poor men, of murdered or proscribed patriots, buildings specially used for industry, and monuments sacred to humanity and to public instruction.

The name of Lyon will be erased from the list of cities of the Republic.

The assemblage of houses which are preserved shall henceforward bear the name of 'Ville-Affranchie' [Free Town].

There shall be set up in the ruins of Lyon a column attesting to posterity the crimes and the punishment of the city's royalists, with the following inscription: 'Lyon made war on freedom: Lyon exists no more – the 18th day of the First month of the Year II of the Republic (9 October 1793), one and indivisible.'

Collot-d'Herbois, a colleague of Robespierre on the Committee of Public Safety, was sent to Lyon along with the ruthless Fouché to dispense revolutionary justice. From a letter from Collot to a fellow Jacobin in Paris.

My friend and brother, our Jacobin brothers are achieving marvels; a letter from Robespierre would please them greatly and would be very effective.

Here we have restored not public spirit, since there is none, but courage, the morale of a few men of energy and of a certain number of patriots who have suffered oppression for too long. We have revitalized justice in republican style, i.e. swift and terrible as the will of the nation. It will strike at traitors like a thunderbolt and leave only ashes. The destruction of one vile and rebellious city will strengthen all the others.

The death of these scoundrels will assure life for generations of free men. These are our principles. We will demolish as much as we can, by cannon-fire and by exploding mines. But as you will realize, amidst a population of a hundred and fifty thousand, there are many obstacles to such methods.

The people's blade cut the heads off twenty conspirators each day and it did not frighten them. We have set up a commission which is as prompt as can be the conscience of true republicans sitting in judgement on traitors. Sixty-four of these conspirators were shot yesterday, on the same spot where they fired on patriots; two hundred and thirty will fall today. Such substantial examples will help to persuade those cities which are vacillating.

Guillon's history of the repression in Lyon, published in 1824, was doubtless exaggerated. But it was based on oral accounts.

THERE is no one in Lyons, whatever their sex or profession, who, having shown wisdom and integrity, can escape the murderous fury of the 'Temporary Commission' abetted by Fouché. To receive a state pension has become a deadly crime. Anyone considered rich deserves to be guillotined. Anyone, man or woman, young or old, who has not contributed toward the expenses of the siege, is condemned to death. All those who held a title, or any post under the monarchy, are executed. All the priests, even those who have not yet taken their final vows, are also executed, because their existence alone recalls the memory of religion. Workers, small shopkeepers, shopworkers, dockers, ignorant labourers, all suffer the same fate.

If one wanted a rough idea of the number of people slaughtered in the Place des Terreaux, it would be sufficient to know that their blood flowed in torrents, the square was flooded by it, so that it was almost impossible to walk across it without staining one's feet. The sawdust spread under and around the scaffold could not absorb so much blood, although it was constantly renewed; so much blood ran in the gutters carrying the sewage all the way to the Rhône and the Saône that they overflowed and it poured into the cellars. Mixing with the very entrails of their native soil and rotting there, it threatened the people of Lyon with the ravages of pestilence, thus adding to all the other scourges which had overwhelmed them during the previous six months.

Among the innumerable citizens shot en masse at the Brotteaux and thrown into the river, there were two who, although wounded, were still alive. Finding the strength to escape from the current, they swam and reached a gravel spit of land where they begged people for mercy; dragoons were ordered to cross over and fall upon them. They finished them off with bayonet thrusts, and left their bodies there to the birds of prey.

From a pamphlet entitled *Letter from the guillotine of erstwhile Lyon to her elder sister, the guillotine of Paris.*

DEAR Sister, I read with wonder a report printed in Paris recounting your miraculous achievements, your admirable feats, and the progress of your work. I was moved to emulate you and, though your junior, I pursued my work with renewed enthusiasm, especially as I, like you, have a burning desire to rout this rabble of bandits and miscreants who have betrayed their country and sworn (in vain) to destroy it. Dearest older sister, your achievements are spectacular, How much praise you must receive!

We were born at the same time, and together we went to work; you have guided my daily tasks but, dearest sister, you must admit that I have despatched these with alacrity. Without boasting unduly, my arm is longer than yours: here in Ville-Affranchie it is quicker. I deal with quite as many as you, and will continue to do so, which is fine I assure you!

Here are details of my work, not to be compared with yours! but nevertheless you will admire my zeal, I am sure. I trim, I chew, I cut up these miscreants, and like you, I send them forth into the next world with a vigorous push. Between 12 October and 22 December I sent no less than 777 of them to the devil, not counting a few who escaped me and were shot instead, but no less dead for all that. Be that as it may, the French republicans are avenged.

Like you, my dear sister I caused them to take their last walk and so I have created ex-nobles, ex-priests, ex-lawyers, ex-municipal guards, ex-merchants, ex-plotters, ex-etc. I am sure you will shudder when you read the enclosed list. I have absolved so many with a final chop of my iron blade.

How many heads in one bag, dear sister! But our work is not yet done. There are many enemies at the heart of the Republic. It is our bounden duty to perform this last service for them, such a pleasant one to fulfil. Never have surgeons achieved such 'beautiful cures'. Your sister. The Lady Guillotine from Ville-Affranchie, formerly Lyon.

Organized in September, the *armée révolutionnaire* was soon bringing dechristianization into the villages and hamlets of rural France, as the account of a local official records.

SEVERAL detachments of this revolutionary army set off for the departments of the south, three of them totalling about three thousand men taking the route through Auxerre. The first unit arrived at Auxerre on 11 November, with cannon mounted on their gun-carriages, caissons, flags, pennants and drums. They were greeted at the St-Siméon gate by a picket from the Auxerre guard, lodged and well supplied by the townspeople, and set off again next morning.

The second group arrived in Auxerre on 13 November in the same style as the first, to be greeted in the same way. Along the way they indulged themselves in all frenzied excesses possible against religious property: they broke down chapel doors, overthrew altars, threw down saints' statues and images. At Ste-Marguerite, a chapel, they committed similar sacrileges and took a copper crucifix which was on the altar; one of their number carried it mockingly, upside down, on a cart, offering it to passers-by to spit on. When a citizen refused, one of the soldiers waved his sabre under his nose and cut off a bit of it.

When they reached the town they continued in the same violent way, mutilating and overturning any stone or plaster crosses and statues they came across, and climbing up towers and church roofs to remove exterior crosses and statues.

In the evening, with the help of ropes and four horses, they tore down a fine cross set in the middle of St Pierre's courtyard, carved with the instruments of the Passion, a monument worthy of our ancestors' reverence which had been erected at great expense.

In order to make sure that the little market towns and villages in the surrounding areas should feel their fury, they split up into various groups which went on next day by side roads. The young libertines of Auxerre imitated them, spreading out to the town boundaries and right across the neighbouring communes, destroying and removing crosses, pictures and statues; nothing escaped their rage, they showed no respect for the antiquity of the monuments; the most touching images served only to stir up their rage, and less than a week sufficed to wipe out all visible signs of Christianity in Auxerre itself and the surrounding parishes.

Dechristianization

As a result of savage penal legislation, few priests who had refused the Constitutional Oath were still in France by the autumn of 1793. Those who remained, or who returned from exile to continue a clandestine ministry, led a miserable, hunted existence.

The constitutional clergy, those who had sworn to uphold the constitution, also suffered from 1792 onwards. As a series of royalist revolts broke out, revolutionaries began to feel that the state church had failed to preach submission to the new regime. Some of the stigma attached to the refractory clergy rubbed off on the constitutionals, and they were caught up in a rising tide of revolutionary anti-clericalism which gained force with the outbreak of war and the fall of the monarchy in 1792. By the summer of 1793 many patriots believed that if the Revolution was to survive, Catholicism, as the tool used by counter-revolutionaries, must be eradicated. A campaign of dechristianization was launched against the Catholic church as well as against the treacherous clergy.

The campaign was taken up by the Paris Commune and its leaders, notably Chaumette, and by Hébert, whose *Le Père Duchesne* had long adopted anti-clericalism as its editorial stock in trade. In May 1793 the Commune stopped the payment of clerical salaries and subsequently tried to prevent the public exercise of Catholicism. It closed churches in Paris and forced over 400 priests to abdicate. Chaumette demanded that the former metropolitan church of Notre-Dame be reconsecrated to the cult of Reason. The Convention hastened to comply and on 10 November a civic festival was held in the new temple, its façade bearing the words 'To Philosophy'.

The most enthusiastic proponents of dechristianization were the *représentants en mission* in the provinces, such as Le Bon in the Pas-de-Calais and Javogues in the Loire. Using local *sans-culottes* as their workforce, they destroyed roadside shrines, stripped churches of their statues, crosses, and ornaments, removed the bells, and then closed the buildings altogether or turned them into stables or storehouses.

Constitutional priests were pilloried in mock religious ceremonies, and forced to renounce their priesthood. Clerical celibacy was denounced. In the Cher, Laplanche forced priests to marry; in the Nièvre, Fouché obliged any who were too old for this to adopt a child or elderly person. Place names were purged of all reference to a Christian past, children were named after republican heroes such as Brutus and Cato, and observance of the new Revolutionary calendar, which

abolished Sunday and Christian feast days, was enforced.

Initially the Convention went along with dechristianization, and deputies expressed approval when communes sent in sacred objects taken from local churches as trophies. But as the movement's excesses began to multiply, some voices were raised in protest. Cambon, in charge of the Finance Committee, feared that the resulting disorders would upset the financial stability he was trying to create. Danton believed that the campaign was alienating France's neighbours and encouraging them to join the allied coalition. In a number of speeches from late November, Robespierre reiterated the principle of freedom of worship. He had no love for the constitutional clergy, but opposed the excesses of their attackers on moral and practical grounds. He believed the campaign offended people's religious sensibilities and drove them into the arms of counter-revolution. Moreover, he had just received information about a foreign plot, in which some of the most active dechristianizers such as Hébert were implicated. Its purpose was to discredit the Revolution by associating it with the wild excesses of secularization. The dechristianization campaign was thus progressively brought under control as the Committee of Public Safety asserted its power over the *sans-culotte* movement.

ABOVE Republican bands and women representing Liberty and Reason paraded in Notre-Dame to mark its dechristianization.

BELOW 'Pluviôse' replaced February in the new secular calendar.

A letter from an individual in Toulon in the autumn of 1793, as the French armies laid siege to the port, gives the vantage-point of the besieged.

Toulon is completely blockaded by republican forces which are repulsed strongly every time the allied troops make some kind of sortie. However, the latter are insufficient in number both to guard all the fortresses, redoubts and other posts and to form an army capable of attacking the besiegers, who as soon as our troops appear take to their heels. These wretched republicans fight like barbarians and massacre any soldiers or officers who are unlucky enough to fall into their hands.

We are awaiting four thousand more men from the Neapolitan force, with a battalion of artillery and a few squadrons of cavalry as reinforcements.

Toulon was the last Federalist stronghold to fall to the Republic, when the French armies occupied it on 19 December 1793. The *représentants en mission* attached to the republican forces made this report to the Committee of Public Safety on 2 January 1794.

In the first few days after our entry into Toulon, citizen colleagues, we were unable to give you more than rough details of the republican army's victory; we hasten to bring you more information which will show the whole world what the courage of republicans can achieve when they are fighting for their freedom.

Since our last letter we have established through the various points of attack what losses the enemy may have suffered, and we have great pleasure in informing you that the figure has reached more than five thousand dead or wounded, not counting the very considerable numbers of prisoners. The speed with which the British embarked resulted in fresh and no less considerable losses; one of their frigates was sunk by the fire from our batteries, and most of their ships were severely damaged; so that the harbour shoreline is covered with their wreckage.

Every day we receive in the harbour vessels laden with supplies; a brig with 18 cannon and five hundred men aboard came in with them; all foreigners on these vessels are made prisoner; all the French are shot as traitors. Exemplary national justice is dispensed daily on the field of battle.

Everyone in Toulon who had been employed in the rebel navy or army, or in the civil or military administration, was shot to the army's manifold shouts of 'Long live the republic!'

Counter-revolution at Toulon and Lyon in 1793

WHERE Federalism persisted longest it tended to harden into overt counter-revolution. As military security and self-defence became paramount, so pronounced royalists assumed control and influenced the outcome of these rebellions. In Lyon the commander of the city's volunteer army was a royalist, the comte de Précy. In Marseille the monarchists sought an accommodation with Admiral Hood, commander of Britain's Mediterranean fleet. Although the great commercial port fell to the government before an agreement was finalized, rebels at neighbouring Toulon signed a treaty with the British, allowing enemy allied troops to occupy the important naval base.

Toulon joined the Federalist revolt at a late stage, in July 1793, as Republican armies closed in on the city and Marseille capitulated. This presented the Toulonnais with a dreadful dilemma: either they surrendered and endured the consequences, or they prepared for a siege behind the heavy fortifications that encircled their city. However, resistance was feasible only if maritime supply routes were opened by arrangement with the enemy fleet. Admiral Hood indicated his willingness to negotiate, on condition that the dockyard was surrendered to him and allegiance sworn to the monarchy. Many citizens – and British seamen – reacted strongly against these terms, but royalist elements were ready to make a virtue out of necessity.

In spite of anxious debate in the sections, or neighbourhood assemblies, and naval mutiny in the harbour, fear of government reprisals dictated the plunge into treason. On 28 August, British and allied forces entered the town and prepared for a long siege. However, Toulon was isolated, Hood received few reinforcements – and it was only three months before besieging Republicans wore down the defenders. The key to recapturing the city lay in occupying the Petit-Gibraltar, a promontory overlooking the port. Although this was generally known, an artillery officer called Napoleon Bonaparte was the only one to pursue the strategy in a determined and successful fashion. Napoleon's part in reconquering Toulon was decisive in his rise to fame; he was immediately promoted to major-general.

Bombardment from the surrounding heights made the city untenable and the British were compelled to withdraw on 17 and 18 December. As they did so panic broke out, with as many inhabitants as possible seeking refuge on departing vessels. Some 7000 or more,

ABOVE Napoleon takes the vital Petit-Gibraltar hilltop at Toulon.

LEFT The fall of Lyon, a prelude to savage repression.

including most of the rebel leaders, fled the stricken city. Severe punishment was meted out to those who remained; there were over 1000 executions and Toulon was stripped of its name, becoming 'Port-la-Montagne'.

At Lyon in October of that year there was even greater repression: fewer people could escape. 'Lyon made war on liberty, Lyon no longer exists', declared the Convention when General Kellerman finally blasted the city into submission after a two-month siege. Although royalist supporters, who saw the revolt as a means of attacking the Republic, were behind the most stubborn resistance, many who were executed as counter-revolutionaries were guilty by association rather than belief. During the winter some 1800 people were slaughtered, many in batches, on the burial grounds of Les Brotteaux, under the direction of *représentants en mission* Fouché and Collot d'Herbois. The punishment meted out at both Lyon and Toulon was clearly intended to have a deterrent effect.

At about the same time, the revolt in the Vendée was being brutally crushed by the 'infernal columns' of General Turreau. Turreau's letter to the Minister of War on 19 January 1794 shows something of how he operated.

My purpose is to burn everything, to leave nothing but what is essential to establish the necessary quarters for exterminating the rebels. This great measure is one which you should prescribe; you should also make an advance statement as to the fate of the women and children we will come across in this rebellious countryside. If they are all to be put to the sword, I cannot undertake such action without authorization.

All brigands caught bearing arms, or convicted of having taken up arms to revolt against their country, will be bayoneted. The same will apply to girls, women and children in the same circumstances. Those who are merely under suspicion will not be spared either, but no execution may be carried out except by previous order of the general.

All villages, farms, woods, heathlands, generally anything which will burn, will be set on fire, although not until any perishable supplies found there have been removed. But, it must be repeated, these executions must not take place until so ordered by the general.

I hasten to describe to you the measures which I have just put in hand for the extermination of all remaining rebels scattered about the interior of the Vendée. I was convinced that the only way to do this was by deploying a sufficient number of columns to spread right across the countryside and effect a general sweep, which would completely purge the cantons as they passed. Tomorrow, therefore, these twelve columns will set out simultaneously, moving from east to west. Each column commander has orders to search and burn forests, villages, market towns and farms, omitting, however, those places which I consider important posts and those which are essential for establishing communications.

The deputies from the Convention sent out from Paris as *représentants en mission* were the moving force behind the Terror in the departments. Carrier at Nantes, for example, was responsible for thousands of deaths associated with the Vendée revolt, notably in the infamous mass drownings in the estuary of the River Loire. The following letter was published in *Le Journal de la Montagne*.

An endless number of miscreants continues to arrive here. The guillotine is too slow, and since shooting wastes powder and shot, it was decided to put a certain number of them in large boats, which are then taken to the middle of the river, half a league from the town, and then sunk; this operation goes on constantly.

On 2 Nivôse (22 November), Carrier himself informed the Convention of this; and on the 8th a message from the Western army seemed to confirm that this method of disposal is being used all along the river; 'Three incurable ills pursue the miscreants: the Loire, the guillotine, and the armies of Westermann and Marceau.'

Laurent, reporting to the Committee of Public Safety from the department of the Nord in December 1793, outlined the kind of things most *représentants* and their agents did.

The city of Cambrai is very short of patriots and one does not know where to turn. The prisons are in a state of disorder and the gaolers go out drinking with the prisoners. I have administered punishments. Among the prisoners there was a battalion commander who was stirring up his guards: I had him taken to Arras. He was one of Capet's tapestry-makers. There are still some other officers in the garrison who have no sense of civic responsibility but are less obvious. There will still need to be a national purging as soon as I arrive.

The churches are stripped bare; the revolutionary ten-day calendar is observed; priests are renouncing their Christian faith; civil marriages are celebrated without benefit of clergy; ecclesiastical trappings are ceremonially burned. Church silver is being dug up from its hiding places. Here and there bags of money are found.

There are still some émigrés around, but they are being tracked down and I have a ferret with a very keen sense of smell: even if it does not find where they are hidden, it discovers their silver.

THE WORLD (London) *20 August 1793*

From the adoption of the Motion made by SIMON in the National Convention, for arresting all the Englishmen in Paris, there is every reason to entertain the most serious apprehension for the personal safety of our valuable Countrymen, who have been imprudent enough to remain in Paris, or in short, in any other part of France.

Fouché: a terrorist en mission

ESTABLISHED in March 1793, *représentants en mission* were in effect liaison agents between the Revolutionary Government and the country at large. These selected members of the Convention, sent out to the department and armies of republican France were the dynamo behind the Terror in provincial France. The Law of 14

Frimaire Year II (4 December 1793) had placed them firmly under the control of the Committee of Public Safety. Yet in practice from mid-1793 down to early 1794, central control was often surprisingly lax, and *représentants* had considerable independence and wide-ranging powers.

The activities of the *représentants* were partly a consequence of the area in which they operated: many of the most terroristic were found in war zones – Joseph Le Bon on the northern front, for example, Carrier at Nantes in the middle of the Vendée region, and Barras and Fréron at federalist Marseille and Toulon. However, political commitment and questions of temperament and personality also mattered: Javogues in the Loire, for example, was a highly volatile, not to say unstable, left-wing Montagnard.

Something of the range and the importance of the activities of the *représentants en mission* in 1793–4 can be seen in the career of Joseph Fouché, at this time an enthusiastic Montagnard, though later to be famous as Napoleon's police minister.

Like so many revolutionaries, Fouché was a member of the generation born around 1760. In 1792 he was elected to the Convention as a deputy for the Loire-Inférieure.

He won lasting notoriety as a *représentant en mission*. His first task, in March 1793, was to help suppress the civil war that had flared up in the west. During the summer he was sent to the Nièvre, a department in central France, on a spectacular mission which forged his reputation as a 'terrorist'. Although a firm believer in a property-owning society, he was keen to redistribute goods belonging to enemies of the Revolution among the poor. His efforts were particularly directed towards the church, which he had formerly served. His spoliation of local churches was justified in terms of the war effort and the need to combat clerical resistance, but it was accompanied by a strong anti-religious ideology: Fouché also played a vigorous role in dechristianization.

During the winter of 1793-4 he was sent to Lyon to organize the repression that followed the defeat of its rebellion. With Collot d'Herbois, a member of the Committee of Public Safety, he was associated with some of the most brutal reprisals of the period. In December and January some 1800 individuals perished for complicity in the revolt, many of them mown down by grapeshot: the dreadful *mitraillades*. Perhaps partly because of this excess of zeal, Fouché was recalled to Paris in the spring of 1794, where, he joined the Thermidorian coalition which overthrew Robespierre a few months later.

Fouché later protested that his terrorist policies were adopted in response to orders from Paris. In this, he was far too modest and underestimated his considerable personal achievement. Despite their idiosyncracies, travelling deputies like Fouché showed a tireless, patriotic commitment, and made an inestimable contribution to the success of the Revolutionary Government in 1793–4.

BELOW The aftermath of *représentant en mission* activity: the burial of enemies of the People in mass graves.

A letter from one of his colleagues describes how the *représentant en mission* Joseph Le Bon at Arras and Cambrai utilized the local revolutionary court to dispense a chillingly terrorist justice.

Le Bon is back from Paris, full of holy rage against the inertia which was impeding revolutionary activities. Straight away a terrifying jury, just like the one in Paris, was added to the Revolutionary Tribunal. This jury is made up of sixty brazen b——s (of which he was one).

A draconian order has brought about the incarceration of all those aristocratic women whose husbands are imprisoned, and likewise of men whose wives are in prison. The Doullens fortress has been requisitioned by a special commission of seven patriots (of whom I was one). The guillotine has not been out of action since then; dukes, marquises, counts and barons, men and women, all falling like hailstones. We have just decreed that we will draw up the act of indictment of all the great aristocrats of Arras first, and then of other places in the department of the Nord. One tribunal will no longer be sufficient, and Le Bon has therefore just added a second section.

Le Bon is only concerned with drawing up acts of indictment, and we others, five or six of us, carry out interrogations or make domiciliary visits where we always make valuable discoveries; we no longer sleep.

Many *représentants* were colourful characters. This description of Javogues in St-Etienne, given by a local official in an unpublished memoir, captures both the extensive powers of such figures and the fear and hatred they inspired.

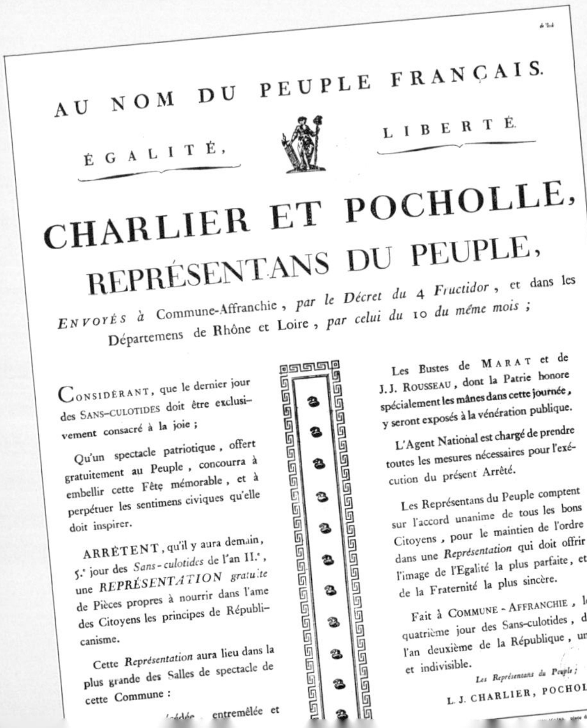

AU NOM DU PEUPLE FRANÇAIS.

ÉGALITÉ, LIBERTÉ.

CHARLIER ET POCHOLLE,

REPRÉSENTANS DU PEUPLE,

ENVOYÉS à Commune-Affranchie, *par le Décret du 4 Fructidor*, et dans les Départemens de Rhône et Loire, *par celui du 10 du même mois*;

CONSIDÉRANT, que le dernier jour des SANS-CULOTIDES doit être exclusivement consacré à la joie;

Qu'un spectacle patriotique, offert gratuitement au Peuple, concourra à embellir cette Fête mémorable, et à perpétuer les sentimens civiques qu'elle doit inspirer.

ARRÊTENT, qu'il y aura demain, 5.e jour des *Sans-culotides* de l'an II.e, une *REPRÉSENTATION* gratuite de Pièces propres à nourrir dans l'ame des Citoyens les principes de Républicanisme.

Cette *Représentation* aura lieu dans la plus grande des Salles de spectacle de cette Commune:

... entremêlée et

Les Bustes de MARAT et de J. J. ROUSSEAU, dont la Patrie honore spécialement les mânes dans cette journée, y seront exposés à la vénération publique.

L'Agent National est chargé de prendre toutes les mesures nécessaires pour l'exécution du présent Arrêté.

Les Représentans du Peuple comptent sur l'accord unanime de tous les bons Citoyens, pour le maintien de l'ordre dans une *Représentation* qui doit offrir l'image de l'Egalité la plus parfaite, et de la Fraternité la plus sincère.

Fait à COMMUNE-AFFRANCHIE, le quatrième jour des Sans-culotides, de l'an deuxième de la République, une et indivisible.

Les Représentans du Peuple;

L. J. CHARLIER, POCHOLLE.

AT six o'clock in the evening, Javogues went to the commune meeting hall at St-Etienne. The municipal body was assembled and there were a great number of spectators. He was drunk as a lord. He made a pretty young girl sit beside him, whom he had summoned to sing a patriotic song. He demanded beer, and gave orders that it should be brought from the cellar of citizen Vincent, who is at the prisons. First came eight bottles of beer; several more trips were made and about thirty bottles, beer and wine, were drunk in the hall. Javogues, the municipal officers and our friends ate sausage and white bread which they had seized from a bakery: they drank beer and wine in the face of people, who soaked up the representative's sermonizing and muttered in their patois, 'Look, look at the b——s! They're getting good and drunk, and we have to pay attention.' The municipal officers and our friends threw pellets of white bread in each other's faces for fun.

One of the spectators remarked to Javogues on the arbitrary taxes he was levying, and he shouted to the leader of the revolutionary guard, 'Bloody hell, come and arrest this b——, I'll have him shot.' Citizeness Fressinette, a spinster, on being told that she had been declared liable to a tax which was greater than her income, hurried to the session to make representations to Javogues; he answered loudly, 'You are a bitch, a damned whore, you have been tossed by priests more often than I've got hairs on my head, your c— must be so big that I could lose myself in it completely.' He went on to say, 'All women are damned bitches, damned whores; they are our piss-pots, etc. etc.' Then he added, 'I'm talking about outrageous royalists.'

To the mayor's daughter, a girl of about twenty, he said, 'You are a fine wench, a damned whore, but a pretty good patriot for all that.' He kissed the young girl sitting beside him at least a hundred times; when he put his hand on her breast, she gave him a good slap and said, 'You're a representative of the people, how can you forget yourself so?' He replied, 'D—— it, don't you see, I'd do less harm getting hold of a hundred tits than stealing a six-farthing *sou*.'

I do not think that such orgies are a good way of regenerating public morals.

There are several beggarly wenches, more down-at-heel than those prostitutes who used to hang around the Paris grain-harbour, who go and visit citizen Javogues, and he has his frolics with them; I am told that one of these tramps has a daughter who calls Javogues her daddy.

The Massachusetts Magazine (Boston), *January 1794*

All France is declared to be in a state of siege, and all foreigners are arrested, and to be held in custody until peace takes place.

The aims of Laplanche, another *représentant* in the department of the Cher, were nothing if not ambitious. Revolutionary enthusiasm was in full flood.

I have spoken of religion and all its mumbo-jumbo; I have spoken out against the bad priests, I have crushed fanaticism and superstition and, at my words, all the chapels, all the crosses, all the holy mangers and wooden and stone saints at the street corners have fallen; everything has been destroyed.

I have suppressed a parish, banned the church, sent the priest back to his former empty presbytery. The bells have come down, only one will remain to give warning of fires and danger.

I have replaced the district administration; it was bad.

I have replaced the judicial tribunal; it was made up of dusty old wigs. In place of this old regime I have installed men of enlightenment and some sans-culottes: *a vine-grower, a shoemaker and a joiner have been nominated, with thousand-fold cries of 'Long live the Mountain!'*

I have kept the municipal council: it is sound.

In place of the lieutenant of gendarmerie I have nominated citizen Desbans.

I have confirmed the existing comité de surveillance; *it is made up of true Montagnards.*

I have taxed the rich for the Revolution; the total of this tax is 249,000 livres.

I have had two bad priests arrested.

I have given orders for the arrest of Romanet, former noble and bodyguard.

I have had corn distributed to those poor souls who had none.

I have given orders that I must have the names of all the needy who have a right to be helped; I will favour the parents, wives and children of the men who are defending the nation.

That is not all, Citizen Representatives; I shall travel throughout the district, I will root out fanaticism, I shall crush the aristocracy, I will bring about the triumph of the Montagnards, I shall tax the rich, and in the end I will enable the people to enjoy the advantages of liberty and equality.

Prudhomme, the editor of *Les Révolutions de Paris*, ceased publication of his newspaper in early 1794 with this rosily optimistic editorial. Was a brave new world at hand?

I swore to cease my *Révolutions de Paris* only when my country was free; I have kept my word.

My country is free, since the French have sworn liberty, equality and indivisibility.

My country is free, since the head of the last tyrant of the French has fallen.

My country is free, since we have a constitution truly republican, worthy of serving as a model to all peoples who would be slaves no longer.

My country is free, since the French make all despots tremble.

My country is free, since the French are able to procure liberty for all other peoples.

My country is free, since none of the abuses of the *ancien régime* exists any more. No more feudalism, no more monarchy, and soon no more superstition.

My country is free, since federalism is destroyed.

My country is free, since the *sans-culottes* have won their rights and now occupy all positions.

The Revolution is over. The people is no longer on its knees, it has risen and has reduced the 'great' to their true stature.

The Revolution can and must be regarded as over, if the *sans-culottes* never depart from its principles.

The Revolution is over, if the Convention does not divide itself, and if the patriots always rally round it.

The Revolution is over, if the patriots know how to be patient in times of shortages.

The Revolution is over, if the *sans-culottes* examine and learn how to distinguish the true from the false patriot.

The Revolution is over, if the virtuous poor are no longer at the mercy of the selfish rich.

The Revolution is over, if the French people truly take to heart the beauties of republican government.

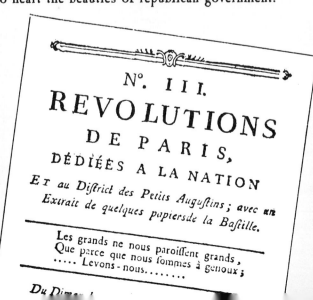

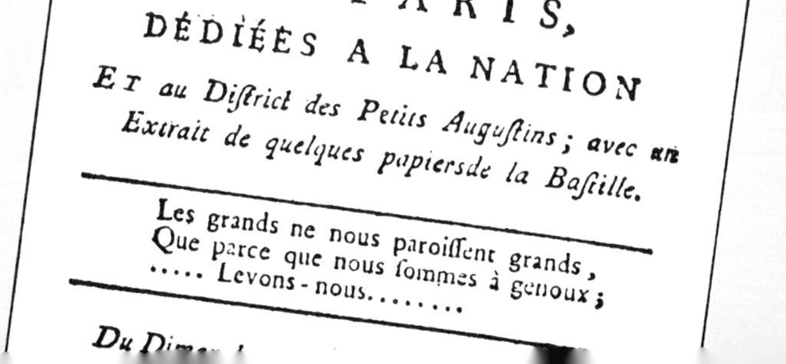

N°. III.

REVOLUTIONS DE PARIS, DÉDIÉES A LA NATION

Et au Diſtrict des Petits Auguſtins; avec un Extrait de quelques papiers de la Baſtille.

Les grands ne nous paroiſſent grands,
Que parce que nous ſommes à genoux;
.... Levons-nous.......

CHAPTER SIX: 1794–1795

The Frozen Republic

At the time of the Festival of the Supreme Being in June 1794, Robespierre urged that the Terror be intensified, to achieve a fairer society. However, he was outmanœuvred by colleagues in the Convention who believed that when the pressures of war eased, the need for terrorist policies would recede. Robespierre was overthrown on 27 July 1794, but France still required a measure of strong central control. Afraid to see a repetition of the levelling policies practised during the reign of Terror, but fearful of a return to the *ancien régime*, the republic remained 'frozen' – the seedbed of Napoleon's military dictatorship.

(*Festival of the Supreme Being*)

The revolution is frozen; all springs of action are checked; nothing is left but red caps worn by intriguers.

The use of terror has desensitized crime, as strong liquors do the palate.

Certainly it is not yet time to do good. We must wait until the general evil is so extreme that opinion in general longs for measures which will lead to good. That which produces the general good is always terrible; to begin too soon appears extraordinary.

The revolution must hold fast to perfect happiness and perfect public freedom, by means of the laws. Each stage, each victory over monarchism, must result in and consecrate a new republican beginning.

The sombre reflections recorded by Robespierre's young colleague on the Committee of Public Safety, Saint-Just, in his notebooks written in early 1794, illustrate a growing concern about the direction the Revolution was taking. At that time, Camille Desmoulins was using used his newspaper, *Le Vieux Cordelier*, as a platform from which to argue for a relaxation rather than an intensification of the Terror.

THE Committee of Public Safety already has power of appointment to all posts, including the Convention's committees, including even the *représentants en mission* sent out to the departments and the army.

What else does it need to dominate or rather to abolish the Convention and rule as a decemvirate, if those deputies it cannot attract by flashing tricolour plumes before their eyes, reward for their adaptability and adulation, can be controlled by fear of being sent to the Luxembourg if they should cause offence? Are there many deputies, are there many men, quite impervious to hope and to fear?

The publisher Nicolas Ruault felt some sympathy for the policy of clemency now preached by Desmoulins and Danton, and viewed the Terror as multiplying its enemies by its increasingly repressive policies.

It is sad to see the patriots destroying each other and thus weakening both their own strength and their cause. Some who have long preached murder and death, who made 'Terror the order of the day', such as Danton and Camille Desmoulins, now feel this so strongly that they are retracing their steps and suggesting 'clemency committees' instead of the revolutionary committees. But the madmen who control the Committee of Public Safety and the National Convention do not listen to them; the scent of the blood they spill gives them courage; they treat Danton and Camille Desmoulins as counter-revolutionaries.

So far these two are the only ones I can see who are returning to common sense, whose revolutionary frenzy is over, who feel remorse for the past or apprehension for the future; they foresee that all these crimes, these bloody executions, may well turn public opinion against the very revolution it began and has supported.

Yet if the Revolution was making enemies by its policies of Terror, it was also, throughout the Spring of 1794, attempting to win adherents by radical social policies. Slavery was abolished following this speech by Danton in the Convention on 4 February.

REPRESENTATIVES of the French people, until now we have only established liberty like egoists, only for ourselves. But today, before the world, we proclaim – and future generations will glory in this decree – we proclaim universal liberty. Yesterday, when the president gave the fraternal kiss to the black deputies, I saw that now was the moment when the Convention must declare our brothers' freedom. Today the Convention has done its duty.

But, having granted the benefit of liberty, we must become as it were its administrators.

Let us refer to the Committee of Public Safety and the Colonial Committee the task of finding ways of making this decree useful but not dangerous to mankind.

We are working for future generations; let us launch liberty in the colonies. Once planted in the New World, it will bear abundant fruit there and put down deep roots.

THE MASSACHUSETTS MAGAZINE (Boston) *September 1793*

A band of blacks of both sexes, attended by martial musick and escorted by a great mob of Parisians, came to the Hall to return thanks to the Legislation for having raised them to the ranks of men.

The President gave the fraternal kiss to an old Negress of 114 years of age, and mother to 11 children. After which she was respectfully conducted to an armchair, and seated at the side of the President.

The abolition of slavery

THE European war preoccupied the armed forces, leaving them little opportunity to defend France's overseas colonies. The Revolution had shattered the naval officer corps and seriously disrupted the navy: even if they had wished to do so, the French would have been unable to break the British and allied blockade and send reinforcements to their valuable overseas possessions in the Caribbean. British naval supremacy soon cut off France's colonial trade, and Britain and Spain seemed likely to seize what they could of the vulnerable French empire.

To survive at all, the colonies would have to look to their own resources, in particular by mobilizing free coloured manpower and even slaves to supplement white republican resistance. In this way British and Spanish attacks might be repulsed and the war carried into their own colonies.

Even before the colonial war began, once Britain had entered the war in February 1793, Brissot had urged the Convention to consider the abolition of slavery. Pragmatism as well as principle was involved: the very survival of the French in the West Indies depended on major concessions to the non-white population. Finally, on 29 August 1793, one commissioner of the French republic in the islands, Léger-Félicité Sonthonax, freed and armed the slaves.

This action brought temporary respite, but only a limited number of slaves were willing to rally to him without knowing the French government's reaction. In the meantime, Britain launched a major offensive in the Caribbean, taking Tobago in April 1793 and going on to occupy Martinique, St-Lucia, Guadeloupe and Port-au-Prince, capital of St-Domingue. On 4 February 1794 the National Convention responded to the British threat by declaring the abolition of slavery in all French colonies. 'By sowing the seeds of liberty in the New World,' exclaimed Danton, 'it will yield an abundant harvest. This is the day on which the Englishman is dead.'

Although the new law did not defeat the British, it hindered their attack. On St-Domingue one of the major rebel slave leaders, Toussaint l'Ouverture, rallied to republican France on hearing the news and, with the sanction of the Republic's representatives, built up a disciplined ex-slave army of 14,000 men. Over the next four years it drove out the Spanish and British and their monarchist allies among the colony's population. In the Windward Islands a small republican force under Victor Hugues broke through the British blockade and reached Guadeloupe, where Hugues issued the Convention's decree and emancipated the slaves. He conscripted them into an army which recovered Guadeloupe and, temporarily, St-Lucia, and carried rebellion into the British islands of Grenada and St-Vincent.

ABOVE Toussaint l'Ouverture, known as the 'Black Jacobin', commander of the slave armies who fought for their emancipation.

In St-Domingue and the Windward Islands the slaves gained their freedom only to be conscripted into the army or put to forced labour to sustain the war effort. This lasted effectively until 1802, when Napoleon renounced the 4 February decree and sought to re-establish slavery. In the French Indian Ocean colonies the emancipation decree was never implemented at all. Nevertheless, the long-term effects of this abolition of slavery were enormous. Race relations would never be the same again: the victories of France's former slaves dispelled the mystique of total white supremacy. The expedition sent by Napoleon after 1802 to bring St-Domingue back to subordination captured Toussaint and sent him back to die in a French prison, but his soldiers resisted and eventually defeated Napoleon's attempts to subdue them. They survived to form the independent republic of Haiti.

The 'Laws of Ventôse', introduced here by Saint-Just in the Convention (26 February-3 March) implied extensive redistribution of wealth. The overthrow of Robespierre and Saint-Just in July 1794 was to prevent this being properly implemented.

THE force of events may be leading us to conclusions we never imagined. Wealth is in the hands of many of the Revolution's enemies; necessity compels working people to depend upon those enemies. Do you think authority can survive if civil relationships depend ultimately on those who are hostile to its form of government? Men who only half make a revolution are only digging their own graves.

Are the people shedding their blood on the frontiers, does every family wear mourning for its sons, in order to make things comfortable for tyrants? You must recognize the principle that in our country no one has any rights who did not help to set it free.

Do away with mendicancy, disgrace to a free State; the property of patriots is sacred, that of conspirators is available for the needy. The needy are the powers of the earth, they have the right to speak as masters to governments which neglect them.

The way to strengthen the Revolution is by making it profitable to its supporters and ruinous to its opponents.

Let us teach Europe that you do not intend there to be one unhappy man or one oppressor on French soil; let this example bear fruit throughout the world; and let it foster love of the virtues and of happiness. Happiness is a new idea in Europe!

I propose the following decree: All the communes of the Republic shall draw up a list of the indigent patriots they contain. When the Committee of Public Safety has received these lists, it will report on the means of indemnifying all these unfortunate people from the property of enemies of the Revolution.

The 'Laws of Ventôse' were followed by the proscription of the Hébertist group, based in the Paris Commune and headed by the editor of the *Père Duchesne*, who had maintained a left-wing opposition to the Revolutionary Government during the winter of 1793-4. As the *Moniteur* recorded, Hébert and his allies were executed on 24 March.

THE execution of the Hébertists took place at about five in the afternoon in the Place de la Révolution. Huge crowds of citizens filled all the roads and

The Jacobin welfare state

THE idea of a welfare state providing relief for every variety of social need from womb to tomb is usually regarded as a distinctively 20th-century phenomenon. However, there are precedents; and the French Revolution was one.

Commitment to an overhaul of the *ancien régime* poor laws emerged as a government priority early in the Revolution. The uprising of 1789 seemed proof enough of the system's failure to cope with mass hunger and distress. The economy had grown fast over the 18th century, but the population had grown faster. Although some individuals did well out of economic expansion, in general terms there was less wealth to go round.

The Constituent Assembly's Mendicity Committee, established to set up a new system of poor laws and chaired by the liberal duc de La Rochefoucauld-Liancourt drew on arguments propounded by Enlightenment thinkers such as Voltaire and Diderot. The church, which had effectively monopolized the distribution of poor relief before 1789, was dismissed out of hand: religiously inspired charitable giving was viewed as fostering idleness and had proved woefully inadequate under the *ancien régime*. La Rochefoucauld-Liancourt argued that social welfare should now become a state concern rather than a private virtue. Central government would fund the relief of social problems from state coffers and according to rational criteria of need. Government-sponsored work schemes would be provided for the able-bodied poor and state pensions

ABOVE A street soup-kitchen: distribution of food to hungry *sans-culottes*.

would be arranged for the 'deserving poor' – the aged and the disabled. Incorrigible beggars would undergo correctional training in workhouses.

However, this ambitious scheme remained unrealized until 1792, when the revolutionary wars stimulated the National Assembly to put its precepts into practice. The Jacobin strategy of – as Robespierre put it – 'rallying the people' meant commitment to radical policies which would win support for the new Republic from the broad mass of the population. This entailed wide-ranging legislation – to fix prices so that the poor could afford bread, to eradicate the last vestiges of feudalism, to democratize education, and so on. A nation-wide framework for pensions was created in March and June 1793; the 'Laws of Ventôse' (February-March 1794) introduced by Saint-Just, Robespierre's main ally on the Committee of Public Safety, decreed that the property of 'suspects' should be distributed among the poor; and an ambitious pension scheme for the rural poor was created through the establishment in May 1794 of a 'Great Register of National Beneficence'.

The welfare system also included types of need neglected or despised under the *ancien régime:* unmarried mothers were offered state pensions rather than society's contempt, and illegitimate foundlings – referred to as

ABOVE The Rotonde de la Villette. Hungry mobs burned similar *ancien régime* customs barriers in July 1789: the Jacobin poor laws were intended to prevent such hunger recurring.

'children of the fatherland' rather than as 'bastards' – became a state responsibility for the first time. Most striking of all, the well-being of soldiers of the republican armies locked in struggle against *ancien régime* Europe and internal counter-revolution became the leading edge of social welfare. A battery of military welfare legislation was introduced. Invalidity and disablement pensions were increased in size and number, and depended on the nature of the injury rather than rank. War widows and soldiers' needy families were accorded unparalleled provision. Military hospitals were organized on a massive scale, and medical resources within the armies improved, ushering in a 'golden age of military medicine'.

These humane and forward-looking reforms did not last: social welfare dwindled when the Revolution lurched to the right after the fall of Robespierre in July 1794. The neutralizing of Jacobinism in political life spelled the end of egalitarian social reforms. The Ventôse decrees were never implemented; the 'Great Register of National Beneficence' ground to a halt; military welfare was no longer a priority; pension schemes were progressively wound up.

squares through which they passed. Repeated cries of 'Long live the Republic!' together with applause were heard on every side. These indications of the people's anger, and the public's satisfaction, were fresh proof of the citizens' love for the Republic, safeguarded by the punishment of these wicked men. So perish all who dare to attempt the restoration of tyranny!

After striking out to the left, the Committee of Public Safety struck out in early April against its main critics on the right, the individuals clustered around Danton and Desmoulins who were calling for a relaxation in the Terror. In letters to his brother, Ruault traces the development of political repression.

The ferocity among the patriots is more savage than ever. The Committee of Public Safety has just had executed some twenty of the most notable revolutionaries such as Clootz, Hébert and Ronsin, commander of the armée révolutionnaire. *The unfortunate Clootz, bowing his head to the blade, cried out, 'Farewell, humanity!' Danton has just been arrested, on the night of 10 Germinal.*

It is because Danton and Desmoulins tried to halt the action of the guillotine that they will have to suffer it themselves. Their good intentions will be snuffed out with their lives. Tomorrow they will be compelled to go before the tribunal of blood which they helped to set up.

It is Danton's misfortune to have recovered some credit among good patriots, and even among people of fashion, since his milder sentiments became known, after he joined with Camille Desmoulins in Le Vieux Cordelier *newspaper to try to stop the massacres of the Revolutionary Tribunal. These two men, leaders of a party become too notorious, had kept some trace of humanity and hoped that an honourable return to good principles might cause their follies, and even their cruelties, to be forgotten. Danton's popularity gave offence to Robespierre, who today is King of the Revolution, High Priest of the Eternal and apostle of the doctrine of the immortality of the soul, which he has had placarded across the entrance to every temple.*

THE TIMES (London), *26 June 1794*

The Convention is detested; the Assignats are inveigled against; but the dread of the guillotine, which falls on the heads of all classes of society, restrains every one by its terrors.

Prisons under the Terror

THE outbreak of the French Revolution had been marked by a popular uprising directed against the state prison: the Bastille, a satisfying symbol of royal tyranny. Within five years the same Revolution had engendered a prison system synonymous with state terror and oppression. The Bastille had disgorged a mere seven prisoners when it fell on 14 July 1789; during the Terror in 1793 and 1794, 7000 inmates passed through the Parisian prisons.

Just as the Bastille engendered a myth of horror far removed from reality, so the Parisian prisons touched and inflamed the imaginations of contemporaries. The groundless belief in a 'prison plot' – that counter-revolutionary prisoners in the Paris gaols would break out and link up with the Prussian armies marching on the capital – triggered off the infamous massacres in September 1792, when vigilante gangs, in the name of popular justice, killed over a thousand prisoners. In the late spring of 1794 huge batches of alleged conspirators were sent to the scaffold.

Nearly fifty institutions served as gaols in revolutionary Paris. Some like the infamous

Conciergerie, on the Ile de la Cité, or the Abbaye had served as prisons under the *ancien régime*; others, like Carmes and St-Lazare, were converted monasteries, convents, educational establishments such as the Collège des Quatre-Nations, or poorhouses like La Salpêtrière and Bicêtre. Some had only a few dozen inmates, others several hundreds; there were five to six hundred prisoners in the Conciergerie in late 1793. Individuals awaiting trial for common-law offences mingled with convicted criminals, but the majority of inmates were people awaiting trial by the Revolutionary Tribunal and anyone judged to be a 'suspect' – that is, hostile to the Revolution and considered a danger to public security. By early 1794, a family relationship to an émigré or a counter-revolutionary could be grounds for imprisonment. One prisoner had done little more than shout '*merde pour la Nation*' in a public place.

Prison life brought a promiscuous mixing of social types. The old divisions often surfaced: there were de luxe cells in prisons such as the Abbaye, and the duc d'Orléans was able to order white wine and oysters for his final meal. But in most cases the looming presence of death dissolved social barriers and produced some strange bedfellows. It was rare for men and women to be strictly segregated, and sexual relations were commonplace. The stimulating effect of imminent death on the libido, plus the fact that pregnancy could bring a stay of execution, contrived some interesting liaisons. There were also other entertainments: a string quartet started up at the Port-Libre prison; illicit opiates circulated to deaden the imagination.

The passage before the Revolutionary Tribunal was usually preceded by transfer to the Conciergerie prison, and from here, too, the tumbrils set out bearing convicted prisoners to the public guillotine. Few were capable of Danton's light-hearted banter with the crowds on 6 April 1794. Yet many displayed stoic courage which made exceptions like Hébert and the duc du Châtelet, who both sobbed uncontrollably on the way to the scaffold, all the more pitiful.

The crowds who witnessed the executions were normally more or less approving, although the speeding up of executions during the 'Great Terror' in June and July 1794 seems to have produced a kind of weariness with the Terror. Most of the gaols were emptied after the fall of Robespierre in late July 1794; but the memory and myth of prisons under the Terror became a lasting legacy of the Revolution.

ABOVE The last roll call of the condemned read out in a prison, as the victims wait to be led out to the tumbril.

LEFT The *cour des femmes* in the Conciergerie, where female prisoners took their exercise – under constant threat of death.

The memoirs of a fellow political prisoner, Riouffe, record something of Danton's reaction to his impending execution at the hands of the Revolutionary Tribunal he had himself helped to establish on 10 March 1793.

DANTON was put in a cell next to Westermann, another of the accused, and never stopped talking. Robespierre had really hoodwinked this frightful Danton, who was a little ashamed of it; looking through his bars he said a good many things he may not have meant, and all mixed with oaths and bad language. Here are some that I remember:

'It was a day like this I had the Revolutionary Tribunal set up, but I ask pardon for it from God and man; it was never meant to be the scourge of mankind. It was to avoid a repetition of the September massacres.

'I am leaving everything in an appalling mess; none of them knows anything about government. In all this frenzy, I am not sorry to have put my name to some decrees which will show that I was no party to it.

'If I left my balls to Robespierre and my legs to Couthon, that would help the Committee of Public Safety for a while.

'Cains, brother-murderers every one of them. Brissot would have guillotined me just like Robespierre. There was a spy who never left me.

'I knew I was to be arrested.

'What proves that that b—— Robespierre is a Nero is that he never spoke so kindly to Camille Desmoulins as he did the night before his arrest.

'In revolutions it's the scoundrels who get the power. Better to be a poor fisherman than a ruler of men. The damned idiots, they will shout "Long live the Republic!" as I go by.'

He also talked constantly about trees, the country and nature.

Danton's execution, here recorded by Ruault for his brother, took place on 6 April 1794.

Danton was the first to climb into the first of the three carts which were to take the group to the Place de la Révolution. He had to wait until all three carts were loaded so that they could go to execution together. The loading took over an hour because Camille Desmoulins struggled a long time with the executioner, and knocked him down twice; he refused to have his hands tied or his hair cut, and they say the gendarmes had to help the executioner overcome Camille's resistance.

During this time Danton was laughing in the cart and nodding to the other condemned men, who were by now bound and placed in their carts, to show that he was being kept waiting too long. He chatted to Lacroix and Hérault, who were next to him, saying in the hearing of the people beside the carriages near the palace courtyard rails, 'What annoys me most is that I am dying six weeks before Robespierre.' Eventually Camille appeared in the cart. His shirt was in ribbons, he was out of breath, frenzied, loudly cursing Robespierre and the Committee of Public Safety and the infamous Tribunal which served these monsters.

The condemned went to their deaths in the midst of a huge crowd of republicans who were there to watch the original founders of their Republic lose their heads. Seeing the procession pass, a woman in the Rue St-Honoré looked at Danton and exclaimed. 'How ugly he is!' He smiled at her and said, 'There's no point in telling me that now, I shan't be much longer.' His face did in fact look like the head of a lion, while Robespierre's is like that of a cat or a tiger.

When they reached the place of execution, they were made to get out of the carts at the foot of the scaffold; they climbed up one by one to be executed and watched as the others died under the blade.

Danton was the last; when he saw the executioner coming for him at the foot of the scaffold, he cried out in a strong voice, 'My turn now!' and quickly climbed the fatal ladder. As they were tying him to the block, he looked calmly at the knife dripping with his friends' blood, and bent his head saying, 'It's only a sabre cut' (a phrase Desmoulins had once used to describe the new method of execution).

Danton is dead, Robespierre triumphant. The tiger has beaten the lion. But the triumph will not last, if we can believe Danton's prediction on his way to the scaffold; and he was a man who understood revolutions.

THE TIMES (London), *10 April 1794*

Danton, who suffered last, displayed to the last moment, all the audacity of a hardened conspirator; like Hebert, he was distinguished by his red collars.

. . . No spectacle can possibly be more horrid than that of the present state of this capital. The streets every where blocked up by beggars . . . A prodigious number of houses untenanted, and shops shut up. Crowds besieging the doors of the bakers and butchers shops. Pits filled with victims who have found a termination of their miseries in the Place de la Revolution, and the police continually on foot for the purpose of new arrests.

The fall of the Dantonists

ONE of the Revolution's most popular and exuberant figures, Georges Danton was executed on 6 April 1794. He had played a major part in the establishment of the Terror, making a famous speech in favour of the Revolutionary Tribunal and serving on the Committee of Public Safety from April to July 1793. But from then on he began to take up a position on the sidelines.

ABOVE Danton defiant, sketched on his way to the guillotine.

His friends were active. In November 1793, Camille Desmoulins launched a new newspaper, *Le Vieux Cordelier*, which was increasingly critical of the Terror, and called for clemency towards suspects. Another long-time associate, Fabre d'Eglantine, was implicated in the financial scandal surrounding the liquidation of the French East India Company, and Danton allowed himself to be fatally compromised in this murky affair. Moreover, the political climate had turned against Danton and his friends.

Robespierre and his supporters on the Committee of Public Safety had destroyed the Committee's main critics on the left, the Hébertists, in March 1794; they were now ready to deal with the Dantonist critics on the right. Although Danton never had a consistent policy, and charges of conspiracy could not be proved, he was potentially a dangerous focus for opposition to the Terrorist government and was linked with Desmoulins' calls for clemency. The Committee of Public Safety decided that he must be eliminated.

The 'Dantonist faction' was manufactured by the government and its public prosecutor, Fouquier-Tinville. Danton was tried with his associates, like Westermann and Desmoulins, but the prosecution added other suspects to incriminate them. The Frey brothers, for example, Austrian bankers, were not in league with Danton, but their presence in the dock supported feeble allegations that he was involved in a foreign plot against the Republic.

Danton defended himself long and loudly at his trial. His thundering eloquence threatened to turn the tables and put the regime itself on trial. The government committees were compelled to speed up proceedings, and the prosecution was authorized to refuse to let the accused speak. Their conviction was, in any case, a foregone conclusion.

ABOVE Camille Demoulins with his wife and child. He died on 6 April with Danton, Chabot, Delacroix and other so-called 'Dantonists'. His wife was guillotined shortly after.

In the growing atmosphere of fear and suspicion, disunity spread even in the two great committees of Revolutionary government, notably over the establishment, in April 1794, of a police bureau attached to the Committee of Public Safety, as highlighted in the memoirs of Sénart, a clerk in the Committees.

IT would be a mistake to imagine that the Committees of General Security and of Public Safety agreed with each other; there was conflict between them and also within each one. In the Committee of Public Safety, for example, Robespierre, Couthon and Saint-Just formed one party; Barère, Billaud and Collot-d'Herbois formed another; and a third consisted of Carnot, Prieur and Lindet.

That committee had spies in the Committee of General Security who told Robespierre word for word everything that happened there. This espionage brought Couthon, Saint-Just and Robespierre still closer together. The latter's fierce and ambitious nature gave him the idea of setting up a general police board, which was no sooner thought of than decreed. After that, the police force of the Committee of Public Safety used to set free anyone arrested by the Committee of General Security, and arrest those whom the latter set free. Thus rivalries and opposition parties began to be evident. Vadier, of the Committee of General Security, employed a known plotter to spy on Robespierre; this was Taschereau, who was a double agent and also spied on the Committee of General Security.

Robespierre attempted to paper over the cracks by persuading the Convention on 7 May (18 Floréal) to institute, with the following decree, a new civic religion, the Cult of the Supreme Being.

THE people of France recognizes the existence of the Supreme Being and of the immortality of the soul.

It recognizes that the appropriate form of worship of the Supreme Being consists in the practice of the duties of man.

Among the first of these duties it places hatred of bad faith and of tyranny, punishment of tyrants and traitors, help for the unfortunate, respect for the weak, protection of the oppressed, to do to others all the good one can and to be unjust to no one.

Festivals will be instituted to place the Divine and the value of their own being before men's minds.

They will take their names from the glorious events of our Revolution and from the virtues that are dearest and most useful to man.

Every year the French Republic will celebrate the festivals of 14 July 1789, of 10 August 1792, of 21 January 1793 and of 31 May 1793.

On each *décadi* (the last of each ten days) it will celebrate the following feasts:
The Supreme Being and Nature - Mankind - the French People - Benefactors of Mankind - Martyrs to Liberty - Liberty and Equality - The Republic - Liberty of the World - Love of the Fatherland - hatred of tyrants and traitors - Truth - Justice - Modesty - Glory and Immortality - Friendship - Frugality - Courage - Sincerity - Heroism - Impartiality - Stoicism - Love - Conjugal Fidelity - Paternal Affection - Maternal Love - Filial Piety - Childhood - Youth - Age of Maturity Old Age - Sorrow - Agriculture - Industry - Our Ancestors - Posterity - Happiness.

Freedom of worship is maintained.

Any gathering of aristocrats and contrary to public order will be suppressed.

If trouble is caused or occasioned by any form of worship, punishment will be rigorously meted out to those who stir it up by fanatical preaching or by counter-revolutionary calumnies or who provoke it by unjust and gratuitous violence.

A Festival in honour of the Supreme Being shall be celebrated on 20 Prairial (8 June). David is instructed to present a programme for it to the Convention.

As the Festival of the Supreme Being planned for 6 June (20 Prairial) to institute the new civic cult approached, Robespierre was the target for two likely assassination attempts. One was by Henri Ladmiral, on 20 May (1 Prairial).

Asked whether he had fired two pistol shots at the person of Collot-d'Herbois with intent to murder him, and which pistol shots misfired?

Reply: That he fired two pistol shots at the said Collot meaning to kill him; that he is very sorry he missed, both his pistols having misfired; that he had bought them in order to kill him and Robespierre as well, and that if he had killed them both, he would have been delighted.

Secret agents and foreign plotters

CONSPIRACY theories had long been rife in France, and the instability created by the Revolution fostered credulity. Four plots were uncovered in December 1790, for example at Lyon and at Aix-en-Provence, and two months later the marquis de Favras was arrested for conspiring to help the royal family escape.

In the spring of 1794 it became widely believed that a fraud concerning the liquidation of the French East India Company was more than just a swindle, and was related to a foreign plot to overthrow the Republic. It also came to be held that ultra-radical and de-christianizing activists were in fact covert royalists.

'Over the years,' Saint-Just reported to the Convention, 'there has been a conspiracy to use the Revolution to effect a change of dynasty.' Furthermore, a member of the Committee of General Security revealed three months later, 'we have proof that all the levers of this Foreign Plot were controlled by someone working for the princes and the coalition tyrants. We now know who distributed the guineas which Pitt sent into France. The atrocious brigand at the heart of this, the most dastardly assault against humanity which the kings of Europe have yet launched, is the former baron de Batz.'

Batz was certainly an inveterate conspirator. A minor nobleman from the south-west, he had been elected to the Estates General in 1789, where he became notorious as a reactionary. During Louis XVI's trial he bribed deputies to vote for an acquittal and, when this failed, laid plans to rescue him en route to the guillotine – and, later, the queen from prison in the Temple. The money for the bribes had come from abroad, from Spain; the Spanish court also funded an intelligence operation in France – the so-called 'Paris agency'. For the next six years a rabid monarchist conspirator, the comte d'Antraigues, continued to receive from the 'Paris agency' information which he passed to the émigré princes and deployed to encourage the European powers to carry through a counter-revolution. Not that Britain needed prompting.'

William Pitt was 'everywhere – like an evil spirit, invisible to human eyes', a deputy told the Jacobin Club in December 1793. His guineas had helped destabilize France in the summer of 1789; they were handed out again in the October *journées*, on the Champ-de-Mars in July 1791 and during the September massacres. 'His agents,' a spokesman for the Committee of Public Safety told the Convention in May 1794, 'are active all over France. They are out to stir trouble in the provinces, to sell Toulon, to counter-revolutionize the Midi.'

ABOVE Toulon, revolting against the Convention, welcomed the English in 1793: Jacobins put this down to Pitt's gold.

Despite these assertions, the British foreign intelligence service was not particularly active from 1789 to 1792. Although gold coins did change hands in the great revolutionary *journées*, they were certainly not British in origin. But after war was declared British foreign secret service expenditure was quadrupled. Naval and military funds were used to collect intelligence and to transport arms and money (mostly forged *assignats*) to capture or suborn ports through which troops and equipment could be poured. The near-impregnable city of St-Malo was a favourite target.

Tinténiac, an agent from London, was in touch in 1793 with the comte de Puisaye, who tried to organize a concerted insurrection in Brittany. Like many of his colleagues, he was taken to and from Jersey by couriers of a network known as *La Correspondance*. From time to time their safe houses near the coast were discovered and yielded apparently conclusive proof that a network of agents linked Pitt and the princes (Provence, Artois and the others), the émigrés and the disaffected in a large-scale conspiracy similar to the one that had fomented insurrection in the Midi.

Unlike the Scarlet Pimpernel, Tinténiac did exist, and there were whole networks of active agents. Their operations added to the dangers besetting the Republic in 1793-4, but their greatest effect was to intensify fear and nourish the suspicion which was used to justify the Terror and the Revolutionary Government.

Could education succeed in creating a new revolutionary man where Terror seemed to be failing? Ambitious educational reforms, including this plan for a military academy put to the Convention by Barère on 1 June (13 Prairial), were never properly implemented.

A severe shortage of both civil and military manpower threatens the Republic.

We must hasten learning and accelerate public military education. The revolution has its principle, and that is to hurry on whatever it needs. Revolution acts on the human mind like the African sun on vegetation.

Today the Convention declares: We will open a military academy, the Ecole de Mars. Three thousand young citizens, the strongest and most intelligent, will fill this new institution. They will come from the new generation, best fitted for study, and devote their blood to their country.

They will all be gathered in a single school; they will live under canvas and eat at the same table, will work in camps under the eyes of representatives of the people.

The basic principle of this resolution is that of a republic, where every citizen is a soldier, each man owes his life to the defence of the fatherland and must make himself fit to serve it well.

Parents must be guided by the principle that children belong first to the general family, the Republic, and only secondly to individual families. Without this principle there can be no republican education.

This appalling doggerel, written by the deranged poet Théodore Désorgues, was personally selected by Robespierre to be the hymn sung at the great Festival of the Supreme Being.

Father of the universe, supreme intelligence,
Benefactor whom blind mortals do not see,
Gratitude knew you; and through that alone
Raised altars to you.

Your temple is in the hills, the waves, the skies.
You have no past, no future; you fill,
But do not occupy, the worlds, and they
Cannot contain you.

Educational reform

REVOLUTIONARY politics were strongly influenced by newspapers and printed materials of all kinds, which depended on a high level of literacy to reach the mass audience for which they were written. Education was therefore a vital issue.

Although the population had become increasingly literate during the 18th century, education had been largely under the control of bodies ranging from the religious teaching orders, which virtually monpolized primary education for the lower classes, to the ancient institutions of the French universities. Under the Revolution, educational reformers aimed to replace the dominance of religious bodies and wealthy, élitist, corporate institutions with places of learning run by the state; its politicians believed that a new system of teaching was crucial to educating the new generation in the republican secularist ideology of France's new order.

When the National Assembly nationalized church property on 4 August 1789, it became virtually impossible for the teaching orders to continue their work – which in any case was made illegal by a decree of 18 August 1793. As a result, in December of that year, the Revolutionary Government decreed the setting up of a network of state primary schools, in which the teaching was largely focused on the educational basics: reading, writing and arithmetic. Attendance was declared compulsory and free for all male children aged between 6 and 8 years old. Teachers were to be paid by each municipality. However, in the financial chaos and religious tensions of the Revolution, relatively few towns and villages either wanted, or could afford to finance, the new state system. By 1794 only 32 out of 557 projected primary schools had been set up, and this sector remained embroiled in religious and local conflicts for most of the nineteenth century.

Secondary schools, many of which had formerly been run by religious orders, were replaced by 'central schools', one for each department. The curriculum was

LEFT Book bindings, as well as their contents, were used to promote republican ideology.

ABOVE The motto of the Republic carved on the foyer of the Ecole de Médecine in Paris.

BELOW The old Latin quarter around the Sorbonne, the centre of student life in 18th-century Paris.

strictly regulated to train mind, hand and eye; from 12 to 14 pupils were taught drawing, natural sciences and living and dead languages; from 14 to 16 they followed courses in mathematics, physics, chemistry and logic; from 16 to 18 they turned their attention to literature, history and legislation.

To replace the universities, which had comparatively few students, the Convention created a system, still in existence today, of Grandes Ecoles to provide high-level professional training: the Ecole Polytechnique for army officers, for example, the industrial school of the Conservatoire National des arts et métiers, the Ecole Normale for teacher training, and three new Ecoles de Santé for doctors and paramedics at Montpellier, Paris and Strasbourg. Public lectures in geology and natural history were given in the National Museum of Natural History, refounded in 1793 from the royal zoological gardens. Institutions such as the Ecoles took in many more students than the old universities, and were crucial in forming the new bourgeois governing class.

Dispel our errors, make us good, make us just:
Reign, reign far beyond the boundless whole;
Bind nature fast to your stern decrees;
Let man have liberty.

> THE MASSACHUSETTS MAGAZINE, (Boston), December 1792
>
> David, who is esteemed the first historical painter that France ever saw, after making a solemn harangue to his pupils, on patriotism and liberty, has dimissed his school, and set off for the frontiers in the character of a common soldier.

The Festival of the Supreme Being celebrated on 8 June – an elaborate pageantry staged by the painter David – seemed to rally the whole nation. Yet the cracks within the façade of national unity were apparent behind the scenes, as the memoirs of the Conventionnel, Baudot, make clear.

AS President of the Convention, Robespierre led the procession. He wore his usual light blue coat and carried a posy of flowers in his hand. People noticed that there was a considerable gap between his colleagues and himself. Some ascribe this to simple deference, others think that Robespierre was using it to underline his sovereignty. I am inclined to think that it was due to detestation of Robespierre.

It seems certain that his downfall was agreed in that triumphal procession; many were well aware of this, and if the gap was not its chief cause, at any rate his opponents made use of it to increase their numbers and convince others of his dictatorship. For the rest, the ceremony ended with an ambiguous speech without strength or vigour, and Robespierre gained nothing from his intended triumph.

The memoirs of the writer Vilate on the same occasion are even more explicit.

WITH what joyful pride Robespierre walked at the head of the Convention, surrounded by a huge crowd, the elegance of his dress responding to the pure radiance of the brilliant day, parading for the first time in the tricolour sash of the people's representative, his head shaded by floating plumes. Everyone noticed how intoxicated he seemed; but while the rapturous crowds shouted 'Long live Robespierre!' – shouts that are a death warrant in a republic – his colleagues, alarmed by his presumptuous claims, provoked him with sarcastic comments.

It was not only members of the Convention who perceived his theocratic intentions; I have this vigorous expression of a real *sans-culotte* from someone who heard it at the Tuileries: 'Look at the b—— it's not enough to be master, he wants to be God as well.'

As if in response to internal dissension, the Committee of Public Safety introduced the infamous Law of 22 Prairial (10 June) restricting the rights of the accused and making it easier to produce death sentences.
As Barère recalled, this intensified the repressive character of the Revolutionary Tribunal, and launched the 'Great Terror'.

IT was on the day after the festival that Robespierre proposed the terrible Law of 22 Prairial, which freed revolutionary justice from its few remaining restrictions, reduced the number of jurors and established real judicial tyranny, or rather a system of murder by the sword of the revolutionary laws. In vain I requested its deferment. Every mind was paralysed by the ascendancy Robespierre had won over the Jacobins, and bent beneath the cruel yoke of the terror he had organized. The law was passed by the silence of the legislators rather than by their agreement.

The dreadful law was put into execution: it was by virtue of its terrifying provisions that the mass executions took place, and that the monstrous medley occurred, of persons of every class, astonished and terrified to find themselves together in the same prisons accused of the same crimes.

Like a growing number of Parisians, Ruault was appalled by the progress of the 'Great Terror', as he writes to his brother on 21 June.

In recent weeks we have seen the deaths of all the greatest and most famous still surviving in France, and the richest too: Chiseul, worthy Malesherbes, all the rest of the Lamoignon family and almost the whole parlement of Paris; the Loménies, Montmorin, the famous Lavoisier and almost all his colleagues the fermiers généraux, *former members of the Constituent Assembly such as Espremesnil, Thouret, Le Chapelier, as well as Mme Elisabeth, sister of Louis XVI, etc. etc. They all died at the foot of a tall and hideous plaster statue called Liberty which has been set up on the remains of the plinth where the effigy of Louis XV stood.*

Jacques-Louis David

JACQUES-LOUIS David, who is usually regarded as the epitome of the revolutionary artist, was not unusual among his contemporaries in promptly embracing the principles of the early Revolution: it is the singular quality of his work that has earned it a consistent place in the iconography of the Revolution.

David had become established as France's leading painter of classical scenes during the 1780s, and in 1790 he was invited to paint the portrait of the mayor of Nantes, a commission which developed into unrealized plans for an allegory of the Revolution from the viewpoint of the Nantes Third Estate. This project was superseded by the 'Tennis Court Oath', sponsored from within the Jacobin Club and then taken over by the National Assembly. Conceived as a vast group portrait, it was intended to be a grand, rigorously contemporary representation of one of the founding moments in revolutionary history; it was never really finished.

His depictions of the revolutionary martyrs Lepeletier de Saint-Fargeau and Jean-Paul Marat (1793) were contributions to the Jacobin propaganda machine, and followed from David's membership of the club and of the Convention itself. The pictures extol the patriotic virtues of the martyred victims, struck down by the forces of counter-revolution: they are timeless commemorative icons rather than portraits.

Although David painted a small number of conventional portraits during the course of the Revolution – initially figures from the *ancien régime* liberal bourgeois world and members of his family – they were occasional pieces, often unfinished. He also produced two unconvincing anti-British caricatures in his capacity as official propagandist.

As a member of the Committees of General Security and Public Instruction, David was put in charge of the festival to commemorate the overthrow of the monarchy on 10 August 1793. However, the most elaborate pageant he staged was the Festival of the Supreme Being held in Paris on 8 June 1794 (20 Prarial II), a month after the cult dedicated to this secular deity had been established. The Being at the head of the new civic religion was a combination of Christian God, philosophical Absolute and political patron saint. All that remained of Christianity was the doctrine of the immortality of the soul; the cult was intended to provide an acceptable substitute for banished Catholicism and to encourage a moral, and therefore political, consensus.

Robespierre, then president of the Convention, was the central character in the pageant, which started with the ritual burning of the figure of Atheism and culminated in a procession to an artificial mountain on the Champ-de-Mars, where deputies gathered around a statue of the French people mounted on a column. In a hymn to the Supreme Being the singers swore never to relinquish arms until the enemies of the Republic had been defeated. Two months later, on 9 Thermidor, Robespierre and his fellow Jacobins, including David, were swept aside.

David lay low until 1799, when he exhibited his next major picture, *The Intervention of the Sabine Women*. A historical allegory on the need for reconciliation, it was also a reassertion of his identity as an artist rather than as a once-proscribed politician. He was quick to identify Bonaparte as a national hero and self-appointed national saviour in *Napoleon Crossing the Alps* (1799), and thus ensure his later patronage.

ABOVE David's self-portrait; the tumour that disfigured his left cheek is just visible.

OVERLEAF *The Intervention of the Sabine Women*, David's huge allegorical plea for national reconciliation after Thermidor.

DAVID

ROMA
ROMA

Is it possible to believe that all those who are sacrificed at her feet are her enemies? What well born, well educated man could fail to support properly organized civil and political liberty. Who will ever believe that Lavoisier and the others were supporters of slavery or tyranny? No, but they were noble, rich and enlightened; they had to be put to death.

The Committee of Public Safety are nothing but leaders of a Jacquerie, sans-culotte *chieftains. This winter and spring the Committee has done marvels for the good of the state and the defence of the fatherland, it has produced fourteen armies out of nowhere, saltpetre, guns and cannon by the thousand, by the million. But now it is making itself detested by the horror and frequency of executions which are quite unnecessary. Whatever sort of government may be in power, it has and always will have its critics, people who dislike it. Is that a reason for killing them?*

The coup of 9 Thermidor (27 July 1794) removed Robespierre and his allies from the Committee of Public Safety and the Convention. This is how the Montagnard deputy Baudot remembered the political atmosphere leading up to the coup.

ROBESPIERRE and Saint-Just were certainly republicans, but too narrowly so, and moreover they were intolerant, despotic, and had no patience with fine distinctions; their mission was bitter, bloody and implacable. Their opponents no longer had to fight for their beliefs but for their lives. Thus in the struggle of 9 Thermidor, it was not a question of principles but of killing.

Members of the Convention who most feared becoming Robespierre's victims in the intensified Terror began to conspire against him, as this letter from the left-wing deputy Joseph Fouché to his sister, 18 July 1794, shows.

Do not be disturbed by the foul slanders they hurl at me; I cannot say anything against their authors, they have closed my mouth. But the government will soon pronounce between them and myself.

I have nothing new to tell you about my affair, which has become that of all patriots since people realized that what the power-seekers are attacking is my unyielding virtue. A few more days, and truth and justice will win a resounding victory.

The Great Terror

THE Great Terror of Paris lasted 49 days, from 10 June 1794, when the Law of 22 Prairial was passed, to 27 July (9 Thermidor), when Robespierre and his associates were overthrown. During that time nearly 1400 men and women were executed – an average of nearly 200 every week. Over the previous 15 months the weekly average had been 22.

The law was prepared mainly by Georges Couthon, a crippled deputy from the Auvergne who was one of Robespierre's closest colleagues on the Committee of Public Safety. Known mainly for his conciliatory, even timid personality, he had an almost mystical faith in patriotic virtue and the capacity of the law to embody such feeling. He distrusted scheming, hypocritical politicians, even those who claimed to be 'friends of the people'. And he was convinced that the defence of France required drastic measures.

The crucial spring campaign of 1794 had started badly for the French. The execution of the Hébertists and Dantonists in March and April had disorientated,

ABOVE A bone guillotine made by French prisoners-of-war in England.

ABOVE A hapless victim of the Terror executed before the crowd.

even dismayed, revolutionary opinion, and it had become necessary to reassert the authority of the Committee of Public Safety over the organs of the Terror throughout France. Although there were moves to centralize repression in Paris, conflicts between different agencies of government, divisions in the Committee itself, unease and fear in the Convention and the recriminations of *représentants en mission*, hurriedly recalled from the provinces, increased tension. When an assassination attempt on the Committee of Public Safety member Collot d'Herbois on 1 Prairial (20 May) was followed three days later by a possible threat to Robespierre's life, nerves became intolerably frayed.

Fear of plots increased and the British were blamed for all setbacks and conspiracies. Severe new measures were taken against the nobility, for example exiling them from Paris. The scene was set for anyone who threatened, or was suspected of threatening, the safety of the revolutionary leaders, to be categorized as an 'enemy of the people'.

Couthon's Law of 22 Prairial reduced the cross-examination of the accused, denied them defence counsel, curtailed the use of oral evidence and allowed judgement by 'moral proof' rather than tangible evidence. Only one penalty remained – death.

The psychological effect was chilling. Justice and humanity were banished: in the eyes of true revolutionaries, these virtues had merely helped the unjust and corrupt to mask their dangerous intentions. To the pure in heart the very success of hypocrites in disguising their 'true motives' was proof of guilt.

Crimes against the Revolution were defined so vaguely – to hinder the consolidation of the Republic, to corrupt public morals, to harm the energy and purity of revolutionary principles – that men and women accused of diverse offences were tried by the Revolutionary Tribunal in batches of fifty at a time. Rich and poor, noble and peasant, duchess and flower-seller were conveyed to the guillotine, often crowded together into the tumbrils which brought them from the Conciergerie prison. The would-be assassins of Robespierre and Collot were executed, linked with 'foreign plotters', currency speculators, debasers of the coinage and of public morals. The poet André Chénier perished, as did the political philosopher Linguet and some Breton peasants whose language their judges could not even understand. Many nobles also died, including fathers mistaken for their sons and vice versa.

Although the French victory over the allied forces at Fleurus on 26 June 1794 effectively removed the threat of invasion, Robespierre maintained that the factions at home – and all signs of vice – had still to be eradicated, an impossible, eternal task.

There were always enthusiastic audiences for public executions in the 18th century – popular legend has it that knitting-women, the *tricoteuses*, crowded impatiently round the scaffold during the Terror – but popular revulsion at the killings certainly grew. The guillotine was moved from the heart of Paris out towards Vincennes; this merely lengthened the route of lugubrious processions through the silent streets and probably reduced the appeal of Robespierre. Though not as bloody as more recent terrors, the 30,000-40,000 who were the victims of revolutionary justice left a painful legacy.

Joseph Cambon, another of the Thermidorian conspirators, scribbled this note to his friends in Montpellier on 26 July, the eve of 9 Thermidor.

It is between Robespierre and myself, tomorrow one or other of us will be dead.

Robert Lindet, a fellow-member of the Committee of Public Safety, recalled the build-up to the coup in the following extract from his memoirs. Like many others, Lindet feared that Robespierre and Saint-Just were plotting to undertake a mass purge of their political enemies within the Convention.

SAINT-JUST had a speech to deliver. He came to the Committee of Public Safety at eight yesterday evening. He refused to tell us the content of his speech, saying it was not finished and he wanted to make some changes. People were afraid this meant a fresh attack. It was decided not to let him speak and to make sure he could not be heard.

This morning, 9 Thermidor, when the session of the Convention began, Saint-Just appeared at the rostrum. The members of the Committee declared that he ought not to be listened to, that he had not shown them his speech. Robespierre demanded that he be heard. People upbraided Robespierre; he replied; it degenerated into an altercation.

The coup of 9 Thermidor was made possible by a temporary alliance between left and right in the Convention. The memoirs of the right-wing deputy Durand-Maillane highlight the moment during the debate in the Convention when it became apparent that Robespierre had lost.

ON 9 Thermidor, a few moments before the famous session, I met Bourdon de l'Oise in the corridor and he shook me by the hand and said, 'Oh, what fine men sit on the right!' I went upstairs to the hall of Liberty and walked there briefly with Rovère; Tallien joined us but he immediately saw Saint-Just at the rostrum and left us, saying, 'There is Saint-Just at the rostrum; we must make an end of this.' We followed him and heard him from his position at the top of the seats where the Montagnards grouped, sharply interrupting Saint-Just and beginning the attack.

9 Thermidor: the fall of Robespierre

BY 9 Thermidor Year II (27 July 1794), personal animosities and political differences divided members of the Committees of Public Safety and General Security. These dissensions proved fatal to Robespierre's followers, who were overthrown not by a popular rising, but by scheming opposition in the Convention.

The Montagnard dissidents were a motley coalition. Some deputies – like the arch-dechristianizer Fouché – feared for their skins because they were already under suspicion. The surviving followers of Danton formed another dissident group, including Thuriot, who shouted at Robespierre in the clamour of 9 Thermidor: 'Silence, murderer! Danton's blood is running from your mouth, it's choking you!'. Robespierre's virtual assumption of the role of high priest at the Festival of the Supreme Being a month earlier had antagonized several deputies: during June, Vadier, a leading member of the Committee of General Security, had tried to ridicule his religious views, by arresting an eccentric prophetess, Catherine Théot, who proclaimed Robespierre as the new Messiah. He and his fellow committee-members were angry that Robespierre and his faction were encroaching on their police powers; the Committee of Public Safety had been entrusted with

ABOVE The Paris Hôtel de Ville under attack on 9 Thermidor.

government reports on the Hébertists and the Dantonists, for example. A further grievance was that in March it had established its own police bureau.

The Thermidorian conspirators were not united. Some envisaged the end of the Terror, others intended to pursue it more rigorously. A few days before the coup, Saint-Just and Barère negotiated a truce between the two committees. On the eve of 9 Thermidor, however, Robespierre called for a purge of both bodies.

His attack on the Committee of General Security alienated the moderates, who feared the dictatorial tendencies of the Committee of Public Safety.

A fiery debate in the Convention culminated in the decision to arrest Robespierre and his followers, but the Paris Commune released them from prison. Robespierre was taken to the Hôtel de Ville. In the Convention, a few members of the Committee of General Security took control and mobilized loyal troops against the Commune. Robespierre was outlawed.

A battle now ensued for control of the *sans-culottes* in the Paris sections. Robespierre appealed to the radicals among them, but he no longer had the support of activists who held him responsible for guillotining their leader Hébert in March. In addition, a new Wage Maximum, promulgated on 23 July, effectively reduced wages in many trades and may have contributed to popular apathy on the night of 9 Thermidor. When the Convention's troops entered the Hôtel de Ville, they met little opposition.

By 3 a.m. on 10 Thermidor (28 July), the building was littered with the debris of the Revolutionary Government. Robespierre's younger brother Augustin had thrown himself from a top-storey window; Couthon had either fallen, or hurled himself, from his wheelchair down the great stone staircase, to lie with a gaping wound in his head. Saint-Just surrendered stoically, but Robespierre, who had tried to shoot himself, was in great pain. Both men were executed, along with over 100 supporters, in the next few days.

Although many left-wing deputies had conspired against Robespierre, it soon became clear that the moderate, rather than the left-wing Thermidorians, were truly representative of political opinion. Tallien triumphed, while the radicals Vadier, Collot and Billaud-Varenne were soon to be under arrest.

ABOVE The Hôtel de Ville today, reconstructed after 1871.

Robespierre went to the rostrum to defend Saint-Just; nothing could be heard but shouts of 'Down with the tyrant! Arrest him!' As this commotion was still coming only from the Montagnard benches, Robespierre turned towards us and said, 'Deputies of the Right, men of honour, men of virtue, give me the right to speak which these murderers are refusing me.' He thought we would thus reward his protection of us. But we had made our choice: no reply and absolute silence until the motion for the arrest of Robespierre and his associates was put to the vote. We all voted for the motion, and so the decision was unanimous.

There was Robespierre, then, all-powerful Robespierre, under order of arrest, arrested, but not quite defeated. He was refused admission to the Luxembourg prison and taken to the Hôtel de Ville, where all his supporters gathered to defend him and to bring down the Convention.

Henriot, commander of the Paris National Guard, arrived after dark with his troops to seize the other members of the Committees of Public Safety and General Security and came to the door of our chamber with guns. We were told of this sudden assault during the deliberations of our evening session. It was proposed that Henriot be declared an outlaw, and this was immediately decreed. If ever I expected to die, it was certainly then. Henriot learned of the decree at once, and instead of attacking us or at least holding us where we were, unarmed and in his power, he withdrew. I could hardly believe it, but it seems that in accordance with the decree of outlawry no one would obey his orders.

During the night of 9-10 Thermidor (27-28 July), Robespierre and his allies, including Parisian National Guard commander Henriot, endeavoured to organize resistance to the Convention. They failed. As this pamphlet account shows, the demoralized group awaited arrest within the Hôtel de Ville. Robespierre had seemingly attempted suicide. He and his allies were to be summarily tried and executed within hours.

THEY went into the Hôtel de Ville and found Robespierre in a room near the session chamber. He was lying on the ground, a pistol shot through his jaw. They picked him up, and some of the *sans-culottes* carried him by his feet and his head; there were at least a dozen round him. They tore off his right sleeve, and the back of his blue coat.

Meanwhile a gendarme found Couthon and fired a pistol into his body. They searched for the rest of the conspirators.

Robespierre was taken to the Committee of Public Safety, still carried by the same men in the same way. He hid his face with his right arm. The procession paused briefly at the foot of the main stairs; inquisitive people joined the crowd; several of the nearest lifted his arm to look at his face. One said, 'He isn't dead, he's still warm.' Another said, 'Isn't that a fine king?' Another: 'And suppose it was Caesar's body! Why hasn't it been thrown on the rubbish dump?'

The men carrying him did not want him touched and the ones at his feet told the others at his head to keep it well up, so as to save what little life he had left. They carried their load up at last to the main committee chamber and put it down on a large table opposite a window; they laid his head on a box full of mouldy ration bread.

He did not move, but he was breathing heavily, and put his right hand on his forehead; clearly he was trying to hide his face; disfigured as he was, he still showed signs of vanity. Sometimes his forehead contracted and he frowned. Although Robespierre seemed half conscious, his wounds were clearly causing him great pain.

Among those who brought him in there were a gunner and a fireman, who never stopped talking to him; they made jokes constantly. One would say, 'Sire, your majesty is in pain,' and the other, 'Well, I think you have lost your tongue, you haven't finished your proposal, and it began so well. Ah, the truth is, you utterly deceived me, you scoundrel.' Another citizen said, 'I only know of one man who understood the art of tyranny, and that is Robespierre.'

Soon afterwards Elie Lacoste of the Committee of General Security arrived; they showed him the prisoners and he said, 'They must be taken to the Conciergerie, they are outlawed.' They were removed.

Next he spoke to a surgeon and told him to 'dress Robespierre's wounds and make him fit for punishment'. The surgeon said that the lower jaw was broken. He put several wads of linen into his mouth to soak up the blood which filled it; several times passed a probe through the hole the ball had made, bringing it out through the mouth; then he washed his face and put a piece of lint on the wound; on this he placed a bandage which went round his chin; then he bandaged the upper part of his head. During this operation, everyone offered his comments: when they put the bandage round his head, a man said, 'Now they are crowning his majesty.' He must have heard all this, for he still had some strength and often opened his eyes.

When the wound was dressed, they laid him down again, taking care to put the box under his head as a pillow, they said, 'until it was time for him to put his head through the little window' (the guillotine).

As the memoirs of the moderate deputy Thibaudeau recall, the overthrow of Robespierre signalled the relaxation of the Terror advocated by Danton earlier in the year. The 'Thermidorian reaction' from July 1794 to October 1795 involved a revival in sociability and ostentation, led by the new rich and by certain fashionable women.

FAMILIES and individuals whom the Terror had isolated began to meet again; social links were re-established. Dinners, balls and concerts were given. Since the possession of wealth was no longer a crime, luxury began to reappear little by little, not in its monarchical profusion but enough to obtain the necessities and pleasures of life. Instead of magnificence and pomp, we had neatness and elegance.

Entertainment then was a pleasure and not a duty. It was undertaken by those who could afford to pay for it, such as bankers, merchants and businessmen. The salons of noble families who had never emigrated were also open, beside those of the new people. For them, it was the pleasure of spending, for the others, the need for sociability, so powerful in France and especially in Paris.

One hoped to find patrons for his business ventures, another to recover his confiscated fortune or to obtain the striking off of his relatives or friends from the émigré lists. All wanted to win that importance gained in the world by contact with powerful or talented and distinguished people.

Paris again commanded the world of fashion and taste; two women renowned for their beauty, Mme Tallien and a little later Mme Récamier, set the tone. This period saw the completion of that revolution in matters of private life which had begun as long ago as 1789. Classical antiquity, already introduced into the arts by the school of David, now spread its influence over women's dress, in the hair-styles of both sexes; the gothic, the feudal, and those bastard and eccentric designs invented by the slavery of courts came to dominate in regard to furnishings.

Mme Récamier owed her success to her own charms. She had the beauty, grace and simplicity of a Virgin by Raphael. Mme Tallien, no less lovely, joined the pleasing liveliness of a Frenchwoman to the rich beauty of a Spaniard. Daughter of M. Cabarrus, a Madrid banker, and wife of M. de Fontenay, a French nobleman, she was arrested at the time of the Terror and owed her life to Tallien; she paid for it with the gift of her hand. Through this union she found herself involved in the Revolution and in politics, where she played the only role proper for her sex and took charge of the department of grace and mercy.

As Mme de Staël's memoirs make clear, the Thermidorian attack on the Robespierrist Terror was accompanied by a revival in royalism. The economy went into a downturn, causing social distress which contrasted with the conspicuous consumption of the new rich. But at least the war threat had receded; in mid-1795 France signed peace treaties with Prussia, Spain and the United Provinces, though fighting continued against Austria and Britain.

THE majority of the Convention wanted to punish some of the vilest of the deputies who had tyrannized over it, but it drew up the list of the guilty with a trembling hand, afraid it might itself be accused of those laws which had served as pretext or justification to so many crimes.

The royalist party was sending agents abroad and found supporters at home through the resentment aroused by the long continuance of the Convention's power. Nevertheless fear of losing the many benefits of the revolution kept the people and the armed forces loyal to the existing authority.

The army was still fighting just as vigorously against the foreigners, and its exploits had already won France an important peace settlement, the Treaty with Prussia made at Basel.

And the people, it must be said, were enduring unheard of hardships with astonishing courage; food shortages and the depreciation of paper money were between them reducing the lowest class of society to abject poverty. If the kings of France had made their subjects suffer half these miseries, revolt would have sprung up on all sides. But the nation believed it was doing this for the fatherland, and nothing can equal the courage inspired by such a belief.

In Paris, the attack on former Terrorists was led by vigilante gangs of youths, the fashionable *jeunesse dorée*, led by the now reactionary deputy Fréron. The memoirs of former Montagnard Choudieu present a left-wing critique of this new force.

FRÉRON gave the watchword to the 'gilded youth' (*jeunesse dorée*), as they called the group he had organized. As a rallying sign these young people wore their hair in what they called 'victim style', that is to say well powdered and braided at the back of the head, in contrast to the style of the patriots who wore their hair short and without powder. In imitation of the leaders of the Vendée they wore coats with black collars; nothing but a white cockade was needed for an open declaration of counter-revolution.

Fréron's army consisted of enthusiastic young men who had never had anything to lose, but claimed to be pathetic victims of the Terror, with a duty to avenge their relatives who had died on the scaffold.

The functions of this group were to police the Palais-Royal and the Tuileries gardens daily, and to sing the 'People's Awakening', every verse of which called for the death of the republicans, whom they called 'terrorists'. The chorus ended with the words, 'They shall not escape us!'

In their leisure moments they amused themselves with a dance which they called a 'farandole'. Anyone who refused to join in was picked up and thrown into the water troughs. Worthy exploits for such an army!

Fréron altered his allegiance but not his character. He demanded in the Convention that the Hôtel de Ville of Paris should be torn down because it had sheltered Robespierre. He also wanted the Jacobins' club demolished.

This anonymous émigré letter points out the divisions within the ranks of the republicans.

The Jacobins have rallied their scattered sons, but their credit is tumbling every day, they are hissed in the public galleries, shunned by society, harried by the public's hatred, their adversaries are gaining ground and have both public opinion and popular support on their side. We are now in the thick of the debate, its outcome will bury the Montagnards, the Jacobins and perhaps the Republic; or else it will guillotine the greater part of the Convention and cause blood to flow from Bayonne to Dunkirk.

What is new in this crisis is that the people as a whole are firmly opposed to the Jacobins. And so the moderates, who are striving to bring down the Revolutionary Government, have the vast majority with them. In the galleries, they talk of the constitution of 1791; in private of bringing back the king. Freedom of the press is beginning to return; primary assemblies are demanded, and liberty to express all opinions.

As for the armies, they know nothing of matters at home. Other passions inspire them – scorn and hatred of foreigners, infatuation with false glory, and that undisciplined emulation which is part of the national character.

Nothing can be expected there, and still less from the royalists; nor from civil war, which is impossible.

As a result of pressure from the *jeunesse dorée*, the Paris Jacobin Club was closed down by this decree of 12 November 1794 (22 Brumaire Year III).

THE united Committees of General Security, Public Safety, Legislation and the Army, decree:

Sessions of the Society of Jacobins of Paris are suspended.

The meeting-hall of this Society shall immediately be locked and the keys deposited at the secretariat of the Committee of General Security.

The return of émigrés to France increased concern about a royalist revival. This letter from the Jura was printed in the *Moniteur* in spring 1795.

The main roads are swarming with émigrés who have borne arms against their country, returning in the same spirit and with the same bitterness which made them leave. Much trouble will come of this, if the government does not take proper steps.

For some days now the émigrés have been raising their heads, and promising help and protection to those who shelter them. I do not know what it means, but they are spreading the word that 'little Capet' will be proclaimed king and all France will wear the white cockade. There will be no disorder, they say, and no one will be punished except some military commanders, such as Pichegru and some others. Thus the brave victors who have defended their country are to be punished by the cowardly rascals who betrayed her.

The jeunesse dorée

THE *jeunesse dorée*, or 'gilded youth', emerged after the overthrow of Robespierre on 9 Thermidor Year II. Also known as *muscadins* (fops), they were young Parisians who had managed to avoid conscription into the republican army after May 1793. The term came to be associated with opposition to the Terror, the rule of the Committees of Public Safety and General Security and the activities of the popular societies, sections and *sans-culottes*. During the winter of 1794 and spring of 1795, the presence of the *jeunesse dorée* on the streets of Paris reinforced the Convention's determination to unravel the system of highly centralized governmental control established in the reign of Terror.

Their social composition was very different from that of the *sans-culottes*. Instead of artisans and shopkeepers, the young men who destroyed busts of Marat, vilified the memory of Robespierre, interrupted performances of republican plays, forced known republican actors and actresses to renounce their political pasts, or fought pitched battles on the streets with reputed *sans-culottes*, were drawn from professional and property-owning circles. Many were minor administrative, clerical or legal officials in the republic's burgeoning ministries. Some owed their positions, and their exemption from the army, to well-placed relatives. Few lived in the radical sections of eastern Paris of the former Faubourg St-Antoine: most had roots in the sections of western and central Paris.

Their political presence owed most to the support they enjoyed within the Convention. There was great political uncertainty during the six months after Robespierre's fall. The events of 9 Thermidor were welcomed as enthusiastically by former political associates of the radical Hébert as they were by those of the more moderate Brissot, Roland and the Gironde. There was a wide consensus in favour of releasing political prisoners, but little agreement on the future course of the Revolution. One reason for the licence allowed the *jeunesse dorée* was that, beyond the general revulsion from the Terror, there were few available alternatives to the Convention. The symbolic political actions of the *jeunesse dorée* – songs, street-fights and the destruction of the insignia of the Year II – seem frivolous in many respects, but they helped to shift the political balance away from the radical policies of Robespierre and the 'Great' Committee of Public Safety. They allowed republicans to vilify the Terror but retain their allegiance to the republic, and royalists to re-enter the political mainstream without making any overt commitment to restoring the monarchy.

Although some members of the Convention, notably Fréron, Tallien and Fouché, were overtly sympathetic to the activities of the *jeunesse dorée*, the majority disowned the frequent street fights in which they were involved. The *jeunesse* failed to make much impact in their attacks on the sectional movement in the popular uprisings of April and May 1795 and, linked with the royalist insurgents in the Vendémiaire Rising on the streets of Paris on 5 October, they were crushed once and for all by Bonaparte's 'whiff of grapeshot'.

ABOVE A *muscadin*, with braided hair and stick for street fights.

Ruault's correspondence makes clear that any hopes pinned on the sickly young 'Louis XVII' were misplaced.

The first to benefit from the effects of 9 Thermidor has been the young dauphin, the wretched child of Louis XVI, still a prisoner in the great tower of the Temple. Until recently the Committee of Public Safety has kept him in the most loathsome and hideous captivity. Obviously it thought him too young to be executed like his father, mother and aunt, and has been trying to poison him with noxious air.

For nine months his constitution has resisted a torment never before used on a child by the most execrable of tyrants. But during this long agony, he has contracted a disease of the bones and nerves which the doctors despair of curing. It is too late; all his finger joints are covered with nodules, his lungs are seriously damaged, his stomach shrunk, he can scarcely breathe or digest food. The unhappy royal child is sinking slowly into the grave.

Fréron, the scourge of former Terrorists in Paris, was nevertheless still a republican. Sent *en mission* to Provence, he published an account of the massacres of former Terrorists by royalist gangs. The White Terror – so-called because white was the emblematic colour of the royal house – was bloodier and more vindictive than even the Great Terror of June-July 1794.

A new terror, far more productive of crime than that from which they claimed to be freeing themselves, now spread like a devouring lava flood in the departments of the Midi.

Marseille, worthy rival of Lyon, disgraced itself by atrocities at which nature sickens. Its prisons, and those of Aix, Arles, Tarascon and almost all the communes of the Rhône delta, were soon crammed with prisoners, most of them detained with no charge specified on the arrest warrants. Royalism too had its 'suspects'. The *représentant en mission* here issued a decree ordering the arrest of all persons suspected of 'terrorism'. God knows what scope that gave to the relentless aristocracy and to private vengeance.

There was not one commune where, following Marseille's example, daggers were not plunged with joy into republican hearts. Everywhere a kind of rivalry stirred up by the Furies, a contest for a prize to outdo all the rest in massacres. Neither age nor sex were spared. Women, children and old men were ruthlessly hacked to pieces in the name of humanity by cannibals who fought over the fragments. The département of the Vaucluse endured the same atrocities. That of the Basses-Alpes, whose people are naturally peaceful, hard-working and law-abiding, did not escape the contagion.

After this, it was not hard to excite people's minds to a fury against anyone who could be called a terrorist. The image of the dangers Marseille had just miraculously escaped obsessed everyone's thoughts. It was necessary in some way to turn the people into criminals. Popular hatred was directed against the ex-terrorists held in Fort Jean in Marseille. Some of the people joined the gangs of hired murderers who went by the name of compagnie de Jésus or compagnie du Soleil.

These vile and savage perpetrators of every kind of murder committed until then penetrated into the deepest cells, they rushed upon their defenceless and starving victims. Daggers and pistols, bayonets and stilettos were not enough – they loaded cannon with grapeshot and fired it point-blank into the prison yards. They threw blazing sulphur in through the ventilators; they set fire to damp straw at the entrances to vaults where scores of prisoners were huddled and suffocated them in the thick smoke. They killed, they slaughtered, they sated themselves on murder.

Bodies already pierced a thousand times were slashed and mutilated, their brains dashed out against the walls. The silence of death was only broken now and again by the murderers' savage cries or the victims' choking sobs. Knee-deep in blood, they could tread only upon corpses, and the last sighs of many a republican were breathed under the feet of the representatives of the people.

Radical journalist Sylvain Maréchal's 'Song of the Faubourgs' was a radical call to arms against the new rich.

Dying of cold, dying of hunger,
People robbed of your rights,
How quietly you murmur;
While the impudent rich,
Whom you spared once in kindness,
Loudly rejoice.

The White Terror

AFTER the fall of Robespierre on 9 Thermidor Year II (27 July 1794), many of the institutions of the Terror were abolished or neutralized. Within days of his arrest, the Convention purged the Committees of Public Safety and General Security of his closest supporters: Fouquier-Tinville, the notorious public prosecutor attached to the Revolutionary Tribunal during the Terror, was arrested on 1 August 1794. On 24 August the concentrated power of the two Committees was dispersed among sixteen new committees of the Convention. Two months later the Jacobin Club was closed, and on 8 December 1794 the Convention decided to readmit the surviving Girondin deputies who had been purged as moderates on 2 June 1793.

Many of those who had welcomed 9 Thermidor were increasingly disenchanted with events. The final abolition of the Price Maximum on 24 December 1794, after a gradual loosening of controls, coincided with one of the coldest winters of the century – the Seine froze and wolves were seen on the outskirts of Paris – runaway depreciation of the *assignat*, and inflation far higher than in 1792 or 1793. All this generalized misery, combined with popular despair at the Convention's policies and general uncertainty over the future, was at the heart of the abortive uprising in Paris on 12 Germinal Year III (1 April 1795).

The rising had more in common with the October 1789 march on Versailles than with the successful insurrections of 1792 and 1793. Crowds marched on the Convention to call for bread and the implementation of the 1793 republican constitution, and petitions were read out from the floor of the assembly. The Convention declared that Paris was under siege. When order had been restored by the National Guard, everyone associated with the Jacobin regime of 1794 was disarmed. Several members of the Committee of Public Safety were deported to Cayenne, in French Guiana, and more than 1600 Parisians had their weapons confiscated.

These events precipitated the White Terror of 1795. It started on 4 May with a massacre of former Jacobins imprisoned in Lyon and continued until 1797. The White Terror was most pronounced in cities along the Rhône valley, from Lyon to Marseille, and in the towns and villages of southern France. Royalists played a prominent role in many of the murders.

The great popular insurrection in Paris, which began on 1 Prairial III (20 May 1795), was a determined attempt to seize power. The crowds, backed by several companies of the Parisian National Guard, initially forced the Convention to accede to its demands for bread and the constitution of 1793. However, by the third day the Convention had marshalled its forces and, for the first time since the spring of 1789, the army was used against the citizens of Paris. The invasion of the Faubourg St-Antoine and the imprisonment of over a thousand former *sans-culottes* was a decisive moment in revolutionary politics.

BELOW The mob in the Convention on 1 Prairial.

Stuffed full of gold, prosperous new men,
Easily, softly, without any pains,
Have taken the hive;
Leaving you free, labouring people,
To eat iron like the ostrich
And try to digest it.

People and soldier acting together
Succeeded in smashing
Throne and Bastille.
Statesmen, new tyrants,
Be afraid of these brothers,
United against you.

I think that my song will
Send me to prison;
This is what grieves me.
The people who sing it, who know it by heart,
Will perhaps bless its author;
This is my comfort.

The *journées* of 12 and 13 Germinal Year III (1 and 2 April 1795) saw impotent popular demonstration directed against the Convention. The main cause of these disturbances, as Ruault recorded in his correspondence, was the high price of bread, which caused hunger and distress to which the government seemed oblivious. A further outbreak on 20 May (1 Prairial) was equally unsuccessful and led to wholesale repression of remaining Parisian radicals.

Paris, 24 Germinal. Public affairs are a thousand times worse in Paris than with you, my dear friend; we are lost here in an immense gulf; between us we have become a hydra with 650,000 heads and the same number of stomachs, which have been hungry now for a long time.

I dare not tell you all the expressions, all the curses heard in the long queues which form every evening, every night, at the baker's doors, in the hope of getting, after five or six hours' wait, perhaps half a pound of biscuit, perhaps half a pound of bad bread, or four ounces of rice, per person.

And yet the four or five thousand men who waste half their working day waiting for this minuscule portion of wretched food, who complained about their poverty and the horror of their existence, are regarded by those in authority as seditious. It has long been known that hunger is seditious by nature; banish that, and these supposedly seditious persons will disappear. They will not break into the august French Senate again, as they did on the 12th of this month (April), to cry, 'Give us bread! Give us bread!'

The flour intended for Paris is stopped on the way and stolen by citizens even hungrier no doubt than ourselves, if such there be within the whole republic. Yet there is no lack of corn anywhere! There is still plenty in store in the departments of the Nord, the Pas-de-Calais, the Somme, the Seine-Inférieure, etc. The farmers absolutely refuse to sell it for paper money; you have to go to them and take linen or table silver, jewellery or gold crosses, to get a few bushels. The wretches! Brutal and grasping yokels!

Discord sits more firmly than ever within the Convention. Now we are back to where we were at the end of April '93, and a hundred times worse as far as financial matters go. Too many assignats, *too much government slackness, too much favour shown to enemies of democracy, too much harshness and cruelty to former patriots, too much personal bitterness . . .*

The army rank and file were often as hungry as the Parisian poor. The consequences of French occupation on neighbouring territories are brought out in this letter from a German inhabitant.

These so-called republicans are every day becoming more inhuman, more immoral, more barbarous; they make war like Huns and Vandals, they send huge armies into our wretched country.

They have no money, no provisions, no supplies, no discipline and the consequences are dreadful and incalculable.

The commanders in chief and other officers too are as tyrannical as the commissaries. They say, 'the Republic isn't paying us, we must live off the conquered countries.'

THE MASSACHUSETTS MAGAZINE (Boston) *July 1795*

Notwithstanding the terrible misery which prevails among a numerous part of the people of Paris, it seems to be felt in a small degree (with an exception of some unhappy wretches, who seem spiritless) the rest of this metropolis wear an aspect of prosperity. The fair sex are more lively than ever; and we see spirited horses, with splendid harness and carriages, though few in number, on account of the dearness of forage.

Thermidor, restaurants and haute cuisine

THE very name 'lobster thermidor' is a reminder that the Revolution proved to be a landmark in the history of French eating habits. Although it did not create the tradition of a distinctively French *haute cuisine*, it gave great impetus to the establishment of restaurants, especially in Paris. From 9 Thermidor onwards, when the Terror was at an end, they flourished as centres of ostentatious consumption, and dishes became ever more elaborate and varied.

Although a number had opened their doors before 1789, and although some owners became famous – Beauvilliers, Robert, Bancelin, Méot and the 'Trois Frères Provençaux' – most restaurants served everyday food in unsophisticated surroundings. From 1789, large numbers of deputies began to arrive from the provinces; they fell into the habit of taking their meals together in the restaurants which sprang up in and around the Palais-Royal and the Rue de Richelieu – a Parisian counterpart to the connection long established in London between parliamentary life and the life of the taverns and coffee-houses. Significantly, the restaurant opened by Beauvilliers in 1784 was called the Grande Taverne de Londres. A newly powerful group, the deputies were well placed to set a fashion. Others – notably the increasing numbers of *nouveaux riches* after 9 Thermidor – followed.

Not everyone was able to eat grandly. Conditions for the masses were often appalling, with leftovers from great restaurants being sold to lesser eating-places and then, in increasingly fetid stages, to the poor. Equality was not the revolutionary virtue uppermost in the minds of diners in the finest restaurants.

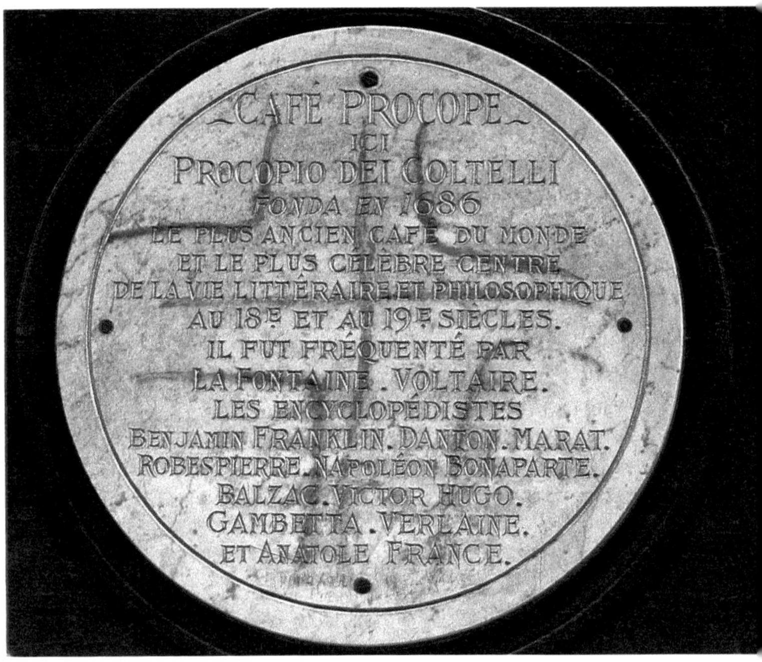

ABOVE The plaque on the Café Procope enumerating its famous patrons, including Danton, Marat, Robespierre and Napoleon. The café is still in business today.

ABOVE The frontispiece of Beauvilliers' *L'Art du Cuisinier*, the summary of his experience, showing a contemporary kitchen.

Many restaurateurs had learned the skills of *haute cuisine* in the kitchens of aristocrats who had emigrated or been executed; Beauvilliers had worked in the household of the comte de Provence, later Louis XVIII, Méot for the prince de Condé, and two of the three Frères Provençaux for the prince de Conti. But it was as restaurateurs that they made their mark on gastronomic history.

The standing of the chef-proprietor of a great restaurant was subtly different from that of the chef in an aristocratic kitchen under the *ancien régime*. Rather than ingratiating themselves with one of a small number of rich employers, ambitious cooks could compete for the custom of a much larger body of diners-out. They did so mainly by inventing an ever greater variety of new dishes. Flavours were delicately blended in preparations that passed through many stages and needed the material and human resources of a more elaborate kitchen than most private chefs had at their disposal.

With a larger restaurant-going public came the beginning of a gastronomic press. The reputation of Paris, by now firmly established in all Europe, soon spread across the world.

In these conditions, fraternity was looking increasingly threadbare and, as Goethe wrote, war seemed to be perpetuating war.

WHAT a noble spirit the French had! Gaily they planted the joyful trees of liberty and promised us not to touch our possessions nor our right to rule ourselves. Our young people burst into transports of joy. The conquering French first won the minds of the men by their vivacity and liveliness, then the hearts of the women by their irresistible grace. But soon the sky darkened; a race of depraved beings, not fit to be the instruments of good, fought each other for the fruits of victory; they massacred one another, subjugated the neighbouring peoples, their new brothers, and sent swarms of rapacious men into their lands. All of them robbed us, despoiled us, seemed to be afraid of nothing but leaving some item of loot until the next day. Our distress was extreme and the oppression intensified hourly; there was no one to hear our cries.

Internally, a truce was secured in the Vendée by a series of treaties with peasant royalist chieftains, such as this one signed at La Prévalaye.

PROCLAMATION of the Catholic and Royal Army of Brittany addressed to the inhabitants of the countryside. 2 Floréal Year IV (21 April 1795).

Brave residents of the country districts, farmers and landowners, hear us.

Peace and concord will take the place of the horrors of civil war and all its accompanying disorders.

We have pleaded your interests. We have obtained from the representatives of the people their promise, their strongest and most unequivocal assurances; you can be certain that they are going to unite at our request to re-establish happiness throughout your countryside.

Prisons in future will only be for wrongdoers; your property and your persons are made sacred by the law; all your sacrifices will have their reward. But peace is made for the happiness of all. We must now think only of the common benefits which will come from free communication on all roads, freedom of markets and of provisioning and exchange.

Having won you all these benefits, and tranquillity in your homes, we consent and agree to the peace settlement proposed to us, in order to give the Convention the means of forming a stable government which shall bring happiness back to France.

On the death of the infant Louis XVII, the comte de Provence became Louis XVIII. In his Verona Declaration of 24 June 1795, he committed himself to a restitution of the *ancien régime* if he was returned to power.

LOUIS, by the grace of God, king of France and Navarre.

To all our subjects, greeting.

In depriving you of a king, whose whole reign was passed in captivity, but even whose infancy afforded sufficient grounds for believing that he would prove a worthy successor to the best of kings, the impenetrable decrees of Providence, at the same time that they have transmitted his crown to us, have imposed on us the necessity of tearing it from the hands of revolt, and the duty of saving the country, reduced by a disastrous revolution to the brink of ruin.

Impiety and revolt have been the cause of all the torments you experience: in order to stop their progress you must dry up their source. You must return to that holy religion which showered down upon France the blessings of Heaven. We wish to restore its altars; by prescribing justice to sovereigns and fidelity to subjects, it maintains good order, ensures the triumph of the laws, and produces the felicity of empires.

You must restore the government which, for fourteen centuries, constituted the glory of France and the delight of her inhabitants; which rendered our country the most flourishing of states and yourselves the happiest of people.

Royalists seeking the return of the Bourbons through constitutional means were increasingly influential in the Convention. They were even, as Thibaudeau records, represented on the Commission of Eleven established to write a new, more moderate constitution to replace the never-implemented Montagnard constitution of 1793.

THERE was a monarchist party in the Commission of Eleven, consisting of Lesage of the Eure-et-Loir, Boissy d'Anglas and Lanjuinais. The other members of the commission were sincere republicans.

The Commission decided unanimously to set the constitution of 1793 aside. Many political writers put forward their projects and ideas. The discussions were friendly and the deliberations calm.

Louis XVII

LOUIS-CHARLES, duc de Normandie, was born on 27 March 1785 and became dauphin when his elder brother died on 4 June 1789. His mother described him at the time as 'a rather highly-strung child who needs to get plenty of fresh air. But essentially he's a cheerful little boy.' Three years later, in August 1792, at the age of seven, he entered the Temple prison. At first the dauphin lived with his family. But on 20 January 1793,

on the eve of the king's execution, he said goodbye to his father; and six months later, one evening in July, Louis-Charles was removed from his mother. The government had decided to move him into 'a separate apartment in the securest section of the Great Tower'. The queen, in any case, was taken to the Conciergerie – and guillotined on 16 October.

Maximum security was required; Louis-Charles was king to some, in principle if not in practice, and plots to free him multiplied. His escape had been Marie-Antoinette's chief preoccupation during her last months; in contrast, his uncle the comte de Provence, attached to the émigré army, issued a proclamation claiming the regency for himself. Fearing that the boy, when older, would constantly try to escape, the Convention decided to give him a properly 'revolutionary' education and wean him from his dynastic inheritance.

For six months Louis-Charles' tutor was a solid *sans-culotte* member of the Paris Commune – Simon the cobbler, who fixed windowboxes and birdcages for the boy. Mentally stressful as this initial 'reprocessing' must have been, his next six months were infinitely worse. Fear of conspiracies involving guards or Commune officials meant there was no tutor to structure the day: games of skittles and quoits in the garden ceased.

Confining 'Capet' to his room was an essential safeguard, but the price was his rapid deterioration.

When delegates from the Convention inspected his quarters first thing on 10 Thermidor (28 July 1794), they found them stinkingly filthy and the prisoner barely able to walk. But although proper feeding arrangements were restored and a 'guardian' appointed, Louis-Charles remained confined indoors, deprived of mental and physical stimulation. He rapidly regressed, preferring a cot to his bed, and by the winter he was seriously withdrawn.

Early in 1795 the Convention debated what to do with a prisoner who was a focus for plots but at the same time a useful bargaining counter in peace talks with Spain and Austria. 'Only one of two courses of action is possible,' the assembly was advised. 'He must either be exiled or held captive.' Exile was rejected, and official silence blanketed the prison once more. In May his guardian reported that Louis-Charles was 'seriously unwell'. After a month of the treatment prescribed by a well-known doctor, his condition worsened, and on 6 June he was moved to a lighter, airier room. He died two days later.

There were rumours that the prisoner had been poisoned, or that it was a substitute, not Louis-Charles, who had died. Pretenders, and later self-styled heirs appeared on the scene, but no one ever claimed to have rescued the boy. His uncle, the comte de Provence, never doubted the young king had died. From Verona on 7 July 1795 he proclaimed his accession as Louis XVIII to a throne which had devolved on him at the death of 'our late king, whose whole reign was spent in captivity'.

ABOVE Simon the cobbler re-educating the young Louis XVII; a contemporary view of one of 'Capet's' guardians.

The new Constitution of 1795 (or Year III) decreed on 22 August (5 Fructidor) brought in the Directory – a five-man executive council. It won swift condemnation from radicals which was echoed in the memoirs of the ex-Montagnard revolutionary Buonarroti.

A mere glance at the Constitution of Year III (1795) is enough to show that the foundation of every part of it is the continuation of wealth and poverty.

First, to silence all claims and to close for ever any opening for innovations which might favour the people, the latter's political rights are abolished or curtailed. The people have no share in the making of laws and no power to censure them; the constitution binds them and their descendants for ever, because they are forbidden to change it.

Certainly it declares the people sovereign, but any deliberation by the people is declared seditious; after confused ramblings about equal rights, the constitution none the less robs the great mass of citizens of their rights of citizenship; and only the wealthy have the right to make appointments to the principal public offices.

The unpopular 'Law of the Two-Thirds' which is here recalled by Mme de Staël accompanied the new Constitution. It stated that former Conventionnels would dominate the two-chamber legislature under the new constitution. It sparked off an insurrection in Paris, the 'Vendémiaire Rising' (4 October 1795), which was ruthlessly put down by the Convention assisted by the young army officer, Napoleon Bonaparte.

THE Convention issued the edicts of 5 and 13 Fructidor, by which two-thirds of the existing deputies were to retain their seats; but it was agreed none the less that one of these surviving thirds should be replaced within eighteen months and the other a year later. This decree severely shocked public opinion and completely shattered the unspoken agreement between the Convention and decent people.

The Parisians attacked the Convention's forces on 13 Vendémiaire, but the result was never in doubt. The Convention's army was commanded by General Bonaparte; his name first appeared in the annals of the world on 13 Vendémiaire (4 October) 1795.

General Vendémiaire

The Vendémiaire Rising came soon after the institution of the Directory, and was the last great insurrection of the Revolution. Centred on the Lepeletier section, around the Paris Bourse, and supported – in contrast to previous protests – by the wealthier western districts, it was a protest against the new Constitution and, in particular, the 'Law of the Two-Thirds', which perpetuated the influence of many of the existing members of the Convention. That assembly used the army – which had replaced the Parisian *sans-culottes* as one of the main motors of the Revolution – to control the streets, under the command of Napoleon Bonaparte. He was the organizing intelligence behind the successful defence of the Tuileries against the rebels, and the architect of his opponents' decisive defeat at the church of Saint-Roch. Four years later, on November 9, 1799, he overthrew the Directory and established a new regime based on his own power.

Although Napoleon consolidated many of the Revolution's achievements, including administrative and legal changes, economic reforms and the abolition of feudalism, much of what was most distinctive and significant about those years perished at his hands. Political life was drained of vitality and meaning. The Rights of Man were turned on their head as discipline, hierarchy and authoritarianism replaced the revolutionary device of liberty, equality and fraternity. Under his rule, France passed into the hands of an autocrat with far more absolute power than Louis XVI had ever enjoyed.

OPPOSITE Napoleon in his twenties; the dashing young officer whose action on 13 Vendémiaire saved the regime which he himself was eventually to supplant.

Guide to further reading

The bibliography of the French Revolution is too extensive to be outlined in a few paragraphs. An indication of the scale and richness of production can be gained from R. J. Caldwell, *The Era of the French Revolution: a bibliography of western civilization, 1789–1799*, New York & London, 1985. Other major works of reference include C. Jones, *The Longman Companion to the French Revolution, 1988*, and S. Scott and B. Rothaus eds., *Historical Dictionary of the French Revolution*, Westport, Connecticut, 1985.

Among general histories, worthy of note are G. Lefebvre, *The French Revolution*, 2 vols, 1961; A. Soboul, *The French Revolution, 1787–99*, 1973; N. Hampson, *A Social History of the French Revolution*, 1963; F. Furet & D. Richet, *The French Revolution*, 1970; J. M. Roberts, *The French Revolution*, Oxford, 1978; and D. M. G. Sutherland, *France, 1789–1815, Revolution and Counter-Revolution*, 1985. Two important, if very different interpretative works are A. Cobban, *The Social Interpretation of the French Revolution*, Cambridge, 1964 and L. A. Hunt, *Politics, Culture and Class in the French Revolution*, 1984.

For an understanding of the origins of the Revolution, we have K. Baker ed., *The Political Culture of the Old Régime*, Oxford, 1987; M. Vovelle, *The Fall of the Monarchy, 1787–92*, 1984; T. C. W. Blanning, *The French Revolution: aristocrats vs. bourgeois?* 1987; P. Campbell, *The Ancien Regime in France*, 1988; J. Egret, *The French Pre-Revolution*, Chicago, 1977; R. D. Harris, *Necker and the Revolution of 1789*, n1986; the classic G. Lefebvre, *The Coming of the French Revolution*, Princeton, New Jersey, 1947; and W. Doyle, *The Origins of the French Revolution*, Oxford, 1980. Important on different aspects of the events of 1789, are G. Lefebvre, *The Great Fear, rural panics in revolutionary France*, 1973 and J. Godechot, *The Taking of the Bastille, 14th July 1789*, 1970.

Works on the politics of the Revolution include L. Hunt, *Revolution and urban politics in provincial France: Troyes and Reims, 1786–90*, Stanford, California, 1978; C. Brinton, *The Jacobins*, New York, 1930; M. Kennedy, *The Jacobin Clubs in the French Revolution* Princeton, New Jersey 1981; R. B. Rose, *The Making of the Sans-Culottes*, Manchester 1983; G. Kates, *The 'Cercle social', the Girondins and the French Revolution*, Princeton, New Jersey, 1985; M. J. Sydenham, *The Girondins*, 1961; A. Patrick, *The Men of the First Republic* (1972); J. Godechot, *The Counter-Revolution: doctrine and action, 1789–1804* (New York, 1971); D. P. Jordan, *The King's Trial*, Berkeley, California, 1979; M. Walzer, *Regicide and Revolution*, 1974; G. Rudé, *The Crowd in the French Revolution*, Oxford, 1959; T. C. W. Blanning, *The Origins of the French Revolutionary Wars*, 1986; and C. Jones, ed., *Britain and Revolutionary France: conflict, subversion and propaganda*, Exeter, 1983.

For the Terror, see R. R. Palmer, *Twelve who ruled: the year of the terror in the French Revolution*, Princeton, New Jersey, 1941; M. Bouloiseau, *The Jacobin Republic*, Cambridge, 1984; N. Hampson, *The Life and opinions of Maximilien Robespierre*, 1974; D. Greer, *The Incidence of the Terror during the French Revolution* (1935); R. Cobb, *The Police and the People, French popular protest, 1789–1820*, Oxford, 1973; and his *The People's armies*, 1988; A. Soboul, *The Parisian sans-culottes and the French Revolution*, Oxford, 1964; C. Lucas, *The Structure of the Terror: the example of Javogues in the Loire*, Oxford, 1973; A. Forrest, *Society and politics in Revolutionary Bordeaux*, Oxford, 1975; W. H. Scott, *Terror and repression in Revolutionary Marseille*, 1973.

Particular aspects of the Revolutionary experience are dealt with in J. McManners, *The French Revolution and the church*, 1969; T. Tackett, *Religion, Revolution and regional culture in 18th-century France*, Princeton, New Jersey, 1986; R. Cobb, *Reactions to the French Revolution* (Oxford, 1972), and his *Death in Paris* (1978); C. Tilly, *The Vendée*, Cambridge, Mass., 1964; A. Forrest, *the French Revolution and the poor*, Oxford, 1981, Jones, *Charity and bienfaisance*, Cambridge 1982; M. Ozouf, *Festivals and the French Revolution*, Cambridge, 1988; and H. Gough, *The Newspaper Press in the French Revolution*, Cambridge, 1988.

For the mid and late 1790s, see also D. Woronoff, *The Thermidorian reaction and the Directory*, Cambridge, 1984; M. Lyons, *French under the Directory*, 1975; and G. Lewis & C. Lucas, *Beyond the Terror, Essays in social and regional history 1794–1815*, Cambridge, 1983.

Sources

Abbreviations used throughout

AHRF *Annales historiques de la Révolution française*
AP *Archives parlementaires de 1787 à 1860*, 1867– . . . (92 vols. to date)
BR B.J. Buchez & P.C. Roux, *Histoire parlementaire de la Révolution française, ou Journal des Assemblées nationales depuis 1789 jusqu'en 1815*, 40 vols., 1834–8.
Moniteur *La Gazette nationale ou le Moniteur universel*, 24 vols., for the period 1789–99.
Rév. fr. *Révolution française*

Place of publication, unless otherwise stated, is Paris for works in French, London for works in English.
Sources are listed as they appear in each chapter. Page references are to passages cited in full or, in some cases, in the form of extracts.

Chapter One

Marquis de Bouillé, *Mémoires*, 1821, pp.112–20.
Barnave, *Oeuvres*, ed. Bérenger de la Drôme, 4 vols.; vol. i, pp.80–4.
A. Brette, *Recueil de documents relatifs à la convocation des Etats Généraux de 1789*, 4 vols., 1894–1915; vol. i, pp.23–5.
E. Sieyès, *Qu'est-ce que le Tiers Etat?*, ed. E. Champion, 1888; pp.123–197.
Brette, *Recueil*, pp.66–87.
J. S. Bailly, *Mémoires*, 3 vols., 1821–4; vol. ii, pp.9–10.
E. Frénay ed., *Cahiers de doléances de la province de Roussillon (1789)*, Perpignan, 1979; pp.366–77.
H. Sée & A. Lesort eds, *Cahiers de doléances de la sénéchaussée de Rennes pour les Etats Généraux de 1789. IV.*, 1912; pp.306–11.
M. Bouloiseau & B. Chéronnet eds, *Cahiers de doléances du Tiers Etat du bailliage de Gisors (secondaire de Rouen) pour les Etats Généraux de 1789*, 1971; pp.228–33.
E. Mallet ed., *Les Elections du bailliage secondaire de Pontoise en 1789*, s.d.; pp.125–6.
A. Blossier ed., *Cahiers de doléances du bailliage de Honfleur pour les Etats Généraux de 1789*, Caen, 1913; pp.41–2.
Mallet, *Elections de Pontoise*; pp.328–30.
P. Boissonnade & L. Cathelineau eds, *Cahiers de doléances de la sénéchaussée de Civray pour les Etats Généraux de 1789*, Cahors, 1908; pp.244–5.
J. J. Vernier ed., *Cahiers de doléances de Troyes et du bailliage de Bar-sur-Seine pour les Etats Généraux de 1789*, 3 vols., 1909–11; pp.632–4.
Frénay, *Cahiers de doléances*, pp.163–4.
L. Lesprand & L. Bour, *Cahiers de doléances des prévôtés bailliagères de Sarrebourg et de Phalsbourg et du bailliage de Lixheim pour les Etats Généraux de 1789*, Metz, 1938; pp.60–2.
Bouloiseau, Chéronnet, *Cahiers de doléances*, pp.192–3.
C. L. Chassin, *Les Elections et les cahiers de Paris en 1789*, 2 vols., 1888; vol. II, pp.589–90.
Marquis de Ferrières, *Correspondance inédite, 1789, 1790, 1791*, H. Carré ed., 1932; pp.37–41.
G. Lefebvre & A. Terroine eds, *Recueil de documents relatifs aux séances des Etats Généraux (mai-juin 1789)*, 2 vols. in 4 tomes, 1953–83; vol. I, pp.66–7.
Marquis de Bombelles, *Journal*, J. Grassion & F. Durif eds, 2 vols., 1978–82; vol. ii, pp.304–6.
Adrien Duquesnoy, *Journal sur l'Assemblée Constituante*, R. de Crèvecoeur ed., 2 vols., 1894; vol. i, pp.304–6.

Chapter Two

A. Young, *Travels in France in 1787, 1788 and 1789*, 1792.
Bombelles, *Journal*; p.308.
Ferrières, *Correspondance*; p.47.
Correspondance secrète du comte de Mercy-Argenteau avec l'empereur Joseph II et le prince Kaunitz, 2 vols., A. d'Arneth & J. Flammermont eds, 1889–91; pp.247–8.
Correspondance secrète inédite sur Louis XVI, Marie-Antoinette, la cour et la ville de 1777 à 1792, publié d'après les manuscrits de la Bibliothèque impériale de Saint-Petersbourg, de Lescure, ed., 2 vols, 1866; vol. ii, p.360.
Young, *Travels*, (9 June 1789).
Moniteur, no. 9, 16–20 June 1789; pp.41–2. no. 10, 20–24 June 1789, p.48.
Creuzé-Latouche, *Journal des Etats Généraux du début de l'Assemblée nationale*, J. Marchant, ed., 1946; pp.130–4.
Cited in A. Aulard, *La Société des Jacobins. Recueil de documents pour l'histoire du Club des Jacobins de Paris*, 6 vols., 1889–97; vol. i, xi.
Creuzé-Latouche, *Journal*, pp.138–40.
Lefebvre & Terroine, *Recueil*; vol. ii, pp.304–5.
Bailly, *Mémoires*; vol. ii, pp.71–3. Cited in BR, vol. ii, p.40.
Madame de Staël, *Considérations sur les principaux événements de la Rév. fr.*, 3 vols., 1830; vol. i, pp.228–9.
Cited in A. Freeman, *The Compromising of Louis XVI: the armoire de fer and the French Revolution*, Exeter Studies in History, 17, Exeter 1988.
C. Desmoulins, *Oeuvres*, 2 vols., 1906, vol. ii, pp.329–31.
F. Gaëtan, comte de La Rochefoucauld, *La Vie du duc de La Rochefoucauld-Liancourt*, 1817. Extracts.
Les Révs de Paris, 4th edn, 1789; pp.9–12.
O. Browning ed., *Despatches from Paris, 1784–90. II (1788–90)*, Camden Third Series xix, 1910; pp.238–42.
Cited in J. Godechot, *The Taking of the Bastille. July 14th, 1789* (1970), pp.280–5.
Creuzé-Latouche, *Journal*, pp.242–5.
Abbé Barbotin, *Lettres*, A. Aulard ed., 1910; pp.48–9.
Bailly, *Mémoires*; vol. ii, pp.159–61.
A. de Lestapis, 'Sur la révolte agraire dans le Bocage normand', *AHRF*, 1955; pp.161–2.
J. Palou, 'La Grande Peur de 1789 à Seyssel sur le Rhône, *AHRF*, 1951; p.190.
P. Vaissière. *Lettres d''aristocrates': la Révolution racontée par des correspondances privées (1789–94)*, 1907; pp.256–7.
Bailly, *Mémoires*; vol. ii, pp.212–7.
Marquis de Ferrières, *Mémoires*, 1821; pp.189–90.
L'Ami du peuple, 21 September 1789.
AP, vol. 8, pp.397–8.
Duquesnoy, *Journal*; pp.299–315.
'Déclaration des Droits de l'Homme et du Citoyen', 26 August 1789.
Comte Beugnot, *Mémoires*, A. Beugnot ed., 2 vols., 1866, vol. i, pp.141–2.
Ferrières, *Mémoires*, op. cit., pp.267–8.
Bailly, *Mémoires*, vol. iii, pp.54–8.
L'Ami du peuple, 5 October 1789.
Duquesnoy, *Journal*, pp.401–6.
Le curé Pous, *Correspondance, 1789–91*, L. de la Sicotière & J. de la Goutine eds, Angers, 1880; pp.32.
Bailly, *Mémoires*, vol. iii, 118–19.

Chapter Three

[Roussel], 'Le Château des Tuileries', cited in BR; vol. iv, pp.198–9.
Bailly, *Mémoires*, vol. iii; pp.139–40.
Gouverneur Morris, *A Diary of the French Revolution*, 2 vols., Westport [Conn.], 1972; vol. i; pp.373–4.
Duquesnoy, *Journal*,; pp.286–9, 411.
BR, 4, 313–5.
Cited in E. Hatin, *Histoire politique et littéraire de la presse en France*, 8 vols., 1860; vol. vii, pp.48–9.
Aulard, *Société des Jacobins Lettres*, vol. i, p.xxix.

P. de Vaissière, *Lettres*, pp.195–6.
AP, vol. 13; pp.178, 189.
BR; vol. 5, p.321.
Cited in J.P. Bertaud, *Les Amis du roi. Journaux et journalistes royalistes en France de 1789 à 1792*, 1984; p.151.
Moniteur, no. 172, 21 June 1790; p.703.
Ibid.; p.704.
Ferrières, *Correspondance*; pp.214–15, 360–1, 375, 428.
Les Révs de Paris, 73, 27 November–4 Dec. 1790.
AP; vol. 54, pp.580–1.
F. Feuillet de Conches, *Louis XVI, Marie-Antoinette et Madame Elisabeth. Lettres et documents inédits*, 6 vols., 1864–73; vol.ii, pp.191–2.
AP; vol.21, pp.80–1.
L'Ami du Roi, cited in J. Gilchrist & W. J. Murray, *The Press in the French Revolution*, Melbourne, Australia, 1971; pp.104–6.
Thomas Lindet, *Correspondance pendant la Constituante et la Législative (1789–92)*, A. Montier ed., 1899; pp.255–6.
BR; vol. 9, pp.152–3.
Bouillé, *Mémoires*; pp.191–2.
Freeman, *The Compromising of Louis XVI*.
F. Feuillet de Conches, *Correspondance de Madame Elisabeth de France, soeur de Louis XVI*, 1868; p.266.
Feuillet de Conches, *Louis XVI, Marie-Antoinette, etc*, vol. ii; pp.234–5.
R. M. Klinckowström ed., *Le Comte de Fersen et la cour de France*, 2 vols., 1877; vol. i, pp.118–9.
Bouillé, *Mémoires*, pp.233–4.
Klinckowström, *Fersen*, vol. i, p.2.
BR; vol. 10, 341.
J. Godechot, *Charles-Alexis Alexandre*, *AHRF*, 1952, pp.136–7.
Klinckowström, *Fersen*, pp.139–40.
Les Révs de Paris, p.102, cited in BR, vol. 10, pp.242–3.
Ferrières, *Correspondance*, pp.360–1.
BR, vol. 10, pp.354–6.
Cited in Lever, *Louis XVI*, pp.596–7.
L'Orateur du peuple, cited in BR, vol. 10, pp.408–9.
BR, 10, pp.394–6.
Ferrières, *Correspondance*, p.395.
Klinckowström, *Fersen*, vol. i, pp.144–5.
Thomas Lindet, *Correspondance*, pp.300–1.
C. Parry ed., *The Consolidated Treaty Series. Vol. 51 (1790–3)*, New York, 1969, p.235.
AP, vol. 30, pp.620–1.
Ferrières, *Correspondance*, p.428.

Chapter Four

Klinckowström, *Fersen*, vol. i, pp.208–9.
Bertrand de Moleville, *Mémoires secrets pour servir à l'histoire de la dernière année du règne de Louis XVI*, 3 vols., 1797; vol. ii, pp.185–6.
F. Mège, *Gaultier de Biauzat, député du Tiers Etat aux Etats Généraux de 1789*, Clermont-Ferrand, 1890; pp.401–2.
N. Ruault, *Gazette d'un Parisien sous la Rév. Lettres à son frère, 1783–96*, 1976; pp.260–3.
BR; vol. 11, pp.131–2.
AP, vol. 34, p.724.
Les Annales patriotiques, 743, cited in BR, vol. 11, pp.241–2.
BR, vol. 11, pp.387–8.
Marie-Antoinette et Barnave. Correspondance secrète (juillet 1791-janvier 1792, A. Söderhjelm ed., 1934; pp.182–3.
AP, vol. 35, pp.436–7.
F. S. Feuillet de Conches ed., *Louis XVI, Marie-Antoinette etc*, vol. iv, pp.369–71.
P. Robinet, *Le Mouvement religieux à Paris pendant la Rév. (1789–1800)*, 2 vols., 1896–8; vol. ii, pp.139–41.
Feuillet de Conches, *Louis XVI, Marie-Antoinette etc*, vol. ii, p.344.
A. Montier, *Robert Lindet, député à l'Assemblée Legislative et à la Convention*, 1899; pp.22–3.
Morris, *Diary*, pp.355–6.
BR, vol. 13, pp.122–4.
Le Patriote français, cited in BR, vol. 13, p.92.
AP, vol. 37, p.686.
C. Perroud, *Lettres de Madame Roland*, 2 vols., 1900–2; vol. ii, p.411.
Lafayette, *Mémoires, correspondance et manuscrits*, 6 vols., 1837; vol. iii, p.405.
Ruault, *Gazette*, pp.279–80.
Vaissière, *Lettres*, pp.487–8.
Les Amis du Roi, cited in J. P. Bertaud, *Les Amis du roi*; p.211.
Klinckowström, *Fersen*, vol. ii, p.234.
Barbaroux, *Correspondance et mémoires*, C. Perroud ed., 1923; p.127.
Choudieu, *Mémoires et notes*, V. Barrucand ed., 1897; pp.458–9.
Vaissières, *Lettres*, p.354.
Chateaubriand, *Mémoires d'Outre-tombe*, M. Levaillant ed., 2 vols., 1949; vol. i, pp.396–400.
AP, vol. 42, p.596.
Klinckowström, *Fersen*, vol. ii, p.289.
Vaissière, *Lettres*, pp.420–1.
Memoirs of Bertrand de Moleville, cited in BR; vol. 14, pp.422–4.
F. Masson ed., *Napoléon inconnu*, 2 vols., 1895; vol. ii, p.395.
BR, vol. 15, pp.231–3.
AP, vol. 46, p.342.
Bertrand de Moleville, *Mémoires*, vol. iii, p.19.
A. Mathiez, *Les Girondins et la cour à la veille du 10 août 1792*, *AHRF*, 1931, p.201.
AP, vol. 47, p.92.
Ruault, *Gazette*, pp.297–8.
A. Aulard ed., *Mémoires de Chaumette sur la Rév. du 10 août 1792*, 1893; pp.38–9.
BR, vol. 17, pp.204–5.
Klinckowström, *Fersen*, vol. ii, pp.340.
AP, vol. 47, p.373.
Vaissière, *Lettres*, p.529.
Théodore de Lameth, *Mémoires*, E. Welvert ed., 1913, p.148.
Klinckowström, *Fersen*, vol. ii, p.346.
Barbaroux, *Correspondance*, pp.224–5.
Choudieu, *Mémoires*, pp.180–2.
AP, 49, 209.
Journal d'une bourgeoise pendant la Révolution, E. Lockroy ed., 1981, pp.288–9.
Vaissière, *Lettres*, pp.551–2.
Correspondance de Madame Roland; vol. ii, pp.434–6.
Cited in Bertaud, *Valmy*; p.276.
Ibid., p.90.
L. Mortimer-Ternaux, *Histoire de la Terreur, 1792–4*, 8 vols., 1862–81; vol. iv. Extract.
Ibid., pp.176–7.
'Campagne in Frankreich 1792' in *Goethes Werke*, L. Blumenthal & W. Loos eds, 1981; pp.234–5.

Chapter Five

AP, vol. 52, p.73. BR 17–18.
Barère, *Mémoires*, vol. ii, 38.
Cited in J. M. Thompson, *English witnesses of the French Revolution*, Oxford, 1939, p.202.
Ibid., p.214.
Ruault, *Gazette*, p.317.
Cléry, *Journal de ce qui s'est passé au Temple pendant la captivité de Louis XVI*, 1823, pp.47–54.
AP, vol. 53, pp.281–2.
Thibaudeau, *Mémoires sur la Convention*, 2 vols., 1824; vol. ii, p.307.
Vaissière, *Lettres*, pp.569, 586.
BR, vol. 21, pp.286–300.
Le pour et le contre. Recueil complet d'opinions prononcées à l'Assemblée Conventionnelle dans le procès de Louis XVI, 6 vols., Year II (1794), passim.
Ibid.
AP, vol. 57, p.468.
Abbé Edgeworth de Firmont, 'Dernières heures de Louis XVI', included in Cléry, *Journal*; pp.216–20.
Vaissière, *Lettres*, p.586.
Le Père Duchesne, cited in BR, vol. 23, pp.311–5.
AP, vol. 58, p.118.
R. Coupland ed., *The War Speeches of William Pitt*, Oxford, 1915; pp.89–90.
AP, vol. 59, p.141.
R. Secher, *La Chapelle-Basse-Mer, village vendéen. Révolution et contre-révolution*, 1986; pp.113–14.
J. Mautouchet, *Le Gouvernement révolutionnaire, 10 août 1792–4 brumaire IV*, 1912; pp.148–9.
AP, vol. 60, pp.389–90.
AP, vol. 60, pp.643.

BR, vol. 25, pp. 131–2.
Thibaudeau, *Mémoires*, pp. 12–13.
AP, vol. 61, p. 378.
M. A. Baudot, *Notes historiques sur la Convention Nationale, le Directoire, l'Empire et l'exil des votants*, Mme E. Quinet ed., 1893; pp. 120, 158.
F. Lebrun ed., *L'Ille-et-Villaine des origines à nos jours*, Saint-Jean-d'Angély, 1984; p. 231.
Vergniaud, *Manuscrits, lettres et papiers*, C. Vatel ed., 1870; p. 153.
Le Père Duchesne, no. 239, cited in BR; vol. 27, pp. 208–12.
Moniteur, no. 147, 27 May 1793; p. 638.
Ruault, *Gazette*, pp. 332–5.
Montier, *Robert Lindet*, p. 104.
Thibaudeau, *Mémoires*, pp. 44–6.
Papiers inédits trouvés chez Robespierre, Saint-Just, Payan, etc, supprimés ou omis par Courtois, 3 vols., 1828; vol. 1, pp. 15–16.
W. Markov & A. Soboul, *Die Sans-Culotten von Paris. Dokumente zur Geschichte de Volkbewegung*, Berlin, 1957; p. 2.
Cited in S. Bianchi, *La Rév culturelle de l'an II. Elites et peuple, 1789–99*, 1982; p. 147.
Markov & Soboul, *Die Sans-Culotten*; pp. 130–2.
BR, vol. 29, p. 327.
BR, vol. 28, pp. 466–7.
AP, vol. 72, pp. 674–5.
H. Wallon, *Les Représentants du peuple en mission et la justice révolutionnaire dans les départements en l'an II (1793–4)*, 5 vols., 1889–90; vol. i, pp. 115–6.
Mémoires pour servir à l'histoire de la Vendée, pp. 114–5.
Secher, *La Chapelle-Basse-Mer*, p. 121.
Mautouchet, *Le Gouvernement rév*, pp. 187–8.
BR, vol. 29, pp. 405–6.
AP, vol. 74, pp. 303–4.
AP, vol. 66, pp. 120–1.
AP, vol. 76, pp. 311.
H. M. Williams, *Memoirs of the Reign of Robespierre* (no date), pp. 71–3.
H. Wallon, *Histoire du Tribunal rév*. Extract.
Papiers inédits, vol. iii, pp. 116–18.
BR, vol. 29, p. 192.
Papiers inédits, vol. i, pp. 313–5.
A. Guillon de Montléon, *Mémoires pour servir à l'histoire de la ville de Lyon pendant la Rév*, 3 vols, 1828; vol. iii, pp. 61–8.
Cited ibid.; pp. 91–4.
Les Révs de Paris, cited in BR; vol. 30, pp. 196–9.
From R. Cobb, *Les Armées révolutionnaires. Instrument de Terreur dans les départements, avril 1793–floréal II*, 2 vols., 1961–3; vol. ii, pp. 661–2.
Papiers inédits, vol. ii, pp. 88–90.
Papiers inédits, vol. iii, pp. 153–4.
H. Wallon, *Les représentants en mission*, vol. i, pp. 220–1.
G. Martin, *Carrier et sa mission à Nantes*, 1924, pp. 297–8.
Wallon, *Les représentants en mission*, vol. iv, p. 56.
Wallon, *Les représentants en mission*, vol. iv, p. 110.
Cited in C. Lucas, *The Structure of the Terror: the example of Javogues and the Loire*, Oxford, 1973, pp. 86–7.
Mautouchet, *Gouvernement rév*, pp. 231–2.
Les Révs de Paris, (1974).

Chapter Six

BR vol. 35, pp. 290–1.
Desmoulins, *Oeuvres*, vol. ii, pp. 294.
Ruault, *Gazette*, p. 346.
J. Guillaume, *Procès-verbaux du Comité d'Instruction publique de la Convention nationale*, 6 vols., 1890–1907; vol. iii, pp. 353.
AP, vol. 84, p. 284.
BR, vol. 33, p. 241.
Moniteur, 5 germinal II, no. 748; p. 2.
Ruault, *Gazette*, pp. 347–8.
Riouffe, 'Mémoires d'un détenu', in *Mémoires sur les prisons*, 1823; vol. i, pp. 67–8.
Ruault, *Gazette*, pp. 348–51.
Sénart, *Révélations puisées dans les cartons des comités de salut public et de sûreté générale*, A. Dumesnil ed., 1824; p. 149.
AP, vol. 90, pp. 140–1.
Mortimer-Ternaux, *Histoire de la Terreur*; pp. 535–6.
AP, vol. 91, pp. 212–4.
T. Désorgues, 'Hymne à l'Etre Suprême' (Year II).
Baudot, *Notes*; p. 4.
BR, vol. 33, p. 177.
Barère, *Mémoires*, H. Carnot & David eds, 4 vols., 1842–4; vol. ii, pp. 202–3.
Ruault, *Gazette*, p. 352.
Baudot, *Notes*, p. 125.
G. Rudé, 'Trois lettres de Fouché', *AHRF* 1967; p. 367.
J. Duval-Jouve, *Montpellier pendant la Rév*, 1879; p. 188n.
Montier, *Robert Lindet*; pp. 248–9.
Durand-Maillane, *Histoire de la Convention Nationale*; pp. 405–6.
'Robespierre et ses complices ramenés de l'Hôtel-de-Ville. Faits recueillis aux derniers instants de Robespierre et de sa faction dans la nuit du 9 au 10 thermidor'.
Thibaudeau, *Mémoires*; vol. i, pp. 128–31.
Mme de Staël, *Considérations*; vol. ii, pp. 146–7.
Choudieu, *Mémoires*; pp. 292–7.
'Lettre d'un émigré sur la situation des choses après le 9 thermidor', cited in Thibaudeau, *Mémoires*; vol. ii, pp. 97–101.
BR, vol. 29, pp. 43–5.
Ruault, *Gazette*, pp. 365–7.
Fréron, *Mémoire historique sur la réaction royale et sur les massacres du Midi*, 1824. Extracts.
S. Maréchal, 'Chanson nouvelle à l'usage des faubourgs' (1795).
Ruault, *Gazette*, pp. 376–7.
Cited in J. P. Bertaud, *Valmy*, pp. 279–80.
Ibid., pp. 278–9.
F. Lebrun ed., *L'Ille-et-Vilaine*; pp. 241–2.
Annual Register, 1795; 000–00.
Thibaudeau, *Mémoires*, vol. i, pp. 179–80.
Buonarroti, *Mémoires sur la conspiration de Babeuf, dite de l'Egalité*, 1828. Extracts.
Mme de Staël, *Considérations*, vol. ii, pp. 152–4.
Thibaudeau, *Mémoires*, vol. i, pp. 264–5.
Ruault, *Gazette*, p. 393.

Glossary

Appel nominal Roll-call of deputies to pronounce openly on the sentencing of Louis XVI in January 1793.

Armées révolutionnaires People's armies: semi-regular units composed of *sans-culottes* militants, 1793–4.

Assembly of Notables Hand-picked assembly of nobles, clerics and municipal officials convened to sanction royal tax reforms in February 1787. They failed to do so, and precipitated the Pre-Revolution.

Austrian Committee The court faction opposed to the Revolution; centred on the "Austrian", Marie-Antoinette.

Assignat Paper currency (initially government bonds) in theory 'assigned' on the nationalised property of the church.

Bailliage Jurisdictional constituency for elections to the Estates General: called sénéchaussée in the south.

Bourgeois Originally a city 'burgher'; by the late 18th century used to denote urban non-noble notables.

Champart Highly detested seigneurial due in kind constituting a fraction of the peasant's grain harvest; abolished in 1789.

Committee of Electors The ad hoc committee established by individuals who had been elected to vote in Paris's deputies to the Third Estate. They grouped together in July 1788 and took over municipal government, becoming the embryonic form of the Commune.

Committee of Public Safety Coordinating committee of the Convention which supervised the war effort and the Terror, 1792–5.

Comités de surveillance Local committees of revolutionary militants entrusted with the enforcement of the Terror in 1793–4.

Commune The municipal government of Paris, 1789–95.

Constituent Assembly National Assembly formed out of the Estates General in the summer crisis of 1789, which existed down to September 1791.

Constitutional clergy Clerics who accepted to take the oath to the Civil Constitution of the Clergy, 1791–2.

Convention The first republican National Assembly in French history, September 1792–October 1795.

Cordeliers Parisian popular society important in the Champ-de-Mars massacre in 1791.

Dauphin Son and heir of the king of France.

Districts Electoral divisions of Paris created for the elections to the Estates General.

Droit de colombier Seigneurial right to own a dovecot; a hated symbol of oppression.

Doubling of the Third The right of the Third Estate (conceded in December 1788) to elect a number of deputies to the Estates General roughly equivalent to those of the other two orders combined.

Federalism Political system allegedly favoured by the Girondins, under which power would be decentralised.

Fédération Demonstration of patriotic fervour, most notably the celebration (Fête de la Fédération) held in Paris on 14 July 1790 to commemorate the storming of the Bastille.

Fédérés Individuals, especially National Guardsmen, sent from the provinces to Paris to celebrate the Fête de la Fédération after 1790. The *fédérés* of 1792 played a major part in the overthrow of the monarchy on 10 August.

Feuillants Moderate constitutional monarchists who left the Paris Jacobin Club following the Flight to Varennes in July 1791.

Gabelle Hated *ancien régime* salt-tax.

Garde-française Royal household regiment which defected to the patriotic party in June–July 1789 and was instrumental in the storming of the Bastille.

Hôtel de Ville City hall. The Paris Hôtel de Ville housed the Commune.

Legislative Assembly Legislature instituted by the 1791 Constitution and which sat from September 1791 to September 1792.

Lettre de cachet Sealed detention order signed by the king, and to be carried out at once, without legal recourse. Used against political opponents under the *ancien régime*.

Livre i) One pound weight; ii) the basic monetary unit of the kingdom, exchangeable against the pound sterling in 1789 at approximately 23:1.

Manège The riding hall attached to the Tuileries palace where the National Assembly held its sessions from 1789 to 1793.

Maximum The set of price-fixing regulations introduced under the Terror, most notably the General Maximum of 29 September 1793.

Milice bourgeoise 'Bourgeois militia': urban militias which in 1789 became the basis of the National Guard.

Montagne, 'Mountain': Name given left-wing deputies (Montagnards) who occupied benches at the top of the steepsided Manège in which the Legislative Assembly and Convention held their sessions.

National Guard Citizen's militia originating in the summer crisis of 1789 with the aim of securing internal order and the defence of the Revolution.

Non-juring priests see **Refractory priests**

Orders The three orders, or Estates, namely the clergy, the nobility and the Third Estate into which *ancien régime* society was conventionally divided.

Parlements The 13 high courts of appeal under the *ancien régime*, which had the right to block unconstitutional royal decrees.

Patriots A title much used in the period from 1787 to 1789 to denote supporters of reform and support of the Third Estate.

People's armies see **Armées révolutionnaires**

Plain Middle-ground moderate deputies who sat in the middle of the steep-sided Manège hall in which the Convention sat.

Popular societies Generic term for popular clubs and societies, many of which were affiliated to the Paris Jacobin Club.

Refractory priests or 'non-juring' priests, those who refused to take the oath to the Civil Constitution of the Clergy in 1791–2.

Représentants en mission Deputies sent out from the Convention under the Terror to rally the provinces and supervise the war effort.

Revolutionary Government Emergency government centred on the Committee of Public Safety which directed the Terror.

Sans-culottes Political movement of small property-owners and artisans active in Parisian politics, most significantly in 1792–4.

Séance royale The 'royal session' of 23 June 1789 at which the king tried to get the assembled Estates General to limit their reforms.

Sections The 48 units of local self-government in Paris, established in May 1790, which became the framework for popular militancy under the Terror.

Tricolore The red-white-and-blue emblem, combining the colours of Paris (red, blue) and that of the Bourbon dynasty (white).

Vendean Supporters of the counter-revolutionary insurrection in western France, centred on the department of the Vendée.

Verification of powers The ratification of credentials of deputies, which became the cause of political deadlock in May 1789, when the Third Estate deputies refused to undergo this process in a chamber separate from the nobility and the clergy.

Veto The right of the monarch under the 1791 constitution to block the national assembly's legislation for up to two legislative sessions.

Biographies

ARTOIS (Charles-Philippe, comte d'), 1757–1836. Youngest brother of Louis XVI, who emigrated on 16 July 1789 and was the most reactionary of counter-revolutionaries in emigration. King of France as Charles X, from 1824 to his overthrow in 1830.

BAILLY (Jean-Sylvain), 1736–93. Brilliant scientist who served as president of the National Assembly in June 1789, presiding over the Tennis Court Oath, then was mayor of Paris down to 1791. He retired to write his memoirs, but was brought back to be executed in Paris during the Terror.

BARBAROUX (Charles-Jean), 1767–94. Sprang to national prominence when he accompanied the Marseille *fédérés* to Paris and took part in the overthrow of the king. Associated with the Girondins, he was purged from the Convention in June 1793.

BARBOTIN (Emmanuel), 1741–?. Curé from northern France who sat in the Estates General and Constituent Assembly.

BARÈRE (Bertrand), 1755–1841. Lawyer, journalist and deputy in the Constituent Assembly and the Convention. Major spokesman for the Committee of Public Safety throughout the Terror.

BARNAVE (Antoine-Pierre-Joseph), 17611–1793. Barrister who with Adrien Duport and Alexandre de Lameth formed the Triumvirate which, from late 1789 to mid 1791, dominated the Constituent Assembly and the Paris Jacobin Club. Led the Feuillant schism from the Jacobins in July 1791. He wrote his famous *Introduction à la Révolution française* while in prison awaiting execution during the Terror.

BARRAS (Paul, vicomte de), 1755–1829. A radical Montagnard deputy in the Convention, he was a vicious *représentant en mission* with Fréron in the Midi while repressing the Federalist Revolt in late 1793–early 1794. One of the conspirators against Robespierre at Thermidor, he played a major role in the late 1790s.

BAUDOT (Marc-Antoine), 1760–1815. Montagnard deputy in the Convention, often away *en mission*.

BERTRAND DE MOLEVILLE (Antoine-François, comte de), 1744–1818. Full-blooded reactionary who served as Navy Minister, 1791–92, and was a secret adviser to Louis XVI. He wrote his memoirs while an emigrant in England.

BEUGNOT (comte Jacques-Claude), 1761–1835. Local magistrate from the Champagne area.

BILLAUD-VARENNE (Jacques-Nicolas), 1756–1819. Left-wing deputy in the Convention, popular with the Parisian *sans-culottes*, who served on the Committee of Public Safety from September 1793 to July 1794.

BOMBELLES (Marc-Marie, marquis de), 1744–1822. Diplomat and courtier.

BONAPARTE (Napoleon), 1769–1821. As a young artillery officer Napoleon was prominent at the siege of Toulon in late 1793, but was briefly imprisoned for Jacobin sympathies in late 1794. His part in putting down the Vendémiaire rising was the beginning of his rise to fame.

BOUILLÉ (Françoise-Claude-Amour, marquis de), 1739–1800. Career soldier who put down the Nancy army mutiny in late 1790 and then acted as secret adviser to Louis XVI for the flight to Varennes.

BRISSOT (Jacques-Paul, 1751–93. Fervent slave emancipationist prior to the Revolution, Brissot sprang to prominence in the Legislative Assembly in association with the Girondin deputies in the call for war. Purged from the Convention as a Girondin in June 1792.

BRUNSWICK (Charles Guillaume-Ferdinand, duc de), 1735–1806. Brilliant career soldier who commanded the Allied forces in northern France in 1792–3.

BUONARROTI (Filipo Michele), 1761–1837. Italian Jacobin associated with extremist radicals in Paris.

BURKE (Edmund), 1729–97, British statesman. A critic of the British government in the American War of Independence, he switched to its enthusiastic support in 1790, his *Reflections on the Revolution in France* becoming the bible of the counter-revolution.

CAMBACÉRÈS (Jean-Jacques-Régis de), 1753–1824. The future Arch-Chancellor of Napoleon was a magistrate who sat in the Convention but lay low for most of the Terror.

CAMBON (Joseph), 1756–1820. Businessman who came to support the Montagnards in the Convention and chaired the important Finance Committee throughout the Terror.

CARNOT (Lazare), 1753–1823. Army officer who served in the Legislative Assembly and the Convention. Elected to the Committee of Public Safety in August 1793, he was responsible for military organisation.

CARRIER (Jean-Baptiste), 1756–1794. Staunch Montagnard in the Convention and sanguinary *représentant en mission* in west France, where he was responsible for the *noyades* in the Loire estuary off Nantes.

CHATEAUBRIAND (François-René, vicomte de), 1768–1826. His reputation as a writer and politician started in the late 1790s, but his *Mémoires d'Outre-tombe* (1849) are an excellent source for the Revolutionary years.

CHAUMETTE ('Anaxagoras'), 1763–1794. Parisian *sans-culotte* militant and journalist, and official of the Paris Commune under the Terror. Executed as an Hébertist in April 1794.

CHÉNIER (Marie-Joseph), 1764–1811. Dramatist and author who was a staunch Montagnard in the Convention, unlike his more famous brother, the poet André, who died on the scaffold two days before the fall of Robespierre.

CHOUDIEU (Pierre-René), 1761–1838. Staunch Montagnard in the Legislative Assembly and the Convention.

CLOOTZ (Anacharsis), 1755–94. Prussian baron who became an enthusiast for the Revolution and was elected to the Convention. Executed as an Hébertist.

COLLOT-D'HERBOIS (Jean-Marie), 1749–96. Actor-manager who became a Parisian activist and was elected to the Convention. A member of the Committee of Public Safety from September 1793, he was responsible (with Fouché) for the repression of Lyon in late 1793. A conspirator against Robespierre on 9 Thermidor, he was later deported for his Revolutionary excesses.

CONCORCET (Jean-Antoine-Nicolas, marquis de). *Philosophe* who was elected to the Legislative Assembly and the Convention. Linked with the Girondins, he was executed along with them.

CORDAY (Charlotte), 1768–93. The assassin of Marat (13 July 1793) was an educated bourgeoise from Caen who identified with the Girondins.

COUTHON (Georges-Auguste), 1755–94. Crippled deputy in the Legislative Assembly and Convention, who served on the Committee of Public Safety and was closely linked with Robespierre, with whom he was executed.

CREUZÉ-LATOUCHE (Jacques-Antoine), 1749–1800. A magistrate who served in the Estates General, Constituent Assembly and Convention. A moderate.

DANTON (Georges-Jacques), 1759–94. Parisian radical associated with the Cordelier Club and the Paris Commune. Minister of Justice on the overthrow of the king, he served in the Convention and supported the establishment of the Terror. By 1794, he was seen as a dangerous moderate and was executed.

DAVID (Jacques-Louis), 1748–1825. Acknowledged as a great artist even before 1789, David threw himself into the Revolution with great gusto, painting the Tennis Court Oath and, elected to the Convention, serving on the Committee of General Security.

DESMOULINS (Camille), 1760–94. Radical journalist and street figure linked with Danton, he was elected to the Convention. His newspaper, *Le Vieux Cordelier*, in late 1793 called for a relaxation of the Terror, and he was subsequently executed.

DROUET (Jean-Baptiste), 1763–1824. The famous post-master of Sainte-Menehould who was responsible for the capture of the royal family at Varennes in June 1791 became a national hero overnight. Elected to the Convention, he proved a staunch Montagnard.

DUMOURIEZ (Charles-François du Périer), 1739–1823. Professional soldier whose Jacobin sympathies won him high command in 1792. Victor at Valmy and Jemappes, he lost the battle of Neerwinden in March 1793 and defected to the enemy after failing to raise his troops against Paris.

DUQUESNOY (Adrien), 1759–1808. Lawyer from eastern France who sat in the Estates General and Constituent Assembly.

DURAND-MAILLANE (Pierre-Toussaint), 1729–1811. Provençal lawyer who sat among the Plain in the Constituent Assembly and Convention.

EDGEWORTH (abbé Henry), 1743–1807. Cleric of Irish extraction who accompanied Louis XVI to the scaffold.

EGALITÉ, see ORLEANS.

ELIZABETH ('Madame'), 1764–94. Sister of Louis XVI who shared his imprisonment and was guillotined during the Terror.

FERRIÈRES (marquis Charles-Elie de), 1741–1804. Cavalry officer from the Poitou who served as noble deputy in the Estates General and then in the Constituent Assembly.

FERSEN (Axel, comte de), 1750–1810. Swedish army officer stationed in France, the confidant and probably the lover of Marie-Antoinette. Planned the flight to Varennes.

FOUCHÉ (Joseph), 1763–1820. The future Police Minister of Napoleon was a teacher attached to the Oratorians before 1789, but soon became a radical. Elected to the Convention, he served as a dechristianizing *représentant en mission* at Lyon and in central France. Threatened by Robespierre, he plotted his overthrow.

FOUQUIER-TINVILLE (Antoine-Quentin), 1747–95. The public prosecutor attached to the Revolutionary Tribunal, responsible for all the major trials, was himself condemned to death by the Tribunal after Robespierre's fall.

FRÉRON (Louis-Stanislas), 1765–1802. Radical journalist and member of the Paris Commune in 1792, Fréron was elected to the Convention, and served *en mission* with Barras in south-east France. A conspirator at Thermidor, he switched to the Right, and organised the *jeunesse dorée* in Paris, which was responsible for the closure of the Jacobin club.

GAULTIER DE BIAUZAT (Jean-François), 1739–1815. Auvergnat lawyer who sat in the Estates General and Constituent Assembly.

GOETHE (Johann-Wolfgang von), 1749–1832. The great German author took a keen interest in the Revolution and accompanied Brunswick's invading army in the Valmy campaign in 1792.

GRÉGOIRE (abbé Henri), 1750–1834. Radical cleric who rallied to the Third Estate in June 1789 and went on to become one of the most important ecclesiastical figures in the Constitutional church. He served in the Convention and survived the Terror.

GUILLOTIN (Joseph–Ignace), 1738–1814. Distinguished physician who in the Constituent Assembly had the guillotine adopted as an allegedly humanitarian means of carrying out the death penalty.

HANRIOT (or HENRIOT) (François), 1761–94. Minor clerk who rose through sectional activity in Paris to become commander of the National Guard in the *journées* of 31 May–2 June 1793. He failed to rally sectional support for Robespierre on 9 Thermidor and was executed the next day.

HÉBERT (Jacques-René), 1757–94. Radical journalist who used his newspaper, *Le Père Duchesne*, to advance his career in the Parisian popular movement. Executed in March 1794.

HOCHE (Lazare), 1768–99. Brilliant general who started life as a stable-boy. Died before he fulfilled his promise.

ISNARD (Maximin), 1751–1825. Prominent Girondin from Grasse who served in the Legislative Assembly and the Convention. Fled arrest in June 1793 and re-entered politics after the fall of Robespierre.

JAVOGUES (Claude), 1759–96. Radical member of the Convention, dechristianizing *représentant en mission* in 1793–4.

LAFAYETTE (Gilbert Motier, marquis de), 1757–1834. Liberal aristocrat who had fought in the American War of Independence and was regarded as a potential French George Washington. After serving in the Estates General and Constituent Assembly, he returned to the army, was appointed to a high command but after trying to lead his men against Paris, he fled to the enemy, who imprisoned him until 1797.

LAMETH (Alexandre, comte de), 1760–1829. Member, with Adrien Duport and Barnave, of the Triumvirate which dominated the Constituent Assembly and the Paris Jacobin Club, 1789–91. A prominent Feuillant after Varennes, his influence declined thereafter.

LAMETH (Théodore, comte de), 1756–1854. More conservative brother of Alexandre de Lameth who served on the Legislative Assembly.

LANJUINAIS (Jean-Denis), 1753–1823. Founder-member of the Breton Club (later the Jacobins) who served in the Constituent Assembly and the Convention. He was increasingly regarded as a Girondin and fled arrest in June 1793, re-emerging after the fall of Robespierre.

LA RÉVELLIÈRE-LÉPEAUX (Louis de), 1753–1824. Member of the Plain in the Convention and important political figure in the late 1790s.

LA ROCHEJAQUELEIN (Marie-Louise de Donnissan, marquise de), 1772–1857. As wife of the Vendean chieftain, the marquis de Lescure she played an active part in the Vendée rising in 1793–4.

LEBON (Joseph), 1765–95. Member of the Convention and violent *représentant en mission* in Arras and Cambrai in early 1794. Executed after Thermidor.

LINDET (Robert), 1746–1825. Norman lawyer elected to the Convention. A staunch Montagnard, he was elected to the Committee of Public Safety, specialising in the enforcement of the Maximum.

LINDET (Thomas), 1743–1823. Parish priest, brother of Robert Lindet, who served on the Constituent Assembly and accepted the Civil Constitution of the Clergy. Elected bishop, he served in the Convention and renounced his priesthood and married.

LOUIS XVI, 1754–93. The king failed to get to grips with the state's financial problems before 1789, and once the Revolution started never ceased to vacillate.

LOUIS XVII, 1785–95. The son of Louis XVI was never crowned, and spent his last years in the Temple prison.

LOUIS XVIII, 1755–1824. The comte de Provence until the death of Louis XVII in 1795, Louis XVIII emigrated in 1791 and commanded émigré armies against the Republic in 1792–4. Restored to the French throne in 1814–15.

MALLET DU PAN (Jacques), 1749–1801. Genevan journalist who acted on a secret mission in Germany for Louis XVI in 1792, and became a major counter-revolutionary propagandist.

MARAT (Jean-Paul), 1744–93. Physician turned radical journalist, Marat edited *L'Ami du peuple*. A member of the Paris Commune in August-September 1792 who was partly responsible for the September massacres, he was elected to the Convention. Assassinated by Charlotte Corday.

MARÉCHAL (Sylvain), 1750–1803. Author, journalist and bookseller closely linked with the Paris popular movement throughout the 1790s, whose atheistical views were especially important in the dechristianisation campaign of late 1793–3.

MARIE-ANTOINETTE, 1755–93. Acquired dignity rather late, after a youth of frivolity and a spell of rabid counter-revolutionary activity after 1789.

MERCY-ARGENTEAU (comte de), 1727–94. Austrian diplomat based in Paris who served as Marie-Antoinette's adviser down to 1791.

MIRABEAU (Honoré-Gabriel Riquetti, comte de), 1749–91. Disreputable Provençal aristocrat who was elected by the Third Estate of Aix to the Estates General and proved one of the shrewdest political strategists of the summer crisis of 1789. He acted as secret adviser to the court from 1790, and when this was discovered in 1792 his posthumous reputation plummeted.

MORRIS (Gouverneur), 1752–1816. American statesman who served as US envoy, then ambassador in Paris after 1789.

NAPOLEON, see BONAPARTE

NECKER (Jacques), 1732–1804. Swiss banker who served as finance minister from 1777 to 1781 and then again from 1788 to 1790. His dismissal on 11 July 1789 triggered off the storming of the Bastille, but though welcomed back in triumph he never got to grips with the Constituent Assembly. He resigned in disgrace and emigrated.

ORLÉANS (Louis-Philippe-Joseph, duc d'. Also known as Philippe Egalité from 1792). Ambitious cousin of the king who dabbled in politics from 1787 onwards, probably intriguing for the succession to Louis. A member of the Convention, he voted the king's death but was himself executed under the Terror.

PAINE (Thomas), 1737–1809. Radical author already famous for his *Common Sense* published during the American War of Independence. His *Rights of Man* (1790–1) was a best-seller, and resulted in his being elected to the Convention. His lack of French reduced his political role and he was imprisoned during the Terror.

PITT (William), 1759–1806. English statesman, who as Prime Minister from 1783 to 1801 and from 1804–6 was the chief European protagonist of the French Revolution.

POUS, 1747–1816. Obscure curé from Languedoc who served in the Estates General and the Constituent Assembly.

PROVENCE (comte de), see LOUIS XVIII

PRUDHOMME (Louis), 1752–1830. Radical journalist, whose weekly, *Les Révolutions de Paris*, from 1789 until early 1794 was one of the most outstanding Revolutionary newspapers.

ROBESPIERRE (Maximilien), 1758–94. Lawyer from Arras whose democratic views in the Constituent Assembly won him a wide popular following. Associated in the Paris Commune after the fall of the king, he was elected to the Convention. He was elected to the Committee of Public Safety in July 1793 and dominated the Convention and the Paris Jacobin Club until his overthrow on 9 Thermidor II (27 July 1794).

ROLAND DE LA PLATIÈRE (Jean-Marie), 1734–93. Royal factory inspector who came to Paris and, through links with the Girondins in the Legislative assembly, achieved ministerial office in 1792–3. He fled arrest in June 1793 and committed suicide when he heard of his wife's execution.

ROLAND (Madame), 1754–93. Her salon was an important ingredient in the political success of her husband. She was tried by the Revolutionary Tribunal and executed in November 1793.

RUAULT (Nicolas). Parisian publisher, whose letters to his brother at Rouen are an excellent source for the Revolution in Paris.

SAINT-JUST (Louis-Antoine-Léon), 1767–94. Fanatical young ally of Robespierre in the Convention and on the Committee of Public Safety who shared Robespierre's fate after Thermidor.

SANSON. Dynasty of Parisian executioners holding office from 1688 to 1847. Charles-Henri (1740–93) executed Louis XVI, while his son Henri (1767–1840) was executioner throughout the reign of Terror.

SIEYÈS (Emmanuel-Joseph, abbé), 1748–1836. Radical cleric whose pamphlet *What is the Third Estate?* won him fame in early 1789. He preferred committee work to public speaking in the Constituent Assembly and the Convention.

STAËL (Anne-Louise-Germaine, Madame de), 1766–1817. The daughter of Necker was in a good position to analyse the early years of the Revolution, but emigrated for the duration of the Terror.

TALLEYRAND (Charles-Maurice de), 1754–1838. Licentious bishop of Autun who became an enthusiastic reformer in the Constituent Assembly, welcomed the Civil Constitution of the Clergy and renounced his bishopric. He spent the Terror abroad, but returned in 1797 to continue his career, ending as foreign minister under Napoleon and the restored Bourbons.

THIBAUDEAU (Antoine), 1765–1854. Silent supporter of the Montagnards in the Convention under the Terror, he came into his own after the fall of Robespierre and emerged as a key political figure in the mid and late 1790s. His *Mémoires* are a good source for the Revolution years.

TURREAU (Louis), 1756–1816. General notorious for the ferocity with which he put down the rising in the Vendée and in western France in 1793–4.

VERGNIAUD (Pierre-Victurnien), 1753–93. Leading Girondin orator in the Legislative Assembly and the Convention. Expelled from the Convention in June 1793 and executed.

WASHINGTON (George), 1732–99. The first US President had become friendly with French officers who fought the British during the American War of Independence.

WILLIAMS (Helen Maria), 1762–1827. British woman of letters swept up into the Revolution when visiting France in 1788. Narrowly escaped execution as a Girondin because of her friendship with Madame Roland.

YOUNG (Arthur), 1741–1820. English agricultural writer who was touring France at the outbreak of the Revolution.

Index

Acknowledgements

Our grateful thanks to the many museums, libraries and individuals, including those listed below, who provided us with illustrations.

(b. = bottom; t. = top; r. = right; l. = left; b.l. = bottom left; b.r. = bottom right)

Archives Nationales, Paris: 100. Musee de Besancon: 34. Bibliotheque Nationale, Paris: 57; 93; 109; 113r.; 125; 129b.; 142/143; 149; 165t.; 169; 179; 185t.; 189; 213; 221; 230; 241r. Bridgeman Art Library, London: 8; 10/11; 14; 18/19; 21t.; 21b.; 24; 53r.; 70/71; 79b.; 95r.; 101t.; 102; 126/127; 135; 141; 143r.; 146/147; 162/163; 175; 177; 183b.; 187; 225; 226/227; 229. Bulloz, Paris: 25l.; 28; 33b.; 77, 114; 117; 130; 142/143; 157; 164; 170; 180; 193t.; 193b.; 205t.; 222; 235; 243. Bibliotheque de Chalons-sur-Marne: 198. Christie's, London: 31r.; 35; 41b.; 45; 47t. Edimage, Paris: 33t. Edimage/Goldner, Paris: 195. Edimedia, Paris: 119; 183t. Flammarion, Paris: 54, 185b.; 198; 209. John Freeman & Co., London: 97; 103; 136/137; 165b.; 239l. Giraudon, Paris: 2; 15t.; 15b.; 26; 37r.; 39t.; 39b.; 43; 50/51; 58/59; 61r.; 63; 69r.; 79t.; 83; 90/91; 101b.; 105; 106/107; 123t.; 131; 139l.; 139r.; 151r.; 154/155; 166; 167; 171; 181l.; 181r.; 182; 191l.; 191r.; 197; 199b.; 203b.; 205b.; 207r.; 208; 210/211; 213; 219l.; 219r.; 241l. Colin Jones: 29; 129t. Hubert Josse, Paris: 27; 31t.; 53l.; 69l.; 73b.; 75; 85; 89; 99; 137r.; 152; 161; 214; 219r.; 237. Mansell Collection, London: 22; 60/61; 67; 111; 113l.; 151l.; 160; 199t.; 217r. Marianne Majerus: 36/37; 47b.; 55; 58t.; 58b.l.; 58b.r.; 70l.; 73t.; 86/87; 115t.; 123b.; 153; 159; 203t.; 215; 216/217; 223t.; 223b.; 231; 239r. Peter Newark's Western Americana, Bristol: 951. Parker Gallery, London: 228. Picturepoint, London: 10; 207t. Victoria and Albert Museum, London: 115b. Wallace Collection, London: 20; 23; 25r.; 41t.; 49.

LA
REP.
FRA
LOI
LA
REP.
FRA
LOI
LA
REP.
FRA
LOI
LA
REP.
FRA
LOI
FORCE
GENIE DE LA GUERRE
GOUT
GENIE DES ARTS
RICHESSE
CONFIANCE ET FIDELITE
GENIE DU COMERCE
PROSPÉRITÉ
GENIE DE LA PAIX
FRATERNITÉ
THALMUD
LIBERTÉ DES CULTES
LUMIÈRE
LIBERTÉ DE LA PRESSE
INDUSTRIE
LIBERTÉ DES PROFESSIONS
PUDEUR
DIVORCE
LIBERTÉ DU MARIAGE
SÉCURITÉ
EGALITÉ DE DEVOIRS
PUISSANCE
NOBLESSE
EGALITÉ DE RANGS
COURAGE
EGALITÉ DE COULEUR
JUSTICE
EGALITÉ DE DROITS